The Higher Education Manager's Handbook

The Higher Education Manager's Handbook 2/e has been substantially updated and reflects important changes that have occurred since its first publication in 2004. In this new edition, Peter McCaffery continues to draw on a wealth of US and UK case studies based in innovative practice. The book offers counsel and guidance on all aspects of the manager's role and provides the navigational tools to successfully operate where the legitimacy of 'management' has often been questioned.

This bestselling guide builds upon its original strengths and remains an engaging, accessible and highly enjoyable read. Written from the unique perspective of the HE manager, it offers practical advice that can be implemented immediately by managers and university leaders at all levels. It addresses the internal ramifications of cynicism and demoralization, and develops the four essential prerequisites to becoming an effective HE leader:

- Knowing your environment
- Knowing your university
- Knowing your department
- Knowing yourself

What's new in the second edition . . .

- New Chapters: 'Leading and celebrating diversity' and 'Enhancing the student experience'
- The key strategic challenges to higher education
- University governance
- Institutional financial health
- Universities as ecologies of learning
- Managing your reputation
- Communicating in a crisis

Higher education managers, team leaders, vice chancellors, provosts, university presidents, department heads and student affairs administrators will find this book to be an irreplaceable resource that holds a permanent 'within hands-reach' position on their desk or bookshelf.

Professor Peter McCaffery is Vice Chancellor and Chief Executive at the University of Cumbria, England.

The Higher Education Manager's Handbook

Effective leadership and management in universities and colleges

Second edition

Peter McCaffery

Routledge
Taylor & Francis Group

NEW YORK AND LONDON

First published 2004
by RoutledgeFalmer

This edition published 2010
by Routledge
270 Madison Avenue, New York, NY 10016

Simultaneously published in the UK
by Routledge
2 Park Square, Milton Park, Abingdon, Oxon OX14 4RN

Routledge is an imprint of the Taylor & Francis Group, an informa business

© 2010 Taylor & Francis

Typeset in Palatino by
Keystroke, Tettenhall, Wolverhampton
Printed by
CPI Antony Rowe, Chippenham, Wiltshire

Library of Congress Cataloging-in-Publication Data
McCaffery, Peter, 1952–
The higher education manager's handbook : effective leadership and management
in universities and colleges / Peter Mcaffery. – 2nd ed.
    p. cm.
Includes bibliographical references and index.
1. Universities and colleges–Great Britain–Administration–Handbooks,
manuals, etc. 2. Educational leadership–Great Britain–Handbooks, manuals, etc.
3. Education, Higher–Great Britain–Administration–Handbooks, manuals, etc. I. Title.
LB2341.8.G7M39 2010
378.1′010941–dc22   2009021853

ISBN 13: 978–0–415–47042–1 (hbk)
ISBN 13: 978–0–415–47123–7 (pbk)
ISBN 13: 978–0–203–86475–3 (ebk)

To Sean and Kyle, so they now know what I do

Contents

Illustrations

Figures

Tables

Boxes

Abbreviations

AAUP	American Association of University Professors
ACAS	Advisory, Conciliation and Arbitration Service
ACCA	Association of Chartered Certified Accountants
ACE	American Council on Education
AGB	Association of Governing Boards
AOB	any other business
ARA	academic-related administration
AUT	Association of University Teachers
BIS	Business, Innovation and Skills
BPS	British Psychological Society
BME	black and minority ethnic
C&IT	communications and information technology
CBI	Confederation of British Industry
CEQ	Course Evaluation Questionnaire
CIPD	Chartered Institute of Personnel and Development
CPD	continuous professional development
CRE	Commission for Racial Equality
CUA	Conference of University Administrators
CUC	Committee of University Chairs
CUCO	Commission on University Career Opportunity
CUPP	Community–University Partnership Programme
CVCP	Committee of Vice Chancellors and Principals – now UUK
DCFS	Department for Children, Schools and Families
DfES	Department for Education and Skills
DGB	degree-granting body
DIUS	Department for Innovation, Universities and Skills
DRC	Disability Rights Commission
DTI/OST	Department of Trade and Industry/Office of Science and Technology
DUMB	defective, unrealistic, misdirected and bureaucratic
ECU	Equality Challenge Unit

EFQM	European Foundation for Quality Management – business excellence model
EHRC	Equality and Human Rights Commission
EQ	emotional quotient
EU	European Union
FE	further education
FTE	full-time equivalent
GMU	George Mason University
HE	higher education
HEA	Higher Education Academy
HEC	Higher Education Corporation
HEFCE	Higher Education Funding Council for England
HEI	higher education institution
HEPI	Higher Education Policy Institute
HERA	higher education role analysis (job evaluation)
HERDSA	Higher Education Research and Development Society for Australasia
HESA	Higher Education Statistics Agency
HMT	Her Majesty's Treasury
HR	human resources
ICT	information and communication technology
IQ	intelligence quotient
IT	information technology
JCPSG	Joint Costing and Pricing Steering Group
KPI	key performance indicator
LEA	local education authority
LFHE	The Leadership Foundation for Higher Education
LGBT	lesbian, gay, bisexual and transgender
LSC	Learning and Skills Council
MBO	management by objectives
MBO	master of the bleedin' obvious
MBWA	management by walking about
MLE	managed learning environment
MoD	Ministry of Defence
NAB	National Advisory Board (no longer current)
NAO	National Audit Office
NHS	National Health Service
NLE	New Learning Environment – at TVU
NSS	National Student Survey
OECD	Organization for Economic Cooperation and Development
OFFA	Office for Fair Access
Ofsted	Office for Standards in Education
OPM	Office for Public Management
OU	Open University
OUP	Open University Press
P4P	Partnerships for Progression
PAC	Public Accounts Committee

QAA	Quality Assurance Agency
QUT	Queensland University of Technology
RAE	research assessment exercise
RBL	resource-based learning
RDA	Regional Development Agency
REF	research excellence framework
RRA	Race Relations Amendment Act
SENDA	Special Education Needs Disability Act
SMT	senior management team
SMART	specific, measurable, achievable, realistic and time-related
SRHE	Society for Research into Higher Education
SSC	Sector Skills Council
STEP	social, technological, economic and political
SWOT	strengths, weaknesses, opportunities and threats
TA	Teaching Assistant
TDA	Training and Development Agency for Schools
THE	*Times Higher Education* (formerly *THES – Supplement*)
TQA	Teaching Quality Assessment
TRAC	transparent approach to costing
TVU	Thames Valley University
UCAS	University and Colleges Admissions Service
UCEA	University and Colleges Employers' Association
UCU	University and College Union
UGC	University Grants Committee (no longer current)
UKeU	UK e-University
USP	unique selling point
UUK	Universities UK
UWS	university-wide services

Preface

The demands made upon higher education managers are greater today than they have ever been. Effectiveness as a university leader requires managers to master four essential prerequisites. They must know their environment; know their university; know their department; and know themselves as individuals.

The Higher Education Manager's Handbook aims to help university leaders to do just that. This new edition has been fully updated to take account of the important changes that have occurred since its first publication in 2004.

It includes two entirely new chapters: one on 'Leading and celebrating diversity' and the other on 'Enhancing the student experience'. The former focuses on leading learning and teaching, student retention, employability and service excellence, while the latter has new sections on widening participation, community engagement and internationalization. There are also entirely new sections on the key strategic challenges facing higher education, university governance, managing your reputation and communicating in a crisis. Like the original, this new edition draws on case study examples of university innovators and offers self-assessment tools in all these areas.

Introduction

The challenge for HE managers

People are always blaming their circumstances for what they are. I don't believe in circumstances. The people who get on in this world are the people who get up and look for the circumstances they want, and if they can't find them, they make them.

George Bernard Shaw

'Management is a punishment from God!' Pilloried in the media for incompetence, badgered by the incessant demands of government bodies and often vilified within their own academic communities, there can be few managers in higher education who cannot have identified with this popular epithet at some stage in their career. And yet, ironically, this sentiment is strikingly at odds with the vitality of the very institutions which this group purports to manage. For while universities have, like other public sector institutions, experienced unprecedented change over the last quarter century, they have been equally successful in facing up to the unprecedented demands that successive governments have placed upon them.

In essence, HEIs have, on the one hand, had to become more accountable for the way they manage their affairs while, on the other, been obliged to cater to the needs of a mass student clientele, rather than those of a privileged few. While this transition in role and function has been neither smooth nor uncontested, HEIs have, by and large, successfully managed to do 'more' (that is, teach more students) with 'less' (fewer resources) while simultaneously maintaining 'quality'. In the UK for example, HEIs have accommodated a tripling of student numbers over the past 25 years while assimilating a 50 per cent reduction in the unit of public funding per student. More than that, HEIs have maintained their international standing in research while continuing to produce first-degree graduates quickly and with low drop-out rates compared to other countries (NAO, 2007; Eastwood, 2008). Universities, then, can quite rightly be proud of their collective achievement. Once perceived as a drain on the public purse, they are increasingly recognized as key contributors to wealth creation and economic well-being.

Where universities have been much less successful, however, is in managing the internal ramifications of these externally imposed changes. Indeed alienation, cynicism and demoralization are currently rife within academic communities (McNay and Bone, 2006; Watson and Amoah, 2007). Witness one Oxford University Professor of English who railed in response to his own question: 'What does the institution of higher education care about?'

> Bleakly observed, the local institution seems to have thrown in the towel. Degree-factory rhetoric is all we hear. New-style university managements are, actually, counter-productive. If you piss off your teachers and researchers you are eating the seed-corn, selling the family silver, sapping the life-blood. You would think our institutions were suicidal, the way they treat us – with the bad pay they collude in, the abolition of tenure they have agreed to, the rash economizings by engineering early retirements of good people, with the weekly questionnaires and the constant abuse of our time and energy and their acceptance of piss-poor TQA-inspired formalisms and abomination of abominations, their utter short-termism (their kow-towing to the silly time-scales of the RAE bods, their iniquitous short-term contracts – you can have your job back at the end of the long vacation if you ask nicely). Managerial cynicism is rampant in higher education as never before. They (THEY) don't care about the poor bloody infantry. . . . People are fed up, they are glad to give up and retire; they are going into internal exile, clock-watching, minimalizing their effort. The government-inspired way, the neo-managerial way, is a mess none of us can survive on.
>
> (Cunningham, 2000)

It is not a surprise then, if no less cause for concern, that a UCU-sponsored (University and College Union) inquiry into university staff well-being in spring 2006 found that 'levels of psychological distress among academics' exceeded 'those in high-stress occupations such as accident and emergency doctors and nurses' (McCall, 2006). Likewise a comparative survey on the 'professional well-being' of the 140 or so officially recognized occupations (commissioned by the Economic and Social Research Council's 'Future of Work' programme) actually placed university teaching professionals at number one in their 'Job Misery Index'. Nor is this grim picture peculiar to the UK. Researchers at Melbourne Business School, for instance, have charted how stress levels in Australian universities have risen dramatically over the past decade, generating an epidemic of work-related illnesses across the country's campuses: an outcome which they attribute to, among other things, the role played by university managers (*THES*, 2000, 2003). It is also the case that the pressure on universities worldwide to embrace yet further change is – and is likely to remain for the foreseeable future – unrelenting. Globalization, information technology, the introduction of variable fees, the emergence of the so-called 'Knowledge Society' and the knock-on consequences of the global credit-crunch all presage a new environment to which universities will have to adapt (HEPI, 2009; Leitch, 2006; Spellings, 2006).

The challenge facing universities then, and in particular individual managers, is a formidable one. Nor can they prepare for it with a *tabula rasa*. On the contrary, as we've seen above, 'management' in universities, unlike in other organizations, has long had its legitimacy questioned. Often depicted by academics ('the managed') as an irrelevant business practice which has no place in the (essentially) collegiate environment of the academic world, this view was, until recently, upheld for the most part by those who occupied such 'management' positions in HEIs. On the other hand, there have been well-publicized instances when 'new managerialism' has allegedly run rampant in its quest to bring the techniques, values and practices of the commercial sector to the university world. Thus where once universities may have been led and managed in an amateurish, complacent or uninformed way, they are now widely perceived as in the grip of an aggressive managerial cadre determined to run HE as a business.

Common to both scenarios is the low status and low esteem which is accorded university management. 'There is no scientific basis to management, therefore it does not deserve to be taken seriously', as the intellectual puts it: a view which is too often compounded in university settings by the disregard that some managers themselves have for their positions when it comes to their own training and development – the notion that somehow 'training is for the second eleven' (Bryman, 2007). Unsurprisingly, the instances of mismanagement and incompetence in universities have exhibited an upward trend. How then – given the prospective changes in the environment, the degree of internal malaise within institutions, and the 'crisis in management' – can university managers hope to manage effectively in such a setting? Indeed, how can and should university managers prepare to meet this challenge?

The purpose of this book is to help HE managers – both academic managers and general managers alike – to do just that. It is based on the research on university innovators overseas which I undertook for the Travelling Fellowship I was awarded by the Winston Churchill Memorial Trust. As a dean of school in a new university, I, like many others with a similar role in the HE sector, had (and now as a vice chancellor of a new university naturally still hold) both a professional and a practical interest in how our institutional counterparts in other countries were responding to the common dilemma which, as I indicated above, we all face no matter where our domicile; namely, how to do more with less while still maintaining quality in an increasingly competitive environment. This study, based on a number of selected universities in the USA and Australia, not only reports the findings of this inquiry, but also seeks to identify the lessons we can learn from these university innovators and in particular those which we can all apply in practice.

It also draws on my own personal and professional experience of crisis management within the context of 'a failing institution', Thames Valley University (TVU). Indeed my initial research followed Tony Blair and David Blunkett's visit to TVU when – in the week after the former had declared at the annual TUC Conference that his three key priorities in government if his party were elected to office would be 'education, education and education' – the then Leader of HM Opposition formally opened the new state-of-the-art Paul Hamlyn Learning Resource Centre on the Slough campus with the rhetorical flourish: 'Why, I wonder, can't every university be like TVU?' At that time, TVU was attempting to establish a self-styled 'New Learning Environment' (NLE): a bold innovation that was to founder, not because the aspiration behind it – to create an education setting which was more learner-centred than teacher-centred – was unsound, but because, as the Quality Assurance Agency (QAA) subsequently pointed out, the scale and speed with which attendant change processes had been introduced (notably, the centralization of academic-related administration and the establishment of an internal market) had undermined the university's infrastructure, thereby placing academic standards at risk.

The whole of this process – the conception, and subsequent unravelling, of the NLE; the QAA's investigation into allegations of 'dumbing down'; the naming and shaming of TVU as Britain's 'first failing university' and the development of the HEFCE recovery plan under the stewardship of Sir William Taylor – conducted, as it was, under intense public scrutiny and in circumstances unprecedented in higher education in the UK, yielded penetrating insights into management practices and processes: both their deficiency and also their efficacy. Not only that, but when contrasted with the examples set by university innovators overseas, it rendered transparent those prerequisites which are essential to effective management and leadership in HE. It is these characteristics which this study seeks to identify. In doing so, it also offers guidance, where appropriate, on tried and tested methods derived from the training programmes and the professional development schemes provided by, among others, the Cabinet Office, the Work Foundation (the former Industrial Society), the Chartered Management Institute and the Chartered Institute of Personnel and Development. Taken together, this study aims to provide HE managers with a 'good practice' guide to effective management.

Its focus furthermore – unlike the bulk of the literature on university management to date – is on the HE manager per se. That is to say, it is written quite deliberately from the manager's perspective. Much of the research in this area in the past – whether conducted by HE researchers, staff developers or management practitioners themselves – has invariably focused on a particular issue or theme (e.g. curriculum, personnel management, staff development, globalization and so on): an approach which while quite legitimate given the conception of the subject matter, and which has very often yielded critical insights into the issue, is also one which has not always rendered them transparent or explicit from the (subjective) perspective of the reader. Put another way, the received wisdom to date offers HE professionals cogent analysis and advice on *what* one could – or should – do in academic environments, but it is implicit, and not explicit, on *how* one should go about doing it.

Ironically, this same trait is also characteristic of the literature which has been designed by management developers and deliberately targeted the middle management HE audience. It is almost as if the same affliction which has affected management development in HE in the past – the (false) assumption that any intelligent, educated individual can manage, and there is therefore no need for training – has also influenced many of those who write about HE for an HE audience: namely, they appear to argue that 'since any intelligent and educated individual *can understand* what we say then *ipso facto* they will *automatically* be able to manage it'. Their conception of management within HEIs is also equally if not more damagingly restrictive, in that they invariably exhibit a consensual acceptance of the status quo in universities and a disposition to regard academic staff as an undifferentiated mass, as well as a tendency to view the role of HE managers as confined solely to responding to the needs of the managed.

In this book I have attempted to overcome the deficiencies of the received wisdom by, on the one hand, conceiving of the academic environment from the holistic perspective of the university manager, rather than in terms of a particular theme or issue (i.e. by making the manager the independent variable of the study rather than the dependent variable as has conventionally been the case) and, on the other, by maintaining an open mind about how such environments could or should be organized and managed: namely, by recognizing that universities do indeed have distinguishing features – the autonomy of the individual scholar; the precedence of subject over institutional loyalty; the strength of tradition and the cult of 'the expert' – but that these characteristics are not so peculiar in themselves that HEIs *have* to be managed in a particular way. And it is for this reason that I have not drawn any particular distinction between so-called academic managers such as heads of subject departments and general (support) managers such as administrators of central services; that, and the fact that such distinctions – as the success of the private for-profit University of Phoenix demonstrates – have more to do with the endemic elitist ethos that prevails within many institutions than they do with the reality of how HEIs will operate in the twenty-first century.

This book, then, seeks to address the needs of all those who manage in HEIs – with a particular emphasis on those who occupy head of department roles – and to make explicit, rather than implicit, the competencies and skills required to be an effective manager. It does not assume that any educated and intelligent individual can be an effective manager *without training*. Nor that universities are unique environments that can only be managed in a special way. And it has been structured and organized accordingly with the manager's world view in mind – the need to master the 'four knows':

- knowing your environment;
- knowing your university;
- knowing your department; and
- knowing yourself.

From the examination of HE in the broader context in Chapter 1 and analysis of HEIs as organizations in Chapter 2, through to the expectations of the role (leading your department; leading by example) and the demands of the role (managing for high performance, developing staff, celebrating diversity, enhancing the student experience, managing change) and finally on to accomplishing mastery of the role: managing up; managing the 'down-side'; managing oneself – each of the chapters provides a commentary and analysis of the particular role aspect under review, and offers advice and guidance on good practice, including case study examples and self-assessment tools.

Taken together, these chapters argue the case for a professional (or 'managerial') approach to people management in HEIs, and the case against amateurist, elitist and reactionary perspectives on university management – that we ought to have the same professionalism in the way we lead and manage people as we do towards our research and teaching. They further seek to demonstrate that 'managerialism' is not necessarily incompatible with collegiality, and to show how 'institutions of learning' can indeed become more like 'learning organizations'. More than that, they aspire to inspire. For history teaches us, as George Bernard Shaw implies, that 'nothing has to be as it is' – maybe that even management can be a blessing, as much as a punishment, from God!

1 Knowing your environment

The university is dead; long live the university.

Times Higher Education Supplement, 11 February 2000

'What is the world's largest business corporation in terms of market value?' It is – as management guru Peter Senge has suggested – not the one you might readily suppose. Not Microsoft or Coca Cola or IBM or General Motors. It is in fact Visa International. As Senge explains, Visa International is a member-owned, non-stock corporation incorporated in the State of Delaware. Governed by the principle of subsidiarity, it has only 3,000 employees – approximately the same number as that of Selfridge's department store in London's Oxford Street. Yet it has a stock market value in excess of $500 billion. In other words, Visa International 'is a business but unlike Microsoft which has an Industrial Age model of organization it doesn't feel like or look like a conventional business' (Senge, 1998). And while Bill Gates has fallen victim to the same (Sherman) anti-trust legislation which thwarted John D. Rockefeller's Standard Oil monopoly, Visa International is a conspicuous exception. It is indeed a novel phenomenon.

Senge's purpose in posing this simple question was threefold: to draw our attention to the significant changes taking place in the nature and organization of business corporations; to remind us that the present may not be an accurate guide to the future; and, equally fundamental, to illustrate that the first prerequisite of effective management is an awareness of one's external environment.

His vignette also highlights the difference in perception between the business world and the academic world. In higher education the prevailing consensus is that we do not really face the same changes as those which confront business. After all, conventional wisdom maintains, universities have a history stretch-ing back centuries, and they have proved themselves to be extremely durable institutions, capable of adjusting to different circumstances while still upholding their traditional ideals. They have, moreover, shown that they can accommodate themselves to the new realities of more recent times – principally, the (negative) governmental economic imperative to do 'more' (teach more students) with 'less' (resources) while still maintaining 'quality' and the (positive) pedagogical imperative to cater to employers' expectations of graduate competence, and students' desire for flexible provision. There is, then, no compelling reason, the argument runs, why universities cannot continue in the same vein in the future.

The problem with this argument, however, is that it ignores both the historical and the contemporary reality of the circumstances facing universities. In the case of the latter, for example, it overlooks the fact that the university is no longer the only type of institution capable of fulfilling the role that it has played in the past – namely that of providing access to knowledge, creating knowledge, and fostering learning in students to enable them to use knowledge. And in the case of the former, it overstates the ancient pedigree of universities, for in truth very few of them are old. In Europe, their ancient heartland, four out of five only came into being in the last century. In the UK fully three-quarters have been established in the course of the past four decades: and 30 of them (the former polytechnics) in a single stroke as recently as 1992. In essence, the bulk of universities are very modern institutions and those that can trace an ancient lineage have survived only because they have changed so much: to such an extent, indeed, that today, universities seek to present themselves as useful to all comers, from international students to regional development agencies. Embracing 'mission stretch', they have acquired 'multiple callings': to broaden student access, enhance student employability, promote lifelong learning, meet quality benchmarks, diversify income streams, improve research rankings and so on. In consequence they have become so diverse, so fractured and differentiated that it seems they are no longer bound by any overarching principles or unitary idea; so much so, as some have argued, that the university as a concept or 'idea' has in fact been rendered meaningless (Barnett, 2000; HEPI, 2009; Scott, 1995, 2008; Smith and Webster, 1997).

It is perhaps not surprising then that many staff in HE have become alienated, and that the prevailing mentality within the sector is survivalist – one of endurance rather than enjoyment; a frustration over a perceived lack of resources, excessive accountability and the erosion of traditional university values (Watson and Amoah, 2007). Some even go further and have suggested that too many universities are imbued with a 'welfarist' mentality; an outlook of 'whingeing and whining' and ultimately one of dependence upon – and, equally, subservience to – the public purse (Melody, 1997). Either way, the most common reaction within the sector has not been to address the broader issue concerning the *raison d'être* of HE other than to constantly reiterate the narrowly instrumental defence line stressing the usefulness of universities to government and industry. Rather, the reaction has often been to engage in mutual recrimination and penny-pinching within institutions on the one hand, and to rail against government and the wider community for failing to appreciate the self-evident value of universities on the other.

The difficulty with this approach, however, is that this outpouring is often matched by a deafening silence outside the sector. Lacking in self-confidence, reluctant to articulate an overriding motivating purpose and contending in a world where hardly anyone is listening, universities, it would seem, are enfeebled institutions facing an uncertain future. Yet the prospect is not nearly so bleak. Higher education is after all a growth industry – the student population at English HEIs, for example, grew from fewer than 1.5 million to over 2 million between 1998 and 2008 – and the education-driven economy of the so-called 'Knowledge Society' is likely to keep it this way in the foreseeable future, credit crunch or not (HEFCE, 2009). We also arguably need an 'idea' of the university more than ever to, as Barnett (2000) puts it, make sense of 'the craziness of the world of super-complexity' in which we now live. The HE Act 2004, too (for all the controversy over the introduction of variable fees, the projected concentration of research in an elite minority of institutions and the lowering of the bar for university title to admit institutions without research degree-awarding powers, including for-profit organizations), has presaged a setting in which universities are encouraged to play to their strengths. Likewise the re-badging of the Department for Education and Skills (DfES) as the Department for Innovation, Universities and Skills (DIUS) in 2007, and latterly as the Department for Business, Innovation and Skills in 2009, does indeed suggest that universities have moved from the periphery to the centre of the government's drive to meet the social and economic challenges of the new millennium: overdue recognition, in fact, of the role UK universities play as one of the nation's biggest earners of foreign currency, bringing in more than £5.8 billion a year in tuition fees, transnational enterprises and other activities (Bolton and Lucas, 2008; HEFCE, 2009). As such, universities have a tremendous opportunity to reassert their importance in the life of the country. Whether or not it is fully taken or spurned will, of course, be dependent on their willingness to practise flexibility on the one hand, while simultaneously maintaining their fundamental values on the other.

This first chapter, then, examines the broader context or nature of the external environment in which HEIs and individual managers alike have to operate. It explains, as a means of understanding the pressures on modern universities and the reasons why they respond the way they do, how universities have come to be where they are today, and includes an analysis of the role of HE and of the key influences or change drivers – globalization, IT, the Knowledge Society, the contractual state, the postmodern challenge – currently affecting HEIs. It also examines the nature of the university identity crisis, the university as an idea, the case for universities and finally the key strategic challenges facing universities.

The role of universities

Universities are both ancient and modern institutions: ancient in the sense that today's universities can trace their first beginnings to those universities – Bologna, Paris and Oxford – founded in the late Middle Ages and are the heirs to this medieval heritage and the traditions and values that goes with it; modern in the sense that it was only in relatively recent times – in the late nineteenth and early twentieth centuries – that universities developed into the form recognizable today, and it was not until a generation or so ago that the bulk of Britain's universities were established. Their evolution, moreover, bears witness to a remarkable series of changes in the role that universities have played: one which is reflective of a close association with (and not, as is often held to be the case, separation or aloofness from) wider developments in society. The ancient institutions of Oxford and Cambridge, for instance – the only established universities in England 200 years ago – were founded as church universities, whose main concern was the training of clergymen and teachers and with it the sustenance of the established Anglican Church. They did not originally seek to encourage progressive science or provide a liberal education – or research either for that matter. The former role was undertaken by the dissenting academies such as the 'godless' University College of London, which was established in 1826 and provided a practical education with an emphasis on science, medicine and engineering (Bolton and Lucas, 2008; Scott, 1995; Schuller, 1995; Coaldrake and Stedman, 1998).

It was the Industrial Revolution, and with it the progressive extension of the franchise and the rise of professional society, which were to be the three key factors in creating the demand for, as well as shaping the development of, a more elaborate university system in nineteenth-century Britain. And it was the civic universities – Manchester, Leeds, Liverpool, Sheffield, Bristol and so on – along with the technical colleges and the mechanics' institutes (which were later to develop into the technological universities and the former polytechnics) which were established to meet it. These three forces – albeit radically extended to embrace the ever-increasing specialization of labour, the universal access to mass entitlement and the ceaseless march of professional 'credentialism' – have continued to mould and shape higher education down to the present day; so much so that the modern university has come to undertake four conventional roles, those of:

- finishing school: the last stage of general education;
- professional school: the training of elite workers;
- knowledge factory: the production of science, technology and ideology;
- cultural institution: the expression of our individual and collective sense of being.

It was the state, though, which was the critical driver in bringing together the different institutions – church, voluntary and public sector – into a coherent higher education system. This development drew on two inter-related processes: the subordination of the autonomous universities on the one hand, and the takeover by the state (or nationalization, if you will) of responsibility for other advanced institutions, on the other. The subsequent abolition of the binary divide between universities and polytechnics in 1992, along with the quadrupling of student numbers in the last 20 years, set in motion a social and political revolution in British higher education; one which has left the system with far more in common with its counterparts in Europe and North America than it had a generation ago.

This transition from an elite to a mass system – or loss of British exceptionalism, depending on your perspective – has been neither smooth nor uncontested and is still also curiously incomplete. For example, in terms of size, there is little doubt that if we apply Martin Trow's (1973) linear model – which defines elite systems as those which enrol up to 15 per cent of the age group, mass systems as those enrolling between 15 and 40 per cent, and universal systems as those which enrol more than 40 per cent – then the UK has acquired the attributes of a mass system. The current age participation index in British higher education, for instance, is in excess of 40 per cent (if we include the UK equivalent of the US Community College student population, namely the post-18 HE provision in further education colleges) and bears testament to the government's long-established target of achieving a participation rate of 50 per cent among under-30-year-olds in 2010.

Much of this growth has been uneven, however, in that it has taken place primarily in the 'new' universities (the former polytechnics) and, moreover, has been based not so much on reaching out to new student populations, but rather on exploiting existing student constituencies more fully. Reservations remain as to whether this growth can be sustained, or whether government aspirations can be met: doubts compounded by the paucity of evidence of viable student demand for new modes of provision (e.g. foundation degrees; 14–19 Diplomas) and the sharp reality facing prospective students that they will have to bear a far greater proportion of the cost of their studies than their predecessors ever did.

Additionally, this growth has still not yet produced the culture change normally associated with the shift to a mass system. The enduring emphasis on the privileged character of student–teacher exchanges; the fervent belief in pastoral intimacy and fear concerning its loss (a peculiarly British phenomenon); and the passionate commitment to a research culture (even though as a university activity it is a relatively recent one) all suggest that – in its 'private life', if not its 'public' one – British higher education remains firmly wedded to elite values and practices no matter if it has become a mass system (McNay, 2006; Scott, 1995).

Nonetheless this expansion – and the universities' and colleges' achievement in accommodating it – has been a remarkable one, particularly since Britain was relatively late in making the shift from elite to mass higher education (the USA and much of western Europe made the transition a generation earlier) and given that it was accompanied by, as we noted earlier, a squeezing of resources, notably a halving in the unit of public funding per student. In the process, the core mission of higher education has been transformed. HEIs have had to redefine their notion of conventional roles such as 'teaching' (where the need to accommodate a more diverse student population has coincided with the emergence of new learning technologies) as well as undertake additional new roles, most notably in the areas of lifelong learning and technology transfer. This transformation, like other developments in the universities' long history, did not emerge in isolation but rather is intimately linked to broader societal and economic trends, drivers which are affecting higher education systems in all developed countries – the UK, Europe, Australia and US alike – in similar ways. It is these critical influences in the external environment which are analysed next.

I THE CHANGE DRIVERS

Globalization

With British banks recording the biggest annual losses in UK corporate history in February 2009 and the prospect of UK public debt 'hitting Armageddon levels (65 per cent of gross domestic product) in 2010–11', few who may have been unfamiliar with globalization could now remain unaware of its consequences – the credit crunch, the housing price slump, the bank and business failures, rising unemployment and the debt legacy to future generations. Equally, with calls for a 'global new deal' to avert 'the worst global recession since the 1930s' through massive state-funded stimulus packages such as the Obama administration's $800 billion, the prospect of tax increases and spending cuts in the mid- to long-term 'is inevitable' – and any public sector manager not planning on this basis, as the chief executive of the UK audit commission put it, 'is living in cloud-cuckoo-land' (Bundred, 2009).

Globalization or 'the intensifying process of economic integration and political interdependence', as Bill Clinton put it in his last speech as US President on British soil (Urry, 1999), is in fact a relatively new term. It is a subject on which few politicians – and UK government ministers in particular – can resist the temptation to say something. And with his eye on contemporary circumstance, the President informed his audience that 'in a single hour today, more people and goods move from continent to continent than moved in the entire nineteenth century'. While his assertion may have been ahistorical – in that it understates the contribution of inventions such as the electric telegraph, the telephone and the railway, and overlooks the fact that the world economy was more integrated a century ago than it is today and that the nineteenth century witnessed the greatest period of voluntary mass migration ever known – his motives were entirely laudable as well as remarkably prescient: namely, to draw our attention to the radical impact this extraordinary process has already had on the established institutions and ideas of the modern world – the market, the state and the individual – and the opportunity, as well as threat, it poses to the current social, economic and political order.

That said, we should also recognize there has been considerable confusion concerning the use of the term 'globalization' – what it is, and what it means. This has arisen in part because the term refers both to global processes (from the verb, to globalize) and to certain global outcomes (from the noun, the globe) and in part because it remains a contested concept. That is, some commentators view it primarily as an economic and political phenomenon, while others place more emphasis on its cultural and environmental dimensions. Thus the term has been used in a variety of ways to refer to (among others):

- the kinds of *strategies* employed by self-serving transnational corporations;
- an *ideology* promoted by capitalist interests seeking a global marketplace unfettered by (national) government regulation;
- an *image* used in the advertising of products (such as airlines, for example) or in recruitment drives for environmental protest groups (as in the 'fragile earth');
- the *basis for political mobilization* on a particular issue: famine relief in Ethiopia, the campaign to save the Amazonian rainforest, etc.;
- the *'scapes'* and *'flows'*, or the means (the fibre-optic cable, the micro-wave channel, the space satellite) and objects (people, information, ideas, messages and images) which now characterize the inter-connectedness of the new global environment.

Globalization, then, is not simply an advanced form of internationalization writ large. Unlike the latter, globalization is at best agnostic about, and at worst positively hostile to, nation states; it celebrates the 'low' worlds (or *Coca-colonization* and *McDonaldization*) of mass consumerism, not the 'high' worlds of diplomacy and culture and, as it is not tied to the past, is subversive of – and not supportive of – the established world order.

As the university is a creature of the nation state – reliant on it for the bulk of its revenue and closely identified with the promulgation of national culture – and has a core business, that of teaching, which has been standardized through the impact of communication and information technology, it follows that globalization presents possibly the most fundamental challenge that the university has ever had to face in its long history (HEPI, 2009; Scott, 1998; Urry, 1999).

The Knowledge Society

Intimately related to globalization is the growing recognition that national economic success can no longer be guaranteed solely by the mass production of consumer goods, or by the physical exploitation of natural assets. Rather, we are becoming increasingly dependent on our ability to create and use new ideas and knowledge. Or, as the Spellings Commission on *Charting the Future of US Higher Education* (2006) put it, 'in tomorrow's world a nation's wealth will derive from its capacity to educate, attract, and retain citizens who are able to work smarter and learn faster – making educational achievement ever more important both for individuals and for society writ large'. New technologies have simultaneously transformed our capacity to store and transmit information. We can now access a far greater range, diversity and quantity of it with greater speed and at our own convenience than ever before. Knowledge, though – and this is often misunderstood – is more than simply information, or access to it. It is about how and why we access it, how we make sense of it and how we engage critically with it. In essence, knowledge is about understanding. It is about 'information put to work . . . it is what enables people to make judgments, create new products, solve problems and interpret events'. And, of course, it has also been the prime *raison d'être* of the modern university. Indeed, in the past century the university – as a producer of knowledge ('research') and as a developer of know-ledgeability ('teaching') – has been a, if not *the*, key knowledge institution in northern and western Europe and North America.

This pre-eminence, however, can no longer be taken for granted. There are now, for instance, alternative sources of authority over knowledge readily accessible through the Internet and television. And while it is the case that high-level training and research have always taken place outside the university and public research system in think-tanks, corporate research and development divisions and so on (indeed half of all spending on HE comes from the private sector), the new Knowledge Society has spawned a proliferation of novel forms of knowledge organization including the 'for-profit university', the 'mega-university' and, especially, the 'corporate university' (and perhaps in future the 'global university'?). Their use of the brandname 'university' may be a compliment but it is also a distinct threat, for these 'new-wave' institutions are earnest competitors for the university's established role. IBM, for instance, spends over one billion dollars per year on research and boasts eight of its own campuses in which it offers its own university-level education. More than that, there is also the threat that other kinds of knowledge organization may yet emerge: institutions that are organized not so much on the university model but on that, say, of management consultancies, market research companies or media organizations. Either way, these new interlopers constitute a formidable challenge which HE will have to rise to meet if it is to maintain its established role (see Box 1.1) (Coaldrake and Stedman, 1998; Daniel, 1996; PA Consulting, 2008).

Social change

Globalization and the Knowledge Society have also generated far-reaching implications for higher education through the way in which they have transformed the nature of both our working lives and our daily lives. In today's education-driven economy the message

Box 1.1 New-wave competitors in higher education

Mega-universities
UK Open University
Academic University Turkey
University of South Africa
Indira Gandhi National Open University, India

For-profit universities
Phoenix, Corinthian Colleges

Corporate universities
BAE, Disney, Ford, Microsoft, Motorola, Unipart

Private HE training organizations
Apollo, DeVry, Kaplan, Laureate Education

Sleeping giants
IBM, News International

is a loud and clear one: 'if you don't learn, you won't earn'. And if you want to prosper, then – given that there are no more 'jobs for life' – you will have to commit yourself to 'lifelong learning' in order to maintain 'lifetime earning'. Thus, whether one likes it or not, higher education has become – and is almost certain to remain – a growth industry. Indeed at the turn of the millennium there were 1.5 million students in Britain, or more than double the total a decade earlier. And the participation of young people has increased from fewer than 1 in 10 to more than 1 in 3 in a generation.

More than that, as the participation has risen the 'employment power' of a university degree has (quite naturally) declined, and this outcome has, in turn, generated a burgeoning demand (as in the 'MBA syndrome') for still more specialist and stronger academic credentials. Hence the surge in growth of ever more postgraduate awards and professional qualifications. Further, the coincidence of this ratcheting (or 'credentialism') with the broadening of professional status has also placed universities in a strong position to cater to the needs of these new professionals in 'enterprise' (entrepreneurs) and 'welfare' (nurses, social workers, etc.), in the same way that they accommodated those of the 'industrial' (engineering) and 'pre-industrial' professions (lawyers, doctors and clergy) (Bargh *et al.*, 2000; Coaldrake and Stedman, 1998).

Whether or not universities will be able to take full advantage of this situation, however – or indeed maintain their existing market share, given the threat posed by the 'new wave' competition outlined above – will be contingent on the extent to which they are willing to respond to public expectations of choice, service and quality. Today's discriminating consumer wants, and indeed increasingly demands and gets, personalized service. And there is little reason to suppose that students are any different. Indeed, as they are more financially pressed than ever, they are likely to be even more intolerant of standardized ('one size fits all') approaches to services and products, such as the expectation that they should conform to the rhythms of a narrow conventional learning environment: attend classes at a set time and place, complete assessments that are often bolted on to courses as an after-thought, and generally learn passively under the overall control of the ('gate-keeper') tutor; in short, an approach which is organized to meet the convenience of the institution and its staff rather than that of the students.

If universities are to meet this challenge, then, as a significant minority have attempted, they will have to fundamentally change the way they currently organize teaching activity. In essence, they will have to turn this existing arrangement on its head, not only to put the student at the centre of the learning process, but also to ensure that provision is tailored to their individual needs. In other words, they will need to establish a learning environment which is much broader and more holistic in scope, one in which students are able to tap a wide range of learning resources (their student peers and library, computing and media facilities) free of the constraints of time and space, organize their learning around assessments which are central to their courses, and above all engage as active participants under the guardianship of the ('facilitator') tutor.

The implications – and also rewards – for universities in taking this initiative are both significant and far-reaching. On the one hand they would have to convince tutors that the transformation in their role – from the traditional one of 'director of learning' (or information deliverer) to that of 'facilitator of learning' (or curriculum designer) – was not merely desirable but essential for success. And on the other they would need to maximize the potential benefits offered by new learning technologies. That is to say, wary of the pitfalls that have already befallen e-banking and e-tailing and indeed the short-lived UK e-university in seeking a 'technological solution' to service excellence, universities would also need to ensure that they embrace a 'conversational' (i.e. 'people-to-people') model rather a 'transmission' ('machine-to-people') model of electronic learning. If successful, then they should flourish in today's service-oriented 'new economy'.

'Contractual' government

A further driver – the one which has had the most profound impact to date – is something that universities have had to contend with since their inception, namely, the nature of their relationship to wider society. Until the second half of the twentieth century, the form and practice of HE was largely a matter of the internal or 'private interests' of the academic community. Since then the state – in the name of the 'public interest' – has taken an increasingly active role in HE, initially to guide, then to steer and direct, and latterly to orchestrate 'the market' in which HEIs operate. A shifting pattern of behaviour, that is, which reflects the change in the way many governments now relate to their citizens: that is, in a contractual manner as much as in the traditional legal and political way.

This contractual view of government, in which the state now purchases services on behalf of its 'clients' as opposed to providing them itself (as it had previously done in the case of publicly owned nationalized industries, for example), has been in the ascendancy since the 1980s. It is most typically associated with the privatization initiatives of the Thatcher government of that period, and the public sector reforms of similar ilk introduced contemporaneously in Australia and New Zealand. This 'purchaser–provider' separation in the management of public services has also of course had a number of far-reaching implications for – and expectations of – the way in which HEIs are organized, governed and managed (Coaldrake and Stedman, 1998).

Efficiency gains

First, and most obvious, as we have seen, has been the financial imperative placed on institutions to do more with fewer resources: to generate, that is, in policy-speak, 'efficiency gains'. And they have in this regard been very successful, managing to accommodate a tripling of student numbers over the past 25 years while assimilating, as the Taylor Report (2001) repeatedly pointed out, 'a 38 per cent reduction [in funding] in real terms since 1989 following a decrease of 20 per cent between 1976 and 1989'. Or, put another way, they achieved an efficiency gain of more than 30 per cent in the 1990s alone, measured in terms of expenditure per student. Not only that, they also managed to sustain – in spite of the unprecedented introduction of means-tested tuition fees and the abolition of student maintenance grants in 1998 – a higher student completion (or lower drop-out) rate than anywhere else (with the single exception of Japan) in the world (Eastwood, 2008).

By the start of the millennium, however, the consensus within the sector was that this momentum was no longer sustainable: not, that is, without damaging 'the continued reputation for quality of our higher education system' (Eastwood, 2008), and particularly since half of Britain's universities were collectively in debt to the tune of £200 million and staff–student ratios had deteriorated from an average of 9 to 1 in 1980 to 17 to 1 in 1998 (or 23 to 1 if funding for research which is included in the average unit of funding is excluded). This view finally prevailed when the government – recognizing the need to 'reverse years of under-investment' – committed itself in January 2003 to increasing public spending on HE by 6 per cent a year in real terms from £7.6 billion in 2003–4 to £9.9 billion in 2005–6. The cash injection was buttressed by a further £1.5 billion a year from 2006 when – in another volte-face on student finance – up-front tuition fees were replaced by a top-up fee of (up to) £3,000 a year and maintenance grants were restored for students from low-income families: thus the government finally introduced in 2006 the measures which the Dearing Inquiry had originally recommended back in 1997.

That said, this income stream cannot be taken for granted. We know, for example, that the government bail-out of failed banks and attempts to pump-prime an ailing economy mean that the fee cap (of £3,000) may not be lifted following the planned review in 2009–10. Besides, Treasury uncertainty over funding institutions in advance of earning back the 'graduate contribution' from students, the very high parliamentary hurdle (the support of both Houses is required for any upward revision) and the absence of political consensus on the issue also suggest it will be far from straightforward thereafter. The government, though, did commit to matching institutions' own fund-raising initiatives (up to £3 million a year for three years) in March 2006; and 'by 2011', Universities Minister John Denham maintained, 'funding for higher education will be 30 per cent higher than in 1997' (Davis, 2009). Meanwhile the debate on where and how further alternative sources of funding may be raised goes on (see Table 1.1) (Watson and Amoah, 2007).

Table 1.1 Funding options for higher education

Option	Strength	Weakness
Increased public funding	• Readily identifiable • Government commitment to acknowledged priority	• No guarantee of government commitment • Electorally unpalatable (allegedly)
Market fees	• Differential ('top-up') fees would accurately reflect the costs of providing teaching • Would encourage diversity amongst HEIs and offer greater choice • The government's chosen option: January 2003	• Would increase graduate indebtedness and threaten student participation • Potentially damaging to access-oriented HEIs • The absence of political consensus
Institutional endowments (or 'perpetual loans') – proposed by Conservative Party, 2001	• £1.6 billion scheme which offers HEIs increased autonomy and independence of action • Could facilitate further development of world-class universities and niche institutions and also the culture of 'giving' (as in the USA)	• Contingent on scale and scope of deregulation permitted by government • May have negative impact on widening participation • Could not be applied universally in the short term • Would create new binary division
Income-contingent graduate contributions (or 'graduate tax') – similar to Cubie below and Australian system	• Abolishes up-front (fee) contributions in favour of fixed repayments shortly after graduation • (unlike Cubie) Endowment fund would meet shortfalls in learning and teaching	• Would increase dependency on public funds and reduce equity in the short-term • May still deter prospective students without incentivizing those who do enrol to pressurize HEIs to provide improved 'value for money'

Option		
The Cubie – Scottish Parliament scheme (same as one immediately above except . . .)	• Endowment fund provides additional support for students	• Raises no extra money for HEIs
Increased maximum fee contribution with income-contingent loans	• Doubling the current fee level (to £12,000) would yield English HEIs an additional income of £800 million	• Government likely to seek clawback of some additional funding • Increases disincentive to study. Unlikely to lead to an improvement in quality
Full-cost fees and scholarships administered by independent trust – advocated by Social Market Foundation	• Would increase institutional autonomy and give students greater influence	• The burden of funding for students would likely remain unchanged
Individual learning accounts	• Would provide greater transparency for individuals and give real meaning to lifelong learning • More a method of building up and distributing many different types of funding to and from individuals	• No ready means of controlling the demand in advance without complex rationing systems • Not a true funding option

Source: adapted from the Taylor Report, 2001.

'Initiativitis'

The second implication of the contractual view of government has been the apparent retreat from central planning, or more accurately a shift in emphasis from overt to covert planning. The higher education funding councils for the home nations (e.g. HEFCE, 1992 to date) are – unlike their ancestor the University Grants Committee (1918–89), which acted as a buffer body between universities and Whitehall and which generated a strategic overview for the sector consistent with universities' core values – nothing other than agents of government. Their role – and there is confusion about this in the sector – is not to lobby or act as a mediator, but rather to implement the government's pre-determined objectives through second-order policies. As their name implies, they are not intended to be planning bodies. Since strategic development is the responsibility of individual HEIs they confine themselves (supposedly) to funding institutions against their own strategic plans rather than seeking to impose any particular system-wide pattern of development (Scott, 1995). Well, that is the case in theory, at least.

Such has been the spate of special initiatives, however, emanating from the funding councils – on access and widening participation; institutional collaboration and restructuring; the development of learning and teaching strategies; the improvement of poor estates; the facilitation of links with business and the community and so on: projects, that is, amounting to £1,470 million or 18.4 per cent of the total funding for HE in England alone in 2009–10 – that one could be forgiven for thinking that HEFCE was indeed HEPCE! The biggest and most controversial of the funding councils' initiatives – accounting for a further £1,572 million or one-fifth of the total funding in England in 2009–10 – is, of course, the Research Assessment Exercise (latterly, the Research Excellence Framework); the four- or five-yearly peer review (or exercise in 'informed prejudice' by 'elitist amateurs' as its detractors put it) of university research output (HEFCE, 2008a; Cohen, 2000). Each of these initiatives is accompanied by the usual bureaucratic paraphernalia and form-filling – the information circular, the consultation document, the invitation to tender, etc. – so much so that for many in the thick of it, it feels like an endless treadmill of bidding rounds and game-playing amid a blizzard of information.

The government's efforts to establish a market in HE have had much the same outcome. The new maximum fee of £3,000 has ironically turned out to be a revised flat-rate fee in practice, with very few institutions charging less and none, so far, charging zero. Competition has emerged between HEIs over the provision of student bursaries and other support incentives rather than the fee levy. Thus we do have 'a market' in HE, if not the one the government or HEFCE had planned or intended. We have also had the same attendant bureaucracy – the reviews of transaction costs and of regulation; notably the formal Access Agreement between each individual HEI and the specially constituted Office for Fair Access (OFFA).

Niche institutions

Even more painful is the realization that these initiatives are likely to be unrelenting. For despite the rhetoric of free enterprise they are, in essence, national planning interventions thinly disguised as quasi-market competition, the chief purpose of which is to establish a more differentiated HE system. This modus operandi is reflected in the funding councils' separation of funding for teaching and for research which, if logically extended, would produce a 'super-league' of (elite) research universities existing alongside but largely segregated from the bulk of HEIs, whose role would be confined primarily to a social one – that of providing (mass) teaching (HEFCE, 2003).

The rationale behind this drive for greater institutional segregation has been the desire to protect elite research universities from the pressures of massification on the one hand, and access-oriented HEIs from the temptations of (so-called) 'academic drift' on the other; or put another way, to preserve and enhance 'excellence' in HE while simultaneously satisfying political and public pressures for mass participation. This aspiration was, of course, most clearly articulated in the 2003 White Paper which anticipated the creation of just such a setting: namely a research elite, centres of teaching excellence, fair access for all and a network of Knowledge Exchanges to promote links between 'non research-intensive universities' and the business community. The Paper notwithstanding, this drive has, to date, not been as successful in practice as national policy makers would have wished.

On the contrary, it could be argued that – formally at least – the HE system has become less stratified, not more. The elite universities, for example, have shown a marked reluctance to forgo their broader social responsibilities, an inclination borne out in the celebrated case of Laura Spence, the Tyneside state school applicant, whose rejection by Oxford, and subsequent acceptance at Harvard, was deemed by the Chancellor of the Exchequer to be an 'absolute scandal'. Irrespective of whether or not this individual student should have been turned down, the furore it generated – 'I have never seen Oxford in such a lather of indignation', as one don put it – showed that although the university may be acutely sensitive to allegations of elitist bias, it also had a keen appreciation of the need for broader student access (Goddard and Tysome, 2000). Likewise the former polytechnics have shown a similar reluctance to forsake research in favour of an existence based solely around teaching. Indeed they have, by and large, sought to expand their research base, in the belief (if not one shared by the authors of the White Paper) that without such activity they would not be taken seriously as universities: an aspiration reflected in the outcome of the 2008 RAE which (by using assessment based on a rating profile rather than a single quality score) 'rewarded excellence wherever it is found' and ensured research funding was, in fact, distributed across universities far more widely than heretofore (Frean, 2008a; HEFCE, 2009).

The government has been more successful, however, in its expectation of universities to take on brand new roles in reaching out to new student constituencies and to the business community in particular. The establishment of science parks as incubators for private enterprise; the commercialization of intellectual property; the provision of consultancy (both to generate income and to assist global economic competitiveness); the development of electronic and distance learning; the extension of continuous professional development provision; the accommodation of lifelong learning and of work-based learning, for example, are all radically new activities which go well beyond the traditional notions of 'research' and 'teaching'. A myriad callings have, in fact, opened up for universities, providing opportunities which institutions have exploited to a greater or lesser extent. Thus differentiation is emerging not so much at the system level – where fuzziness, which was the norm even before the binary division between universities and polytechnics was abolished in 1992, has increased still further – as at the institutional level. Put another way, it would appear that we have all become niche institutions or, at least, are expected to be so; that 'instead of trying to do everything', we should, as HEFCE advises, 'focus on what we do best' – even though, ironically, the Knowledge Society is evolving in the exact opposite direction – to an environment in which easy categorization and ready-made demarcation are conspicuous by their absence (Bargh *et al.*, 2000; PA Consulting, 2008; Scott, 1995, 2008).

Accountability

'Paper, paper, everywhere', 'Trial by paper' and 'Academics swamped by bureaucracy' are familiar press headlines which bear testament to a further – and also bitterly contested – implication of the government's contractual relationship with HE, namely, the former's insistence that the latter should adhere to new forms of accountability. This expectation, derivative of the expansion of provision in HE, has a number of sources. One is the financial imperative that, since HEIs receive over £8 billion of public money a year they should do their utmost to deliver 'value for money', a performance indicator which is monitored by the national funding councils. Another is quality assurance, the view that academic quality cannot be guaranteed if it is exclusively reliant on academic self-regulation; that quality ought to be managed, rather than assumed, in order to demonstrate that provision is 'fit for purpose', the monitoring of which is undertaken by the Quality Assurance Agency (QAA).

Still another is the desire for greater transparency – that stakeholders have a 'right to know' and should therefore have access to accurate, consistent and comprehensive information on HEIs, enabling them to make informed choices: a process which is invariably aided and abetted by the publication of university league tables in the national media. In consequence, HEIs have found themselves required to respond to external requests for information, inspections, audits, submissions and bids for funding from an increasing variety of stakeholders: the QAA, HEFCE, the Higher Education Statistics Agency, the Teacher Development Agency, the National Health Service, European Commission, Research Councils and so on (see Figure 1.1). Though this requirement is no different to that expected of other public sector institutions – and is in fact symptomatic of the emerging audit society which has developed as a corollary of the nascent Knowledge Society – it has had a more profound impact on HEIs for a number of reasons.

First, universities, and in particular the traditional ones, have had a longer and deeper attachment to institutional autonomy and professional collegiality than other comparable public sector organizations, an ethos reinforced in the past by the emphasis placed on planning resources (inputs) but undermined now by the current vogue for auditing policy (outcomes). Second, the strength of this tradition has meant that these new requirements have (rightly or wrongly) been widely perceived as having replaced a self-governing system based on trust among competent professionals with one based on a presumption of mistrust and incompetence – a perception, accurate or otherwise, which has, not surprisingly, had a predictably depressing effect on morale within universities. Third, the other reservations prevalent within universities concerning audit – that the processes are overly bureaucratic, time consuming, expensive and needlessly stressful – were apparently borne out in the funding council's own review. Their initial review inquiry found that the cost of accountability was approximately £250 million – or 4 per cent of the £6 billion of

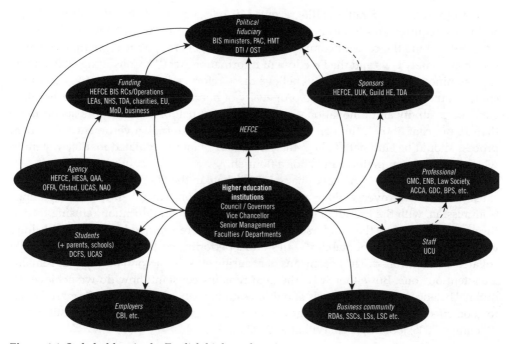

Figure 1.1 Stakeholders in the English higher education sector

Source: adapted from HEFCE, 2000b.

public funds which HEIs received in 2000 – but since 'the overall regime [was] a patchwork of legacy requirements from different stakeholders, responding to different concerns, at different times, with little overarching design, coordination or rationale' they concluded this investment 'represents poor value for money both for stakeholders and for institutions'. Further, the review team found that – among other things – the regime encouraged 'inappropriate behaviour' (such as game-playing, positional planning and short-term opportunism); contributed to 'planning blight' (by exacerbating uncertainty); placed academics' professional reputations (and even their careers) at risk; and fostered a 'something for something' culture which incurred costs in administering extra funding which were, ironically, often disproportionate to the extra money awarded (HEFCE, 2000b; Smith and Webster, 1997).

The reviewers recommended, therefore, that a new paradigm be established – an investor/partner model – for the relationship between HE funding agencies and institutions: one which was less burdensome and less interventionist and which in channelling demands on HEIs through a single body (the funding council) would eliminate 'the duplication, confusion and conflicting demands of overlapping systems' symptomatic of the current accountability regime. The implementation of this recommendation through the work of the Higher Education Regulation Review Group (the so-called 'single conversation') has – along with the QAA's much trumpeted 'lighter touch' for institutional and subject review – been broadly welcomed. Indeed these measures have led to a further 20 per cent reduction (on top of the 25 per cent between 2000 and 2004) in the cost of accountability between 2004 and 2008 to £190 million – or

2.4 per cent of the c. £8 billion HEIs received in 2008 – even while still accommodating additional requirements (for example, from the Office for Fair Access); though this figure does not include the costs of complying with more general public regulations such as health and safety laws and the Freedom of Information Act (PA Consulting, 2009). Even so, a significant number in HE still believe these reforms do not go far enough. On the contrary, they argue that given the propensity of bureaucratization to stifle rather than enhance creativity and innovation – and the fact that half of all academics spend more than 15 per cent of their time on administration – the external government assessment process should be eliminated altogether, in favour of an unregulated market system in which freedom, competition and choice flourish.

Much the same concerns have shaped the debate in the USA. Indeed, accountability caused more controversy than any other issue among members of the Spellings Commission, with the President of the American Council on Education refusing to sign the final report rather than endorse the Commission's recommendation of establishing uniform measures of accountability with student performance data that would be centrally collated and controlled. The best means of ensuring effective accountability thus remains a contentious one. But either way, the goal remains constant: how do we achieve the optimal balance between the needs of public assurance (that funds are spent properly and to good effect) and those of private governance (of the health and interest of institutions) (Spellings, 2006; Jobbins, 2006; Williams, 2007).

Active management

A final implication of the emerging audit culture – and one which has been equally divisive in consequence – has been that universities have been compelled to be far more proactive in the way they manage their affairs. Two generations ago, universities were self-governing collegial communities of scholars presided over by vice chancellors whose *raison d'être* was essentially that of ceremonial figurehead. Their autonomy went un-challenged and their affairs were 'administered' by a bursar and a registrar whose combined complement of staff rarely exceeded 10 per cent of the total payroll of the typical 1950s redbrick university. Today, universities operate as professional bureau-cracies with vice chancellors whose authority rests more on managerial competence than it does on collegial charisma, and who wield power akin to their role – and to that of their counterparts in the private sector – as the institution's chief executive officer. External intrusion has become a daily fact of life; university departments have become 'basic units' and 'cost centres'; and 'central services' administration now consumes well over one-third of the average university budget. More than that, universities have acquired the typical organizational panoply – the mission statement, the guiding principles and strategic plan, the corporate brand, etc. – characteristically associated with that of contemporary private sector enterprise. And, in many instances, they have sought to apply techniques, values and practices derived from the commercial sector. Simply stated, the 'donnish dominion' has been supplanted by managerial sovereignty (Halsey, 1992; McNay, 2006).

Governmental expectations that new universities (the former polytechnics) would take on additional responsibilities (for industrial relations, estates management and strategic planning) subsequent to incorporation, and that all universities would both generate efficiency savings and adhere to new forms of accountability, have, as we have noted, played a significant role in precipitating this volte-face in institutional management. It would be wrong, however, to assume that governmental pressure was the sole driver. On the contrary, the growth of managerialism is as much attributable to the internal dynamics of institutional development as it is to any external pressure. Institutional expansion alone on the scale that we have witnessed (the size of the average British university today, *c.* 17,000, is more than double that of 40 years ago) would have required that universities be far more actively managed than had previously been considered necessary. As it is, it is more than simply a matter of size. Universities have also become increasingly complex institutions. The relentless specialization and sub-specialization of scholarship, the acquisition of new roles (such as technology transfer and lifelong learning), and the formation of collaborative partnerships with FE institutions and private enterprise have all contributed to making universities far more heterogeneous than in the past. In addition, the redesignation of the former polytechnics as universities in 1992 also diluted the organizational exceptionalism still further. For all these reasons, then, universities would – government pressure notwithstanding – have been obliged to manage their affairs in a much more self-conscious way than hitherto (Bargh *et al.*, 2000; Scott, 1995).

Either way, the very fact that universities do need to be managed in a more proactive way has meant that issues concerning the internal operation of universities – principally, how should universities be optimally organized and how should they be managed (in an entrepreneurial or collegial way, for example) – have assumed far greater importance and significance in contemporary HEIs; a theme which we will return to later.

Academic specialization and postmodernism

The two final change drivers have, unlike the previous ones, arisen from within rather than outside HE, one – the ever-increasing specialization of scholarship – as a consequence of the growth of knowledge, and the other – postmodernism – as an intellectual challenge to the prevailing (modernist) epistemology of knowledge. The former trend is one which has, in turn, given rise to the professionalization of knowledge, to the practice, that is, of scholars writing primarily for a specialist audience, invariably their academic peers, rather than a generalist one. It has become a common and generally accepted practice.

Postmodernism, on the other hand, has been a more contentious and less well-understood phenomenon. A significant minority view it as so much 'academic globaloney': as a change in form and style, rather than one of any real substance. And indeed its very nature – its lack of coherence and its opposition to Big Ideas of the past and present – does not make it easy to define. The origins of postmodernism are obscure, though it appears the movement sprang from a seemingly disparate range of sources: the apparent demise of grand ideologies; the idea of post-industrial society; the theories of the post-structuralists (Derrida and Foucault); and the aesthetic reaction against the 'international style' of modern architecture. Its foundations, that is, are united more by what they reject – modernist discourse – than by what they have in common with one another. Put another way, according to the postmodernists, the relationship between the researcher (the subject) and the object of study is a lot more delicate and complex than modernists have assumed to be the case. Indeed in the postmodern view modernist research is fatally flawed because of the way in which language is used – *unproblematically* – within this discourse to picture the essentials (atoms, neurons, economies, etc.) of 'reality', so much so, in fact, as to call into question the very notion of objectivity which has underpinned all traditional methods of scientific inquiry to date (Reed and Hughes, 1992).

The impact of postmodernism in practice, then, has been profound. In subverting the conventional belief in the possibility of objective knowledge and scientific truth, it has not only undermined the epistemological basis on which the modern HE system developed, but has also spawned an academic environment characterized by *difference*; i.e. one in which – in the absence of any particular hierarchy of subjects or notion of authoritative knowledge – a plurality of mutually contestable knowledges (or 'multi-vocalism') prevails. Or, put another way, it has precipitated a transformation in the organization of knowledge in universities away from what has been termed Mode I knowledge (traditional, homogeneous, hierarchical subject disciplines rooted in an apprentice–master relationship) towards Mode II knowledges (which are non-hierarchical, pluralistic, transdisciplinary, fast-changing and socially responsive to a diversity of needs). This trend has itself been compounded by the relentless drive towards ever-increasing subject specialization (Smith and Webster, 1997).

In practice, these two drivers have had a largely unsettling effect on academic communities. On the one hand, postmodernism has not surprisingly reduced, if not in all cases, the confidence and self-esteem of many intellectuals in their work – in both what they produce and the value of it. And on the other, specialization has brought about a decline in the number of intellectuals who write for the wider public, for the simple reason that it fosters scholarship which places a premium on writing for the sake of professional advancement at the expense of contribution to public affairs. Indeed, the scale of fragmentation in many disciplines is such that sometimes academics, even within the same faculty, cannot discuss their areas of expertise without misunderstanding. And this is particularly manifest in areas such as the post-structuralist school of thought where self-styled 'radicals' (usually securely tenured at renowned universities) proffer opinions in language which is excessively and unnecessarily convoluted, self-referential and socially exclusive: in rebarbative jargon in short. And it is these same 'radicals', ironically, who have repeatedly railed at the language used by proponents of 'new managerialism' (Jacoby, 1997).

In consequence, then, the university community has become ensnared by its own peculiar notions of intellectual expertise. Many intellectuals have retreated to this private world apparently unable or unwilling to engage with a wider public and public issues. And this is at a time when, as we have seen, universities have come under greater public scrutiny than ever before. It is as if the university has 'lost the plot' just when it can least afford to. More than that – in challenging the ethical base as well as the epistemological one on which the university rests – postmodernism has shorn the institution of any particular value structure. Thus we cannot assume any longer that the contribution of the university is necessarily a given 'cultural good'.

ISIS

the consequences of the other change drivers
organizational exceptionalism, the acquisition
wave' competitors – it is readily apparent why
ve concluded that the university faces a crisis
nal decline. Today, these commentators argue,
gs in a mass system. Yet it does not stand for
ny essential qualities. As such, the university
pt and as an institution.
esents is self-evident. It goes to the heart of
the response from the academic community
as Smith and Webster (1997) put it, 'passive'.
pose or unifying theme for HE for the reasons
justify themselves primarily, and indeed not
e contribution they, and their graduates, make
ation. Frustratingly, however, this message is
Others, by contrast, maintain we need the 'idea'
d that a broader and more profound case can
w the prospect is not nearly so bleak. On the
o prosper than it is to wither in their future

of the university? What case can we make in defence of the institution?

The university as an 'idea'

The irony of today's condition – the absence of a commanding model or expressive vision of the university – is that it is an entirely novel experience in the institution's long history. For in the past, indeed, HE has always been supported by a number of just such ideas: visions, that is, which are invariably invoked by those seeking to defend the university ideal.

The first and also the most famous was, of course, the one embodied in Cardinal Newman's *The Idea of a University* published in 1852. A former Oxford tutor and Anglican convert to Catholicism, Newman's vision was of an institution that was not a tool of business, the state, or indeed (to the surprise of his sponsors) the Church. Universities needed 'elbow room', Newman argued, in which to pursue 'a knowledge which is its own end . . . liberal knowledge': not to train up imperial rulers, as has sometimes been argued, but rather to cultivate in its students the values of civilized reflection. In Newman's view, then, knowledge is valuable for its own sake, not for the uses to which it could be put. And his university ideal – in keeping with the scholastic tradition of the medieval university – was that of a setting in which knowledge and culture, with a special emphasis on classical Greek culture, were conserved and passed on. His university is therefore strictly non-utilitarian: one in which there is no place for either professional training or indeed organized research. Rather it is teaching which is the activity at the heart of what Newman calls 'the business of a university' (Pelikan, 1992).

A second model, and one in marked contrast to Newman's ideal, was the research university. Initially conceived by the Prussian education minister Wilhelm von Humboldt as an instrument for national rebuilding in the wake of the Napoleonic Wars, the university, in this model, drew on science as well as philosophy, and prioritized graduate research ahead of undergraduate teaching. Centred on the all-powerful departmental professor, this model – in which graduate students served their apprenticeship for the PhD in much the same way as journeymen had done in the medieval guild – also embraced academic freedom and student freedom of choice. With such success it was soon adopted elsewhere, notably the United States where the Humboldtian university was most clearly epitomized in the establishment of Johns Hopkins University (1876), Clark University (1887), Stanford University (1891) and the University of Chicago (1892).

The German notion of the university as an instrument of national culture fell into disrepute with the rise of fascism in the 1920s and 1930s, and it was left to the existentialist philosopher Karl Jaspers to reassert the independence of the institution. 'The University', he wrote famously in *The Idea of the University* (1946), 'is a community of scholars engaged in the task of seeking truth'. In Jaspers's scheme the transmission of culture was based strictly on critical enquiry but interestingly, unlike Newman, he did not believe that the university should be preoccupied solely with the pursuit of 'pure learning'. There was room in Jaspers's university for professional education too.

A third model was that of the 'modern' university, a concept developed by the American educationalist and former Johns Hopkins graduate Abraham Flexner in his *Idea of a Modern University* published in 1930. Reacting against the dominance of what he termed the 'service station' role of universities – the expectation that universities should provide vocational education and demonstrate their practical usefulness to the country – as well as his perception that much university research output was of poor quality – Flexner argued for the establishment of a 'modern' institution, which combined the ideas of Newman and von Humboldt within a 'unity of purpose' to pursue excellence. Flexner's 'modern university' ideal exerted, as one might expect, a very powerful attraction at the time of its publication, one indeed which has persisted in many quarters undiminished to the present day. This is in spite of (or maybe because of) the ideal's antipathy to mass participation, and the fact that, as Clark Kerr pointed out as long ago as 1960, Flexner (like Newman) was describing an institution that had already ceased to exist (Kerr, 1963; Coaldrake and Stedman, 1998).

A fourth model was the multiversity developed by Clark Kerr, President of the University of California, and celebrated in his *Uses of a University* published in 1963. Kerr's model, symptomatic of the idealistic aspirations of post-war American society, conceived the university as having not one single community but multiple ones: viz. different communities of students, different communities of academics and external communities of alumni, government, business and so on. His multiversity is a city – a 'City of Intellect' – in which staff and students identify with particular subcultures rather than with the whole. This conception Kerr sought to make reality, first through the building of a multi-campus public research university system, unique in not having an official flagship campus, and second as the architect of the 1960 California Master Plan for Higher Education. The latter, called a 'treaty' by Kerr, outlined a vision for the entire state – to spread opportunity to all its young citizens, to raise the skill levels of human resources and so on – and established a three-tier system, each tier with its own function and specialization. Thus the elite campuses of the University of California offer world-class research and teaching facilities; the California State University concentrates primarily on undergraduate teaching; and the state's many community colleges provide low-cost and locally focused access to higher education. The Plan attracted admirers and critics in equal measure but remains the classic example of a stratified system of HE provision and is potentially the source of renewal – as recognized in the 2003 White Paper – for a vision of HE in the twenty-first century (Kerr, 2001).

The home-grown British response to the same forces which produced a mass system in the USA saw the establishment of the 'Polytechnic Experiment' (1965–92), on the one hand, and the creation of the green-field campus sites of the county (or Shakespearian) universities – York, Lancaster, Warwick, Sussex, Essex and Kent – on the other. These twin initiatives combined a visionary aspiration (largely unmet) to redraw the map of learning with the more pragmatic (and eventually successful) goal of providing vocational and technical education (Scott, 1995).

The case for universities

Contemporary HE is heir to all these earlier visions – but, as we noted earlier, a dispossessed one. For there is nothing today to match these past visions which have, to varying degrees, been either undermined or discredited. It is, however, possible to identify some elements which testify to the uniqueness and special value of the institution – and why ultimately universities matter. In the first instance, we need to remember, as Daniel Bell (1966) began reminding us 40 years ago, that what gives our universities their defining purpose is that *they retain a near monopoly of the granting of credentials*. And while this purpose may be fraught with risk – in that potentially it could reduce the university to being a servant of the professions, employers and industry – the very fact that universities have maintained a virtual monopoly in the awarding of legitimate credentials testifies to the vitality of academia.

Second, universities – the virtual campus notwithstanding – are particular sorts of gathering places. And even in the postmodern era, when knowledge is uncertain and contested, they remain *the primary site of cultural engagement; a physical locale* where people come together to engage in intellectual endeavour. Third, and more problematic, is the – unashamedly and unapologetically modernist – contention that, in spite of postmodernist claims to the contrary, the university remains *the locus of disinterested research, scholarship and teaching*; a guiding principle which should underpin all institutions bearing the name. This is not inconsistent with the 2003 White Paper's view of universities having different priorities and in some instances maybe even a 'teaching only' brief. Such a conception indeed would mark the reassertion of what Newman always maintained was the (single) core activity of universities.

Fourth, the uncertainties of the new postmodern age, a 'world of supercomplexity', have bestowed, as Ronald Barnett (2000) points out, a new set of responsibilities on universities. There is the need to reorganize research to engender daring new frames of understanding; utilize pedagogy that enables us to understand the character of this world; empower individuals both within itself and in the wider society to live purposefully amidst supercomplexity. Put another way, the university should complement critical thinking – what it always has done – with critical self-reflection and critical action, and in that way establish itself as *a site of the continuing formation of critical being*; that is, as *an emancipatory institution* which empowers students on the one hand, and acts as *a key instrument in maintaining an open society* on the other (Bolton and Lucas, 2008; Smith and Webster, 1997).

Taken together, these distinctive features offer a basis for revivifying the university both as a concept and as an institution: to enable it potentially to fulfil a uniquely significant role that no other type of institution could properly provide in a free and responsible society. And when we combine these with the significance which the institution holds – as an object of aspiration and as a crucial *rite de passage* – for an increasing proportion of the population, as well as the practical contribution which universities make (summarized in Box 1.2), then the future prospect is indeed a bountiful one.

It remains the case, however, as we have seen, that to make it so universities will have to redefine themselves to operate successfully at the forefront of change. They must ensure flexibility, that is, while still maintaining loyalty to traditional values. If they do not, then they run the risk of being overwhelmed and will have no one but themselves to blame for the outcome. Institutional management and the professoriate alike, then, have a shared responsibility to ensure that universities take the former path. If successful there is no reason why universities cannot be more important than ever in the future.

Box 1.2 The functions and aims of universities

Functions
- Pursuit of research and scholarship
- High-level specialized education and training
- Fulfilling the workforce needs of the 'expert society'
- Performance of leadership roles in intellectual activities
- Provision of services to the region and immediate community
- Acting as a screening mechanism for entry to the professions
- Operating as an avenue for social mobility

Aims
- To generate a highly educated and trained population
- To generate a population able to work and live together. The British universities' concept of collegiality, and their strong pastoral systems, help to promulgate the ideal of a civilized society, able to settle dissent through democratic and rational means
- To generate a society that reflects certain inherent moral values
- To transmit a shared culture – one which is not in any way inconsistent with the ideal of cultural diversity
- To preserve and transmit knowledge
- To assist in spreading the benefits of informational and technological advances
- To enable its graduates to play an active part in wealth creation of the nation
- To generate a population skilled in the wide range of specialized activities necessary to sustain a complex society

Source: adapted from Bolton and Lucas, 2008; National Conference of University Professors, 1996; Talloires Declaration, 2005.

III THE KEY STRATEGIC CHALLENGES FOR UNIVERSITIES

If they are to be successful, however, then universities will need to consider and address the specific strategic challenges facing the HE sector (see Tables 1.2 and 1.3). Each of these challenges varies, of course, in significance for different HEIs depending on their particular circumstances, but no HEI can say that any of these issues do not apply to them – from those that affect every institution in general (e.g. the projected 15 per cent drop in the number of UK 18-year-olds by 2020; the Leitch (2006) target of equipping 40 per cent of the UK workforce with 'higher level skills' by 2020) to those that will generate a much more varied response across institutions (e.g. research and widening participation). Indeed the 'mission stretch' which HEIs have been subject to over the last generation means that in order to prosper each HEI needs to be proactive in fashioning its particular response to each and every one of them, appropriate to the context. And what is equally striking is that these key challenges facing HEIs are indeed broadly similar across all developed countries, as indicated in the findings of the various national inquiries into HE that respective governments have commissioned: for example, the Spellings Commission (2006) in the USA; the Dearing Committee (1997), the White Paper (2003) and the Leitch Review (2006) in the UK; the West Committee in Australia (1997–8); the Tertiary Education Review in New Zealand (1997–8) and the National Commission in post-apartheid South Africa (1995–6) (Watson and Amoah, 2007).

Table 1.2 The key strategic challenges for your university

Equality and diversity
- Meeting statutory requirements
- Going beyond legal compliance
- Internalizing diversity as a core university value
- Fostering diversity among partners

Student numbers
- Planning – the demographic challenge
- Growth, consolidation, contraction

Widening participation
- 'Fair access'; low-income groups; minority populations
- Student bursaries; support incentives
- Student retention: open door, not a revolving door
- Local partnerships; progression accords; curriculum mapping

HR
- Demographic trends; retirement peak; generational changing of the guard

University values
- What do we stand for – really?
- What do we want to be known for?
- How will we behave to one another as a learning community and a living community?

Funding
- Variable fees; fee review
- Friend-raising; fund-raising
- Diversifying income streams
- Full economic costing

Marketing
- Market positioning
- Brand identity
- Proactive strategic communication
- Reputation management
- League table positioning

Competition
- Local, regional, national, international
- Alliances, collaborations, mergers

Table 1.2 Continued

- Twenty-first-century academic
- Succession planning
- Pay and reward framework
- Academic promotion scheme
- Performance management
- Staff experience
- Employer of choice

Resources and estates development
- Sustainable facilities and services
- Web-based; web-enabled
- Future-proofed
- Value for money
- Project and programme management
- Stakeholder satisfaction

Governance
- Implementing code of good practice
- Financial sustainability
- Monitoring institutional performance – KPIs
- Risk management
- Governance effectiveness

Sustainability and corporate
- Social responsibility
- Serving broader political, social, ethical and cultural agendas
- 'Greening the campus'
- Civic engagement
- Enhancing community capability
- Economic and social regeneration
- Business and enterprise

Business and enterprise
- 'Third stream' activity
- Knowledge transfer
- Employer engagement
- The skills agenda

- Academic portfolio fit for purpose

Learning and teaching
- The new 'information-age mindset'; lifelong learning
- E-learning; learning through work
- Harnessing the learning network: home, campus, place of work, local community
- Students as producers of learning as well as consumers of learning
- Staff as facilitators of learning as well as directors of learning
- Graduate employability

Enhancing the student experience
- Quality 'customer care'
- Personalized service
- Student satisfaction

Management of research
- Research excellence framework
- Research contracts and careers
- Academic pipeline

Internationalization
- Student recruitment
- Franchises, collaboration and partnership
- Competition: private providers
- Learning, teaching and curriculum

Accountability
- Quality assurance, enhancement and accreditation
- Data transparency to inform student choice
- Meeting student and employer expectations

Source: adapted from LFHE, 2004.

Take, then, each of these challenges in turn. What are their implications for your university? your department? What do you need to do to meet the challenge of the new HE?

Table 1.3 Traditional higher education and the new HE

Traditional HE	*New HE*
Competition: other universitites	Competition: everywhere
Student as apprentice scholar	Learner as customer (and producer)
Delivery in the classroom	Delivery everywhere
Technology as an expense	Technology as market differentiation
Institutional-centric	Market-centric
18–25-year-old audience	Lifetime learner
Terminal degree	Lifelong learner
Mode 1 knowledge	Mode 2 knowledge
Take what is offered	Courses on demand
Academic calendar	Year-round campus
Course as 3–4 year revenue	Course as business plan
Teacher as director of learning	Teacher as facilitator of learning
Academic as 'jack of all trades'	Academic as specialist
Multicultural	Global
Diversity as problem	Diversity as strength
Process-compliant	Outcomes-driven
Public subsidy	Portfolio management
Peer review	Quality 'kite marks'
Producer of knowledge	Agent of learning
Organized by subjects	Organized for solutions

2 | Knowing your institution

The University is a community of scholars engaged in the task of seeking truth.

Karl Jaspers, 1923

I find the three major administrative problems on campus are sex for the students, athletics for the alumni and parking for the faculty.

Clark Kerr, President, University of California, 1958

'This proposal, you know, might have to go to a Congregation.' This constantly reiterated mantra came to haunt John Kay soon after his appointment as the founding Director of Oxford University's Said Business School in 1996. His brief – to introduce a new subject into an ancient institution – was a difficult one, but given that the project was being underwritten by an external sponsor – in the form of a £20 million gift – and since Kay himself was a long-standing Fellow of St John's College and therefore familiar with 'the Oxford way' – his task should have been, as he anticipated, rendered more straightforward. And indeed it was initially, for Kay's immediate priority, to establish a developmental strategy, was enthusiastically endorsed by colleagues (Kay, 2000a).

When he sought to advance the initiative further, however, through the implementation of an agreed action plan, Kay found that the university had no mechanism for proceeding with such discussions. Instead he was advised to turn his strategy document into specific proposals which could then be considered by relevant committees: a disastrous consequence, from Kay's perspective, for none of these committees had an overarching brief, and his initiative would be tackled piecemeal fashion. Worse still, they were all averse to reaching a definitive conclusion anyway. Indeed Kay discovered that the Oxford committee system had elevated the avoidance of decision-making into an art form. The 'eight oars of indecision', as Kay dubbed them – deferral and referral; procedural objection; the wider picture; evasion; ambiguity; precedent and denial – were all techniques which were invariably deployed by committee members to thwart his proposals (Kay, 2000b).

In exasperation, Kay turned to those university officials who held executive titles only to find they did not have executive functions or authority. Even his suggestion that they hire a project manager to oversee the construction of the building – a normal business practice – was overlooked in favour of appointing yet another committee of academics solely for this purpose. As a last resort Kay could have appealed to Congregation – the 'parliament' of all the Oxford faculty, some 3,000 in number and the source of ultimate authority in the university – but he knew this would be fruitless as this course of action had been repeatedly recommended to him by opponents, in the knowledge and spirit that 'you haven't got a hope in hell of getting this through so you might as well give up now'. Kay opted to resign in frustration in 1999 and become a Fellow once more of St John's College. The University restructured its operations the following year (devolving decision-making and resource allocation to the local level) and it was left to Anthony Hopwood, Kay's successor, to establish the Said Business School as a major intellectual and physical centre of the institution (Kay, 2000a).

Kay's experience highlights how Oxford's greatest strength – academic freedom and innovation flourishing within a federalist, organic and diverse structure ('the collegiate academy') – is also potentially its greatest weakness: an inability to grasp change as opportunity. From our perspective, it also underlines the importance, for a manager, of understanding the nature of your organization *even when you believe you know it well enough already*! Kay's detractors argued that he did not do enough either to work with the grain of a complex academic institution, or to convince others of the efficacy of his vision for a US-style business school operating on the banks of the Isis. To be an effective manager, then, you must have a keen appreciation of the distinctive features and nuances of your institution, notably its climate, structure, politics and culture.

We should also recognize that, despite the tendency to treat HEIs as if they are all organized along similar lines, no two institutions are alike. The participative democracy that characterized Oxford's deliberations over Kay's proposals, for example, contrasts markedly with the way in which decisions were reached under a former Vice Chancellor at Bradford University. Here there was no ambiguity, or much else. The Vice Chancellor simply exercised his executive authority without any reference to others, on the basis that the deadlines for response set by the HEFCE 'means that there is no time for democracy' (Ramsden, 1998). This sharp divergence in practice also illustrates how the management of HEIs has become increasingly differentiated. More than that, several HEIs have pioneered new paths of development. Some have sought to establish themselves as an 'entrepreneurial university' or 'business excellence university' while others have attempted to become a 'virtual university'.

This second chapter then considers the institutional context or nature of the internal environment in which individual managers have to operate. It explains, in general, how HEIs have come to be governed and managed as they are today and, in particular, the nature of organizational culture peculiar to HEIs. In doing so it offers analytical tools which managers can use as a means of understanding their own individual circumstances and context. It also examines exemplars of the new models of institutional organization (the 'entrepreneurial university', the 'virtual university' and so on) and speculates on the alternative ways in which HEIs might develop and organize in the future: the University 2025.

The management of HEIs

A 'community of scholars' or a 'degree factory'? These two epithets – and the contrast in connotation associated with them – have come to characterize the increasingly bitter debate in academia on how universities are, or should be, organized. The 'community of scholars' – and its depiction of autonomous professionals pursuing knowledge for its own sake within a collegial academy, where authority is derived from academic expertise – has always been, and still is, a powerful and evocative ideal to most academics. The 'degree factory', by contrast, conjures up an image of the university as a large corporate identity where functions and resources are consciously 'managed', and where the concepts of relevance and service have primacy.

The reality, however – historical and contemporary – is more complex than this simple dichotomy suggests. While it is true that the term 'management' is relatively novel in higher education – it was first used with reference to institutional planning in the late 1960s – it is also the case that (Oxford and Cambridge apart) there was significant lay involvement in the government of 'old' universities from the outset. Put another way, contrary to popular belief, most 'old' universities, although autonomous in the sense that they are not state institutions, have not always been run by academics. The ancient Scottish universities of Edinburgh and Glasgow, for instance, were controlled by their respective town councils until well into the nineteenth century. And the governing councils of most civic universities established in Victorian England were dominated by networks orchestrated by founding patrons and their heirs – Chamberlain in Birmingham, Wills in Bristol and Palmers in Reading (Warner and Palfreyman, 2001; Scott, 1995).

It is, in fact, possible to discern, as Scott has demonstrated, four main phases in the internal government of 'old' universities: civic (late nineteenth to early twentieth century); donnish (1920s to early 1960s); democratic (late 1960s to 1970s) and managerial (1980s – to date) (see Table 2.1): a pattern of development which is indeed more evolutionary than revolutionary, each phase reflecting the (quite logical) response which universities made to the changing environmental circumstances they encountered. The donnish phase, for instance, emerged as a consequence of the state's growing stake in HE and the subsequent change in source of university income – from town council and industrial subsidy, and student fees (symptomatic of the civic era) to direct state 'block' grants meted out by the UGC set up for this very purpose in 1919 (until 1989). Under the new funding arrangements the influence of founding patrons waned and power passed from lay councils to academic senates. The elite collegiality characteristic of this donnish phase was in turn challenged by the student protests of the 1960s, and the increasing heterogeneity of staff and student populations of the 1970s. The democratic phase proved to be short-lived, however, and the managerial university emerged in the 1980s as a response to a newer, harsher environment, characterized by fewer resources, greater accountability and increased complexity. Viewed historically then, this current managerial phase is not a radical departure from the past – nor should we assume it is an eternal one. It has, as we noted earlier, been as much a positive response to institutional growth and development as a defensive one to manage successive cuts in public funding.

'New' universities have arrived at a similar point, though by an entirely different route. Originally local authority institutions, by and large, they only acquired independent status in 1989. Consequently they do not have the same deep-rooted attachment to

Table 2.1 The government and management of UK universities

	Phase period	Civic: late nineteenth to early twentieth century	Donnish: 1920s to early 1960s	Democratic: late 1960s to 1970s	Managerial: 1980 to date
'Old' universities	Characteristics	• Dominance of lay patrons and governing council	• Elite collegiality; VC & senior professors • Pre-eminence of Academic Senate; supervisory lay council	• Democratic collegiality • Extension of democracy to staff and student 'rank and file'	• Reordering of internal authority • Senior management influence increases; effective (if not formal) power of organs of academic self-government decreases • Heads of department as line managers. Formation of senior management teams (SMT)
	Management	• Non-issue	• Minimal 'lightest of light touch'	• Consensus	
	Administration	• Skeletal	• Subordinate	• Professionalized (CUA)	• Managerial cadre (including planning, strategy)
	Role of vice Chancellor	Chancellor substitute Ceremonial figurehead	Charismatic leader Institution-builder	Chief executive Crisis manager; political lobbyist; returns officer; efficiency champion; fund raiser	

Table 2.1 Continued

	Phase period	Municipal: pre-1989	Transitional: 1970s to 1989	Corporate: 1989 to to date
'New' universities	Characteristics	• Local authority institution No form of institutional democracy	(i) Establishment of academic boards in HEIs (ii) Gradual devolution of local authority responsibilities (iii) Creation of national policy environment, via National Advisory Board (NAB)	• Polytechnics established as free-standing institutions (1989) Creation of unified university system (1992) • Establishment of new smaller governing bodies with majority of independent members (a closed corporation)
	Management	• Under-developed Bureaucratic hierarchy regulatory		• Fully fledged. Pre-eminence of SMT 'overshadows' Academic Board
	Administration	• Key functions the responsibility of local authorities		• Professionalized and formalized; takeover of local authority residual responsibilities (industrial relations, estates management, strategic planning)

Source: adapted from Scott, 1995; Bargh *et al.,* 2000.

institutional autonomy and collegiality which prevails in 'old' universities. Their academic boards, for instance, are, despite their formal power, comparatively lightweight compared with their equivalent – the academic senates – in the traditional sector, and are often overshadowed by powerful senior management teams. Their governing bodies too – given that the independent member majority appoints their successors (in a similar vein to a closed corporation) – are arguably not sufficiently accountable either. Nor do 'new' universities enjoy the financial security which underpins many of their 'older' counterparts. Cambridge, for example, in 2001 was worth 170 London Guildhalls in financial terms (Sanders and Goddard, 2001).

Significant though these differences are, management systems and practices in 'new' and 'old' universities are no longer so dissimilar. Line management has become the norm in both types of institution. They each invariably have a 'Vice Squad' – a senior management team of Pro-Vice Chancellors and Deputy Vice Chancellors with specific portfolios of responsibility – and are headed by a Vice Chancellor whose role, in most cases, is now firmly a chief executive one. It is also the case that the majority working in higher education understand and accept that institutions have had to be more actively 'managed'. Where there has been criticism (and often rightly so), and why managerialism has attracted such opprobrium, is because of the *way* in which institutions have handled this process. The style of management in these instances has almost always clashed with the prevailing institutional culture. *Effective* management, on the other hand – one that harnesses the commitment and skills of all staff – is contingent upon getting the 'fit' between management style and organizational culture right. That is, ensuring that the management style – whether it be formal, rational, consensual, hard-driving or political, etc. – harmonizes with, rather than rubs against, the distinctive character of the institution. Without it institutions will never realize their full potential.

The style of management is invariably set from the top. Let us first consider then, in more detail, the formal governance of HEIs, as a means of understanding the institutional context in which you have to operate.

The governance of HEIs

> Governance concerns power. It is about who is in charge; who makes decisions; who has a voice; and how loud is that voice.
>
> Henry Rosovsky, Dean of Faculty,
> Harvard University, 1990 (cited in Ehrenberg, 2004)

> The governance of higher education is complex, arcane and often antipathetic to modernization and outward-looking strategic change. Universities complain vociferously about the burdens imposed by the demands of public accountability and the vagaries of ministerial policies. But in practice these external constraints are at least matched by the sea anchors of internal procedures, committee structures and institutionalized conservatism that characterize most universities. Whether externally imposed or internally generated, the driver for most governance arrangements has been the maintenance of due processes.
>
> (PA Consulting Group, 2008)

Openness to contradiction is part of the genius of universities. The freedom to enquire, to debate and to criticize and to speak truth to power, whether it be the power of government, of those who fund the university, or those who manage it, is central to the vitality of the university and its utility to society. It is crucial that university governing boards understand this essential source of institutional strength, that they are steadfast in its support, strong in its defense and are not seduced by the fallacy of managerial primacy: that things that make management difficult need to be removed or reformed. An easily governed university is no university at all.

(Bolton and Lucas, 2008)

What is governance?

Governance in higher education has been variously defined as 'the structure and processes of decision-making', 'the establishment of policies to guide the work of the institution' and 'the constitutional forms and processes through which universities govern their affairs' (Tierney, 2004; Shattock, 2006). Not surprisingly, it has been a contentious issue both within and without universities ever since their inception, and never more so than today as universities seek to adapt to the unprecedented change that confronts them. 'Too arcane in its traditions'; 'too unresponsive to the demands of the modern world'; 'too corporate and too capitalistic': these refrains have become commonplace criticisms in recent times and suggest that universities still have much to do to meet the challenge of governance (Burgan, 2004; Kezar, 2006).

How institutions address this challenge depends in the first instance on their legal status – whether they are public or private, whether they operate for profit or not – and on the legal requirements placed on them by their charter or articles of incorporation. In the UK there is not one single tradition but several:

- the distinctive Oxbridge model in which the primacy of academic self-governance is derived from the medieval concept of a guild of masters;
- the medieval (or 'ancient') Scottish model – centred on Aberdeen, Edinburgh, Glasgow and St Andrews – based on a clear separation of power between courts and senates with provision for a rector elected by students;
- the civic university model – or classic English bicameral system with the court as the overall governing body, a council as the executive governing body (operating like the court of a Scottish university) and an academic senate – first introduced in Manchester in 1880 with lay majorities on the court and council, and a senate made up solely of academic members;
- the post-1992 Higher Education Corporation (HEC) model, first established under the Education Reform Act, 1988, when the former polytechnics became corporations independent of local authority control (and were subsequently designated universities in 1992). The HEC is characterized by a unicameral structure – a board of governors restricted to a maximum of 24 members – in which all corporate power resides. That is, in contrast to the civic university model where the corporate body is comprised of the whole university (court, council, staff, students, graduates), in the HEC the governing body itself is the corporation (CUC, 2009; Shattock, 2006).

Tradition notwithstanding, what is more striking has been the *external* pressure placed on universities to conform to a single uniform pattern – the corporate sector one – irrespective of whether institutional governance is protected by charters and statutes or not. The received wisdom tells us that this is not only the most effective way of enabling universities to meet the challenges of an increasingly complex, politicized and market-driven environment, and of maintaining institutional stability, integrity and reputation, but also gives recognition, long overdue, to the fact that universities are themselves significant businesses (HEIs, after all, create over a half-million jobs and contribute more than £45 billion a year to the UK economy (Tollyfield, 2007). It is only fitting and proper, therefore, that we should take a lead from the corporate sector on how we should govern our institutions.

Thus, from the Jarratt Report's (1985) recommendations (reflecting on how universities accommodated the Thatcher government 'cuts' of 1981) that the vice chancellor should be recognized 'not only as an academic leader but also as chief executive of the university', that heads of department should be appointed to their role, rather than elected by their peers, and that the balance of councils' and senates' roles should be readjusted in favour of the former; to the establishment of the Financial Memorandum in 1988 (the annual contract between the funding council and a university for the education of a set number of students against a financial allocation) which made the governing body, not the institution, responsible for its delivery, and again to the Dearing Report's (1997) proposal of a Governance Code of Practice for universities with the recommendation that the size of pre-1992 university councils should be limited to 25, with an obligation to review their own effectiveness and that of their institutions at five-yearly intervals – a recommendation revived by the Lambert Review (2003) and adopted by the Committee of University Chairs (CUC) for the first time in their revised guide of 2004 – the message has been a consistent one: that universities are best served by a single *unambiguous* governing body of uniform size (CUC, 2009; Shattock, 2006; Watson and Amoah, 2007).

While the CUC code, for example, is voluntary – and advocates the figure of 25 as a 'benchmark of good practice' rather than a literal requirement – it incorporates a 'comply or explain' approach. That is, as Lambert put it, 'all institutions should disclose in their annual report when their governance arrangements do not conform to the code and explain why their governance arrangements are more effective'. The expectation then is that pre-1992 universities in particular should, in essence, endow their governing bodies (whose size has already been reduced to around 33 through self-regulation) with the same kind of unicameral powers of direction that pertain in the post-1992 universities, which themselves are closely modelled on the private sector company board (Shattock, 2006). A CUC survey conducted in 2008 confirmed that two-thirds of UK HEIs had adopted the CUC code and a further 17 per cent had done so with amendments (Schofield, 2009).

Universities in the USA, likewise, have adopted a similar unicameral structure or 'corporate' model of governance. There is a remarkable diversity within higher education in the USA – public; private; research universities; liberal arts colleges; state universities; community colleges and so on. Indeed there are no less than 19 different structures for higher education systems across the 50 states, ranging from California, which (like Connecticut, Louisiana and Nebraska) has three separate systems to organize its institutions: one for research universities; a second for masters' universities and baccalaureate colleges and a third for community colleges, all coordinated by a state-wide board, to Georgia and Wisconsin, which combine all institutions into one state-wide system. Even so, the common denominator in all cases – whether there is a consolidated governance system, a segmental system or campus-level system, and whether the institution, like Harvard (1636) and Yale (1701), pre-dates the nation or not – is that US universities are governed by boards of trustees, regents or similarly titled entities, holding the status of corporations and comprised principally of lay representatives. The University of Michigan, for example, has a board of nine members including the university president and eight regents elected in biennial state-wide elections. Princeton University, by contrast, has up to 40 trustees, 13 elected by the alumni and the remainder elected by the board as either (four-year) term trustees or charter trustees (with 10-year terms), in addition to the president and the governor of New Jersey (Hermalin, 2004; MacTaggart, 2004).

What is striking here again is that while Harvard, Yale and the other colonial colleges may be among the oldest corporations within the English legal tradition, state colleges and universities have, voluntarily in this instance, almost invariably copied this model – from the founding of the University of Virginia (1819), the 'first real state university', onwards – even though there was no legal requirement for them to do so (Heller, 2004). This outcome has been, as one might have anticipated, a deeply divisive one, and begs the question: are university governing boards very much like corporate boards of directors? Can the model of corporate governance – 'the system by which companies are directed and controlled' – really apply to universities?

While the analogy is an easy and indeed fashionable one to make, there are significant differences we ought not to overlook. First, most public companies would expect to have a roughly equal number of executive and non-executive directors. In universities only the vice chancellor or president is an executive member of the board – and not always then. In the US, presidents are as likely to be excluded as included in board membership. Equally, non-executive directors of public companies are recruited for their knowledge and understanding of the particular business or industry. In universities few board members have direct experience of higher education. They literally are lay people who bring their particular expertise from outside the core business.

Thus the composition and membership of university governing bodies preclude them from fulfilling the requirements of a company board – *for they cannot do so on their own*. They need the detailed involvement of senior members of the academic community if they are to be effective as a board – hence the totemic significance of *shared governance* (Mortimer and O'Brien Sathre, 2007). In a university setting then, and this is most important, governance is not perceived solely as the way in which governing bodies operate (as is often the case in the corporate sector) but as a process that embraces many more levels across the institution – senates and academic boards, faculty boards, departmental meetings and so on. And good governance is about ensuring all these levels work well. A distinguishing characteristic that many would maintain is only right and proper since the functions of a university are very different from those of a company, and therefore require a different style of governance and management if they are to be successful (Ehrenberg, 2004; Shattock, 2006).

How does governance work?

In theory, it appears to be relatively straightforward. The CUC Governance Code of Practice (2009), for instance, is very explicit in this regard:

> The institution's governing body shall adopt a Statement of Primary Responsibilities which should include provisions relating to:
>
> - approving the mission and strategic vision of the institution, long-term business plans, key performance indicators (KPIs) and annual budgets, and ensuring that these meet the interest of stakeholders
> - appointing the head of institution as chief executive of the institution and putting in place suitable arrangements for monitoring his/her performance
> - ensuring the establishment and monitoring of systems of control and accountability, including financial and operational controls and risk assessment, clear procedures for handling internal grievances and for managing conflicts of interest
> - monitoring institutional performance against plans and approved KPIs, which should be where possible and appropriate, benchmarked against other institutions.

Let us be clear then. The responsibility of the board is to govern, not to manage, and there is a world of difference between the two. Governance is about setting the conditions for, and holding to account, the university executive. Management, in contrast, involves responsibility for the effective operation of the institution and the achievement of its goals, within the policies and procedures approved by the board; the effective use of its resources and creative support of the highest standards for teaching, research and enterprise (CUC, 2009).

In addition, in pre-1992 universities, the senate (50 to 100+) is typically 'the supreme academic authority of the university' responsible for regulating and directing the academic work of the university, while in post-1992 universities the academic board (normally no more than 30 but exceptionally up to 40 members, with at least half made up of senior management post-holders) is responsible for academic affairs including academic standards, subject to the 'overall responsibilities' of the governing body and the vice chancellor for these matters. Thus its role is typically an advisory one with regard to academic activities and the resources needed to support them (CUC, 2009).

In the US a similar division of labour is apparent in the American Association of University Professors' (AAUP) classic Statement on Government in Colleges and Universities, which encapsulates the critical principle of shared governance. First published in 1966 and commended by the American Council on Education (ACE) and the Association of Governing Boards (AGB), the AAUP's statement is widely regarded today as the standard for desirable procedures of campus governance at US colleges and universities. In essence, shared governance means that academic decisions (student admissions criteria, staff recruitment and promotion, curriculum development) are delegated to the faculty; administrative decisions (acquiring resources and planning expenditures, designing, building and operating facilities) to the management (or 'administration'), and responsibility for accountability and public policy (compliance with federal, state and local laws, fiduciary responsibilities) to the governing board (Duderstadt, 2004).

Theory is one thing. In practice the model has not always worked as intended for a number of reasons:

- First, *one size does not fit all.* There is not only a remarkable diversity in the forms of governance used by universities and colleges reflective of their history and tradition, there has also been increasing differentiation among them. Thus in the USA, for example, the nation's 4,100 universities and colleges have gradually separated into four functional categories: the 100 or so major research universities from Yale to Berkeley (where faculty governance has crumbled at the university, if not the local level); the 120–150 smaller private liberal arts colleges (*c.* 3,000 students, where shared governance is most closely practised); the huge multifarious array of state colleges and universities, regional private colleges and universities and colleges of art, technology and business (where governance and management vary greatly); and community colleges, less well-endowed private colleges and proprietary schools (where there is little tradition of shared governance) (Ehrenberg, 2004).

  There has been similar differentiation among the UK's 160+ HEIs: from the 38 major research-intensive universities of the so-called Russell Group (20) and 1994 Group (18) (where shared governance is most closely practised) to the 32 teaching-led regional universities of Million+ (typically former polytechnics where shared governance is weakest).

  In both countries institutional diversity and functional segregation mean it is much more difficult (even if it were desirable) to apply a single standard for governance in higher education.

- Second, while many accept that shared governance is one of the essential guiding principles for higher education – a corollary of and indeed essential prerequisite for the concepts of academic freedom and peer review, *there are multiple and conflicting interpretations of what the term means.* Some view it as a *legislative* model grounded in the formal structures of decision-making (such as faculty boards, senates). Others see it from a *symbolic* perspective – that shared governance is not so much about the formal rules, but rather the ways in which these are interpreted through working together. Still others emphasize that shared governance is essentially a process of genuine *consultation*, while a final group view it from a *communicative* perspective – that shared governance is about cultivating a common understanding of institutional goals and direction and how individuals and departments contribute to this greater unifying good. These various perspectives inform individual behaviour and, in the absence of consensus, leave us with a particular conundrum. If we are to realize effective shared governance we must meet the challenge of how best we can work with these competing definitions (Tierney, 2004).

- Third, *shared governance in practice has been innately conservative.* Each of the key constituencies has always had, as Clark Kerr identified, if not decision-making authority then at least veto power. And, as Kerr noted ironically, the only choice that cannot be vetoed is the status quo! While this conservatism may have contributed to the longevity of many institutions, it has also acted as a constraint on their ability to respond to changing circumstances and future demands (Kerr, 2001).

- Fourth, *while the dividing line between governance, management and faculty may be clearly understood, it is not always so easy to discern in practice*. Thus, for example, everyone might agree that a decision on the academic character and mission of the institution speaks of governance, just as a decision on the allocation of staff workloads speaks of management, and that on the promotion of research, faculty. But what of a more complicated decision to construct, say, a new building and the subsidiary decisions: where to locate it on campus? who and what teaching and research facilities should be housed within it? what should be its architectural style? and so on. Such decisions implicate all three key constituencies and demonstrate the need for all sides to act in good faith, in a dialogue of shifting accommodation and mutual respect. The difficulties arise, of course, when they do not, and turf problems abound, which is why trusteeship or governorship has occasionally been likened to marriage – 'a learn-as-you-go enterprise' (Freedman, 2004).
- Finally, and most importantly, *the unprecedented changes confronting universities today are exposing the flaws in this traditional approach to university governance*. Governing boards face a serious challenge in their ability to understand and govern in this new environment. A task made even more difficult as universities increasingly 'hollow out' their activities or shrink their traditional core (full-time faculty, student services, library) while expanding their peripheries (outsourcing partnerships, discrete research institutes, sponsored research, licence and patent activity, corporate training), leaving governing boards with 'a paradox of scope', or less control over more things (Tierney, 2004; Mortimer and O'Brien Sathre, 2007).

This condition is made more difficult still, particularly in the USA, by the increasing politicization of governing boards (for example, attempts to restructure the curriculum to stress a specific ideology or eliminate social commitments such as affirmative action) (Kezar, 2006). There is an old saying that no institution can be better than its governing board, and the fear is that present circumstances will discourage the most experienced and dedicated citizens from serving on these bodies. Likewise, faculty participation has become increasingly difficult to achieve in university-wide governance, if not at the local level. Caught in between is the university leadership whose responsibility (considerable), compared with its corporate sector equivalents, is not always matched by its authority (modest). It should not surprise us that research studies into the work of governing boards have found that 'effective governance is a relatively rare and unnatural act' (Chait *et al.*, 1996; Duderstadt, 2004). See Box 2.1.

What can universities do to enhance governance?

- *Accept that the diversity of institutions is such that pluralism, rather than standardization, should be the norm in governance* – that given their varied histories and traditions, their size, scope and status, institutions should – and will – differ in the way they run their affairs. Be confident in doing so.
- *Set the right course.* The single most important contribution that governing bodies can make (alongside the appointment of a vice chancellor or president) is to identify

Box 2.1 How does governance work in your university?

Good governance is 'shared governance' and requires good management. It is about ensuring that governance at all levels works well. A thorough understanding of the governance arrangements in your university will give you critical insight into how your institutional context is shaped by them and an awareness of how you can influence them and, most importantly, help you maximize the contribution you can make in your role.

1 What are the formal powers, duties and responsibilities specified in your university charter or articles of incorporation – for the governing board? senate/academic board? president/vice chancellor?

2 Who are the members of your governing board? How are they selected – by nomination, election, other? Who selects them? What expertise do board members have and how is this used?

3 What is your university's mission? How was it developed? How is it reviewed? Is it fit for purpose? Does your university's mission explain why the university exists (its purpose); the university's competitive position (its strategy); the values the university believes in and the standards and behaviours expected of staff?

4 Does your university have key performance indicators (KPIs)? How are these developed and disseminated? What use is made of them?

5 What is your university committee structure for governors/trustees, academic faculty and management? Which ones are the key committees? Why?

6 What groupings and networks are important outside the formal university committee structure? Why?

7 How is the senior management organized in your university (e.g. the President's executive board; VC's advisory group; senior management team; senior academic/administrative committee; Monday morning club)? What effect do the style and function of this group have on your university – and on you in your role?

8 What opportunities are there for mutual learning between governors/trustees, academic faculty and management (e.g. joint committees; special task groups; open meetings and conferences; away days; buddy scheme)?

9 How are decisions made at the university level? The local level? How are these decisions disseminated?

10 What are the contentious issues on which governors/trustees, academic faculty and management disagree? What do these disagreements tell you about the difference between theory and practice in governance? the distribution and exercise of power in your university?

11 What is the academic structure and organization of your university (e.g. subject disciplinary groups; units; divisions; departments; schools; faculties)? What is the rationale for the present structure? How does this structure facilitate or impede staff participation, consultation and decision-making?

12 What is the internal 'business model' chosen by your university? Is it centralized or devolved? The university as a unitary corporation with faculty/school divisions; the university as a holding company with faculty/school subsidiaries; the university as a loosely coupled system with single department autonomy; or, other? How does this model affect you in your role?

13 What can you do to enhance governance in the forums you belong to?

and articulate a clear and coherent mission for their institution – an inspiring purpose and distinctive niche. From this, all else should follow.

- *Agree the basic principles and values that should guide institutional decision making*. These might include the principle of *subsidiarity*, in which decisions are made at the lowest level consistent with expertise and accountability. Complemented by the principle of *externality*, which recognizes that the benefits and costs of a decision accrue not only to the members of the community making the decision, but also to the broader community they serve. Academic freedom, openness to new ideas and the commitment to excellence are also likely to be on everyone's list. What about those values and practices, however, such as shared governance; promotion, tenure and post-tenure review; performance management; performance-related pay; collective bargaining?

- *Foster a working partnership between faculty and governing boards based on mutual respect rather than the exercise of power*. The most positive and least contentious of the Jarratt Committee recommendations was for the creation of a joint committee of governors and academic senate devoted to planning and resources – these have become de rigueur in pre-1992 universities. Extending this principle further not only builds confidence and mutual respect but also brings together mutually reinforcing expertise. Post-1992 universities are experimenting with joint governing body/ academic board conferences, while in the USA faculty engagement has been enhanced through the establishment of university-wide special task forces (or 'Kleenex structures') that help solve a major problem (e.g. student retention) or provide advice on a significant issue (strategic priorities; internationalization; graduate programmes) and then dissolve (Ehrenberg, 2004; Shattock, 2006; Schofield, 2009).

- *Balance responsibility with authority and recognize that everyone does not, nor should they expect to, have a say on everything*. In particular by defining more precisely the 'terms of engagement' in the consultative process, as a means of improving and speeding up institutional decision-making. For example, by determining those areas in which the special expertise of faculty requires their consent (e.g. academic programmes and policies), those areas in which faculty advice would be sought and considered but would not necessarily be authoritative (e.g. funding priorities), and those areas in which faculty are not especially authoritative at all (e.g. car parking, photo-copying).

- *Recruit governors with the necessary expertise*: self-evident perhaps, but more difficult in the USA where trustees are often political appointments or elected representatives, and there is little or no tradition of staff or student representation on governing boards, which are a given in the UK. Common to both the USA and the UK, however – and glaringly different from the private sector – is the relative absence of educators on governing boards. A recently retired vice chancellor, or president of another institution, could be an extremely valuable addition to any board.

- *Develop key performance indicators that are not only genuinely SMART (specific, measurable, achievable, realistic and time-bound) but are also integrated with strategic planning, and the performance of the senior management team*. The CUC has identified two top-level summary indicators (or 'super KPIs') (institutional sustainability and academic profile/market position) along with 10 top-level indicators of institutional health (for example, the student experience and learning and teaching; research; staff and human resource development; estates and infrastructure; and so on) as a guide for helping governors to monitor their institutions. Many universities have developed, or are in the process of developing, their monitoring frameworks. That said, KPIs can often be dangerously simplistic and open to contrasting inter-pretations if not carefully thought through. For example, are low admissions criteria symptomatic of a poor institutional reputation or a commitment to widen access and participation? Is high expenditure on the library evidence of a necessary commitment to research, or an overprovision of staff as against materials, or indeed an over-expenditure on journals concealing an under-expenditure on student texts? There is also a danger of KPIs being yet another tick-box exercise, or simply an internal target-setting process, if developed without reference to the wider world (Port, 2008).

All constituencies have a common interest in establishing and assessing performance levels and, while formally owned by governing boards, performance reviews need to be undertaken jointly with senior management and faculty if they are to be effective instruments of good governance quality assurance. They should provide a clear picture of where a university stands, in comparison with other institutions of like characteristics, and also identify priorities for action for strategic planning which can be used in reviewing the performance of the senior manage-ment team (Shattock, 2006).

- *Remember all the benefits your governing body could – and should – bring to your institution.* See Table 2.2.
- *Consider and evaluate if your governing body has the necessary 'enablers' to meet the challenge of effective governance.* See Table 2.3.
- *Recognize that the key to effective governance is not so much structural as cultural.* Received wisdom tells us there is no single optimal design for a governance structure, or indeed for the organization of academic disciplines, departments or the university itself. Indeed, when Enron collapsed in December 2001, with the loss of billions of dollars of debt hidden by complex and dubious accounting practices, it was not for want of a proper governance structure, for it had a highly financially literate company board and a well-established audit committee – and the same can be said of Lehman Brothers at the time of its collapse in September 2008. Rather, what distinguishes exemplary boards – large or small – is that 'they are robust effective social systems which may or may not follow the good governance hand-book' but which do 'take into account the culture and norms of the organization they govern'. That is, they recognize that multiple ways of interpreting shared governance may well flourish but, rather than seeking to dissuade individuals from their own views, they work creatively with them from a cultural perspective (Shattock, 2006).

In other words, improving governance is about paying attention to the 'soft stuff' rather than the 'hard stuff' of institutional life. It is about demonstrating trust by initiating dialogue, being transparent on how decisions are made, developing a common language, 'walking the talk' (by saying what you mean and doing what you say) and nurturing a

Table 2.2 Distinguishing features of an effective university governing board

Competency dimension	Characteristic	Adds value (by)
Contextual	Understands and takes into account the culture and norms of the institution it governs: there is governor induction and orientation; educational opportunities outside formal board meetings; relevant data provision and information and informal social events with staff and students	Modelling desired behaviours
Educational	Ensures that governors are knowledgeable about the institution, the profession, the board's roles, responsibilities and performance: there is clarity of role, an effective committee system, careful selection of the board chair, on-going board evaluation and collective responsibility	Monitoring progress and performance
Interpersonal	Nurtures the development of governors as a working group, attends to the board's collective welfare and fosters a sense of cohesiveness: there is a culture and associated values which guide the way the board works	Creating opportunities for the president 'to think aloud'
Analytical	Recognizes the complexities and subtleties of issues and accepts ambiguity and uncertainty as healthy preconditions for constructive dialogue: there is acknowledgement that an easily governed university is no university at all	Encouraging experimentation
Political	Accepts as a primary responsibility the need to develop and maintain healthy relationships among major constituencies: there are positive working relationships with key external parties and internal ones too, including that between the board chair, university president and university secretary (the key 'triad') and also between the board and the university more generally	Facilitating effective decision-making
Strategic	Helps the institution to envision a direction and shape a strategy: there is a common vision and purpose; a strategic plan and key performance indicators with agenda-setting regarded as an activity run jointly by senior management and the board	Helping senior management determine 'what matters most'

Source: adapted from Chait *et al.*, 1996; Kezar, 2006.

Table 2.3 Assessing the effectiveness of university governing boards

Enablers of effective governance	Outcomes of effective governance

1 Requisite leadership and board member engagement
  • the approach, style and motivation of the board chair
  • the support of senior management for effective governance
  • the quality of interaction between the chair, the president and university secretary and among board members
	Holding the senior management to account to ensure that:
	1 The Strategic Plan is achieved
	2 Financial health is achieved
	3 Accountability and regulatory requirements are met

2 Requisite governance structures and processes
  • the roles and responsibilities of board members are clear, understood and accepted
  • the decision-making structure is fit for purpose
  • delegated responsibilities have appropriate reporting mechanisms
  • meeting arrangements are fit for purpose
  • size of membership is appropriate to meeting the board's role and responsibilities
	4 Academic and service provision are quality assured
	5 Risk assessment is implemented and innovation supported
	6 Institutional reputation and competitiveness are enhanced
	7 Confidence in institutional governance is demonstrable

3 Effective board membership
  • members are recruited with sufficient skill, experience, motivation and diversity of background
  • the skills and experience of members are utilized
  • induction and on-going professional support and development are fit for purpose
  • regular review and appraisal of member performance
	8 Senior management is itself supported and challenged in a constructive manner

4 Commitment to vision, organizational culture and values
 • the institutional vision, mission, culture and values are known, understood and accepted
 • the principles of good conduct in public life are accepted and practised
 • core academic values are known, understood and supported

5 Effective performance monitoring and measurement
 • KPIs are agreed and adopted
 • the strategic planning process informing performance measurement is fit for purpose
 • institutional performance is benchmarked with relevant peer HEIs
 • the performance of the board itself is measured

6 Effective information and communication
 • information provided is timely, accurate and presented in as effective a way as possible to enable the board to discharge its responsibilities
 • communication between the board and senior management, the university at large and key external stakeholders is fit for purpose

Source: adapted from Schofield, 2009.

core institutional identity. This way is also the best guarantor of meeting the single greatest threat to shared governance – that faculty are no longer willing to invest time and effort in making it work (Tierney, 2004; Mortimer and O'Brien Sathre, 2007).

Sensitivity towards and understanding of institutional culture are essential pre-requisites not only of effective governance but of effective management too. But what is organizational culture – and how can we manage it?

The culture of HEIs

What is culture?

A notoriously slippery concept to define, 'culture' has been invoked by 'all persons to mean all things'. Traditionally, it has been used as a reference guide to (as well as judgement on) patterns of societal development; though nowadays it is employed more usually as a (non-judgemental) means of differentiating between societies as well as organizations. Common to both approaches is the notion that culture is a distinct (static and fixed) entity: a unitary phenomenon which has clearly defined attributes (derived from beliefs, stories, norms, rituals and so on) and which all nation-states and organizations possess.

More recent perspectives in organizational science, however – like those in anthropology, sociology and new social history – view this interpretation of culture as being unduly mechanistic; one, that is, which fails to convey either any sense of dynamism with regard to workplace activity, or any real understanding of it from the insider's viewpoint. Advocates of this revisionist school argue that culture should in fact be conceived, not as a distinct static entity, but as a dynamic social process; i.e. an on-going and proactive 'process of reality construction that allows people to see and understand particular events, actions, objects, utterances, or situations in distinctive ways'. In other words, such revisionists consider organizations to *be* cultures as opposed to *having* cultures; that culture is, in essence, a process rather than an entity (Morgan, 2006; Frost *et al.*, 1991; Allaire and Firsirotu, 1984).

Either way, it is a lot more complex, as Figure 2.1 illustrates, than the popular conception of the term which prevails within organizations, that culture is simply 'the way we do things round here'. Organizational culture is indeed reflective of – and embedded in – the 'working out' of a variety of powerful influences: the distribution of power within the organization; the way in which work is structured and controlled; the attachment to history and tradition; the 'ownership' of the organization; the rituals, routines, stories, symbols and gossip which shape everyday working life and so on, all of which profoundly affect, and are affected by, the 'mindset' and behaviour of staff and management. Culture is thus a combination of values, structure and power which has implications for every aspect of an organization's operations, its external relationships and ultimately the realization of its institutional mission.

Academic cultures

Drawing on Karl Weick's (1976) characterization of the classic collegial academy as a 'loosely coupled system' and Charles Handy's (1993) categorization of organization

Stories	Staff	Systems
Beliefs and values	Mindset	Organization structures
Rituals and routines	Behaviour	Power structures
Symbols	Skills	Management style

Figure 2.1 The cultural web of an organization

Source: adapted from Alexander, 2001.

cultural types, Ian McNay (1995, 1996) has developed a model which helps us not only to interpret the nature of organizational culture peculiar to HE, but also to explore how HEI cultures have changed over time. McNay's model – based on the degree of 'tightness' or 'looseness' on two dimensions: policy definition and control over implementation (see Figure 2.2) – generates four organizational types of HEI, each with its own distinguishing features (see Table 2.4).

Type A, with loose policy definition and loose control over implementation, is the *classic collegial academy*. Here the focus is on freedom to pursue professional and personal

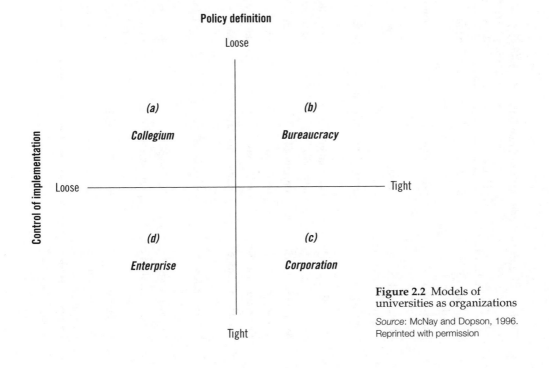

Policy definition

Loose

(a) Collegium   *(b)* Bureaucracy

Loose ———————————————— Tight

(d) Enterprise   *(c)* Corporation

Tight

Figure 2.2 Models of universities as organizations

Source: McNay and Dopson, 1996. Reprinted with permission

(left axis) Control of implementation

Table 2.4 Summary characteristics of four university models

Factor	Collegium	Bureaucracy	Corporation	Enterprise
Dominant value (Clark, 1983)	freedom	equity	loyalty	competence
Role of central authorities	permissive	regulatory	directive	supportive
Handy's (1993) organization culture	person	role	power	task
Dominant unit	department/individual	faculty/committees	institution/senior management team	sub-unit/project teams
Decision arenas	informal groups networks	committees and administrative briefings	working parties and senior management team	project teams
Management style	consensual	formal/'rational'	political/tactical	developed leadership
Timeframe	long	cyclic	short/mid-term	instant
Environmental 'fit'	evolution	stability	crisis	turbulence
Nature of change	organic innovation	reactive adaptation	proactive transformation	tactical flexibility
External referents	invisible college	regulatory bodies	policymakers as opinion leaders	clients/sponsors
Internal referents	the discipline	the rules	the plans	market strength/students
Basis for evaluation	peer assessment	audit of procedures, e.g. IS9001	performance indicators	repeat business
Student status	apprentice academic	statistic	unit of resource	customer
Administrator roles: servant of . . .	the community	the committee	the chief executive	the client, internal and external

Source: McNay, 1995.

goals uninhibited by external constraints. Discipline-based departments headed by senior professors are the dominant organizational unit and evaluation is by peer review. The management style is permissive and consensual and students are regarded as apprentice academics.

Type B, the *bureaucratic* university, has a loose policy frame but exercises tight control over implementation. Its focus, as one would expect, is on rules, regulations and procedures. The management style is formal-rational and decision-making is formalized in committees. Evaluation is based on external audit and students are perceived as statistics.

Type C, the *corporate* university, exercises tight control over both policy and implementation. Here the focus is on loyalty to the organization and in particular to the senior management team and chief executive, who are the dominant institutional unit. The management style is political-tactical and decision-making is centred in senior management working groups. Evaluation is monitored through performance indicators and students are seen as units of resource.

Type D, the *enterprise* university, combines a tight policy frame with loose control over activity. Its focus is in competence and its orientation is as much external as it is internal. The management style is supportive of devolved leadership and decision-making and is centred on project teams. Evaluation is based on attracting repeat business and students are treated as valued customers.

Research in the UK and Australia suggests that in broad terms HEIs have – as a consequence of the changes in the environment they have faced over the last two decades – moved in a clockwise direction from A to B to C to D, a pattern of development which is consistent with the environmental 'fit' (evolution-stability-crisis-turbulence) associated with each of the four cultures. It would be wrong to assume, however, that this pattern is either a universal or a consistent one. Cambridge and Imperial College, London, for example, have arguably moved from A to D without passing through B or C. It is also the case that none of these different cultures are mutually exclusive and it is likely that all four coexist in most HEIs (Bolden *et al.*, 2008; Coaldrake and Stedman, 1998; McNay, 1995).

What is your university or college culture?

The point is: what is the nature of the organizational culture which you work in? There are no easy answers. We need to recognize that there are difficulties in examining culture whatever one's perspective. Insiders, as well as outsiders, find it difficult to analyse simply because so much of culture is 'taken for granted'. Or as Edgar Schein (2004) memorably put it: 'Culture at its deepest level is the assumptions we do not see'. And for all that, it is *your* perspective which may, or may not, tally with that of your colleagues. For this reason you may wish to share the activities which follow with the other members of your department.

1 One simple yet very effective way of realizing 'hidden' staff perceptions – as the UK Open University has demonstrated (Russell and Parsons, 1996) – is to ask staff to draw their own individual picture of the institution as they perceive it. You should then share these pictures with your own and discuss the outcomes (see Figure 2.3).

1 The normalistic chart

The conventional hierarchy; everything has a place and everything knows its place.

2 The octopus

An instance of failed synergy; nothing fits and nothing seems to work.

3 The dinosaur

The head – the SMT – thinks it knows where it's going
The body lumbers on.

4 The medieval painting

Inter-departmental tribal warfare; winners and losers (and no students).

Figure 2.3 Images of university organization

2 Another more structured approach – given that organizational cultures, as Tony Becher (2001) reminds us, operate in three arenas: front-of-stage (the public arena); back-stage (where deals are done) and under-the-stage (where gossip is purveyed) – is to attempt to articulate these 'official' and 'unofficial' cultures (see Table 2.5). The questionnaire outlined in Box 2.2 is designed to help you do this: to develop, that is, your own 'fine-grained' understanding and analysis of your own institution still further.

   Again, you can complete this questionnaire either on your own or share it with colleagues. If the latter, examine the differences between their responses and your own. More importantly, try and establish the reasons for these differences and identify what you can do about them.

3 The questionnaire completed, use the scoring mechanism in Box 2.3 to quantify your perception of the current 'cultural balance' of your institution.
   • Think of your institution as it was five years ago and repeat the scoring exercise.
   • Anticipate how your institution will develop over the next five years and repeat the exercise again.
   • Plot the outcomes to determine the shift in your organizational culture.

   Compare your analysis with:

   (a) the sequential pattern of development (A-B-C-D) implied in McNay's model. Has your institution followed the same path? If not, how do you account for the differences?
   (b) those of your colleagues. Where do you agree? disagree? Are the differences significant? Is the management style consistent with the organizational culture?
4 Repeat the first three activities and on this occasion focus solely on your own department or unit rather than the whole institution. Compare the outcomes.
   (a) In what ways is the culture of your department or unit similar to and different from that of your institution? Account for the differences.
   (b) What are the strengths and weaknesses of your institutional culture? departmental culture?
   (c) Is your perception consistent with those of your colleagues? What are the key differences? Do they relate to your management style? Do you need to change it?

The management of culture?

A systematic examination of our organizational culture then yields a number of significant benefits. It enhances our own self-realization, gives us insight into the hidden perception of others, and ultimately develops our understanding of the 'social reality' of the institutional context in which we have to operate.

   Understanding organizational culture, however, begs the question – should it be changed in some way? And, if so, what can we do to change it? Certainly many in the private sector reason that – since the creation and maintenance of a 'strong' organizational culture is a critical determinant of company success – 'managing culture' must be an

Table 2.5 Understanding the culture of your HEI: an illustration

Gossip and the informal stories that provide everyday conversation yield a penetrating insight into organizational culture – in themselves and in the messages they convey. For example:

HEI	Conversation theme	'Message'
'New' university, south-east England	Q What's the difference between the Vice Chancellor and the rest of the staff? A He's chauffeur-driven and we are all student-driven!	There is one law for some and another for the rest of us.
	The removal of the staff pigeonholes from X campus	Irrefutable proof of the management conspiracy against dedicated staff
Regional research university, eastern USA	The 'meat-axe administrator' and his refrain: 'We already did that yesterday!' They slough it off here, slough it off there, slough it off everywhere.	It's a Darwinian jungle in this state and we're ahead of the game. Outsourcing is all the rage here and we could be next.
Regional research university, north-eastern USA	He (the President) used to come out of the 'puzzle palace' with a guard of honour. It was like Moses coming off the mountain with the tablets (the Strategic Plan).	Who knows what the executive does or thinks; you can't get near them. Collegiality? You gotta be kidding.
University of technology, eastern Australia	A lot of the staff here have greater credit card bills than the debt of the university.	Whatever else this university can be accused of – financial laxity isn't one of them.
Research university, eastern Australia	You need the personality of a Sherman tank to survive as Head of Department here.	Its rough, its tough and there is no end in sight. The industrial model is just not suited to an HE environment.
Research university, western Australia	X has just been R............d	Given a severance offer he couldn't refuse. We don't carry any 'deadwood' here, no matter what you might think.
Regional university, south Australia	I've been parking my car under that tree for 8 years or more.	The latest change initiative can just go hang. 'Wake me when it's over.'

Box 2.2 Understanding the culture of your HEI: questionnaire

The culture of your institution is embedded in the images, metaphors, beliefs, values, norms, rituals, language, stories, legends, myths, and other symbolic artefacts that decorate and give form to the experience of everyday working life.

Think about your institution.
How would you describe its culture?

Try to be systematic in your analysis by identifying specific examples of the symbolism in use:

What are the principal images or metaphors that people use to describe your institution?

_____
_____
_____
_____

What *physical impressions* do the organization and its artefacts create? Does this vary from one place to another?

_____
_____
_____
_____

What are the dominant *stories* or *legends* that people tell? What messages are they trying to convey?

_____
_____
_____
_____

What kind of *beliefs* and *values* dominate your organization (officially . . . unofficially)?

_____
_____
_____
_____

What are the main *norms* (i.e. the do's and don'ts)?

_____
_____
_____
_____

What are the main *ceremonies* and *rituals* and what purposes do they serve?

_____
_____
_____
_____

What *language* dominates everyday conversation (e.g. buzzwords, clichés, catch phrases)?

_____
_____
_____
_____
_____

Think of three *influential people*: in what ways do they symbolize the character of your institution?

_____
_____
_____
_____
_____

What *reward systems* are in place? What 'messages' do they send in terms of activities or accomplishments that are valued, and those that are not?

_____
_____
_____
_____
_____

What are the favourite topics of *informal conversation*?

_____
_____
_____
_____
_____

What are the *identifiable subcultures* in the organization? How are they differentiated?
Are they in conflict or in harmony?

_____
_____
_____
_____
_____

What *impacts* do these subcultures have on the organization? What functions do these groupings serve for their members? Is the overall effect on the organization positive or negative?

_____
_____
_____
_____
_____

Box 2.3 Understanding the culture of your HEI: scoring mechanism

Each of these items contains four descriptions of organizational features. Please distribute 100 points among the four descriptions according to how similar the description is to your own institution. None of the descriptions is any better than the others; they are just different. For each question, please use 100 points.

In question 1, for example, if (a) seems very similar to mine, (b) seems somewhat similar, and (c) and (d) do not seem similar at all, I might give 70 points to (a) and the remaining 30 points to (b).

1 Dominant characteristics (Divide 100 points)
  My institution is
  (a) a very personal place. It is like an extended family. People seem to share a lot of themselves.
  (b) a very formalized and structured place. Bureaucratic procedures generally govern what people do.
  (c) very competitive in orientation. A major concern is with getting the job done. People are very production and achievement oriented.
  (d) a very dynamic and entrepreneurial place. People are willing to stick their necks out and take risks.

2 Organizational leader (Divide 100 points)
  The University Vice Chancellor/Principal/President is generally considered to be
  (a) a mentor, a facilitator, or a parent figure.
  (b) a coordinator, an organizer, or an efficiency expert.
  (c) a hard driver, a producer, or a competitor.
  (d) an entrepreneur, an innovator, or a risk taker.

3 Organizational glue (Divide 100 points)
  The glue that holds my institution together is
  (a) loyalty and commitment. Cohesion and teamwork are characteristic of this organization.
  (b) formal procedures, rules, or policies. Maintaining a smooth-running organization is important.
  (c) an emphasis on production and goal accomplishment. Marketplace aggressiveness is a common theme.
  (d) a focus on innovation and development. The emphasis is on being at the cutting edge.

4 Organizational climate (Divide 100 points)
  The climate inside my institution
  (a) is participative and comfortable. High trust and openness exist.
  (b) emphasizes permanence and stability. Expectations regarding procedures are clear and enforced.
  (c) is competitive and confrontational. Emphasis is placed on beating the competition.
  (d) emphasizes dynamism and readiness to meet new challenges. Trying new things and trial-and-error learning are common.

5 Criteria of success (Divide 100 points)
  My institution defines success on the basis of
  (a) its development of human resources, teamwork and concern for people.
  (b) its having unique or the latest 'products' (in teaching, research and consultancy). It is a product leader and innovator with a keen interest in stakeholder satisfaction.

(c)   efficiency and equity. Dependable delivery, smooth scheduling, low-cost production and the maintenance of standards are critical.

(d)   its position in the external league tables. Being number one relative to the competition in the marketplace is a key objective.

6   Management style (Divide 100 points)
The management style in my institution is characterized by
(a)   teamwork, consensus, and participation.
(b)   security of employment, longevity in position, and predictability.
(c)   hard-driving competitiveness, production and achievement.
(d)   individual initiative, innovation, freedom, and uniqueness.

Score
(a) collegium
(b) bureaucracy
(c) corporation
(d) enterprise

Source: adapted from Cameron and Quinn, 2006.

effective way of generating competitive advantage. Not all such efforts are successful, however. Far from it. Too often such initiatives have foundered because they have been based on the (arrogant) assumption that (as an entity) culture, like dough, can somehow be consciously moulded by senior managers sitting above the fray. More successful have been those instances which recognize culture as a process which embraces all players within the organization (Trowler, 1998; Frost *et al.*, 1991).

In either case, the lesson learned is to remember that: 'our actions speak so much louder than our words'. Thus, it would make little sense – and serve to foster deep antipathy – for an HEI to have, say, a mission statement extolling how much the institution valued excellence in teaching, if the criteria it used for staff recruitment and promotion were based solely on performance in research. Put another way, we can all contribute to sustaining, or shaping, our organizational culture by the way in which we act. Our actions demonstrate to others what we really value. And in the context of HEIs the criteria we use for recruitment, promotion and redundancy, and the way in which we respond to critical incidents and institutional crises, celebrate achievement, operate budgets and so on all send important signals which reinforce or alter the perception of others. These may, in turn, affect their outward behaviour and indeed inner consciousness. This is an issue we will return to in Chapters 3 and 9 when we discuss leadership and the management of change respectively. Some HEIs, however, have deliberately and purposefully sought to adopt a particular organizational model. And it is to these types of institution we turn next.

The entrepreneurial university

The notion that a university could, and should, be run along the same lines as a private business company is one many academics view with horror. Such a proposal is invariably dismissed for one, if not all three, of the following reasons. First, it is maintained that if universities were to embrace a commercial ethos then the consequences for the concept or *idea* of the university would be dire. For in such a setting universities would have no core business, and no responsibilities, and ultimately would be reduced to the totality of market opportunities on offer. Thus the 'soul of the university' would simply wither and die in this environment (Pratt, 2000). Second, it is argued that even if universities wanted to adopt this approach then the *practical* differences between them and commercial enterprises – the tradition of consensual management; the primacy of quality over profit; the greater degree and range of accountability; the tension between academic freedom and commercial confidentiality; the political interference in policy making; the difficulties in measuring value and outputs, and so on – would render this aspiration nigh-on unworkable. And last, it is recalled that the *legal* status of universities – typically that of a registered charity – would preclude such a possibility ever gaining credence.

These barriers, however, have not dissuaded all universities from taking this path. Far from it. 'Caught in a cross-fire of expectations' at 'a time of disquieting turmoil with no end in sight', universities, as Charles Vest, the President of MIT, put it, are 'overextended, under-focused, over-stressed and under-funded' (cited in Clark, 1998). The pressure on them to innovate is considerable, if not overwhelming. Indeed such is the overload of demands on universities – to accommodate more students and different types of students; to satisfy the lifelong training needs of an ever more specialized labour market; to assimilate the careening growth of knowledge; to do 'more' with 'less' and so on – that, as Burton Clark (1998, 2004) argues, universities have little option but to take an entrepreneurial path if they wish to secure their future. To do nothing at all would be to run the risk of institutional breakdown: a far more daunting prospect, surely, than the inherent dangers associated with entrepreneurialism.

As it is, some universities have taken the lead in this regard and there are five European ones in particular – Warwick (England), Strathclyde (Scotland), Twente (Netherlands), Chalmers (Sweden) and Joensuu (Finland) – which Clark has identified as role models worthy of emulation: innovators, that is, which all sensed the need to transform their traditional character by becoming 'more enterprising, even aggressively entrepreneurial'. In the case of Warwick, for example – one of seven new 'green-field' research universities founded in the 1960s – the university's 'tough-minded recognition' that the Thatcher government of the 1980s 'had become an undependable university patron and often a hostile one' led it 'to work hard to place the institution in an independent posture – to stand on its own feet by earning its way': an institutional idea whose enthusiastic adoption has enabled the university to generate almost half of its income from non-governmental (or third-stream) sources, and establish Warwick as 'the success story of the (English) university world'.

Strathclyde has reaped a similar reward for its endeavours. Different in pedigree to Warwick, this Glasgow institution – a former mechanics institute turned technical college and eventually technological university – chose to adopt its traditional ideal of '200 years of useful learning' in confronting the contemporary prospect of 'death by a 1,000 cuts'. So successful was this initiative that the ideas of useful learning, strategic research and technology transfer have 'come together as a belief system that has become an all-university culture'. And the university, no longer Scotland's poor relation, has taken on a semi-comprehensive form in which three of its five faculties (business, education and the arts) are now concentrated in research, teaching and service outside science and technology (Clark, 1998, 2004).

Joensuu, a modest regional university in rural Finland, was – in sharp contrast to Warwick and Strathclyde – positively encouraged by the government to experiment with innovations in university management, notably the radical idea, for the highly centralized Finnish national system, of doubly decentralizing budget-based control all the way down to the departmental level. The university's early acceptance of a second novel innovation – of flexible staff workloads – has secured Joensuu's burgeoning reputation as a 'piloting' institution, one which operates significantly differently from those in the traditional Finnish style. Of humble origin, Joensuu has successfully 'strengthened its sense of self and its place in the world'.

Chalmers University of Technology also established a distinctive identity for itself when, in 1994, it chose to become a 'foundation university', an institutional definition which virtually all other Swedish universities were unable or unwilling to consider. This 'opt-out' from a national system characterized by 'central government controlled standardization' caused a sensation, but one which the university desired in order to gain 'simultaneous right of disposition over all resources', 'a more flexible organization' and to have 'greater opportunity for our own organizational and financial initiatives'. Grounded in the idea that the university should have 'a plurality of special places for innovative behaviour', Chalmers has flourished as a 'one-of-a-kind' institution (Clark, 1998, 2004).

Twente, the last of the five, is arguably the most ardent subscriber to this particular model of development. A provincial Dutch university founded in the 1960s, Twente, responding to growing marginality and fuelled by a desire to evolve from an 'education university' to a 'research university', defiantly declared itself in the early 1980s to be '*the* entrepreneurial university', a term of which it initially barely knew the meaning in practice. It turned out to mean two things – an 'attitude' and a sense of 'doing business on one's own account and at one's own risk'. The consequence was that Twente achieved its goal, and in 1996 hosted the inaugural meeting of the new European Consortium of Innovative Universities.

The similarities between these innovators are not confined solely to the nature of their response. They also extend to the manner in which they sought to transform themselves: namely, even though these innovators may have differed markedly from one another – in terms of their institutional origins and character, the nature of their national settings and the stimulus which prompted them to action – they all chose to adopt common 'organizational pathways of transformation'. The five elements of these pathways, Clark argues, are not only characteristic of these particular innovators but 'constitute an irreducible minimum' for any prospective university which seeks to follow in their path.

The strengthened steering core

The first element involves recognizing that universities cannot continue to be managed in the conventional way they have been in the past; not, that is, if they wish to respond effectively to the overload of demands placed upon them. In order to do so universities must develop a capacity which they have conspicuously lacked in the past, namely the ability to steer themselves. Elite universities, of course, can afford to ignore this imperative (though likely not indefinitely) and continue to rely on their outstanding reputations and political clout for maintaining resources and status. All other HEIs, however – the wannabes, the marginal and the desperate – do not have the benefit of this luxury. A strengthened steering core then – which enables the institution to respond more quickly, flexibly and consistently to expanding and changing demands – is thus a necessity. And in the case of the five innovators, the key to their achievement in this respect lies, as Clark demonstrates, in the nature of the cores they established: ones which not only embraced *both* central managerial groups *and* academic departments, but which also reconciled new managerial values with traditional academic ones.

At Warwick, for example, the university has – and indeed prides itself on – a 'flat structure' of a (strong) centre and (strong) departments linked together by a web of central committees, notably the Vice Chancellor's Steering Committee, the Earned Income Group and the Senate Budget and Resources Committee. Faculties and deans are conspicuous by their absence. At Strathclyde a 'soft' centre characterized by 'a lassitude of purpose' and with responsibility diffused 'in a rabbit-warren of over 50 committees' was replaced in 1987 by a University Management Group (UMG) or 'private sector model of management'. The UMG was the institution's considered response to the 1985 Jarratt Report on the (in)efficiency of British universities and it 'became the action group that could get-up-and-go'. It reports to the Court and Senate, but is a creature of neither.

This process of strengthening institutional steering capacity was, of course, not unproblematic. At Warwick, for example, there was bitter student and staff protest against what some regarded as the establishment of *Warwick University Ltd*, while at Strathclyde faculty 'warriors routinely stalled' reform initiatives by vetoing 'disagreeable issues' (Clark, 2004). Why these changes were ultimately accepted at Warwick and Strathclyde is because each took pains to ensure that faculty were directly represented – by departmental chairs or elected pro-vice chancellors and deans – on these central cores. In this way, 'management points of view, including the notion of entrepreneurship, were carried from centre to academic heartland, while faculty values infiltrated the managerial space'. And, in consequence, all members of these cores 'worked to find resources for the institution *as a whole*'.

The expanded developmental periphery

The second element derives from the belief that academic departments by themselves can no longer do all the things that a contemporary university has to do and that the latter therefore must make up the difference: namely, by reaching across old university boundaries and seizing the initiative to develop links between itself and the wider world. This activity has, as in the case of the five innovators, typically focused on the establishment of professionalized outreach units – on knowledge transfer, industrial contact, intellectual property development, continuing education and the like – and the creation of externally oriented (Mode II knowledge-based) research centres.

At Warwick, for example, the university's 'developmental periphery' embraces:

- the Warwick Manufacturing Group, which has sales of £80 million a year and 500 companies and governments worldwide as customers;

- a conference business which generates £12 million a year from 2,000 en-suite bedrooms;
- a science park 'hothouse' which accommodates 65 high-tech companies employing more than 1,500 staff;
- a fully fledged business school of international repute;
- an arts complex that attracts 250,000 visitors a year.

Similarly at Strathclyde 'peripheral' activity has centred on:

- a Research and Consultancy service which has facilitated the creation of 22 spin-off companies (more than any other Scottish university) and the collection of £7 million a year from intellectual property rights;
- an Institute for Drug Research which generates £2.5 million a year in royalties and 20 research centres including leading-edge ones in the social sciences and European regional development.

While the focus is similar in each of the five cases, the same cannot be said of the way in which these activities are organized. New outreach administrative units and research centres are sometimes closely linked to the steering core and academic departments and sometimes not. There is no one way, no one model. What these development peripheries have done, though, in all five instances is bequeath a common legacy: namely, they have moved each of the five innovators towards a dual structure of basic units in which (specialist-based) traditional departments are supplemented by (project-based) centres linked to the outside world. They have, in effect, spawned a matrix-like structure which fulfils the institutional need to acknowledge the continued importance of discipline-based academic departments on the one hand, while simultaneously enabling it to cater for the growth of the service role of the university on the other.

Developed further, an enhanced periphery could indeed, in organizational terms, move a university towards the character of a shopping mall. And while it might add to the organizational complexity of an institution, this is, arguably, a minor inconvenience compared to the benefits an enhanced periphery brings, not simply in economic terms, as an income generator, but also in academic ones too – in its contribution to new modes of thinking and problem-solving, to interdisciplinarity and the production of useful knowledge and so on.

The diversified funding base

The third element arises from the broad acceptance that the traditional and staple source of funding for HEIs – i.e. government – is no longer either reliable or munificent. On the contrary, mainline institutional support from government, as a share of total budget, has declined virtually everywhere. Not only that, the emergence of 'contractual' government has robbed universities of the ability to plan for the long term with any degree of confidence. Enterprising universities recognize this trend and turn it to their advantage. That is, rather than passively fall in line with a government-determined agenda (experiencing parallel financial increases and decreases as government stimuli wax and wane) they actively intervene by deciding to pursue additional sources of income. In other words, they accept and promote as their maxim a general truth offered by two percipient American observers (Babbidge and Rosenzweig, 1962) over 40 years ago that: 'a workable twentieth-century definition of institutional autonomy [is] the absence of dependence upon a single or narrow base of support'.

Our five innovators are no exception. They each set out – with remarkable success – to build a diversified funding base, initially, by competing more vigorously for research grants and contracts from second-stream sources (Research Councils), and latterly by systematically constructing an ever widening and deepening portfolio of third-stream sources, which stretched from industrial firms, local governments and philanthropic foundations to royalty income from intellectual property, earned income from campus services, student fees and alumni fund-raising. By the mid-1990s each of the innovators had reduced its dependence on government as a funding source to the extent that third-stream activities accounted for a significant proportion – Strathclyde 51 per cent, Warwick 47 per cent, Joensuu 27 per cent, Twente 21 per cent and Chalmers 20 per cent – of their overall income. This achievement is an invaluable one as it offers the innovative university far greater freedom for manoeuvre than that enjoyed by its less enterprising counterpart. It not only increases total resources but also allows a university to 'roll with the punches' (a loss here is made up by a gain there), to build up reserves, to borrow additional monies and ultimately to take innovative steps, as Warwick did when it used accumulated surpluses from its earned income to fund 50 new research fellowships aimed at 'further enhancing and strengthening the University's research reputation'.

Diversified funding, however, does not come without a price. The perennial debates within universities, for example concerning the internal disposition of funds raised through diverse sources – over the range and amount of central top-slicing, the degree of institutional cross-subsidization and so on – are invariably, and legitimately, contentious. It is, though, a price worth paying, for without diversity in financing universities would lose the ability to be adaptable, to make choices, and with it, in effect, the opportunity to be better-focused institutions.

The stimulated academic heartland

The fourth element recognizes that, while traditional academic departments may no longer be able to do all the things that a contemporary university has to do, they are still vitally important in the shaping of an institution's future. For they constitute the heartland where traditional academic values are most firmly rooted and, therefore, where entrepreneurial innovation is most likely to fail. This is not to say that the traditional heartland is characterized by the absence of enterprising action. On the contrary, virtually all science and technology departments have become entrepreneurial to some degree, as have some social science departments and even humanities departments. The point is that such enterprising action has typically been unevenly spread within institutions. The entrepreneurial university, by contrast, is one in which enterprising activity is widely diffused across the academic heartland.

The key to the latter's achievement lies as ever – as in the case of the five innovators – in the way that entrepreneurial activity is fostered, not by hard managerialism but rather by maintaining and even increasing collegial integration: by bringing faculty, that is, into the central steering groups, and by insisting on faculty–management collaboration throughout the process. At Warwick, for example, such collegial entrepreneurialism manifested itself in a number of ways: through the establishment of a pioneering university-wide graduate school; through the creation of the institutional research fellowship scheme; through the building of numerous research centres under departments and the melding of the periphery (e.g. the Warwick Manufacturing Group) with traditional academic departments (such as engineering). In each case – characterized as 'the Warwick Way' – an initiative was identified, a framework developed and a leading academic (or 'product champion') was 'given their head' to realize the opportunity (Warner and Palfreyman, 2001).

At Chalmers, likewise, it was a science professor who pioneered the Chalmers Innovation Centre and inspired 'the transfer of new product ideas and new technology from university to industry'. And at Strathclyde the university has been able to file over a dozen patents from the work undertaken by the Department of Electronic and Electrical Engineering, its leading academic department. At Joensuu, the university relied on 'dialogue' and 'information systems' – to monitor departmental 'inputs' (sources of support, unit costs) and 'outputs' (degree completion, course coverage, research productivity, etc.) – as means of asserting the broader institutional interest and its successful piloting of budgetary-based departmental self-regulation.

In all of these instances, the innovators were more than simply inclusive. They empowered individuals and departments to take responsibility for their actions and to establish their priorities. In this way, they successfully managed to 'install a spirit of collegial entrepreneurialism' by 'unhooking collegiality from defence of the *status quo* and the love of the *status quo ante*' and orienting it in favour of adaptiveness and change (Clark, 2004). In return, the innovators were rewarded with – and entrepreneurial universities are characterized by – *selective* substantial growth in their basic units.

The integrated entrepreneurial culture

The fifth and final element recognizes that entrepreneurial universities are not only differentiated in operational terms from their less enterprising counterparts, but also in a cultural sense – in the ideas, values and beliefs they espouse. Put simply, entrepreneurial universities accept the notion that change and adaptation constitute a continuous and never-ending process and typically develop – as in the case of the five innovators – a work culture which reflects this proposition, one, that is, which successfully reconciles (not jettisons) traditional academic values with newer managerial ones.

Cultural transformation of this order does not, of course, occur overnight. In the case of the five innovators this process developed in all instances over a period of at least 10 to 15 years. Indeed they each have 'a story' (or *saga*) to tell – of institutional perseverance in the face of adversity – which has itself become part of their cultures. And they all, in turn, have shared a common pattern of cultural transformation: namely, all five innovators moved along the same 'ideational road', from the initial teasing out of a working *idea*, to the cultivation of institutional *beliefs*, the dissemination of a new *culture* and the formation of a new unifying *identity*; or as, for example, in the case of Warwick, from the tentative notion propagated in the early 1980s that the institution should 'earn' its way, to the growing belief in the efficacy of the earned income approach; its unprecedented success in this regard and the collective acceptance of this modus operandi

– 'the Warwick Way' – celebrated, literally and symbolically, on the twenty-fifth anniversary of the university's founding. At Strathclyde, the leading idea was not nearly so well defined, but in time the initial managerial idea expressed in a distinctive central steering group, a productive periphery, and an entrepreneurial 'spirit' in some heartland departments became folded into a generalized belief system of 'useful learning', a doctrine which, like that of Warwick, was at the centre of the university's bicentennial celebration in 1996.

These new belief systems did not emerge in isolation from other institutional structures and processes. On the contrary, they were sustained by the practical development of the other elements. In other words, the first four elements provided the *means* by which these transforming ideas became operative. And herein is the key to the innovators' success – and the lesson to be drawn by those seeking to emulate them. Namely, successful transformation is contingent on the interaction of *all* of the elements – not one or two, but all five of them. It cannot be achieved, for example, by simply relying – as advocates of top-down approaches might have it – on a strengthened steering core: each of the elements by itself can make little difference. The capacity for transformation lies in their collective interaction (Clark, 1998).

Such has been the success of the five innovators in this regard that they have not only managed to transform their organizations internally but have also been able to sustain it through what Clark describes as the mutually reinforcing 'dynamic of reinforcing interaction, perpetual momentum and collegial volition' (Clark, 2004), to such an extent indeed that they are characterized by 'a steady state of institutional change' rather than one of inertia or preservation of the status quo. In short, they have all achieved what they set out to do: to have more control over their destiny. Neither state-led nor market-dictated, they typify the new self-reliant, self-steering university.

They are not the only ones in this regard. In the USA many universities acquired a steady state of change over the last generation. Stanford University for example – initiator of, and academic anchor for, Silicon Valley with spin-offs such as Sun Microsystems, Netscape, Cisco Systems and Yahoo – has emerged as the foremost entrepreneurial university in the world. Though not as integrated with new technology start-up businesses as Stanford, Massachusetts Institute of Technology (MIT) likewise has generated 175 new enterprises in its immediate vicinity – the Route 128 (circumferential highway) complex – and is the locus of the region's economic development: 'the Massachusetts Miracle'.

Beyond these two leading private universities, there are two flagship state universities. The University of Michigan has managed to move from being a 'state-assisted university' to a 'privately-financed public university' (or self-reliant public university) by becoming the largest performer of academic research and development of all US universities, private or public. It has succeeded to such an extent that the state contribution to the university is less than 20 per cent of its overall income. University of California, Los Angeles (UCLA), too, has become a 'federal-grant university' more than a 'state-supported university' with a multiplicity of research centres, institutes and labs derivative of a very wide base of initiative-generating faculty interests.

Again, North Carolina State University has sought to differentiate itself further from its neighbours, Chapel Hill and Duke, by building a new framework – the Centennial campus – which offers a new model of how to go beyond technology transfer and the normal output of trained graduates towards a more thorough integration of academia and industry on its joint-use campus. Georgia Institute of Technology ('Georgia Tech') has also sought to develop university–industry collaboration aimed at generating economic growth in its home state. Host to the 'Yamacraw' project (a coalition of the state, its six principal public and private universities and 12 Georgia corporations), focused on high-tech services and employment, Georgia Tech is committed to 'becoming the country's foremost public technological university'. In all these cases, Clark identifies three distinguishing characteristics that set these institutions apart: their deliberate attempts at self-reliance, their build-up of high research intensity and their ingrained willingness, spurred by competition, to compete vigorously for institutional prestige (Clark, 2004).

Beyond the USA and Europe, Monash University has emerged as the leading entrepreneurial university in Australia. Here the transformation has been teaching-led rather than research-led. Born in the 1960s in the shadow of the University of Melbourne, Monash avidly seized opportunities opened up by the government's creation of a New Unified National University System in 1987 (when 73 HEIs gave way to 36 public universities): to increase first undergraduate education in the local region and, more spectacularly, its international provision both on-site and offshore. What all these innovators demonstrate is that their success has been achieved by harnessing collegiality, not spurning it. They have shown that entrepreneurialism need not compromise traditional academic values; that it may actually present universities with the best alternative in the difficult circumstances now facing them.

The virtual university

Attractive as this proposition may be, it is not the only option universities have been considering. An equally compelling vision to many in higher education has been the notion of the 'virtual university'. Unlike the entrepreneurial university which emerged as a reaction to a negative economic imperative (the universal squeeze on funding), the virtual university is usually perceived as a positive response to a technological driver and pedagogical need. That is to say, faced with rising demand and rising expectations (students' desire for flexible provision, employer requirements of graduate competence and so on) – with, in effect, the challenge of turning 'mass time' into 'quality time' for students – universities tend to view the enabling potential of new technologies as a godsend. They can provide them, that is, with the practical means – and arguably the only realistic one – of increasing scale at a sensible cost without sacrificing quality (Gourley, 2004). Not only that. Such technologies, if intelligently adopted, would enable them to meet the newly emergent challenge posed by corporate universities such as the 'big six' in the UK – Body Shop, British Aerospace, Ford, Motorola, PricewaterhouseCoopers and Unipart – and a host of others in the USA including McDonald's Hamburger University, the Disney Institute, Microsoft and Sears.

Not surprisingly, HEIs have mobilized to capitalize on this incentive and a conspicuous minority have broken new ground in establishing themselves at the forefront of 'borderless education'. Early pioneers such as the University of Melbourne, Deakin University, Columbia University and New York University, for example, established their own private subsidiaries – Melbourne University Private Ltd, Deakin Global, Columbia Fathom.com and NYU Online – in order to enable them to operate more flexibly and to extend their international reach (CVCP, 2000; Robins and Webster, 2002).

Others joined with like-minded HEIs in developing new international consortia, often in collaboration with commercial organizations. *Universitas 21*, for example, initially established in 1997 as an informal network of elite research-intensive universities from the UK, the USA, Canada, Australia, New Zealand, Hong Kong, Singapore and China, is now an incorporated British company seeking to position its 18 university members world-wide as a 'global brand', one in which, as Alan Gilbert, then Vice Chancellor of Melbourne University and founder of the original network, put it – in classic marketing speak – 'the centuries old brand value of the individual partners is invested in an international cross-jurisdictional brand signifying and symbolizing a singular level of quality and quality assurance' (Cohen, 1998). It also established a joint-venture company with Thomson Learning, a subsidiary of the Thomson Corporation, and launched its own online university: U21 Global. Eurospace 2000 was another consortium that likewise sought to establish a virtual campus and distance education network, in this instance to support 'learning on demand' by bringing together 45 European universities, and a host of private enterprises (including Alcatel, IBM and Philips) and international agencies, to facilitate the delivery of lifelong learning.

Such was the initial enthusiasm that the British government invested £62 million in developing its own UK e-University (UKeU) to be 'the flag-carrier', as Education Secretary David Blunkett put it in February 2000, that would deliver online degrees from UK universities to the rest of the world. Not all these initiatives managed to live up to their initial hype. U21 Global launched its first MBA in 2003 and has 3,000 students based mostly in India, China and the Middle East against an initial expectation of 500,000 students by 2011. Columbia University's Fathom.com and NYU Online have foundered – as indeed did the UKeU in April 2004, having attracted just 900 out of a projected 5,600 students. In taking 'a supply-driven approach rather than a demand-led one' combined with 'an inability to work in effective partnership with the private sector' (Sun Microsystems) and 'a woeful lack of formal market research' (for example, failing to forge a partnership with the British Council), the UKeU project was condemned by the Commons Education and Skills Committee as 'a disgraceful waste' of public money (Lipsett, 2005; Maslen, 2006).

Other HEIs, by contrast, have sought to broaden their use of new technologies beyond that of course delivery to include their own internal operations in order to become not simply web-based but also *web-enabled*. Again, such initiatives have not always produced the outcome that was anticipated. Visionaries at three north-east England universities, for instance, found that when they attempted to harness new technologies – in developing a new finance and human resources management information system (Newcastle University), extending the work of the Learning Development Services unit (Sunderland University) and promoting excellence in the use of C&IT (Northumbria University) – electronic processes 'did not displace traditional ways of doing things but simply co-existed in a tense symbiotic relationship'. They adjudged that far from leading to a break-up of the traditional university, new technologies actually require 'a re-institutionalization of the university as a more corporate kind of organization where goals, roles, identities, rules and operating procedures are made more explicit': that is, a far more 'concrete' organization, ironically, than the one currently existing in many universities. They concluded that the quest for the virtual university is a fruitless one, for the premise on which it is based – 'a university without walls' – is flawed (Goddard, 1999).

While it may well be that the idea of the virtual university underestimates how universities as institutions (currently) work, and perhaps overstates what communication technologies can do, it would be premature to discard the notion altogether (van Ginkel, 1995), particularly since we already have successful exemplars of this model in operation: institutions, that is, characterized by the fact that they have all differed from the traditional university since their inception. One such virtual university we should acknowledge and which is very well known is, of course, the UK Open University. Established in 1969 to provide higher education opportunities to individuals whose circumstances did not permit conventional full-time residential study, the Open University fused the technologies of correspondence education with those of broadcasting and a unique student support network. An open (no formal entry requirements at undergraduate level) and distance learning institution whose courses cost 40 to 60 per cent less than conventional face-to-face provision in the UK, the OU today boasts 'an academic community on which the sun never sets'. It currently has more than 164,000 students in 41 countries – including Hong Kong, Malaysia and a number of Eastern European countries, including Russia – 80,000 of whom are networked to the OU, and to each other, from home computers (Daniel, 1998; Gourley, 2004)).

One of a dozen or so mega-universities, the OU is still very much an industrial model of higher education delivering a mass product to a mass audience. While it may be a virtual university, in that it functions indepen-dent of physical location, it does not operate as a 'virtual corporation': one which is flexible, tailored to individual or corporate needs and fluid in structure. It is precisely this attribute which is the hallmark of our second virtual university exemplar: the University of Phoenix, the most famous private for-profit higher education provider in the United States. A subsidiary of the Apollo Group first accredited in 1978, Phoenix deliberately positioned itself to respond to what it saw as the failure of most traditional institutions to consider the adult population. And it has sought to differentiate itself from the traditional university ever since, not simply in its provision of an online library to complement its online campus but also through its:

- 'cornerstone philosophy' – to focus on providing professional education for working adults who have established personal and professional goals (rather than the younger college student still deciding on a career);
- organization of curriculum and pedagogy – programmes are offered on a year-round basis with students studying courses sequentially (rather than concurrently) over a five- to eight-week period in an atmosphere of 'concentrated immersion'. Classes mirror business practice and students are grouped into problem-solving teams and self-help study groups;
- modus operandi – a small administrative centre and an army of 6,000 non-tenured part-time teachers ('working practitioners' hired on the basis of what students will learn rather than their academic credentials) provide specialist training 'anytime, anywhere' to individual and corporate clients alike via a network of 170 campuses and 300 corporate sites (in 37 states) situated, for convenience's sake, on the edge of freeways and in shopping malls.

Initially derided as the founder of 'McEducation', Phoenix currently has a national enrolment of 300,000 students – including 150,000 registered (in class sizes of nine) with Phoenix Online – making it the largest accredited private institution in the United States. And with a stock market valuation of $11.4 billion – equivalent to the endowment fortune of Yale University, America's second wealthiest college – the leading provider in its field, its unabashedly mass-market focus is reflected in its ($150 million) acquisition of the naming rights to the stadium of the NFL's Arizona Cardinals (de Alva, 2002; Philips, 2007).

Phoenix's success, like that of the OU, is attributable, then, not so much to new technologies per se, but to the way in which they have been harnessed and *integrated* – as a *means* to an end, rather than an *end* in itself. While operationally differentiated from one another, neither has forgotten (unlike some enthusiasts of e-learning) that learning is, in essence, a social activity, and that the key ingredient is not computers but rather the *interaction* between student and tutor and between students and their peers. They have as such sought to organize themselves around a genuine (dialogue-based) *conversational* model of learning rather than the traditional (tutor-centred) *transmission* model or (environment-simulated) *constructivist* model so characteristic of the many initial – and ultimately disappointing – institutional attempts at Internet delivery (Laurillard, 2001). They also recognize that learning in the future will be as much network-based (university–home–place of employment–local community) – something which the Dearing Inquiry failed to grasp – as it is campus-based. And their market performance bears testament to the fact that a virtual university – based on such principles – can indeed deliver 'more' for 'less' without sacrificing quality: a lesson not lost on others such as the University of Illinois's new $20 million online Global Campus initiative which is seeking to emulate some Phoenix practices (Philips, 2007).

All this is not to say that the apocalyptic predictions proffered by futurists and management gurus like Alvin Toffler (1991) and Peter Drucker (1993) – that 'the big university campuses will become relics' and 'the college won't survive as a residential institution' – will come to fruition. Far from it. It is more probable, as we noted in Chapter 1, that the university will still retain a physical manifestation – a particular sort of gathering place. Indeed, the greatest threat to the hegemony of the residential university ideal has not, ironically, been the prospect of a 'virtual take-over' based on innovations in new technologies, but rather the increasing tendency of universities to recruit students from their home region, or, more accurately, the growing propensity of students (well over one-half of all undergraduates in the UK) to apply (largely for reasons of financial constraint) solely to those universities based in their locality. Either way, the virtual university, like the entrepreneurial model, offers universities yet another alternative with which to respond to the unprecedented circumstances now confronting them. What, though, of the university of the future: what might the reformed post-millennial university that has adapted to this new environment look like – the university of 2025?

The university of 2025?

Projecting forward is, of course, a hazardous business. It would be very easy, for example, to get carried away, as some futurists have done, by the prospect of a techno-fantasy in which modems take over from people, databases from discourse, and computers from culture. More sober reflection anticipates four alternative paths of development: one – the 'post-Fordist' university – grounded in changes in the way the university is internally managed; two others – the 'core university' model and the 'distributed university' system – based on the break-up of the traditional university as we know it; and finally, universities in 'an ecology of learning' centred on universities exercising positive and forward-looking leadership in a sector transformed from without, from the outside-in. These four institutional variants offer competing visions of the future university. Let us consider each in turn.

The post-Fordist university

The first anticipates the emergence of a post-managerialist culture within universities, a transition that is similar in scope to that of the last two decades, during which managerialism replaced collegialism as the dominant cultural form within most UK universities. Managerialism, then, it is foreseen, will in turn suffer a similar fate to that which befell collegialism – and be replaced by what Peter Scott and David Watson (1994) have dubbed a 'strategic' (or 'reflexive') culture.

This presumption, they argue, is a logical corollary to the massification of HE in that it recognizes that institutions have to be managed differently according to their size and complexity. Thus, where once it may have been appropriate (say) for small elite HEIs (*c.* 7,000 students), with uncomplicated missions, to be managed along collegial lines, this was no longer possible with the emergence of a mass system characterized by heterogeneity and diversity and large-scale institutions (*c.* 10–20,000 students). Equally, the managerialism characteristic of this transition will no longer be suitable, Scott (1995) maintains, as HEIs evolve beyond 20,000 FTEs. Indeed, increasing size, complexity and differentiation within institutions will 'compromise the need for strong centralized direction' and senior management, once the locus of most decision-making, will 'shrink to a slimmed-down strategic core'. That is, its role would be limited to safeguarding the financial (and legal) integrity and academic mission of the university while providing management services to its basic units, which would enjoy far greater operational freedom beyond that of responsibility for devolved budgets. Consequently institutional hierarchies would become much flatter and may even be replaced by loosely coupled networks.

In essence, Scott and Watson anticipate universities evolving in much the same way as many successful private corporations have done (and particularly those knowledge-intensive enterprises which employ highly skilled workers) by developing an institutional setting which facilitates flexibility and synergy while accommodating volatility. Such a setting bears the hallmarks of an organization commonly typified as 'postmodern' or 'post-Fordist'. This new transition to a strategic culture they stress, however, would neither represent a return to old-style collegiality, nor a retreat from managerialism, but rather 'a reinterpretation and recombination of both to meet the radically different challenge of managing mass institutions'.

The core university model

Our second institutional variant anticipates, by contrast, a very different HE environment. Principally, a framework would be established in which universities – reconfigured to have as their primary role the commissioning of courses and programmes – would invite bids from newly self-employed academic staff to teach them. Such a setting – the brainchild of the Office for Public Management – could and should be created, the OPM argue, by restructuring higher education along the lines of the NHS. This means, by accepting the academic community for what it is – a world in which tutors cling resolutely to their autonomy and to their subject loyalties – and seeking to change it from without, not within, namely by 'reformulating the staff "contract", both legal and psychological, to reflect this underlying reality' (Albury, 1997).

In this new environment academic staff – perhaps in partnerships, consortia, trusts or other organizational forms based on particular subjects, disciplines or approaches: the Progressive Particle Physics Partnership, the Renaissance in the History of Art Trust – would be free to tender for the delivery of courses and programmes in any number of universities and colleges. They would also have the freedom to choose (the exigencies of making a living notwithstanding!) *not* to teach subjects in which they were uninterested, as well as to pursue other activities (e.g. research and consultancy) which they personally valued. Equally, universities – now reduced essentially to their senior managers and administrative support – would be able to create real choice for students by offering courses which they demand rather those which staff want to teach. And the key, and by no means trivial, task for senior managers would be to act as champions of the 'stakeholders' of their university or college, by developing strong forms of engagement with potential students, targeted communities, employers and relevant agencies to ensure the needs of these various parties are met.

The establishment of such an environment would in effect turn the HE 'business' on its head, making it market-driven rather than producer (supply)-driven. In this sense the proposal is a logical extension of the 'contractual' view of government which, as we noted earlier, has emerged as the dominant orthodoxy in the management of public services over the last two decades. For staff in HE it would herald the 'end of tenure' and the 'start of tender'. Implementation, however, may be another matter for this very reason. Tenure enjoys iconic esteem in academia, particularly in the USA, and any proposal which seeks to drastically reshape the contract between academic staff and institutions, as this one does, could only be successful if there was sufficient strength of political character and will to carry it through.

The distributed university system

Our third alternative also anticipates the emergence of a new configuration within HE and again, like the second variant, envisages a radical change in the contractual status of academic staff. The change, however, in this instance, is a second-order outcome rather than the prime motivating factor. The distributed university system takes as its cue not the legal and psychological reality of the staff contract, but rather the needs of all learners (electronic as well as face-to-face): for access to communities of scholars on the one hand and the acquisition of credentials from universities on the other. It recognizes that the digital age will change the relationship between these two and that as such the days of the traditional (and inflexible) monolithic university are numbered.

Indeed the model – as propagated by two Californian cybernetics researchers (Brown and Duguid, 1996) – envisages the university system broken up into its four main constituent parts: a degree-granting function, academic staff, campus facilities and students. These elements may have hitherto been considered all part of a single institution but have in reality no inherent reason (historical precedent notwithstanding) to be so or remain so. Take them apart, and the system of HE would become much more *flexible*, particularly for the learner. In such a setting, for example, the university's role would be confined primarily to that of granting credentials, and as a degree-granting body (DGB) the 'new' university would own little beyond its own administrative competency and a building in which to house its staff. Thus liberated of the need to make the massive capital investment that a university requires now, these DGBs would be able to evolve to meet the needs of students, faculty and employers far more easily than their predecessors.

Faculty, likewise, would be free to become independent contractors. Like doctors who contract to NHS Trusts, they would have to find DGBs to sanction their teaching and, like doctors, they might find more than one to do this. They could also contract either individually or in teams, but would not (as now) all have to assemble in one place. As for payment, remuneration could be linked to the type of teaching (lecture, tutorial, research seminar, etc.) or the teacher's ability to attract high-quality students to the DGB. Alternatively, as in the case of eighteenth-century academics such as Adam Smith, scholars could simply collect a fee directly from the students they personally attract. Equally flexible arrangements could be put in place for research.

Facilities would probably look very much like the campus of today, the significant difference being that they would be quite independent of either the DGB or the faculty. As such, the physical campus – if it is to survive and prosper – would have to ensure that the standard of its facilities was of sufficient quality to attract the students, staff and DGBs within its region. Conversely, faculty and students would not have to travel to their DGB, but might travel to be close to superior facilities. Nor would they be locked into one set of facilities. In well-endowed areas, for instance, some faculty and many students might well use more than one facility.

For students *choice* grows dramatically if the university is broken up. Their central choice would involve finding a DGB appropriate to their needs. Such a decision would, as it does now, draw on a whole array of factors: the DGB's insistence (or not) on conventional campus life; its willingness to accredit prior experiential learning; the exchange value of the degree in question; the presence and commitment of quality staff and so on. Once the choice is made, students would then have the option of how they would like to study: online, offline; home-based, campus-based or work-based; in class, with mentors or on their own; or simply a mix of all the permutations on offer. They would not, however, have to commit to working with the faculty of a single campus or a single region. In essence, a student's university career would not be through a particular place, time or preselected body of academics, but, rather like their current explorations of the Net, through a network of their own making yet endorsed by the DGB and its faculty.

This model, then, does not anticipate the wholesale destruction of the university system. On the contrary, it seeks to combine the strengths of the old conventional system with the resources of the new digital age: the local and the distant, the real and the virtual. And it does so in such a way as to enhance flexibility and freedom, competition and choice.

Universities in 'an ecology of learning'

Our final alternative is one in which universities redesign the conventional building blocks of higher education and reassert themselves in their different ways (consistent with their mission, history and potential) as 'agents of learning, rather than simply providers of knowledge' (PA Consulting, 2008).

The emerging new social and economic system – or 'global ecology of learning built upon open, engaged communities of learning' (PA Consulting, 2008) – embraces and transcends the conventional transactional economy of knowledge dissemination and exchange. As such it is less concerned, PA Consulting (2008) argues, with maximizing the dissemination of *outputs* (research publications, students taught, knowledge products sold to business and the like) so characteristic of the traditional economy of learning than it is with generating *outcomes* (opportunity, creativity and innovation) that can feed back into the continuous growth and sustainability of the whole system.

If universities are to flourish, the consulting group maintains, it will be contingent on them 'being recognized as special in this turbulent environment' – fulfilling a distinctive role that no other player can provide. This, in turn, will entail universities forsaking their traditional producer-led, self-defined model of organization in favour of one that moves the institution from public subsidy to portfolio management; from peer review to quality 'kite marks'; from pedagogy to partnership; from academic subjects to solutions; and from knowledge to learning.

The role of government would be critical here too – not so much in seeking to shape or to control the system as in encouraging the development of an outward-looking, socially engaged HE sector. Either way, the challenge remains for 'the sector to transform itself from *without*, from the outside-in, while remaining true to its defining values of independence and learning' (PA Consulting, 2008; their italics).

Whether or not the university of the future will look anything like this picture, or that of the post-Fordist or the core university model, we cannot tell. But what is clear is that these models, along with the virtual and entrepreneurial ones, do offer universities a genuine way forward. That is, they each offer a model of the university that does not seek to preserve the glories of the past but, rather, to use what is appropriate and relevant for the future. And for that they should warrant our undivided attention, if not agreement. For what is certain is that the traditional university will not remain as it is today.

3 | Leading your department

As I went to bed at about 3 a.m., I was conscious of a profound sense of relief. At last I had the authority to give directions over the whole scene. I felt as if I were walking with destiny, and that all my past life had been but a preparation for this hour and for this trial.

Winston Churchill on becoming Prime Minister, 10 May, 1940

Seven weeks later and France had fallen to Hitler's armies, a shattering blow that left Britain to fight on alone. Clementine Churchill wrote to her husband on 27 June 1940: My Darling Winston, I hope you will forgive me if I tell you something that I feel you ought to know. One of the men in your entourage (a devoted friend) has been to me and told me there is a danger of your being generally disliked by your colleagues and subordinates because of your rough sarcastic and overbearing manner. . . . I was told 'No doubt it's the strain' – I cannot bear that those who serve the Country and yourself should not love you as well as admire and respect you. It is for you to give the Orders and if they are bungled – except for the King, the Archbishop of Canterbury and the Speaker you can sack anyone and everyone. Therefore with this terrific power you must combine urbanity, kindness and if possible Olympic calm. . . . Besides you won't get the best results by irascibility and rudeness. They will breed either dislike or a slave mentality. Please forgive your loving devoted and watchful Clemmie.

'Winston Churchill', Ed Morrow, the American broadcaster based in London in 1940, observed, 'mobilized the English language in defence of the free world against the tyranny of Nazism – and much else besides'. In Clemmie, Churchill was fortunate to have a devoted partner unafraid to remind him that the qualities of sound leadership were needed more than ever in a time of crisis. And, great leader that he was, Churchill had the good sense to heed such wise counsel. 'God knows where we should have been without him', commented Field Marshal Lord Alanbrooke of Brookeborough, Chief of the Imperial General Staff, in his memoirs, in 'deep-rooted admiration' of the way in which Churchill's leadership averted defeat in 1941, as the nation's darkest hour turned into its finest (Alanbrooke, 2001; Churchill, 1996; Soames, 1998).

It is of little wonder then that Churchill – and leaders of similar ilk such as Franklin D. Roosevelt, Mohandas Gandhi and Martin Luther King Jr. – should have been the subject of so many research inquiries into leadership. If we can identify the distinguishing characteristics which set leaders of this stature apart, it was reasoned, then we can look for these factors when selecting future leaders. These endeavours were not nearly so straightforward in practice, however. On the contrary, the quest to reach an under-standing of leadership – on its nature and essence, its style and meaning, its exercise and practice – has come to resemble the pursuit of the Holy Grail. The source of the difficulty, as Warren Bennis (cited in Syrett and Hogg, 1992) puts it, lies in the fact that 'leadership is an endless subject and endlessly interesting because you can never get your conceptual arms fully around it . . . I always feel like a lepidopterist chasing a butterfly.' And as is often the case in such pursuits, opinion on the subject has moved full circle. Thus where leadership was once perceived as the preserve of the few who were born to the role it is now widely regarded as an attribute that can be acquired – or learned – and therefore open to all (Bolden *et al.*, 2008).

Leadership has itself, in the process, become a growth business, not least for HEIs themselves. University business schools have become veritable 'cash cows' for their institutions as literally hundreds of courses on the subject have been established worldwide, usually in response to overwhelming demand from private organizations which themselves have, in turn, often set up their own in-house leadership development programmes. All these programmes, to a greater or lesser extent, have been created in the quite correct belief that leadership and management capacity is a critical determinant of organizational success. Many argue, and most agree, that this holds equally true for the public sector and the private one. As the late Tory Education Minister Sir Keith Joseph used to say, the nearest thing we have in education to a magic wand is an outstanding head-teacher. And this is even more the case given the new tough environment in which public services now operate, one in which consumer demands for tailor-made service, employee expectations of empowerment and governmental insistence on 'value-for-money' all vie for attention, under the critical gaze of voracious media.

Either way, it is a principle that the government has taken to heart and rendered a lynchpin of their public sector 'modernization' agenda. And *prima facie* there appears to be good reason for them doing so. For we now live in a time when the National Health Service sends patients abroad for treatment as a means of easing congested waiting lists, rail safety is seriously questioned, passenger complaints are at an all-time high and so on. We should be wary, however, of a knee-jerk reaction in which a 'private sector knows best' approach – or copycat management style – is adopted. After all, much the same pejorative discourse on the management and provision of public services dominated the politics and newspapers of all major cities in nineteenth-century Britain and America. And yet today their legacy is widely regarded as the 'unheralded triumph' of the Victorian Age (Teaford, 1984).

We should also remember it is now broadly accepted that effective leadership is as much contingent on *context* as it is on personal attributes and qualities. That is, leadership is not simply a matter of who one is, or what one does, but also involves doing the right thing at the right time in the work environment. This applies to HE just as it does to every other working situation, public and private. The point is: how can one lead in a university setting? What is the nature of leadership in such an environment? In what ways do leadership and management differ in HE? Can one be a leader as well as a manager? How should you lead?

These questions have too often been ducked within HE in the past. HE is not immune from the forces sweeping across other parts of the public sector. Nor do we do ourselves any favours pretending otherwise. Too much academic leadership, as we noted earlier in the Introduction, has been characterized by unprofessionalism: excessively lax and unresponsive at one extreme, and dumbly aggressive and assertive at the other. Both kinds have had devastating consequences in practice. This chapter, and those that follow, seek to confront these issues and address this deficiency.

This third chapter explores the concepts of leadership and management, outlines the similarities and differences between them and articulates the nature of leadership in theory. It also demonstrates how leadership can be applied in practice within the HE context by focusing, in this instance, on leadership in the formulation of departmental strategy.

Leadership versus management

> Leaders do the right thing, managers do things right.
> Peter Drucker, 1974

Some commentators use the terms 'leadership' and 'management' interchangeably as if they were synonymous with one another, while others use them in a very deliberate sense to convey that they are, in fact, quite different. Still others regard one (leadership) as a subset of the other (management). In academia we tend to shy away from using the terms altogether! It is not surprising, then, that the lay person's conception of these terms – like that of academia – is very often an unclear one, if not downright muddled. It is a misperception we need to straighten out.

Organizational effectiveness, it is broadly accepted, is dependent upon both capable leadership and sound management. It does not follow from one or the other, only from the successful combination of the two. Their very complementarity, however – as the *sine qua non* of organizational success – has often prevented us from recognizing that there is indeed a very real difference between the two. It is exemplified not only in the characteristics and activities of managers and leaders, but also in the perceptions of them in the workplace, as well as in the origins of the words themselves (Turner, 1998).

'Manager' is derived from the Latin *manus* (or 'hand'), which is the root of the sixteenth-century Italian word, *maneggiare*, referring to the handling, training and control of horses. British soldiers subsequently brought the word back from Italy and applied it to the handling of armies and the control of ships, vital duties performed by people who became known as 'managers'. The word gradually came to be applied to anyone who had a responsibility for organizing activities and controlling their administration. And the activities or functions associated with it – planning, staffing, budgeting, coordinating, decision-making and so on – came to be the guiding principles (and organizational theory) on which the classic business corporation was later formed. This association of management with 'gaining one's ends' through control and organization and perhaps, too, by implication, manipulation also helps explain why, in some HE cultures, the term is often perceived as a pejorative one – indeed as 'a dirty word'.

While management is unfairly (and wrongly) viewed as a simplistic, unnecessary and bureaucratic process, leadership, by contrast, is invariably portrayed as a difficult and noble art. The word 'leader' is derived from *laed* – a word common to all the Old North

European languages – meaning 'path', 'road', 'course of a ship at sea' or 'journey'. A leader is, therefore, someone who accompanies people on a journey guiding them to their destination, and, by implication, holds them together as a group whilst steering them in the right direction. Present-day dictionaries typically define a leader as 'one who rules, guides or inspires others'.

This linguistic dichotomy is also mirrored in the workplace perceptions of these activities and analyses of these roles as reported in two national surveys (see Box 3.1). The key difference between the two, exemplified best perhaps in Drucker's (1974) phrase – 'leaders do the right thing [and] managers do things right' – also highlights the symbiotic nature of their relationship. That is, there is limited value in doing things right if you don't know where you are going. And equally, it is of little use knowing where you're going if you haven't got the wherewithal to get there. The roles, however, are not wholly mutually exclusive and we should be wary of exaggerating the differences between them, and likewise of concluding that an effective manager cannot also be an effective leader or, conversely, that a charismatic leader will necessarily be a poor manager. Each role, after all, poses challenges which draw on complementary sets of competences (see Box 3.2). It also may not be a question of being one or the other. Indeed,

---

Box 3.1 Workplace perceptions of leaders and managers

Managers
Viewed as:
- planners
- controllers
- implementers of policy
- resourcers
- administrators
- people who are results-oriented

Leaders
Viewed as:
- motivators
- enablers
- mentors
- communicators
- innovators
- people who are energetic

A manager
- is a copy
- administers
- maintains
- focuses on systems and structure
- relies on control
- has short-range view
- asks how and when
- has his/her eye on the bottom line
- accepts the status quo
- is the classic good soldier
- does things right

A leader
- is an original
- innovates
- develops
- focuses on people
- inspires trust
- has long-range perspective
- asks what and why
- has his/her eye on the horizon
- challenges the status quo
- is his/her own person
- does the right thing

Managers
- plan and budget
- organize and staff
- control and solve problems
- establish order

Leaders
- set direction
- align people and groups
- motivate and inspire
- produce change

Source: adapted from Turner, 1998.

Box 3.2 The leadership and management challenge

Leadership

Style	Strategic vision	Team building	Influencing	Environment building
e.g. making a personal impact, leading by example	e.g. creating a vision of the future and deciding how best to meet objectives by focusing on outcomes	e.g. inspiring people to work together and give of their best	e.g. using negotiation and persuasion to achieve desired outcomes	e.g. creating the conditions to foster creativity, innovation and risk-taking

Management

Change	Complexity	Networks	Ambiguity	Learning
e.g. assessing drivers, communicating, envisioning and delivering	e.g. processing information and ideas	e.g. using others to leverage results, share best practice and learn	e.g. handling difficult situations with limited information	e.g. drawing on experience and new ideas to improve results

the everyday expectation in the workplace is that individual post-holders will be capable and proficient in both. And this is particularly the case for those holding departmental (or 'middle-management') positions, where leadership and management functions are more closely integrated than at the broader institutional level.

The situation in HE is no different even if we would like to think otherwise. The traditions of academia, like those of other professional groups, have long upheld a separation between leadership and policy making on the one hand, and policy implementation and administration on the other. A distinction which was manifested clearly in the traditionally separate roles of academics (whose domain included academic leadership and policy formation) and administrators (whose domain included advice on policy and the responsibility for policy execution), and one which lives on in the nomenclature which is still often used, even today, to differentiate between the two. Thus, whether the post is head of a service department of a physical support character (such as residential accommodation or estates), or one essentially academic in nature (such as registry or the library), or indeed an academic department outright, all three post-holders are invariably lumped together (and sometimes by the occupants themselves) under the catch-all 'administration' (Warner and Palfreyman, 2001). It is only relatively recently that the title of 'manager' has been conferred in some of these areas. It has not always been accepted without reluctance – and the national representative body is still entitled the Association of University Administrators rather than what would be the more accurate epithet: Association of University Managers. It is also even more unusual for a 'dean' or 'head (chair) of department' to be styled 'academic staff manager' or something similar. Even so, the world beyond academia would readily recognize – if the organization of HE was more transparent – that the functions being carried out by these post-holders are very much analogous to those carried out elsewhere in the public and private sectors, by leaders and managers. But what is it that makes for effective leadership and management?

Being an effective leader and manager

> Go to the people
> Live amongst them
> Start with what they have
> Build on what they know
> And when the deed is done,
> The mission accomplished
> Of the best leaders
> The people will say,
> 'We have done it
> ourselves'
>
> Sun Tzu, Chinese philosopher, *c*. 500 BC

> [The general should be] ingenious, energetic, careful, full of stamina and presence of mind . . . loving and tough, straightforward and crafty, ready to gamble everything and wishing to have everything, generous and greedy, trusting and suspicious.
>
> Xenophon, Greek historian, 504 BC

Leadership is one of those rare topics – like war and peace, with which it has been particularly associated – which has enthralled and fascinated scholar and public alike, ever since records began. This attraction remains as powerful today – if perhaps not more so – as it has ever been. Popular debate on the subject dates back as far as Homer and his peers, while the first scholarly output can be traced to Plutarch and the biographies of great persons he penned in the first century AD.

Proper scientific research on leadership, however, only really began at the start of the twentieth century. Since then, literally thousands of formal research studies have been carried out which have, in turn, spawned a whole host of theories. Nevertheless the mystique of leadership has remained intact, for none of these theories has fully explained the phenomenon. Rather, the inquiries that generated them were as much a reflection of the way in which our assessment of leadership roles has changed over time, as they were an impartial examination of the intrinsic nature of the subject itself (see Table 3.1) (Sashkin, 1995).

Either way, the quest to determine just what makes a leader effective – and the reason the subject is still so compelling (that, and the corporate and societal needs of the new millennium) – is because it remains as elusive today as it has ever been. This is not to say our understanding of leadership has not advanced. On the contrary, the substantive research to date has yielded an array of illuminating insights into the subject. And it is to an initial consideration of this work we turn first. What can the received theoretical wisdom tell us about leadership and management in practice?

The 'great person' approach

The first serious researchers into leadership (in the 1920s) assumed, as alluded to earlier, that effective leaders were born, not made, and as such set out to identify their distinguishing traits. This so-called 'great person' approach (the individuals were nearly always male, but not exclusively so) dominated research inquiries for the next two decades and gave birth to what critics later dubbed the 'myth of the heroic leader'. Based on the concept of the military hero, this cult was buttressed by the reading public's penchant for biographies – and has been bolstered still further in recent times by the contemporary practice of head-hunters who, in seeking to 'fit' (literally, 'the right person to the right job'), have lent even greater credibility, however unwittingly, to the mystique of searching for the 'great person'. Such inquiries have generated all kinds of epiphenomena: the greatest American presidents were stubborn and grumpy; the British boardroom executive today is more than likely 'a mummy's boy', and so on (Brodie, 2001; Frean, 2001). They have also indicated that leaders were generally a bit smarter, a bit more outgoing, slightly more inventive, and even a little taller than the average. None of these traits, however, or any others, has stood out sufficiently to be clearly or strongly associated with leadership.

Behavioural theories

The focus of leadership research therefore changed. By the late 1940s researchers were less concerned with identifying individual traits of leadership – who leaders are – and more interested in leadership behaviour: *what leaders do* and how they do it; their actions and the style in which they perform these actions. These inquiries identified two essential aspects of effective managerial leadership: *task-oriented* behaviour (the importance of leaders providing clear instructions and directions) and *relationship-oriented* behaviour

Table 3.1 Overview of twentieth-century theories of leadership

Period	Theory/approach	Theme	Advocates
Up to late 1940s	Trait theories	Leadership ability is innate and linked to personal qualities	Hunt (1992)
Late 1940s to late 1960s	Behavioural theories	Leadership is associated with behaviour and style	Adair (1983); Blake and McCanse, (1991); Likert (1967); Mintzberg (1973)
Late 1960s to present	Contingency theories	Leadership is affected by the context and situation	Fiedler (1978); Hersey and Blanchard (1992); House (1988); Vroom and Yetton (1973)
Late 1960s to present	Power and influence theories	Leadership is associated with the use of power	Bass (1985); Bennis and Nanaus (1985); Burns (1978); Kouzes and Posner (1995; 2003)
1970s to present	Cultural and symbolic theories	Leadership is the 'management of meaning'	Deal and Kennedy (1982); Smith and Peterson (1988)
1980s to present	Cognitive theories	Leadership is a social attribution	Cohen and March (1986); Hunt (1992)
1990s to present	New leadership theories	Leadership is linked to organization building and transformation	Kakabadse and Kakabadse (1998); Senge (1995); Turner (1998)
1990s to present		Leadership is a distributive phenomenon	Gronn (2000); Spillane (2006); Woods (2004)

Sources: adapted from Middlehurst, 1993; Kakabadse and Kakabadse, 1998; Bolden *et al.*, 2008.

(the need for leaders to provide personal support and encouragement). Initially it appeared that the puzzle of leadership was finally resolved. For if everyone simply learned how to engage in these two types of leader behaviour, and did so with sufficient acumen, then there would be no shortage of successful leaders. In practice, however, the benefits of such leadership proved to be quite limited and did not ensure outstanding performance on the part of either followers or leaders.

Situational leadership

The emphasis within research therefore shifted again, and the 1960s witnessed the emergence of a new perspective which stressed the importance of situational factors (or 'contingencies'); the nature of the task, the type of external environment, the abilities of followers and so on. If effective leadership is not *who they are* or *what they do*, it was reasoned, then perhaps it arises from the interaction between leaders, followers and situations and involves leaders *doing the right thing at the right time*. The most influential of these contingency theories has been the situational leadership model developed by Hersey and Blanchard (1992), which also forms the basis of – and lends its name to – one of the most widely used management improvement approaches in the world today.

In essence, Hersey and Blanchard argue that a leader's style – whether 'participating', 'delegating', 'selling' or 'telling' – varies according to the degree of a subordinate's ability and willingness to undertake the task at hand. And their model reflects this proposition. That is, it incorporates the two dimensions on leadership behaviour we identified above and also includes a third: an environmental variable denoting follower 'maturity' or 'readiness'. Managers can then use the model not only to assess the willingness and capability of followers to do a job, but also to determine what combination of task and relationship behaviour will be most effective in a particular situation. Indeed, in emphasizing the importance of flexibility in leadership behaviour (in contrast to earlier searches for an all-purpose leadership style) and by demonstrating the potential for facilitating follower 'maturity' this model gave managers their first real *practical* insight into enhancing their effectiveness as leaders. The model is readily understood and managers find it as relevant and useful today as their predecessors did when it was originally conceived (see Figure 3.1).

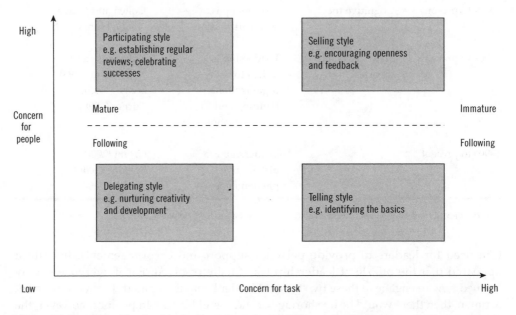

Figure 3.1 Situational leadership: leadership style and follower 'maturity'

Source: adapted from Middlehurst, 1993; Hersey and Blanchard, 1992.

Transformational and transactional leadership

Further insight came from an unlikely quarter, if not an unfamiliar source – the American historian, James MacGregor Burns (1978) in his examination of distinguished national, social and moral leaders. In Burns's view, such leaders were successful because they were able to transcend the customary (Hobbesian) norms of traditional leadership – i.e. the self-interested *transaction* of rewards and benefits in exchange for compliance and loyalty – by engaging with their supporters on a 'higher' plane, by appealing to their altruistic motivations (to their notions of liberty, justice, equality and the like) rather than their self-interested ones of money, status, praise and so on. In doing so, a cycle of mutual reinforcement was set in train, in which both leaders and followers raised each other's motivations and sense of purpose to such an extent that their behaviour and aspirations were *transformed* well beyond their original expectations. This notion of leadership – as transformation – was, of course, not a new one. The emotional appeal and power of leadership based on charisma (or 'god-like gift'), for instance, is an idea of ancient pedigree. Particularly germane at moments of crisis, it is also one which we have indeed witnessed ourselves in recent times, in the aftermath of the atrocities of September 11th, 2001, and again in the stunning election victory of President Barack Obama in November 2008.

Burns's critique, however, provided us with the first clear delineation between leadership as a moral process – or *transformational* one – as distinct from that which is essentially *transactional* or exchange-based in nature: a distinction which some argued mirrored the essential difference between leadership and management (they were, in Burns's view, the opposite ends of his transactional–transformational continuum). This view is disputed by others, notably Bass (1985) and Kotter (1990), who persuasively argue that transactional strategies, such as rewards for good performance, are not only compatible with transformational leadership but indeed, as we noted earlier, are an essential corollary to it if organizational effectiveness is to be realized. Where the substantive difference between leadership and management really lies, these commentators imply – and this is significant – is in the way in which these individuals are *perceived by their staff*. For while a management relationship can be conducted in a cool, job-oriented and perfectly satisfactory (transactional) manner to both parties a leadership relationship cannot. The latter, if it is to succeed – that is, if followers are going to give their consent to be led (or transformed) – has to involve the emotions. Thus for effective managers to become equally effective leaders there must be warmth, inspiration and a stirring of the blood in their relationship with their staff.

For this reason still others have used Burns's typology as the basis for developing new approaches to leadership in practice. These models of new leadership – the visionary leader, the 'learning organization' leader, the liberating leader and the discretionary leader – have come to dominate contemporary thinking on the subject. All these approaches are grounded to varying degrees in transformational theory and as such this literature is often suffused with a quasi-religious, moralistic fervour. What practical insights, though, do they offer us on effective leadership?

Models of new leadership

The visionary leader

Based on the work of Warren Bennis (Bennis and Nanaus,1985), James Kouzes and Barry Posner (2003), and Marshall Sashkin and W.E. Rosenbach (1993), Visionary Leadership Theory is the most comprehensive attempt to focus Burns's initial ideas on organizations. Its exponents argue that if leadership is to be effective then it has to be based on not just one but three major aspects of transformational leadership: behaviours, personal characteristics and organizational culture-building activities. The implication is a clear one. To be an effective leader you must have the requisite qualities listed in Box 3.3. Daunting as this may initially appear, however, the model's advocates do insist that these qualities are all competences we can learn to develop: that the goal of the self-actualizing visionary leader is indeed within reach of all of us.

The 'learning organization' leader

The role and nature of leadership as well as the expectations of it are, as one would expect, different in the context of the learning organization. Popularized in the 1990s by Peter Senge (2006) among others, the learning organization was grounded in the widespread belief that 'the rate at which organizations learn may become the only sustainable source

---

Box 3.3 The visionary leader

The behaviours, personal characteristics and culture-building activities common to all effective transformational leaders

Behaviours
1 Focus: providing a clear focus on key issues and concerns, i.e. on the right things
2 Communication: getting everyone to understand this focus through effective organizational communication practices
3 Consistency: acting consistently, over time, so as to develop trust
4 Respect: demonstrating, through actions, care and respect for the organization's members
5 Empowerment: creating empowering opportunities that involve the organization's members in making the right things their own priorities

Personal characteristics
1 Self-confidence: a grounded belief in one's ability to make a positive difference
2 Being comfortable with empowerment:a grounded belief in the ability of others to make a positive difference
3 A long-term vision span (c. 10 years)

Culture building
A propensity for building strong cultures by instilling assumptions, values and beliefs that support four key organizational functions: managing change, achieving goals, coordinating teamwork and maintaining a vibrant organizational culture.

Source: adapted from Sashkin, 1995.

of competitive advantage in the future'; that in a context of rapid change only organizations capable of flexibility, adaptability and productivity could expect to flourish. As such, many enterprises sought to establish themselves as 'learning organizations where people continually expand their capacity to create the results they truly desire, where new and expansive patterns of thinking were nurtured, where collective aspiration is set free, and where people are continually learning to see the whole together'.

The implications for leadership in such settings are quite profound. In the first instance, Senge (1990) argues, would-be learning organizations need to abandon the traditional conception of leadership (one that is 'based on assumptions of people's powerlessness, their lack of personal vision and inability to master the forces of change, deficits which can be remedied only by a few great leaders') and embrace a new view that centres on 'subtler and more important tasks'. In Senge's model, leadership is focused on three critical roles – those of *designer*, *teacher* and *steward* (or servant). These functions in themselves are not new, in the sense that they each have antecedents in the ways leaders have contributed to building organizations in the past, but in the context of the learning organization they take on new meaning since they demand new skills: to 'build shared vision', 'surface and test mental models' and develop 'systems thinking' (see Box 3.4).

Leadership is also a distributive phenomenon in Senge's model. That is, if organizations really wish 'to tap people's commitment and capacity to learn at *all* levels', then leadership must be devolved throughout the organization via a web of executive leaders, local line leaders and internal networkers. Only then, when these leadership criteria are met, Senge maintains, will enterprises have the opportunity to establish a learning organization: to become, that is, masters of 'generative' learning and not simply of 'adaptive' or survival learning (Senge, 2006).

The liberating leader

The concept of the leader as liberator developed, like that of the 'learning organization' leader, as a response to the sweeping changes in the external environment (in working patterns, access to information, the nature of competition, global economics and so on) which has affected all organizations over the last decade. In this instance, however, the source of competitive advantage was perceived to be not so much the rate of organizational learning, as the degree to which organizations 'unlock the potential and creative energies of all their employees', or, put another way, the extent to which they establish a 'liberating organization', one which 'creates a climate of trust, empowerment and stability by devolving authority and responsibility and harnesses the latent energy within its walls' (Turner, 1998) (see Box 3.5).

In this environment, leadership, as in Senge's model, is not confined to the top. Indeed, in its outright rejection of position, status and hierarchy and its commitment to 'democracy at work', the 'liberating organization' takes Senge's notion of devolved leadership a stage further – by fostering liberating leadership at all levels. Such leadership – as the name implies and as the ideal behavioural profile outlines – is modelled on the assumption that effective practice is about *what leaders do and the way they do it, which in turn reflects what they believe* – self-belief, belief in and beliefs about others, and belief in fairness (see Box 3.6). Liberating leaders then jettison old-style command-and-control ways of working. They

Box 3.4 The leader's new work: building learning organizations

The learning organization
Based on five disciplines (or component technologies)
Each 'discipline' is a series of principles and guiding practices to master:

1 Personal mastery
2 Mental models
3 Building shared vision
4 Team learning
5 Systems thinking – the conceptual cornerstone that integrates the first four

New roles of leader
Leader as designer – teacher – steward

New skills of leadership
Building shared vision
- encouraging personal vision
- communicating and asking for support
- visioning as an on-going process
- blending extrinsic and intrinsic visions
- distinguishing positive from negative visions

Surfacing and testing mental models
- seeing leaps of abstraction
- balancing inquiry and advocacy
- distinguishing espoused theory from theory in use   → *ACTIONS vs. WORDS*
- recognizing and defusing defensive routines

Systems thinking
- seeing inter-relationships, not things, and processes, not snapshots
- moving beyond blame
- distinguishing details complexity from dynamic complexity
- focusing on areas of high leverage
- avoiding symptomatic solutions

Source: adapted from Senge, 1990.

create situations where continuous improvement can occur; demonstrate, by their own behaviour, how people can be liberated to maximize their skills; recognize the need for continuing change and urge everyone to meet the challenges that this brings; and, finally, act as facilitators, coaches and supporters, encouraging those closest to the tasks to take their own decisions.

Dismissed by some as a fanciful New Utopia, the model is viewed by its supporters as 'a managerial blueprint for the new millennium': one that can be customized to meet the needs of all organizations. And given the substantial number of organizations that have successfully adopted it there is every reason to believe they may well be right.

Box 3.5 Characteristics of the liberating organization

Feature	Purpose
A flat organizational structure	to cut out functionalism, bureaucracy and the worship of status
Inversion of the pyramid	leaders and managers support employees who interface directly with customers, i.e. 'leadership from behind'
Organizational democracy	to value the contribution of all alike and to promote their self-esteem; colleagues not subordinates
A liberating climate	to encourage healthy development and growth
Genuine empowerment	the unequivocal transfer of authority, responsibility and resources to those closest to each group of tasks
A 'blame free' culture	to use mistakes as learning opportunities, not to levy punishment
Self-managed teams	independent workgroups with the authority and responsibility to achieve their agreed targets
Mutual trust	the rock upon which all effective working relationships are built
Ownership	established through shared information, the provision of user-friendly procedures and the celebration of successes
Vision	an inspirational view of the future, communicated to all, that acts as an organizational head group, lighting the path ahead
Values	the principles, beliefs and standards to which the organization holds
Communication	to be open, comprehensive and without hidden agendas; clarifying rather than clouding and natural without affectation
Development	an integral part of working, managing and leading. Coaching and encouragement to learn are second nature
Innovation	sensible risk-taking is encouraged and fear is banished
Attitude	proposed changes are seen as challenges to be met and managed rather than opposed

Source: adapted from Turner, 1998.

The discretionary leader

The 'liberating organization' and the 'learning organization' concepts both share a belief in the ability of individuals to shift perspectives and make themselves and their organizations more effective. The same is equally true of the concept of the discretionary leader, though in this case the focus is not so much on the 'one-size-fits-all' approach to leadership, characteristic of the two grand schemes above, but rather on the scope for – and use of – discretion on the part of individual leaders per se.

Box 3.6 Profile of the liberating leader

Liberates	• Does not blame people for mistakes
	• Encourages the people closest to the job to take their own decisions
	• Listens to their staff
	• Encourages full and open communication
	• Operates systems based on trust, rather than suspicion
	• Encourages staff to develop new ideas
Encourages and supports	• Accepts responsibility for the actions of their staff
	• Gives praise where it is due
	• Recognizes and acts to minimize other people's stress
	• Supports staff when they need support
	• Regularly meets with individuals to clarify direction
	• Makes people feel important and shows that they have faith in them
Achieves purpose	• Achieves results
	• Agrees demanding targets with individuals or teams
	• Consults those affected before making decisions
	• Is willing to take unpopular decisions in order to move forward
	• Seeks out future challenges/opportunities
	• Regularly communicates an inspirational view of the future
	• Constantly seeks to improve the way things are done
Develops people and teams	• Encourages other people to learn
	• Encourages people to work together as a team
	• Regularly meets with the team, as a whole, to review progress
	• Takes time to develop and guide their staff
	• Deals effectively with breaches in standards of behaviour
	• Treats other people's mistakes as learning opportunities
Example to others	• Actively encourages feedback on their own performance
	• Communicates an air of enthusiasm
	• Works on their own learning
	• Practises what they preach
	• Openly admits mistakes
	• Sets a good example to others by their own behaviour
Relationships built on trust	• Does not put self-interest before the interests of their staff
	• Keeps promises and does what they say they will do
	• Is in touch with, and sensitive to, people's feelings
	• Is calm in a crisis, and when under pressure
	• Is honest and truthful
	• Does not take personal credit for other people's work
	• Is always fair

Source: Turner, 1998.

Taking its cue from Socrates, that no one remains 'within a box' unless they are bounded by their own perspective, the discretionary concept recognizes that – while the scope for discretion is more limited at the lower levels of an organization where roles are more prescribed – individual leaders in all cases can and indeed should draw on the wide range of approaches open to them in fulfilling their roles. And the key to effective leadership in fact lies in *the flexibility as well as ability of leaders to utilize the most appropriate approach according to the context in which they operate*. In other words, the concept recognizes that not only do different organizations require different types of leadership but, since modern-day organizations are invariably characterized by diversity, dissension and difference, then leaders also need to be able to reconcile contradictions *within* the same organization. In addition, since no one individual, no matter how gifted, is likely to be able to fully appreciate the different requirements of different contexts, this model also emphasizes the need for leadership based on, and around, teamwork (Kakabadse and Kakabadse, 1998; Kakabadse, 2001).

These emphases – on the individual and collective contextualization of leadership – constitute, the model's advocates maintain, the best way forward for organizations seeking to master the internal and external repercussions of the 'new economy'. And, by implication, those individual leaders who choose not to exercise their discretionary roles will, like their organizations, suffer the consequences.

Guiding principles of leadership and management

A definitive understanding of leadership, then, continues, as we have seen, to elude analysts. And some maintain that the subject will remain an unexplained phenomenon in perpetuity. Even so, these four models of 'new leadership', along with the received wisdom to date, do provide us with a series of pointers to the nature and exercise of leadership in practice. They constitute a set of guiding propositions, if you will, which can aid us in seeking to be effective leaders and managers in practice. These can be summarized as follows:

1 Leadership and management are not mutually exclusive. There is no reason why an effective manager cannot also be an effective leader and vice versa. And the workplace expectation – particularly at departmental level – is that individual post-holders will be proficient in both capacities. Whether an effective manager does indeed become an effective leader is determined, in the final analysis, by the way they are perceived by their staff ('followers'). It is your colleagues who determine if you are a leader.
2 Leadership is not confined to – or vested in – a single great figure. Nor is it the preserve of – or related to – formal positions in an organization's hierarchy. Rather it is a distributive phenomenon. The skills of leadership and the exercise of leadership can exist at all levels in an organization. *Ipso facto* it is incumbent on those who wish to be genuinely effective to foster these qualities within their department. Effective leaders grow people; bad leaders stunt them.
3 The stereotypical young, dynamic whiz kid is no more representative of effective leadership than is the traditional 'captain-of-the-ship' conception of leadership. Both

notions are as unfounded as they are outdated. Leadership is as much to do with groupings and group behaviour – the formation and operation of top teams, departmental teams, project teams and so on – as it is to do with individuals and individual behaviour.

4 Leaders are, by and large, made, not born. They are learners and as such can be helped to develop themselves, in particular to master the key competences associated with transformational leadership, all of which can be learnt, namely:
   - visioning skills, including creative thinking
   - critical evaluation and problem-detection skills
   - communication and linguistic skills
   - expectation-management skills
   - empowering skills
   - the confidence to challenge traditional ways of working.

5 The mastery of competences and the development of self-confidence, however, are not in themselves sufficient to guarantee effective leadership – unless individuals are also motivated to that end: that is, to use power and influence (publicly) to benefit the organization and its members, rather than simply (privately) to satisfy their own personal desire for power, status and achievement.

6 The essential attributes of an effective leader are much the same whatever the environment. It is the context (the organization's particular needs) and the leadership approach taken which are the key variables. Consequently, effective leaders seek to utilize their discretionary role to the fullest extent. In doing so, they recognize:
   - what works in one context may not do so in another (and equally, what makes you successful in one job may not necessarily do so in another);
   - the need to develop and maintain both a flexible and a broad mindset able to cope with multiple different contexts;
   - the importance of harnessing this (rational) mindset with an equally well-developed sense of emotional intelligence; that is, of tackling both the 'hard' stuff and the 'soft' stuff together with a similar degree of insight and maturity. (Too often in the past leaders have been off balance one way or the other. Maximum strategic insight is of little use if combined with limited (emotional) sensitivity. Equally, emotional maturity will only get you so far and no further if you lack strategic organizational insight. One needs to complement the other if leadership is to be effective.)

7 Effective leadership is a dynamic process and at best a transformative one. It is about, as the industrialist John Harvey-Jones put it, 'lifting people's vision to a higher plane, raising achievement beyond what might normally be expected and getting extraordinary results from ordinary people' – and in the process also transforming oneself as a leader through continued reflection, self-development and personal change (Turner, 1998).

8 Finally, effective leaders – and aspiring ones – accept they will be judged on the results or outcomes they produce, not simply the leadership competences they possess.

Leading and managing in HE

> To rephrase the corny words of the song, you have to do it your way.
> John Monks, TUC General Secretary

In applying these principles, it follows that if individuals are to be effective leaders then they must, in the first instance, understand both themselves and the particular context in which they operate. And this is as true for prospective leaders and managers in HE as it is for aspirants in other environments. Our examination of leadership in HE begins therefore with those who occupy, or aspire to, such roles; that is: you and your particular HE environment. The questions set out in Boxes 3.7 and 3.8 are designed to help you 'reach within yourself', to probe your modus operandi, to increase your self-awareness and reflect on your state of being. Their purpose is to provide you with an initial self-assessment, an on-the-spot 'health check' of how you are doing in your role.

Box 3.7 Conversations with yourself

Take each question in turn, take time to reflect on it and write down your answers on a sheet of paper. Discuss the accuracy of your judgements with someone whose opinion you value and trust.

- What is expected of me in my role?
- How am I doing in my role?
- How do I know?

[These are the basic questions which every employee in any organization should be able to answer – including those who work for you. If you have difficulty answering them fully, you should consult the individual you report to immediately.]

What do I stand for; what are my values; do they match those of my HEI?
- *What or where is the level of fit?*

Do I have the right level of dissatisfaction with the status quo and the way things are?
- *Do I challenge the way things are?*
- *Do I encourage others to do so too?*

What are my comfort zones and how, if I choose, do I move out of them?

Do I aim big and just fall short, or aim smaller and hit the target?
- *How do I set goals and are they the right ones?*
- *Do I really stretch myself?*
- *How much do I push boundaries?*
- *Is my mindset 'better safe than sorry' or 'nothing ventured, nothing gained'?*
- *Do I aim for the upper reaches of the possible or the lower level of the impossible?*

How much am I engaged in Activity and how much in Action?
- *Do I mistake being busy with making things happen?*
- *How much of what I do is tangential to actually achieving things?*
- *Do I do things because I am interested in them or because they need to be done?*

What motivates me to act?

How much of the day do I spend thinking about the past – the present – the future?
- *Do I have to feel right about the past before taking action in the present to create the future?*
- *Do I live out of my imagination or memory?*

Do I know how to hit my pause button?
- *Do I suspend assumptions and preconceptions?*
- *Do I know what winds me up and how to stop that from happening?*
- *In what ways do I add/destroy value?*
- *What mindsets usually drive me?*
- *Do I have a mind which is usually open to new possibilities?*
- *Do I have a positive inner voice?*
- *Do I know when not to interrupt others but to listen to their ideas?*
- *Do I hear what people are actually saying?*

How do I get that 'fresh feeling', how do I declare myself satisfied, how do I close the loop?
- *Am I satisfied at the end of each day that I have done all I can and draw a line under it?*
- *I got a 'fresh feeling' when I moved house, changed jobs, moved offices, completed that project, etc. How could I have that feeling at the end of each day?*

How could I redefine the issues and problems that face me?

How do I feel each evening when I walk through the door at home?
- *How long does it take me to unwind?*
- *How do I recharge my batteries?*
- *If someone asks me how the day has gone what do I usually say?*

What do I put my energy into?

How do I dance on a shifting carpet?
- *Do I move ahead with change or feel like the rug is (sometimes) being pulled from under me?*
- *Do I strive for step change or incremental change?*

Where will I be in five years' time?

What do I want to achieve with the rest of my life?

Now look in the mirror, literally . . .

What image and what example do I convey to others day to day about the quality of life I lead?

Are they the right ones? How should I change them?

There are more formal and systematic ways of conducting a self-assessment which you should also consider. Indeed there are literally scores of such instruments on the market. The most popular and widely used include:

- Visionary Leader Behavior Questionnaire (Sashkin, 1995): a survey which enables you to compare your own perceptions of your approach to leadership with those

Box 3.8 The top 10 'stoppers and stallers' obstructing effective leadership

Consider each of the following 'stoppers and stallers' which have been identified as the most common obstacles to effective leadership. To what extent, if any, do these factors apply to you? How do you propose to overcome them?

• Failure to build a team	• the most common shortcoming
	• failure to give credit to staff, to say thank you or to encourage them
• Arrogance	• an asset on occasion at some levels, otherwise a drawback
• Lack of composure	• failure to handle pressure or stress well
	• tendency to become sarcastic, hostile or abrasive when things get tough
• Lack of ethics	• failure to recognize where the limits of proper behaviour lie
	• losing the confidence of others in the organization
• Betrayal of trust	• saying different things to different people
	• not keeping promises
• Poor administration	• being bad at the detail
• No strategic thinking	• the converse of the previous fault; tendency to concentrate exclusively on tactics and detail
• Over-managing	• checking up on subordinates all the time
	• demanding constant information on how things are going
• Failure of networking	• failure to maintain external links or to keep up with what others are doing
• Inflexibility	• failure to adapt; an expectation that increases with seniority yet can become more difficult with age

Source: adapted from the Work Foundation, 2006.

who work for you (subordinates), alongside you (peers) and who you report to (your line manager): it provides '360 degree contextual feedback' on your leadership behaviour, your leadership characteristics and your effect on the organization as a leader.

• Myers-Briggs (Personality) Type Indicator (Myers and Myers, 1977; Quenk, 1999): an instrument which enables you to assess the deeply held ways – Extrovert or Introvert; Senser or Intuitive; Thinker or Feeler; Judger or Perceiver – in which you prefer to work, and hence is an indicator of how you are likely to behave in practice in solving problems, reacting to change, communicating and so on.

• Thomas-Kilmann Conflict Mode Instrument (Thomas and Kilmann, 2002): a mechanism which enables you to assess the styles you have learned to develop

(Competing, Accommodating, Avoiding, Collaborating and Compromising) in handling workplace conflict.

These three instruments, while useful in their own right, are especially incisive – given the critical insights they yield on quite different aspects of behaviour – when used in conjunction with one another. And this has become common practice across the private sector and parts of the civil service and public sector. They can also be just as illuminating for teams as for individuals and you may wish to consider using them with your own team or a team of your peers, say the senior management team.

However, a health warning is in order. Such instruments can generate feedback and outcomes which some people, and maybe even you, find hurtful or offensive. The key, of course, is not to take offence or to deny the validity of the feedback, but rather to act on it appropriately. Not everyone, however, will be able to do so. For this reason, then, you should enlist the support and help of your management and staff development adviser, or alternatively a reputable career management consultant, before undertaking this initiative. You should not be deterred, however, for the received wisdom to date indicates that the benefits of this activity – both collectively and individually – have far outweighed any particular drawback.

This theme of self-assessment and the implications for learning and development for ourselves, as well as others, is one which we will return to in chapters 4 and 11. For the moment, we turn to perhaps the most critical aspect of your role, indeed of any leader's role. It both contributes to, and is shaped by, your own environmental context: i.e. the articulation of a strategic vision for your department.

Establishing a vision: developing a strategy for your department

Vision without action is a daydream, action without vision is a nightmare.

Japanese proverb

We live in an age when even a humble sandwich bar cannot open without the fanfare of an accompanying statement of mission or vision. The strength of this trend is matched only by the degree of scepticism which such gestures often engender in their intended audience. Why they have been received in this way is not difficult to discern. Invariably the design of a single individual or group, and often prone to grandiose new-age rhetoric – if not outright slogans – such statements have quite rightly been regarded as unmerited claims, or unwanted impositions or both by staff and customers alike.

It is also a pattern from which HEIs have not been immune. Their initial attempts to articulate their institutional missions in the early 1990s, for instance, generated statements which, as one reviewer put it, were either 'unashamedly publicity instruments' or declarations 'of a five year plan' or, worse still, 'definitions of the management's role within the institution, not the institution's role within HE'. Such initiatives above all bred 'confusion and fudge' while spawning apathy and dissent in equal measure (Earwaker, 1991). As relative latecomers to this activity, HEIs have also been surprisingly slow, compared with organizations in the private sector, to learn and adapt after this initial experience. This may in turn be symptomatic of the resistance to the idea of diversity which persists in UK higher education.

Either way, the prevailing scepticism surrounding notions of 'mission' and 'vision' both within and outside HE, and their collective debasement in the literature on management, cannot and should not detract from the fact they are vitally important, if not desperately important for HE, given, as we noted earlier, the overwhelming pressure on HEIs to change and to diversify. Indeed vision, as we have seen, is at the heart of leadership. A vision is a 'dream', not a pipe-dream but a realistic long-term ambition: a picture of the future that you want to produce. For example: where do you see your department headed? What could it achieve? How could it be special? distinctive? cutting edge? Envisioning necessarily calls for creativity, imagination and optimism. More than that, it also requires animation, inspiration and passion on your part if it is to enlist others in 'building a shared vision' and agreeing to a strategy which realizes this vision. How, though, should you set about this task? That is, how do you develop a strategic vision? And how do you engender collective ownership of it?

In the first instance, we need to recognize there is no single right way. Some commentators, for example, argue that vision springs from the 'collective mind' of the staff group and it is the role of the leader to tease out and articulate these latent ideas. Others maintain the exact opposite: that such visions emanate from the ideas developed by the head of department who then encourages staff to develop a commitment to them. Nearly all agree, however, that shared visions are unlikely to emerge from a series of formal departmental meetings called 'To develop a Strategic Plan' (Ramsden, 1998). In reality, the way they emerge varies according to the nature (the culture, needs and organization) of the particular institutional context. Thus what method works in one environment may not do so in another, and vice versa.

The common variable in all cases is the ability and willingness of the leader to take the initiative – and this applies to developing the content of a strategic vision, in the first instance, as much as it does to the building of a consensus around it. In the case of the former, if not the latter, there is indeed a set of guiding principles or a common framework which you can, and may in fact be expected to, follow, given that HEIs are now invariably held externally accountable – in the UK since 1992, for example – for producing their own particular institutional plans. Put another way, HEIs in common with other organizations all (or in the great majority of cases) adhere, nuances of style and approach notwithstanding, to a framework which is broadly similar: a three-stage cycle, that is, of planning, documentation, and implementation and monitoring, each with its own particular sub-elements which together provide a comprehensive guide to the process of strategy formulation (see Figure 3.2).

What is strategy?

All this begs the question – what is strategy? Why do we need it? What is its purpose? How should you formulate it in your department? 'Strategy' is another of those terms in management which has come to mean many different things. In essence, the origins of the word relate to 'generalship' and political leadership and the process involves standing back from day-to-day activities and taking an overview from the perspective you hold: e.g. organization-wide, departmental, personal and so on. In the case of work, it is 'about defining and agreeing the nature of your organization or department'. Or as Alexander (2001) suggests, it is 'the framework which guides those choices that determine the nature

Figure 3.2
The strategic
planning process

Source: HEFCE, 2000a.

and direction of the organization. It is what an organization wants to be'. The role of strategy then essentially is to:

- facilitate strategic decisions: by providing a framework for choosing;
- arrest strategic drift: by acting as a prompt to assess progress and to identify, build and maintain a leading edge;
- foster coordination: by providing a mechanism for reducing wasted and conflicting efforts;
- enhance motivation: by generating a sense of being in control, on a winning path.

Strategy involves alignment between three elements:

Aims

Capabilities

Opportunities

Figure 3.3 Strategy as alignment

Or, put another way, strategy at its simplest – and this is important as it is often overlooked when participants are embroiled in the process – involves, at whatever level, the alignment of three basic elements: aims, capabilities and opportunities (see Figure 3.3). Historically, each element has in turn been regarded as the critical focus of strategy: 'aims' in the 1960s by those who believed that once a mission was established and people were 'on board' everything else would follow; 'opportunities' in the 1970s and early 1980s by Michael Porter and the Boston Consulting Group, who maintained that salvation lay in mastering the forces of competition in the external environment; and, latterly, 'capabilities' by those who argue that organizational success is contingent first and foremost on the effective mobilization and integration of all internal competences and resources. Nowadays all three are regarded as significant, with no one element being more highly regarded than any other – the critical aspect now being their mutual integration rather than their sovereign singularity (Porter, 1998; Mintzberg *et al.*, 2008).

The strategic planning process

Step 1: Identify the four or five key aims, capabilities and opportunities of your department – as you see them

This simple overview provides us with the ideal starting point for a preliminary analysis of your department. As head of department it is incumbent on you to take the initiative in this regard, in part because your colleagues and those at the head of your institution will expect you to, and in part because you should be at least as informed, if not better informed, than either group on the particular capabilities and opportunities in your area. But most of all because as a putative leader the articulation of a departmental strategic vision should, in the first instance, begin with you – your own *personal* perspective. This is not to say that you should foist your view on your colleagues but rather that, if you want them to engage in an informed and meaningful way in this process, then you need to put yourself through the same searching self-examination that you expect of them. The alternative, of simply asking staff 'blind' to express their views, will – like an ill-informed student seminar in the hands of a poorly prepared tutor – generate little heat, even less light, excite no one and fail to do justice to the full range of opportunities and issues in the broader environment.

Furthermore, if you are going to be transformative, this self-examination also provides you with the opportunity to kindle your own passion and beliefs in what your department can achieve beyond the mundane. You should express a genuine conviction that which is visible to others and which they can share. In Senge's (1990) terminology you need to 'surface and test' your own 'mental models' first as a means of 'building a vision' you can believe in, as well as potentially share with others.

Using the overview, then, reflect on and write down the four or five key aims, capabilities and opportunities for your department as you perceive them. What assumptions do your perceptions rest on? Are they accurate ones? Are you satisfied all your responses reflect (genuine) reality and not simply wishful thinking or in-house rhetoric? Is there a match between your aims, capabilities and opportunities? If not, how will you achieve alignment?

Step 2: Examine your department systematically and comprehensively

Examine your department from each of the different perspectives – 'scanning', 'analysing' and 'generating ideas' – of the strategic planning model (Figure 3.2). Test, develop and refine your initial self-assessment accordingly.

You are now in a position to probe, develop, test and refine your ideas further – and just as likely add to them. To do so you need to undertake a more systematic full-blown examination of your department, one that encompasses not simply what are often referred to colloquially as SWOT (strengths, weaknesses, opportunities and threats) and STEP (social, technological, economic and political factors) analyses, but all the elements and sub-elements of the strategic planning process identified in Figure 3.1. Thus you need to both research and analyse your department from each of these different perspectives as outlined and exemplified in Table 3.2 (Luffman *et al.*, 1996). An alternative way of conceiving this process – and an extremely useful one for conventional subject depart-ments – is the directional policy matrix developed by Sizer (1982). You can use this matrix to assess the strengths of your own subject area in relation to that of other subjects within your institution, as well as of your counterparts in other HEIs (see Figure 3.4).

Step 3: Critically review the mission statement and strategic plan of your HEI

Whichever way you choose, there is a recurring theme or constant variable to which you need to give the most careful consideration, as it is often the greatest single source of difficulty. We have already alluded to it earlier; it is the degree of 'fit' between your departmental perspective on strategic orientation and that of your institution in the broader sense. We noted in the last chapter how an analysis of organizational culture can generate critical insights into the context in which you operate. In this instance you need to examine in fine detail the more formal aspects of your institution. That is, you need to

Table 3.2 The strategic planning process illustrated

1 Scanning

Purpose	Research and analysis	Example of outcome
(i) Environmental (STEP) scan To discern changes in the business environment which are either planned or emergent and which will affect the department.	Social developments	The level of mature student participation in HE remains high but has – again – not risen for the third consecutive year, indicating the local market has indeed reached saturation point. Emergent growth in the number of young, white-collar professionals – a new potential market for CPD provision.
	Technological developments	Impending launch of new 'managed learning environment' (MLE) using Blackboard platform is likely to transform programme delivery and prevailing teaching orthodoxy. Strong potential for improvements in both quality and resource efficiency. (Immediate need for staff training and development.)
	Economic change	Funding Council decisions – to claw back money on basis of unmoderated student target numbers (rather than the revised figure) and to withdraw financial support for units of assessment graded 3b in the RAE – will impact disproportionately on the department. Threat of course closure and job losses. Buoyant currency exchange rates in Asia may yield even greater international student numbers. Specific skills demand in key business sectors in local and regional economy still unmet, a shortfall we could make good.
	Political change	Government commitment to 50% participation rate for 18–30-year-olds provides opportunity to develop 'partnerships for progression' (P4P) with our local FE providers and the elaboration of our own sub-degree provision.

Table 3.2 Continued

1 Scanning

Purpose	Research and analysis	Example of outcome
(ii) Internal resource assessment To ensure that the resource needs of plans are identified and can be met (i.e. the strategy is deliverable).	Staffing resource	Staffing establishment currently fully utilized. Reliant on cadre of part-time staff to deliver 20% of core teaching activity.
	Staff skills	Majority wedded to conventional pedagogy. Use of ICT a minority interest. Almost all are dedicated researchers though expertise is limited in commercial and outreach activity.
	Learning resources	Existing stock more aged and incomplete than ever. Uniform configuration of physical facilities reinforces conventional pedagogical style. Potential for resource-based learning – and MLE – untapped.
(iii) Institutional mandate To ensure there is a 'fit' between the departmental strategy and your institution's overall strategic operation.	Core value/'mission'	To excel as a dynamic learning community'. 'Access and opportunity'. 'The pursuit of excellence'. 'To be No. 1'. 'Entrepreneurialism'. Indeterminate, unknown, 'no sense of mission'?
	Strategic orientation	(Business Planning Sequence:) Plan → Act → Evaluate (Defender) Act → Evaluate → Plan (Prospector) Evaluate → Plan → Act (Analyser) Act → Plan → Evaluate (Reactor)

2 Analysing

(iv) Market position To locate the department in comparison to other HEIs as well as to other departments within our university.	Teaching and research performance	Outstanding reputation for teaching reflected in 'excellent' TQA assessment (23/24) though performance rating in RAE (3b) below what we had anticipated (3a/4). Overall a 'consolidated' market position compared with our rivals elsewhere and relative to the other departments across our university.
(v) Portfolio analysis To identify the most – as well as the least – successful areas of our provision.	Academic programme portfolio	Applying the university's new costing and pricing model to our departmental courses indicates that: 80% are consistently successful in academic and financial terms; 10% are successful academically but not financially (our 'loss leader' access programme to attract local mature entrants; our singular Master's programme); 10% are successful financially but not academically (our unacceptable drop-out rate – 30% – on the postgraduate diploma); 0% consistently unsuccessful in academic and financial terms (not applicable).

3 Generating ideas

(vi) Action plan To identify areas for action based on analysis.	New activities	Articulate and develop new short course portfolio aimed at young, white-collar professionals keen on CPD.
	Improvements to existing activities	Reappraise postgraduate diploma and develop local action plan to improve student retention. Develop closer links with – local commerce and industry. Develop closer links with – local commerce and industry. Develop joint projects with – local commerce and industry. Deploy designated staff – to develop RBL and to utilize Blackboard – to help propel change and to promote greater teaching efficiency.
	Discontinuance of selected activities	Replace our singular Master's programme with a series of Master's pathways based on a common foundation year programme.

Figure 3.4
The strategic directional policy matrix

Source: Sizer, 1982; Porter, 1998

- Market size
- Market competition

- Market prospects
- Cost effectiveness
- Optimal staff resource
- Demographic patterns
- National significance
- Government policy

- Stakeholder attitudes
- STEP: Social, Technological, Economic and Political trends
- Employment prospects
- Image and perception

SUBJECT AREA ATTRACTIVENESS

UNIVERSITY STRENGTHS IN THE SUBJECT AREA	High	Medium	Low
High	'A Star' Overall expansion	Selective growth/ niche specialization	'A Cash Cow' Consolidation
Medium	Selective growth/ niche specialization	Consolidation	Contraction and planned withdrawal
Low	'A Problem Child' Consolidation or planned withdrawal?	Contraction and planned withdrawal	'A Dog' Plan withdrawal and redeploy

UNIVERSITY STRENGTHS IN THE SUBJECT AREA

- Size of department
- Market size and share
- Market image and reputation
- Number of applications
- Nature and diversity of student body
- Graduate employment
- Cost effectiveness
- Staff profile
- Teaching assessment
- RAE publications
- Research and enterprise income
- Research and enterprise potential
- Range of partnerships
- Other resources: human, financial, material

put aside any scepticism or prejudice you have and critically review the mission and strategy of your HEI.

Such matters, as we noted earlier, have often courted publicity and controversy in equal measure – and with them, to be frank, a good deal of nonsense too. The penchant for mission statements, for example, parallels the trend towards 'flatter', less hierarchical organizations. And their publication has invariably been designed to exert a centrifugal 'pull' within this new type of institutional environment. If a mission statement is to be useful or effective, however, it has, as Colin Marshall, former chairman of BA, put it, 'to be much more than an outline of good intentions and fine ideas. It should offer a framework for the entire organization. The values which drive the organization and the belief that the organization has in itself and what it can achieve' (quoted in Luffman *et al.*, 1996). Indeed, conventional wisdom suggests that any mission worth its salt must have four discrete qualities, namely an expression of:

- purpose – *why the organization exists*: an inspiring purpose which avoids playing to the selfish interests of one or another set of stakeholders;
- strategy – *the organization's competitive position*: the identification and specification of the organization's strategic position;
- values – *what the organization believes in*: the moral and cultural values of the organization identified and expressed in such a way as to engender pride in all employees;
- standards and behaviours – an indication of *the standards and behaviours expected of staff* in pursuing the organization's strategic goals.

So, ask yourself the following questions:

1 To what extent does your HEI's mission statement measure up against these four criteria? Where is it deficient? Why? When was it last reviewed and revised?
2 Turning to your institution's strategic plan you need to consider the degree of synchronization between this and the mission statement. Is the strategic plan a logical corollary to your HEI's mission statement? What and where are the gaps? Are they significant?
3 How does your HEI define its market position according to its strategic plan? As a Star (high growth; high market share), a Cash Cow (low growth; high market share); a Problem Child (high growth; low market share) or as a Dog (low growth; low market share) (Porter, 1998)?
4 How does your HEI view its environment according to the plan? As a Defender (of its market position), a Prospector (for market growth) or as an Analyser (of its market position)? Or is it a Reactor (out of step altogether)? What are the implications of this market position and strategic orientation (Miles and Snow, 2003)?
5 To what extent does the plan exhibit symmetry and consistency between the 'first-order' (or 'upstream') strategies which identify your HEI's long-term objectives; 'second-order' ones which affect the institution's operation; and finally, 'third-order' (or 'downstream') strategies which determine the most appropriate use of human resources? What are the implications of any inconsistencies (Boxall and Purcell, 2002)?

6 What does your HEI's strategic plan imply about the stage of the organizational life-cycle of your institution: entrepreneurial – collectivist – formalized and controlled – or adaptive (Cameron and Quinn, 2006)?

7 What else does your institutional plan tell you? About the assumptions and forecasts on which it was based – the integration (or otherwise) of supporting strategies – the capacity for genuine self-critical scrutiny and for stretch (i.e. the scope of institutional ambition) and so on?

Putting together these answers should provide you with significant insight into the self-perception of your HEI. It should demonstrate that there is an informed and meaningful stratagem – as in the case of the University of Leeds for example (see Table 3.3) – to underpin your HEI's claim to be a 'research-led' institution, a 'community university' or 'opportunity university', etc. If not – though this is unlikely – you should seek immediate clarification from your institutional planning director or your line manager. If you are still not satisfied then you may want to consider mounting a challenge to the rationale. If so you are likely to make more headway if you remember that (in spite of appearances to the contrary) planning documents are meant to be 'living documents' and not unchanging formal monoliths set in stone for the duration of their span.

Step 4: Examine the degree of 'fit' between your departmental perspective on strategic orientation and that of your HEI

Assuming there is indeed consistency in your HEI's claim, you now need to determine where and how your perspective on your department's strategic orientation measures up against that of your institutional one. There should be an alignment, if not perhaps in the fine detail, between the broad aims, opportunities and capabilities of your department as you see them, and those of your HEI. Put another way, there should be sufficient scope within your HEI's strategic plan to enable you to develop a departmental perspective which, while customized to your particular circumstances, fits comfortably within this overall institutional framework. Again, if not you need to consider why. Are the differences matters of style or substance? If the latter, you should go back and review your own perceptions once more. If these remain unchanged then you need to consider the implications – political as well as practical – of these differing perspectives and be prepared to spell them out when it comes to articulating your view of the options facing the department.

In practice, substantive differences in the rationale underpinning departmental or institutional strategies are relatively infrequent. More often than not the relationship between the two is characterized by symmetry and consistency. Where significant – and critical – differences do arise, however (and not surprisingly), is over the extent to which the rationale is perceived to match the everyday reality of institutional life.

Put another way, you may have a mission statement and strategic plan and it may even be pinned to the wall, but far more importantly do the staff in your department – and across your HEI – have *a sense of mission*? Are they driven by a sense of purpose? Are they aware of how to realize it? In management speak, is the 'Espoused Theory' consistent with the 'Theory-in-Use'?

Table 3.3 Strategy map of the University of Leeds

Vision	By 2015 our distinctive ability to integrate world class research, scholarship and education will have secured us a place among the top 50 universities in the world		
Purpose and values	We are a research-intensive University which strives to: • create, advance and disseminate knowledge • develop outstanding graduates and scholars to make a major impact upon global society		Values: Academic Excellence, Community, Inclusiveness, Integrity, Professionalism
Stake-holders and partners	[--------Our research sponsors expect---------] …high quality research of importance to society / …the best externally recognized experts in their field / …to deal with a University with a reputation for delivery and professionalism	[----Students – as lifelong members of our University community expect----] …to study at a first-class University recognized for its strong, enduring reputation / …to learn from academics at the cutting-edge of knowledge / …an education that creates excellent career opportunities / …a stimulating environment that supports personal development	
Key themes	Enhance our international performance and standing	Achieve an influential world-leading research profile	Inspire our students to develop their full potential	Enhance enterprise and knowledge transfer
	Increase the input of our international activities	Deliver international excellence in all our areas of research	Deliver excellence and inspirational learning and teaching	Enhance performance and value derived from enterprise and knowledge transfer
			Translate excellence in research and scholarship into learning opportunities for students	

Table 3.2 Continued

Create sustainable recruitment of high quality international students	Develop selected peaks that deliver world-leading performance	Provide an exceptional student experience	Contribute to the enrichment of society on a local to global scale
	Create new research and innovation led international strategic collaborations	Increase participation of those who can benefit	

Strategic enablers			
	[------------------------------------Improving our effectiveness------------------------------------]		
	Build strategic partnerships that add significant value	Provide first-class facilities	Create time for academic development	Improve core systems and processes	Manage organizational performance

	[-------Financial sustainability-------]		[-----------------------------Valuing and developing all our staff-----------------------------]	
	Aggressively grow research income	Grow additional sources of profitable income to invest in our future	Develop leadership skills in a wider range of staff	Ensure effective communication and ownership of values and strategy at all levels
	Manage resources to deliver strategic priorities	Ensure all faculties and schools are able to generate surpluses for re-investment	Proactively attract and retain high quality staff	Manage performance and support the development of all staff

Source: Arthur, 2008.

Step 5: Measure the rhetoric against the reality

Measure the 'Espoused Theory' (the rhetoric) against the 'Theory-in-Use' (the reality), the knowledge of mission against a 'sense of mission'. Design and formulate your strategic options accordingly – from the perspective of your colleagues. The perceived differences between institutional rhetoric and everyday reality go to the very heart of why mission statements have attracted so much opprobrium – and you need to be especially sensitive to such concerns if you wish to avoid a similar fate in the case of your department. As we all view the world through a different lens so you need to give careful consideration to the style as well as the substance of the options you see facing the department. You will get short shrift from your colleagues, for example, and rightly so, if you propose objectives which, while consistent with your institutional plan, seem hopelessly out of kilter from their perspective; and doubly so if you couch them in language which, while echoing your HEI's mission, does not resonate with it.

This is not to say you should bow to the status quo or qualify your ideals either. Far from it. Visions and strategic plans – if they are to succeed – are necessarily positive. They anticipate the realization of an idealized and desirable future state. Equally, they are not concerned with the negative: the problems of the here and now, the raking over of past mistakes or the outlining of reasons why aspirations cannot be realized. Even so, you must remember that if your departmental vision is to be realized then your colleagues will need to believe in it as much as you do. Consequently you should articulate your vision in the first instance from their 'world-viewpoint', not one derived from the 'infallibility' of your institutional mission plan, or in anticipation of a leap of faith or wholesale conversion to it.

Yet we should also be wary of being overly sceptical or certainly cynical in this regard. HEIs have tended to make heavy weather of their institutional mission plan. Universities are too large and too complex, it is often argued, not to say peculiarly distinctive – *sui generis* – and as such are not always conducive environments in which to generate a sense of mission among staff. Evidence from the private sector, however, indicates that this does not always have to be the case; that such reasoning is indeed seriously, if not fatally, flawed. BP, to take one example, has an organizational infrastructure of global proportion, as one would expect of a world leader in the supply and distribution of oil. It has also set itself an ambitious global mission – to be performance-driven, progressive, innovative and green. What is equally impressive, however, is the way in which these core values have been disseminated within and across the organization. Indeed first-hand investigation confirms that whether the BP respondent is a Norwegian fitter on a North Sea oil rig, a Belgian engineer in a Dutch oil refinery or a Spanish operative in a Madrid filling station, each is similarly imbued with an acute understanding and genuine commitment to the company's mission and its values. If BP is able to generate a sense of mission – in spite of the size, complexity and sweep of its global operation – then there is no reason, in theory, why HEIs cannot do likewise.

In the case of your department, then, it is important you strike a balance between the need to engage your colleagues on the one hand, and your impulse to embrace your institutional mission on the other. This is something only you can judge, based on your understanding of your colleagues and the extent of their knowledge and commitment to the institutional mission. You should then articulate your departmental perspective accordingly. Whatever the style or substance of your deliberations, you should aim to develop a paragraph or 5–6 bullet points for each of the following sequential elements of the strategic process:

1 Where are we now? Analysis (not navel-gazing)
2 Where could we go? Option formulation (not generating confusion)
3 Where do we want to go? Option selection (not post-rationalizing)
4 What will help us get there? Engineering coherent support (not changing the rules)
5 What do we do today? Implementation (not fire-fighting).

It is important that you go through each of these stages step by step. You should resist the temptation to skip any of them. That way you will avoid the danger of making assumptions about the status quo on the one hand, and underestimating the potential for – as well as implications of – future developments on the other. In doing so, you should also, as we noted earlier, accentuate the positive. The alternative is to run the risk of lapsing into navel-gazing, generating confusion and becoming mired in fire-fighting (Luffman *et al.*, 1996; Mintzberg *et al.*, 2008).

Step 6: Assessment of risk and setting key targets

You should remember to build in to your perspective two aspects which have not always been given due consideration in the past but which are nowadays increasingly expectated, if not required, by statutory authorities: i.e. an assessment of risk, and an indicative list of your key targets.

In the case of the former, you should outline the risk implications for embarking on your proposed course of action and, equally important, the consequences of *not* undertaking it. The rationale for such risk assessment is to help avoid excessive risk-taking on the one hand, and to facilitate the seizure of new opportunities on the other, while simultaneously reassuring stakeholders that you are unlikely to be blown off-course by unforeseen circumstances. The irony, of course, is that in the case of many HEIs the greatest single risk facing them is their actual *fear* of taking a risk in the first place.

As for target-setting, the idea, quite correctly, is to provide you with an indicator of progress towards your goal (how we will know when we've got there), an incentive for achieving it and a means of monitoring your collective activity. Such targets, it is commonly accepted, are most effective if they are SMART: i.e. specific, measurable, achievable, realistic and time-bound. And you may well have had experience in developing objectives of this nature in the past. If so, you will know that in practice targets which claim to be SMART may be anything but; that is, they are often written to satisfy 'the system' (rather than address the real task at hand), are invariably inflexible and frequently set goals that are either too high or too low (Rose, 2000). You should take extra care, then, to ensure you do not fall into the same trap: i.e. you should develop your indicative targets in such a way that they are not DUMB – defective, unrealistic, misdirected and (perhaps worst of all, simply) bureaucratic.

Step 7: A 'shared vision' for your department

Your personal perspective on the department completed, you are now in an informed position to undertake the most difficult task of this whole process: that of securing the agreement of your colleagues on the best way forward for your department.

Your research and analysis of what the department could and should do will count for naught if you are unable to engage your colleagues in establishing a 'shared vision' on your collective future. There is, as noted earlier, no single right way. However, our understanding of leadership – together with the examples of good practice extant in some HEIs – do provide us with a way forward. You have anyway already taken steps to help you in this regard – through your own self-assessment ('paving the way' – the 'first leadership act' in Senge's view (2006)); and in your willingness to 'encourage the heart' by articulating your vision from your colleagues' perspective. You now need to go further and test your 'mental model' with them.

More than that, in order to 'enable others to act' you need to encourage your colleagues to put themselves in your shoes and develop their own indicative 'mental model' of the department. This need not be a grand design, simply a one-page summary of their visions and strategies for the department. Either way, their critique of your perspective along with their own conceptualization should enable you to revise, enhance and maybe even dramatically reshape your own initial ideas. This interchange between an individual leader's ideas and the collaborative thought of colleagues is at the heart of vision formation, and it is contingent on your willingness – as a putative transformational leader – to invite your colleagues to share in the process of leadership.

Strategic planning in practice

We can see these elements and processes at work in the institutional examples of good practice offered by Northeastern University, Boston, and George Mason University, Virginia.

Northeastern University, Boston

Northeastern, a large private 'national research university' that is 'student-centered, practice-oriented and urban' with 'a strong community service mission', set itself the goal (as part of its 'self-study for re-accreditation') of 'creating a New Home for Faculty': a 'home' which envisages faculty working in new ways; where 'mentoring, advising, collaboration and curriculum development are recognized, assessed and rewarded along with teaching, research and scholarship as integral elements of professional performance' (Baer *et al.*, 1998). The experience of departments in attempting to make this vision a reality provides us with an illuminating insight on the variation in approaches to departmental planning. Two model ones in particular – the departments of Mathematics and Cardiopulmonary Sciences – highlight the difference.

In the case of Mathematics – a large department with an international research reputation and a heavy service load – the Chair found it virtually impossible, in the first instance, to generate any interest on the part of his colleagues in the process. Indeed they felt threatened by the prospect of defining departmental goals consistent with the university's mission, as if they were 'losing control over one's life' as one faculty member put it. To overcome this difficulty the Chair did two things. One, he sought to make the process more meaningful by focusing preliminary discussions on an issue (or 'hook') of particular interest to the whole department, in this instance the hiring of junior faculty. And two, he attempted to give 'ownership' to the department by asking one of his colleagues to write a first draft based on the debate. The tactics worked. Staff estrangement was arrested and turned around. The process of draft writing and circulation, feedback and revision soon developed its own momentum and a collective agreement was finally reached. From the Chair's viewpoint the key to this successful outcome was 'to listen and feel the emotions of people in your group, to find an appropriate activity that stimulated the interests of the group and to move ownership of the process in ever widening circles'.

In Cardiopulmonary Sciences, by contrast – a smaller department oriented towards applied research and professional development – the attraction of a new and different setting (and with it the prospect of greater professional fulfilment) exerted such a 'pull' on staff that the Chair had no difficulty in arousing staff interest. On the contrary, her main concern was how best to harness this enthusiasm. After consulting colleagues she arranged for staff to work through their initial ideas in groups of two or three. She then organized a series of departmental retreats (or 'away-days') at which these ideas were presented, discussed and ultimately voted upon formally (all votes having equal weight) by every department member. While, in theory, a high-risk strategy in itself – in that there was no guarantee that staff would necessarily vote for goals consistent with the university's mission – the Chair found that, in practice, this was not the case. Not only that but the goals which the department finally adopted were those on which there was near unanimity. Indeed, she concluded that the process had made her department 'feel more like a team than ever before'.

George Mason University, Virginia

George Mason University (GMU) has sought to improve staff participation and commitment in a similar way; in this instance, in developing a strategic plan for the institution as a whole. A 'commuter school' catering for minority populations in the Washington DC metropolitan area – yet based ironically in America's wealthiest county (Fairfax, north Virginia) – GMU is relatively under-funded compared to its more illustrious state neighbours: the University of Virginia, William and Mary and Virginia Tech. What it lacks in tradition and continuity it has sought to make up, with commendable drive and ambition, by aiming to be 'if not the biggest, then the best managed university in the world'. In this spirit and in a conscious attempt to foster community-building, the university's executive charged a faculty group task force with the job of identifying the objectives – or alternative scenarios if you will – which the university could and indeed should set itself.

Working to the brief set by the Provost's office – to establish attainable goals; to focus on audit, dialogue and 'friend-raising'; and to include alumni, the local

Round Table and legislators in the consultation – the group produced a visionary guide, *Engaging the Future* (Wood *et al.*, 1997), which outlined a range of viable alternative options open to the university. Put another way, they posed the questions, anticipated future scenarios, and above all established a framework for institutional discussion and decision-making. They also included concrete recommendations which were subsequently adopted, notably: the creation of three-year faculty secondments for senior scholars to the Provost's office; the launch of a video-based 'constituency conversation' on university citizenship; the establishment of a credit-based staff development account for individual faculty members, and the formation of a 'New Century College' aimed at providing 'the finest small college education in the context of a large state university'.

Such has been the success of this initiative, indeed, that the Commonwealth of Virginia has adopted it as mandatory practice for all universities in the state – including William and Mary and others: an instance of one-upmanship that we should certainly not begrudge, given we can all learn and benefit from it. Indeed, it is a model of best practice we could and would all do well to follow.

4 | Leading by example

I know that I can save the country and that I alone can.

William Pitt

. . . Is that right?

George W. Bush left the White House as he entered it – amid controversy, latterly in addressing the global financial crisis, and formerly as the 'minority' victor in the most controversial presidential election since the Hayes–Tilden contest of 1876. In between his popularity plummeted as US intervention in Iraq faltered. It was not, of course, meant to turn out this way – particularly for a president who, compared to many of his predecessors, had only a moderate interest and understanding of foreign affairs when he came to office. And while it is difficult to recall events prior to 9/11, the Bush administration did initially pull off a remarkable coup.

Though he was widely expected to struggle from the outset because of the nature of his election victory, many sceptics – including much of the Washington media – were openly baffled at the smooth way the new President moved into the old office, at how the White House became more akin to 'Bush Corp': an organization defined by a business culture with the President as chairman of the board.

Much of the explanation for this remarkable turn-around was in fact due to the sole, but significant, characteristic which differentiated Bush Jr from all 42 of his predecessors (as well as his successor) in the office. Sons may have followed fathers (as in the case of the Adams) into the White House before – as have 26 lawyers and seven soldiers for that matter – but George W. Bush was the first president ever to hold an MBA. And while his business career may not have been an untrammelled success, he did manage to apply the lessons he learnt at Harvard Business School to the business of running a government to telling effect in his first year of office.

His management style bore all the hallmarks of the MBA handbook, from the appointment of Cabinet members (chosen on the basis of complementary expertise combined with an element of rivalry, alongside imperfectly defined portfolios, to foster 'creative tension' among advisers) to the approach to strategy (one theme per week, one speech per day) to the insistence on a strict code of dress and behaviour. Bad language, poor timekeeping and 'dress down' Fridays were made taboo. On the other hand, staff were encouraged to follow the President's lead and not overdo the overtime – to maintain in effect the balance in their lives between commitment to work and responsibility to family and community.

It was a management style which perceived politics as being a matter of performance goals more than motive, and of results more than process. For Bush the business of government was just that – less a matter of ideology than a theory of management. His job, as he saw it, was to sell 'the plan', get the right people to put it in motion and then stand back: a modus operandi most clearly visible in the 'corporate' relationship that existed between President and Vice-President; between Bush, the chief executive officer who dealt with the broad-brush strategy, and Dick Cheney, the chief operating officer who put it into practice.

Now while it is the case that Bush may well have been motivated to differentiate his administration from the informality characteristic of his immediate predecessor – his adoption of MBWA ('management by walking about') and the use of joshing nicknames could be interpreted (as indeed it was) as a deliberate 'charm offensive' to wrong-foot his opponents – it was equally the case that his actions demonstrated an astute business-based manoeuvre, one that reaped him a handsome dividend in his first hundred days and of which we should all take heed. That is, irrespective of whether one shares Bush's conception of politics or the beliefs espoused by his administration, the style, tone and manner in which he reorganized the White House provide us with an exemplary model of leadership, of how to undertake a new role, shape it to your design and make it your own: in Bush's case to live up to his own maxim that 'a good executive is one that understands how to recruit people and how to delegate. How to align authority and responsibility, how to hold people accountable and how to build a team' (Macintyre, 2001). His failing here, of course, was his inability to sustain this modus operandi throughout his term of office.

This practice of reflecting on leadership – of how one should embrace a new role or tackle an existing one – is not often found, unfortunately, in HE. Indeed, to judge from a leadership study of UK university vice chancellors it is a practice conspicuous by its absence. As exemplified in the typical response which researchers met when they probed individual vice chancellors on their preferred or adopted leadership styles: 'I don't really think about these things frankly. I just try and get on with the job. Basically I don't read books about it. I just get on with it' (Bargh *et al.*, 2000). It may be – and one would like to think it is – that the VCs in this case study do not simply rely on 'playing it by ear', that they do in fact consciously deliberate on their modus operandi but did not feel inclined to admit doing so for reasons of culture or personal modesty. Either way, the point is that it is an activity we ignore at our peril. Private sector organizations indeed set such store by it that they invariably hire coaches to ease new post-holders through this process, an investment they willingly and regularly incur in the knowledge that the benefits which accrue will far outweigh the initial expense. In HE the hiring of coaches is beyond the reach of many HEIs, yet, even if it wasn't, it is doubtful many would regard it as a priority for funding. For, as we noted earlier, leadership and management within HE are bedevilled by the low status and esteem in which they are almost universally held. This parlous situation is exacerbated still further by the tendency of some managers to treat their role as if it were a temporary distraction from their 'real' work of teaching and research (see Box 4.1).

Box 4.1 'New manager assimilation': San Diego State University

Not all universities are hesitant or sceptical of hiring external consultants to facilitate the assimilation of new managers. San Diego State University is a case in point.

The context
The desire of the newly appointed University President 'to take charge' – 'to begin building strong, positive and productive working relationships' with his eight-strong Cabinet of top administrators. His predecessor had served 20 years in office.

The approach
The external facilitator – hired to help in the leadership transition – meets with each of the Cabinet members for 45 minutes on a one-to-one basis. The one-to-one meetings are organized around a common set of questions (see below) which the new President has agreed in advance with the facilitator. Ground rules provide for anonymity. The facilitator concludes the process by convening the entire Cabinet group, including the new President, and summarizing the outcomes.

The findings
1   What do we want to know about the new President?
   * He came from a state college – does he understand research, graduate education and Division I athletics?
   * He seems to have a consultative management style – how does that really work?
   * How will he utilize the Cabinet?
   * What does he need from us?
   * How will the campus relate to the system administration now?
   * Is he Dr Weber? Stephen? Steve?

2   What should he know about us?
   * He has a terrific faculty and staff.
   * We have an entrepreneurial culture, which may be resistant to change.
   * Our mission and identity need clarification.

3   What does he need to know to be successful here?
   * Use your transition process to convey messages about the future of the campus.
   * Become highly visible in the community.
   * Bond with the faculty and the staff as soon as you can.
   * Consultation is important, but don't forget that the President must make the executive decisions.
   * You will be given an extended honeymoon – don't squander it!

4   *What significant issues need to be addressed quickly?*
   * Establish and define your presidency, asap.
   * Get 'up to speed' on athletics!
   * Don't be afraid to delegate.
   * Make any planned personnel changes asap.
   * Improve our planning and budgeting processes.

5   What specific suggestions do we have for addressing the issues we have identified?
   * Develop a shared vision and value system for us to use in decision-making.
   * Don't get 'used up' in your first year – save a little for the ' third act'
   * Get to know us – use us to help advance your agenda – work with us as a team.

The feedback

Participants agreed the transition dialogues did facilitate an extremely valuable exchange of information in a way that was far less protracted than would be the norm. More than that, however, they also enabled:

- the President to signal he was 'eager for the views of senior officers and valued their feelings as professional colleagues';
- Cabinet members to be more 'self-confident and comfortable in delivering bad news or identifying problems and issues that needed resolution';
- Cabinet meetings to proceed 'with less game playing and more honest conversation';
- the 'top team' to approach an immediate crisis incident (a campus triple homicide) with 'a higher degree of readiness and effectiveness' than would otherwise have been possible.

Source: adapted from Krinsky and Weber, 1997.

We all have a collective responsibility to address this malaise and as individual managers can do so, in the first instance, through the personal example which we set – the way in which we conduct ourselves; the style, tone and manner we set in managing day-to-day affairs; the ways in which we support colleagues, handle meetings, make decisions, resolve conflict, establish standards and so on. To be an effective manager requires you to give serious consideration to these issues. Put another way, if you are to make a real difference to your colleagues and make a distinctive contribution to your institution – and also, critically, one that meets with your own satisfaction – you need to consider these matters in a deliberative, reflective and self-conscious way. This fourth chapter seeks to help you do that by systematically examining these particular 'public' aspects of your role, namely the establishment of a modus operandi, the chairing of meetings, the making and taking of decisions, the handling of conflict and the building of teams.

Paving the way

> 'I wish some power the gift would gi'e us, to see ourselves as others see us'.
> Robbie Burns

One of the most difficult things to learn – and one of the last things we ever learn about ourselves – is the personal impact we have on those around us. Yet without such self-knowledge we cannot begin to determine how effective we are in our roles. Our path to self-realization, however, has been made still more difficult in recent times. For, like it or loathe it, we cannot ignore the fact that we operate in a radically different political and social world from our forebears, one which seemingly celebrates fame over originality, 'image' over 'reality', style over substance, sound-bite over reason and 'spin' over news-story.

Plotting a course of action in such a setting is no easy task. It requires that you are genuinely attuned to the needs and feelings of others as well as your own. Indeed, leadership development programmes nowadays are less about testing the leadership capacity of individuals through various outdoor pursuit challenges and the like, and more concerned with getting participants 'to reach inside themselves' to find the leadership style of their own that would most successfully mesh with their organization. We began to explore this issue in the last chapter and identified a variety of ways you could gain more self-knowledge through formal feedback instruments (such as the Visionary Leader Behavior Questionnaire, the Myers-Briggs (personality) type indicator and the Thomas-Kilmann conflict mode instrument) as well as in conversation with the person who knows you best – yourself.

We can – and you should – extend this journey of self-exploration further in order to prepare you for the role you have undertaken.

1 Emotional intelligence

First, examine that aspect of your personality which will have a critical bearing on whether (or not) you will be successful, namely not so much your IQ – a common mistake made in gauging individual's leadership potential, not least in universities (as in 'x is highly intelligent and must therefore be able to lead') – but rather your EQ. Popularized by American psychologist Daniel Goleman (1996), 'emotional intelligence' is defined as the ability to perceive one's own feelings and those of others. Thus the more emotionally intelligent person is characterized by a high sense of self-worth, an ability to express and understand their emotions and to understand their personal values. They also tend to be more aware of their own strengths and limitations, to recognize these things in people working around them and to accommodate them. Such individuals invariably outperform their less sensitive counterparts and not surprisingly EQ is now felt to be as – if not more – important than IQ in determining professional effectiveness and progression (Dann, 2008). How, though, do you fare? Box 4.2 enables you to assess your own level of emotional intelligence, a task you need not approach with undue hesitancy, for if you do not score as well as you hope you can always take remedial action, since it is still possible to significantly increase your EQ (unlike your IQ) in later life.

2 Your preparedness for the role

A more conventional way of assessing your preparedness is to examine your degree of competence for the role. The management competence framework, outlined in Box 4.3, is a generic template which one UK new university has developed to clarify to managers the (benchmark) standards of performance expected of them; to help them assess their performance and to guide them in determining their development needs. You should take each of the nine core competencies in turn:

- Grade yourself Strong–Average–Weak against the skills and qualities in each sub-category.
- Determine your overall average for each of the nine core competencies.
- Discuss your profile with a 'critical friend', someone whose opinion you value and trust. In what aspects are you strong – less strong – under-developed – undeveloped? Focus on the gaps and the weaknesses in your profile. What can you, ought you to, do about them?
- Commit to an action plan to address them.

Box 4.2 Emotional intelligence questionnaire

Test your emotional intelligence. Tick a single response to each question then add up your score.

	Never	Rarely	Sometimes	Routinely	Always

AWARENESS OF FEELINGS
Recognizing one's emotions and their effects.

	Never	Rarely	Sometimes	Routinely	Always
1 Do you know which emotions you are feeling, can you say why and accurately label them individually?	❏	❏	❏	❏	❏
2 Do you recognize the chain from experiencing an emotion to taking action based on it (i.e. the links between your feelings and what you think, do and say)?	❏	❏	❏	❏	❏
3 Do you recognize how your feelings affect your performance, the quality of experience at work and your relationships?	❏	❏	❏	❏	❏

PERSONAL INSIGHT
Knowing one's key strengths and frailties.

	Never	Rarely	Sometimes	Routinely	Always
1 Are you aware of your strengths, weaknesses and emotional boundaries in relationships?	❏	❏	❏	❏	❏
2 Do you consciously make time to be reflective?	❏	❏	❏	❏	❏
3 Are you open to candid feedback, new perspectives, continuous learning and self-development?	❏	❏	❏	❏	❏

	Never	Rarely	Sometimes	Routinely	Always

SELF-ASSURANCE
Sureness about one's self-worth and capabilities.

	Never	Rarely	Sometimes	Routinely	Always
1 Do you present yourself with self-possession; have poise but with warmth?	❏	❏	❏	❏	❏
2 Can you celebrate diversity in teams, voice views that are unpopular?	❏	❏	❏	❏	❏
3 Are you decisive, able to make sound judgements using emotional and analytical information, despite uncertainties and pressures?	❏	❏	❏	❏	❏

SCORING

ALWAYS: Add 4 points for every tick. ROUTINELY: Add 3 points for every tick. SOMETIMES: Add 2 points for every tick. RARELY: Add 1 point for every tick. NEVER: No points.

Score 36–27

Congratulations. You have a high to exceptional awareness of your own emotions, thought and resulting behaviour. You would have the ability to reflect on incidents that did not go well or as expected and analyse your part in that sequence of events.

Score 26–18

Well done but reflect on the reasons why you put a 'sometimes' response. Think about questions you could ask others in future to check out what their motive is for their behaviour or their responses to you. Try to stop yourself from repeating mistakes.

Score 17–9

You may be puzzled by the way you act or the responses you get from others. You may feel misunderstood a significant amount of the time. Enlist the help of a friend to develop a plan for taking steps to improve yourself.

Score 8–1

You are very honest. Showing integrity is a great EI strength. You would benefit from a course to help you to increase your self-awareness. Your score shows you are not particularly aware of how or why you behave the way you do.

Source: adapted from Dann, 2001; 2008.

Box 4.3 Performance expectations of senior managers at one UK 'new' (post-1992) university

Strategic ability
- balances immediate needs against longer-term objectives
- ensures day-to-day tasks and activities are clearly linked to the longer-term aims of the business
- develops a coherent picture of the school's/UWS's contribution to overall university goals and communicates this
- influences and contributes to wider university issues

Leadership
- creates and secures commitment to a clear vision
- initiates and manages change in pursuit of strategic objectives
- is visible, approachable and earns respect
- inspires and shows loyalty
- builds and supports a high-performing team
- acts decisively, having assessed the risks
- accepts responsibility for the actions of the team

Communication
- negotiates effectively and can handle hostility
- is concise and persuasive orally and in writing
- listens to what is said and is sensitive to others' reactions
- chooses the methods of communication most likely to secure effective results
- is comfortable and effective in a representational role
- builds, maintains and uses an effective network of contacts

Judgement and decision-making
- ensures necessary information or evidence is collected and weighs the value of advice against its source
- assesses the degree of the risk in major plans and decisions, and balances against potential disadvantages
- takes timely decisions in uncertain situations or based on limited information, where necessary
- evaluates the potential impact of a decision on school/UWS priorities or on broader university objectives
- remains objective in assessing information when under great pressure

Management of people
- develops staff to meet challenging organizational needs
- establishes and communicates clear standards and expectations
- delegates effectively, knowing when to step in and when not to
- makes best use of skills and resources within the team
- gives regular face-to-face feedback and recognition
- addresses poor performance, builds trust, good morale and teamwork
- responds to feedback from staff
- secures commitment to change through appropriate involvement of staff

Management of financial and other resources
- secures value for money
- challenges existing practices and leads initiatives of new and more efficient use of resources
- negotiates for the resources to do the job, in the light of wider priorities
- commits and realigns resources to meet key priorities
- uses management information to monitor/control resources
- demonstrates commitment to using IT as a resource

Delivery of results
- defines results taking account of customer or other stakeholders' needs
- manages relationships with customers/other stakeholders effectively
- organizes work processes to deliver on time, on budget and to agreed quality standards
- strives for continuous performance improvement and encourages others to do the same
- assesses and manages risk
- monitors performance and incorporates feedback in future plans

Personal effectiveness
- adapts quickly and flexibly to new demands and change
- manages own time well to meet competing priorities
- shows resilience, stamina and reliability under heavy pressure
- takes a firm stance when circumstances warrant it
- is aware of personal strengths and weaknesses and their impact on others
- shows commitment to own personal and professional development
- offers objective advice without fear or favour
- pursues adopted strategies with energy and commitment

Expertise and professional competence
- earns credibility and influence through depth and breadth of expertise
- ensures that decisions are informed by relevant technical/specialist expertise
- understands and operates effectively within the university framework
- accepts personal responsibility for quality of professional work
- gives professional direction to others
- seeks and applies best practice from other organizations

3 Your image

A further, and by no means trite, consideration as to your 'roadworthiness' is image – your own image and that of your immediate surroundings. We cannot overlook the fact that one of the consequences of living in an increasingly image-conscious age is that first impressions really do count – particularly at work, and especially when dealing with external clients. Conventional wisdom, for instance, tells us that when we walk into a meeting, people form an impression which is based 70 per cent on our personal image, 23 per cent on the sound, pitch and modularity of our voice and just 7 per cent on the content of what we're actually saying (Hanscombe, 1998).

If you are to make the right impression then attention to your image is as critical as any other aspect of your role. Put another way, it is as important to 'look the part' and 'feel the part' as it is to 'fit the part'. This is not a question of acquiring an expensive wardrobe or of becoming 'the packaged executive'. Such techniques – like the penchant for 'power-dressing' in the 1980s – are rarely sustainable or desirable for they are, at bottom, transparently manipulative. Rather, it is a matter of reflecting on the example you convey to others about the quality of life you lead. It is about projecting a positive image – thinking positively and being positive. This is not always easy for everyone. Indeed we're all familiar with the individual who has the unfortunate tendency to enter a room as a kind of walking apology – 'Sorry, it's only me'. Again, however, as with emotional intelligence, there are ways in which we can cultivate such positive habits and we will be exploring them later in Chapter 11, 'Managing yourself'. And while it might mean you do indeed need to refresh your wardrobe, the important point is that your credibility with colleagues and clients is intimately related to the image you project. You will get back, be it positive or negative, what you give out.

Equally, the impression others have of you is often informed by your surroundings as much as by yourself. Therefore you also need to cast a critical eye on your immediate working environment – notably your office. If you have one – and we tend to assume it is essential we do, even though it may not be – what does your office say about you? Is it a stimulating or stale environment? Organized or disorganized? Tidy or cluttered? Bright or dull? Green or barren? As Churchill once said, 'we shape our buildings and afterwards our buildings shape us'. The same can be applied to offices if we allow them to. You therefore need to consciously reflect on the 'messages' your office gives to colleagues and to visitors about you. Does the way in which you have utilized the space, decorated the walls, furnished the surroundings and personalized it convey what you really want? For example, if you have a desk – and again we tend to automatically assume we should have one even if it may not be necessary – how is it positioned? If it is in the centre with you behind it and your visitors made to sit in front of it, this may convey the sense that you like to be the 'controlling adult' of your environment. Alternatively, they may feel you are an insecure manager with something to hide – or both. Place it alongside one of the walls and the position of your desk conveys a quite different impression. One of a person who is willing to share their space on an equal footing with others while simultaneously maybe running the risk of being thought a soft touch. The point is you need to ensure that whichever way you choose to organize your office – and we will pick this issue up again later – it reflects your personal style.

4 Approaches to leadership

In developing your own way forward you also, as we noted earlier, need to consider aspects not only of yourself but of your institution: its distinguishing characteristics, its climate, structure, politics, culture and so on. You then need to determine which leadership approach is likely to have the most successful effect in your working environment. Some such as Senge (2006) argue that 'taking a stand' is the first leadership act. And he argues that the 'learning organization' is a 'good idea' but will remain only that unless, and until, individuals make a conscious and deliberate choice to build such organizations. There are, as we have seen, other models on which you can draw – the visionary leader, liberating leader, transformational leader, transactional leader and so on. The general management literature is also awash with sage advice on everything from *Thriving on Chaos* (Peters, 1987) to the *One Minute Manager* (Blanchard and Johnson, 2000). Three further generic perspectives are worth considering. One, Stephen Covey's *The Seven Habits of Highly Effective People* (1989), because it is one of the few successful codes of behaviour to have stood the test of time, and because it also provides you with a sound reference point to question your actions (see Box 4.4). A second, Kouzes and Posner's (2003) leadership challenge model, for the same reasons (see Box 4.5). And the third – a transformational leadership model for the public sector – because it offers an approach more closely suited to universities than probably any other, one which not only recognizes the critical differences (in governance and management and accountability) between the public and the private sector (principally, the lack of clarity and greater complexity of the former compared to the latter), but also reflects the variation in the perception of leadership of those who work in the two areas (see Box 4.6). In the private sector the greatest expectation of the leader is to be a role model, while in the public sector the most important prerequisite for a leader appears to be what they can do for their staff, a tendency that closely resembles the model of leader as servant (Alimo-Metcalfe and Alban-Metcalfe, 2002).

This is not to say, however, that leadership is simply about meeting staff needs. On the contrary, it suggests that while individuals may ascribe characteristics such as charisma, vision, courage, passion and so on, to (distant) leaders these are not necessarily the same qualities they value in their own (immediate) boss. Here, it would seem, public employees set greater store on line managers who have particular attributes: namely, being sociable, open and considerate of others; having a sense of humour; being credible in their field of expertise; being intelligent; and setting high performance standards for themselves and for others. In other words, they value leaders who set an example by 'practising what they preach' (see Box 4.7). In this context, then, leadership is about engaging others as partners in developing and achieving a shared vision and enabling staff to lead. It is about creating a fertile supportive environment for creative thinking and for challenging assumptions about the status quo, as well as having genuine sensitivity to the needs of a broad range of internal and external stakeholders. It is in short the transformational model of leadership – that of the *democratic* leader who seeks to take an organization through change while transforming people's beliefs in themselves and encouraging leadership in others. This approach also has clear implications for management and the role managers are expected to play: i.e. not so much a case of 'hands on' as 'hands off' (see Box 4.8). Conventional wisdom also indicates a striking symmetry between leadership effectiveness in universities on the one hand, and transformational

Box 4.4 The seven habits of highly effective people

In *The Seven Habits of Highly Effective People*, Stephen Covey identifies seven key steps that will lead to truly effective behaviour, whether at work or at home.

The first three habits are 'private' steps the individual must take personally before being able to achieve significant results in the outside world. The next three habits are 'public' activities for the public realm where interaction and, crucially, interdependence are called for. The final habit is to stay fresh.

- **Be proactive.** Covey does not use the term proactive in the more recent sense (where it is synonymous with 'active'). He genuinely means taking responsibility for your life and your actions. A key principle for Covey here is that 'between stimulus and response people have the freedom to choose'.
- **Begin with the end in mind.** This means having clear goals and knowing what it is you want to achieve. Covey even suggests drawing up a personal mission statement that is based on your most valued principles.
- **Put first things first.** Effective management of time, tasks and responsibilities. This includes developing trusting working relationships, delegating effectively.
- **Think win/win.** Creative problem-solving, not aggressive negotiating or feeble passivity. The approach transcends current difficulties and finds alternatives.
- **Seek first to understand . . . then to be understood.** Covey talks about 'empathic listening'; allowing others to express themselves, letting them know they are being listened to and understood.
- **Synergize.** This for Covey is the 'miraculous' part – catalysing, unifying and unleashing the greatest powers within people. The whole is greater than the sum of its parts.
- **Sharpen the saw.** This is about renewal and staying fresh. The man struggling to cut down a tree is too busy to sharpen his saw, so it takes him far longer.

If you observe these seven habits, Covey believes you can constantly renew yourself. Beyond that the leadership challenge – or Eighth Habit – Covey identifies is to 'inspire others to find their voice' by modelling the right behaviour, path-finding shared vision, aligning goals and systems for results and genuinely empowering those around you.

Source: adapted from Covey, 1989; 2004.

Box 4.5 Five practices of effective leaders

- **Modelling the way** – leading by example, living your values
- **Inspiring a shared vision** – developing a compelling vision of the future
- **Challenging the process** – yearning for improvement and willingness to experiment, to learn
- **Enabling others to act** – promoting collaboration, building trust and empowering others
- **Encouraging the heart** – recognizing and celebrating achievement

Source: adapted from Kouzes and Posner, 2003.

Box 4.6 Characteristics of the transformational leader in the public sector

Leading and developing others

- Has genuine interest in staff as individuals; values their contributions; develops their strengths; mentors; has positive expectations of staff abilities
- Trusts staff to take decisions and initiative on important matters; delegates effectively; develops potential; supportive of mistakes
- Approachable and not status-conscious; prefers face-to-face communication; accessible and keeps in touch
- Encourages staff to question traditional approaches to the job; encourages new approaches/ solutions to problems; encourages strategic thinking

Personal qualities

- Transparency: honest and consistent in behaviour; more concerned with the good of the organization than personal ambition
- Integrity: open to advice, criticism and disagreement; consults and involves others in decision making; regards values as integral to the organization
- Decisiveness: decisive when required; prepared to take difficult decisions and risks when appropriate
- Charisma: in touch; exceptional communicator; inspires others to join them
- Analytical and creative thinking: capacity to deal with a wide range of complex issues; creative in problem-solving

Leading the department/organization

- Inspiring communicator of the vision of the organization to a network of internal and external stakeholders; gains the confidence and support of various groups through sensitivity to needs and by achieving organizational goals
- Clarifies objectives and boundaries; team-orientated approach to problem-solving, decision-making and identifying values
- Has a clear vision and strategic direction, engages various internal and external stakeholders in developing; helps others to achieve the vision

Source: Alimo-Metcalfe and Alban-Metcalfe, 2002.

Box 4.7 Leadership by example

To lead by example you must ensure you:

- work hard to high standards
- actively encourage feedback on your own performance
- communicate an air of enthusiasm
- help out/walk the job
- work on your own learning
- practise what you preach
- openly admit your mistakes
- set a good example to others by your own behaviour
- are *corporate*
- don't compromise yourself

- don't panic
- don't let it get you down

You should never say . . . (and should try to resolve):

- no one tells me
  - what's going on
  - what my exact job is
  - what my responsibilities are
- the university should do . . .
- it's not down to me

Box 4.8 The new public sector manager

As public bureaucracies evolve:

From mechanistic organizations which build on:

- rules
- procedures
- job descriptions
- structures
- rationality
- planning
- management by objectives
- control

To more human organizations which build on:

- values
- meanings
- commitments
- shared understanding
- rituals
- communication
- learning
- collaboration

Then the role of the *new manager* moves:

From
Close Control – 'hands on'
The manager as:

- supervisor
- expert
- director
- controller
- constraint

To
Remote Control – 'hands off'
The manager as:

- resource
- coach
- catalyst
- explorer
- orchestrator
- boundary manager
- networker
- champion
- politician
- negotiator
- conflict raiser/resolver

leadership in the public sector and Kouzes and Posner's leadership challenge model, on the other (see Box 4.9).

Either way, the options are for you to consider and the choice of approach is yours to make. Ultimately it is about finding out what works for you. There is, as we noted earlier, no magic formula for leadership and management. In developing a personal style,

Box 4.9 Effective leadership in higher education

Conventional wisdom indicates that the distinctive features of leadership effectiveness in HE are characterized by the intensity of academic staff expectations. That heads of department will:

- Seek to maintain staff autonomy
- Consult over important decisions
- Foster collegiality with regard to both decision-making and mutual cooperation
- Fight the department's corner with senior managers and through university structures

How to lead
- Provide a clear sense of direction; strategic vision
- Create a department structure to support the direction
- Foster a supportive and collaborative environment
- Be trustworthy
- Have personal integrity
- Have credibility as a role model
- Facilitate participation in decision-making, consultation
- Provide communication about developments
- Represent the department and proactively advance its cause
- Respect existing culture while seeking to realize the vision of the department

How not to lead
- Fail to consult
- Do not respect existing values
- Act in ways that undermine collegiality
- Do not promote the interests of those for whom you are responsible
- Be uninvolved in the life of the department, the university
- Undermine autonomy
- Allow the department to drift

Source: adapted from Bryman, 2007.

however, which is consistent with your beliefs and values and with your working environment, you will be well on the way to becoming an effective leader and manager. How, though, does this (theoretical) effectiveness translate into your (practical) day-to-day activities? It is to these seemingly mundane – yet in terms of your ultimate success, critically important – aspects of your role we turn next.

Meetings, meetings, meetings

> I chair from the front.
> Margaret Thatcher

> Wilt stared out of the window at the new Electronics building and wondered for the umpteenth time what it was about committees that turned educated and relatively intelligent men and women, all of them graduates of universities, into bitter and boring and argumentative people whose sole purpose seemed to be to hear themselves speak and prove everyone else wrong. And committees had come to dominate the Tech.
> Tom Sharpe, *Wilt on High*, 1984, p. 2

Meetings are one of the most – if not *the* most – distinguishing characteristics of university life. Whereas in business such commonplace gatherings are rightly regarded as an important part of work, in academia caricature has elevated them into a celebrated art form. This satirical tradition, stretching from F.M. Cornforth at the start of the last century to Laurie Taylor in this, tells us 'what everyone knows' about HE – that it is beset by committees in which people spend hours of their time while someone takes minutes (Lucas, 1995; McNay, 1996), an activity whose prodigious consumption of time many staff believe – and with good reason – is an unwelcome distraction from their 'real and proper work'.

Academia is, of course, characterized by a far greater range of forms of authority than business. Indeed Burton Clark (1983) has identified no fewer than nine forms of authority in academic settings. Four are based on disciplines (personal rulership (professorial); collegial rulership (professorial); guild authority; and professional authority); two are characteristic of institutions (trustee authority and bureaucratic authority); and three operate at the level of the system (bureaucratic authority, political authority and what he calls 'system-wide academic oligarchy'). These various forms of authority – and the stakeholders they represent – help explain why HEIs have developed an elaborate network of committees to accommodate them. But this development in itself is not the root cause of staff disaffection. After all, there is an equally long-standing commitment to collegiality within academic cultures, and with it an express (and to outsiders, probably excessive) desire that consultation and decision making are both extensive and mutually deliberative processes.

The real source of staff grievance appears to lie in the fact that this 'system theory' is too rarely adhered to in practice. Critics, for instance, invariably complain that committees often have an unclear remit or are poorly controlled, or both; that they are sometimes used as devices to, at one extreme, deliberately stall or avoid reaching a decision, or, on the other, disguise the fact that decisions have already been made elsewhere. Collegiality, as the latter implies, is breached as much as it is honoured in practice and as such can alienate a significant minority of staff. More than that, collegiality also allows negative (as well as positive) attitudes and behaviours to flourish unchecked, which the determined and the unscrupulous are free to exploit, without being held to account. When other new forms of authority are introduced into such a setting – and in particular ones such as that exercised by managers which many insiders regard as illegitimate – it should not surprise us that staff perceive them as yet another unwarranted and unwanted intrusion on their autonomy, their time and their energies (McNay, 1996; Ramsden, 1998).

The challenge for managers, then, is a considerable one. Indeed credibility in your authority will stem from:

- the way in which you determine to schedule meetings (or not);
- the types of meetings you hold;
- the way in which they are organized;
- the manner in which you chair them.

Your mastery of these critical key skills, moreover, will enable you to enhance not only your effectiveness as a leader *within* your department or service but also – given that performance targets nowadays are invariably dependent on a far greater degree of internal collaboration than hitherto – your contribution as a member representing your area in different forums *across* the institution. How to do it though?

To meet or not to meet, that is the question

It is widely accepted that the committee culture symptomatic of academic institutions is, as we noted earlier, simply a reflection of the plurality of forms of authority and of the collegiate tradition that persists within them. The harsh reality, however, is that this culture is also fuelled by those who enjoy, or have most to benefit from, such gatherings: i.e. managers and others in authority. Indeed it is not uncommon to come across managers who pride themselves on having diaries that are 'wall to wall' with meetings. It is as if they have adapted Parkinson's Law and expanded their number of meetings to fill the amount of time they have available. It is a mistake you will also find yourself making unless you exercise the most stringent self-discipline.

After all, we need to recognize that meetings can be *seductive* in the sense that they are social occasions in which you meet with other colleagues, they get you 'out of the office'; they can fill you with a sense of importance, are often relatively undemanding and usually free from interruption. They can also be a fatal attraction. For they can delude you into thinking that 'I am busy, therefore I must be being effective'. Nothing, however, could be further from the truth. Being occupied is not the same as making things happen. Activity is not the same as taking action. Indeed, as a 'rule of thumb' Senge (1998) maintains that as a manager you should divide your time in roughly equal proportion between that spent in meetings and that devoted to action outside them.

Is a meeting really necessary?

This is the first question you should ask yourself when either planning to hold a meeting yourself or having been asked to attend one organized by others. What is the purpose of the meeting? What do you want to get out of the meeting? What do you want others to get out of the meeting? What would be the consequences of *not* meeting? Are you meeting for meeting's sake? Could you not instead send an email, a voicemail, a memo, make a telephone call or write a report?

You should not proceed with a meeting unless you are able to respond positively to these questions. And if it has been arranged by another you should seek clarification from the Chair prior to the meeting as to its purpose. If not satisfied, you should lobby other attendees and challenge the purpose at the meeting itself or (so long as your interests are not threatened) opt not to attend and give your reasons why.

That said, we need to recognize of course that meetings can have very different purposes and that there are indeed many different types of meeting:

Purposes of meetings

All meetings serve one or more of four main purposes:

1 information-giving: 'have I got news for you?'
2 information-gathering: 'what do you think of this?'
3 decision-making: 'what are we going to do?'
4 problem-solving: 'how should we resolve this?'

They are also invariably used to satisfy one or more of the following objectives:

- to test colleagues' reaction to information given (inviting opinion);
- to gain their acceptance of the given information;
- to identify the need for further information;
- to pool ideas and experience on a particular subject (to learn from one another);
- to gain understanding of each other's point of view (to gain cooperation);
- to give individuals the opportunity to test their ideas and attitudes with those of others (and possibly change them);
- to build group morale.

Types of meetings

Meetings can vary, too, in many different ways according to:

- size: large, small, mass or one-to-one;
- status: formal, informal; official, unofficial; open, closed; academic or management;
- scope: team-, group-, unit-, department-, faculty- or institution-wide;
- function: steering group or working party; exam board or user group; think-tank or project team; mitigation panel or public forum; course committee or staff seminar, etc.;
- nature: brainstorming or briefing; presenting or discussing; monitoring or evaluating; negotiating or consulting; lobbying or assessing, etc.

You need, therefore, to give careful consideration as to how you want to organize meetings in your own area. You should not fall into the trap – as so many others do – of assuming that the 'all-purpose meeting for all staff' is the most appropriate – nay, only viable – way to manage the work of your department. Such gatherings can indeed improve team spirit and resolve difficulties. Too often, though, they waste time (and money), increase hostility, treat 'acorns and oak trees as if they were alike' and skim over deep divisions among staff. You can take much of the heat from such meetings – and simultaneously make them more meaningful and effective – by preparing your audience sufficiently beforehand, by arranging to hold, or have others hold, different meetings (as suggested above) to satisfy different purposes: small advisory meetings, say, to gather and exchange information; others to test new ideas; still others to develop policy papers and so on.

You also need to consider the types of meetings you intend to have with staff on a regular basis – team briefings, team meetings, all-staff meetings, one-to-ones, and so on (see Boxes 4.10 and 4.11). Their nature and frequency will depend on the size and complexity of your department or service.

- If, for instance, your department is a relatively small (under 15) stable single-site operation you should anticipate holding all-staff meetings either once a term or twice a semester, and one-to-ones with one or two individuals who have a particular and significant responsibility every other week: e.g. subject coordinator, course leader, team leader.

Box 4.10 One-to-one meetings: key features

Why have them?

One-to-one meetings offer you one of the most effective and efficient ways to manage your department while developing your own management team at the same time.

You should aim to hold them with the two to three individuals in your department who have a particular and significant responsibility either for an activity (e.g. Admissions, Research, Community Links) or the management of staff (e.g. Team Leader, Programme Leader, Subject Coordinator).

Key features

You need to ensure, if you are to achieve your goals, that your one-to-ones:

- are scheduled on a regular basis, typically one hour every other week (a great time-saver and not a time-waster, for regularity ensures that you and your colleagues do not feel obliged to interrupt each other every time a development arises);
- are literally (rather than virtually) a face-to-face discussion in private;
- cater for a discussion which reviews the whole of the role, not just a single aspect of it;
- are structured meetings and not just a casual chat;
- include a discussion of the past, present and future (up to three months in either direction);
- are a genuine two-way dialogue aimed at assessing and reviewing the effectiveness of both parties as a partnership;
- have outcomes (revised or amended targets, agreed deadlines, etc.) that you record briefly in writing on a file note: specific action points to be picked up and to form the basis of your next regular meeting.

Source: adapted from Moores, 1994; Adair and Thomas, 2008.

Box 4.11 Team briefings: key features

Why have them?

Team briefing, as the term implies, is more like a systematic flexible drill than a conventional meeting. A well-established practice which has its origins in the commercial sector, it has been increasingly adapted to good effect in public sector organizations, including HEIs. Briefings, of course, have an obvious practical application if you are responsible for a university-wide service but they can and have been used equally well by academic leaders, who tend to place more emphasis on the format (the 5Ps) of the briefing and play down the enforced formality of these occasions (often substituting half-hour informal meetings over lunch in their stead).

Either way, team briefings can be particularly useful in helping you to:

- correct misunderstandings within your group;
- reduce the effect of damaging rumour, of the grapevine, etc.;
- seek cooperation from your colleagues in preparing for change;
- improve the commitment and morale of group members;
- reinforce your role as leader and manager of the department.

How do they work?
- face-to-face; to facilitate a free range of Q and A;
- small teams (four to 15 people);
- regular: 30 minutes every other week or once a month depending on circumstance;
- relevant: the focus and information must be on the 'here and now' if the briefing is to command sufficient interest and commitment.

Format: the 5Ps
- ▶ Progress: how we are doing in relation to our targets (budgetary, planning, admissions, etc.)?
- ▷ Policy: new initiatives; changes in policy, systems and routines
- ▷ People: who is coming, who is going and why; promotions; scholarly activities; publications; professional development opportunities
- ▶ Points for action: what do we have to do before we meet again? Agree on who will do it
- ▷ Praise: for the group and for individuals as appropriate

▶ at every briefing
▷ not necessarily at every briefing

Source: adapted from Moores, 1994; Adair and Thomas, 2008.

- If you have responsibility for a university service your meetings with staff should be of greater frequency, typically every other week – and you may like to consider alternating them with team briefings.
- Likewise if your department is a large academic one with multiple programmes on different campuses and a diverse range of interests, you should anticipate holding additional staff meetings and alternating them between sites. You will also need to build in additional one-to-ones to ensure you embrace the full range of your department's interests and responsibilities, e.g. with your research director, enterprise activity coordinator, community liaison officer and so on.

Now that you have decided the combination of meetings, both regular and occasional, which best suits you and your department's needs, you face a more difficult task still – that of conducting them.

Effective chairing

Academics are fond of remarking that management is little more than common sense. If that were so, then the poor reputation of meetings – chaired by academics as well as managers – suggests it is a commodity in relatively short supply in universities. Staff complaints as we noted earlier are manifold. The most common being:

- an unclear remit: lack of a clear purpose or objective;
- the absence of an agenda, or a poorly prepared agenda, or an over-ambitious agenda;
- held at the wrong time, with the wrong people, or in the wrong environment;
- behavioural problems: getting side-tracked, going round in circles, individual soap-boxing and gamesmanship, time-wasting and waffling;
- interruptions from outside the meeting: messages, phone calls, etc.;

- too lengthy, no time-frame;
- no agreed actions; poor minutes.

These complaints, however, are all attributable to a common source – poor organization and control on the part of the Chair. You will be well on your way to being an effective Chair if you do not fall foul of any of the above. To that end, you should treat these serial complaints as a checklist of don'ts.

Put another way, the effective Chair pays due regard to the planning and organization of all aspects of the process, not simply part of it. They recognize that a successful outcome is as much dependent on what is done *before* the meeting as it is on what happens *during* it, and equally on what action is taken *after* it. They place equal value and importance on each stage.

Before the meeting

You should:

1 Plan

Be clear about your precise objectives and why you need the meeting. Meetings, as we've noted, often lack such objectives. Indeed they are invariably no more than a list of activities: e.g. discussion of the latest government initiative on Widening Participation and so on. The real objective would be the desired outcome from this activity: e.g. 'to elicit people's point of view', 'to agree a course of action', 'to plan one', 'to decide a response', etc. That is, the objective should be clear, explicit and challenging (and not implied, vague or non-existent). Objective setting is critical, for without one it is unlikely the meeting will have an appropriate structure, and the structure of the meeting should flow logically from your objectives.

List the subjects for:

- information giving (this may entail clarification: either way, this aspect should be kept to a minimum; circulate via email, voicemail or internal post instead);
- information gathering;
- decision making;
- problem solving.

2 Inform

Anticipate which people and what information may be needed. In identifying participants you need to take the following into account:

- The ideal meeting size is probably around seven to 10 and certainly no more than 15 (formal rules governing the membership of Academic Boards and Senates notwithstanding).
- Meetings are not just time-consuming but very expensive too. Do your participants need to be there the whole time, or simply for a single item?
- If you need information you should ask individuals to prepare a 'position statement' in advance of the meeting, on one to two sides of A4 (max.) in bullet-point format.
- You should ensure that everyone knows what is being discussed and why.

There is nothing so irritating or so unnecessary as for individuals to be asked to assemble in ignorance of the matter at hand. It not only guarantees a 'cold start' to any meeting but also limits the potential contribution of participants from the outset.

3 Prepare

- Draw up a logical agenda and circulate (with papers) in good time, i.e. at least 48 hours in advance.
- Schedule the most important, difficult or contentious items first to catch people when they are fresh.
- Try and save a 'high-note' item for the end to send people away in an up-beat mood. (Or in the event that the meeting does not go well you should at least be prepared to thank participants for their honesty.)
- Do not permit 'any other business' (AOB) – other than important announcements – unless it is cleared with you before the meeting. Otherwise you run the risk your meeting will be hijacked. It also encourages sloppy practices and time wasting. To give of their best, participants need to be forewarned of an issue, not confronted with it 'on the spot'.

Estimate the length of the meeting – up to one hour preferably, certainly no more than two – and allocate time for each item on the basis of its importance. Some Chairs also advertise this time limit for each item, though it is a practice that can backfire as it leaves you open to challenge – for being presumptive, manipulative, etc. – which itself precipitates yet more time wasting. A more prudent course of action is to set a time limit for the meeting as a whole and to start the meeting at an unorthodox time – at a quarter to or a quarter past the hour rather than on the hour. That way you convey the message to participants that time is important to you and also to them.

Determine and establish the most suitable physical setting for the meeting. It may seem self-evident that the actual layout and configuration of the meeting rooms can make a critical difference, yet it is surprising how often in practice this is left simply to chance – typically an inheritance from the room's former occupants. You should be proactive in this matter. Ideally you should hold your meetings in a convenient place in surroundings that are reasonably comfortable (but not too comfortable!) and arrange the seating in such a way that you have a clear view of everyone and they in turn have one of you and of everyone else. In other words, you should avoid the political gamesmanship inherent in the meeting configurations of some universities – the raised platform, the 'top table', the 'over-long' rectangle, the elongated tuning fork, the linear ranking and so on. Depending on the circumstance, there may be occasions (e.g. to facilitate group consultation or formal negotiation or team-building, etc.) when you need, or want, to alter the group dynamic. In this case you should consider assigning places to named individuals or alternatively breaking up the collective group into smaller sub-groups organized around different tables (for example, laid out in a circular fashion or, in management parlance, 'cabaret style'). The point is you should consciously reflect on the optimal physical configuration that will help you to realize your meeting's objectives.

During the meeting

You should aim to keep control:

- of the subject under discussion;
- of the people at the meeting.

This is far easier said than done. All your planning and preparation, however, will have been in vain if you fail to do so. Consequently you need to recognize that one of the main reasons why Chairs fail in their duty is due to the inherent contradiction within their role: namely the expectation they should, as Chair, remain uninvolved, disinterested and impartial and suppress the impulse to intervene, even though they invariably have a direct and personal stake in the discussion in hand. In reality few can resist the temptation to participate. Getting involved in the subject matter of a meeting, however, while simultaneously chairing it are two quite different things that simply do not mix.

And it is, of course, the case that some Chairs deliberately choose to ignore this contradiction (often those intent on outright manipulation) while others bask in it (usually those eager to parade their knowledge; the so-called 'sage on the stage') and still others (those who through misunderstanding, lack of self-esteem or other personal shortcoming) flounder on regardless. All these examples of poor practice – of role models not to follow – are familiar to many in HE (see Box 4.12). To avoid joining them you must 'manage this

---

Box 4.12 Chairing meetings: chairs we have endured . . . role models *not* to follow

- **The pedant**   Sticks to the script and nothing but the script. A stickler for protocols and obsessive about procedures rather than the process. Can't see the wood from the trees and doesn't let others in who can.
- **The 'populist pretender'**   A dedicated follower of fashion: unstintingly politically correct. Poses as 'man of the people' yet support for social inclusion and mass participation does not extend to those around the table. Speaks 'left of centre', acts well to the right.
- **The philosophizer**   Conducts a meeting as if it were a tutorial. Takes (academic) 'heart on sleeve' very seriously. Boldly goes where few have gone before. An interesting and diversionary journey which never arrives at a destination.
- **The 'fat controller'**   Often well-meaning but has not graduated beyond traditional pedagogic style. Applies a didactic approach which yields predictable outcomes: apathy, boredom and non-engagement on the part of the majority.
- **The benevolent dictator**   A charming and engaging character who leaves nothing to chance. Has it all 'done and dusted' beforehand, presents the group with a fait accompli and lines up the troops accordingly.
- **The dictator**   As above though without the style, wit, grace or charm. An unadorned bully.
- **The functioning cipher**   Suffers from a distorted perception of corporate responsibility. Acts as a cipher for a higher authority. Abrogates responsibility for any decision or action. Adds nothing, contributes nothing and alienates everyone.
- **The 'collegio-phile'**   Wants to please all the people all the time. So wedded to – and self-conscious of – the collegiate tradition is paralysed by indecision for fear of upsetting any colleague. More led by the gang than a leader of the gang.

contradiction' in a positive and constructive way. How? By conceiving of your role as that of 'facilitator' rather than 'chair'. These terms are invariably used interchangeably to describe the conduct of meetings yet they are in practice very different types of modus operandi (see Box 4.13).

As facilitator you are more 'a guide by the side' and less 'the sage on the stage'. This is not to say, however, that you have to deny any interest in the issues at stake, or have to adopt a laissez-faire approach to proceedings. On the contrary, you are there as 'custodian of the process', to guide the meeting in an informed and transparent manner. Thus, for example, you don't go into the meeting and say 'What shall we do?' You go in and give a sense of direction; you present the case, outline the alternatives and say 'We can do a, or b, or c – what do you think?' To do otherwise is to abrogate your responsibility (see Box 4.14).

Put another way, it is your duty to:

- first of all, enforce time discipline, so start the meeting on time – 'on the dot'. Make no allowances for latecomers: i.e. start as you mean to go on;
- clarify the objectives at the outset and check that all participants have a shared understanding;
- introduce each topic (the 'what') succinctly by putting it into context and explaining the purpose or objective (the 'how') and outlining the alternatives (the 'means');
- use your 'internal clock' to control the pace of the meeting so that the time allotted is proportionate to the gravity of the issues at hand;
- keep the discussion to the point; ask questions of clarification and summarize at frequent intervals;
- conclude each topic with a summary of what has been agreed or decided;
- conclude the meeting by recapping the actions that have been placed on individuals and checking that all participants have a shared understanding.

These responsibilities are well known but, as we've said earlier, are not necessarily well done. The way in which you have physically configured the meeting should help you in this regard. And while there may be no substitute for experience, there are some

---

Box 4.13 The differences between chairing and facilitating a meeting

The chair system	**The facilitator system**
Chair often has a direct and personal stake	Is impartial, looking only for a successful outcome
Relies on rules and procedures	Is rooted in common sense and courtesy
Identifies each idea with its owner	Uses teams and group dynamics
Calls for immediate valuation of input	Requires deferred judgement
Controls the flow of ideas and inputs	Ensures a free market for contributions
Is commonly rooted in mistrust	Is transparent, with no hidden agendas
Frequently is 'win-lose'	Aims for 'win-win' and consensus
Is open to manipulation	Ensures good behaviour, protects individuals
Underpins the 'sage-on-the-stage'	Offers a 'guide by the side'

Box 4.14 The five stages of decision-taking: the five Cs

As guardian of the decision-making process, you should:
- rehearse by yourself the five different stages involved in the solving of problems and the taking of decisions;*
- be prepared to lead your colleagues through the same process – the five Cs.

1 Consider the issue and clarify the facts	• Don't immediately react to the problem or issue. Take time to think about it. • What is the problem or decision? Have you got all the facts? What additional information do you need? • Who is involved in the problem or decision? • How urgent is it? Must it be done now? What would happen if it were delayed? • Are you dealing with the actual problem or just the symptom? • What is the effect of the problem? What is the real cause? • Why has this situation arisen?
2 Consult with your colleagues	• Use the meeting to draw on the existing experience and skills of your colleagues. • Generate ideas, options, scenarios, alternatives. • Identify the outcome you would like.
3 Commit to a decision	• Summarize the options available to you. • Elaborate the pros and cons of each option. • Make the decision.
4 Communicate the decision	• Take the action you have decided on. • Communicate with all the individuals involved who will be affected by the action – email, voicemail, memo, briefing, 'walk the job'. • Explain the rationale for your decision and the process by which it was reached. • Be assertive in helping to sell the decision.
5 Check and evaluate the implementation	• Monitor that the agreed actions are in fact being carried out. • Has the problem or issue been solved? • How can you avoid it reoccurring? • What have you learned from the process? • How can you pass that knowledge on to others?

In practising the five Cs you will avoid the most common causes of *bad* decision-making:
- complacency
- taking the easy way out
- prejudice.

Note: * Decisions, that is, which require reflection and consultation – not the predictable operational ones which form part of the everyday norm or the ones you need to take in an emergency.

Source: adapted from the Work Foundation, 2006; Adair and Thomas, 2008.

practical guidelines you can follow which will make your task that much easier and your performance as Chair more effective. Seek to establish ground rules for your meetings: e.g. to start and finish on time; no food or drink; no mobile phones; no *Blackberry* emailing; no interruptions and no side-bars when an individual is talking; a three-minute time limit for each speaker, etc.

Just as teachers face the difficult task of individualizing learning in a mass system of HE, so you as Chair must respect, value and foster contributions from all meeting participants. Ideally, all colleagues should feel able – and be encouraged – to contribute in an open, honest and enthusiastic way. As not all colleagues will be so inclined you also need strategies to hand to deal with the many varied and idiosyncratic characters who populate university gatherings (see Box 4.15).

Do stick to a systematic approach to discussion – specify the issue or proposition; produce or hear the evidence; hear the arguments for and against; summarize the arguments; come to a conclusion or verdict; decide and record what action to take.

Box 4.15 Chairing meetings: contributors you will recognize . . . and must handle

- **The rustler**   Always has papers ready and prepared for the meeting they've just come from and the meeting they're going to next but never the one they're actually in now! As such, constantly rifles through their material. Pin down quickly and identify papers for them lest distraction persists.
- **Chatterer**   Already thinks they're at the next meeting. Always wants to hold a separate meeting to the one they're actually attending. Shame them into silence by asking their opinion on the item they were not listening to. Remind them of the no side-bars rule.
- **The late arrival**   Usually a recidivist. Do not make any allowances unless justified. Put them 'on the spot' soon after they arrive. They may reform their habit sooner rather than later.
- **The doomsday merchant**   'The department is doomed. The university is doomed. We're all doomed'. Don't necessarily take the interjection seriously. Test out the views of others. Carefully dissect the nature of the issues at hand. Stick strictly to the facts, not opinion.
- **The cynic**   'Who gives a stuff anyway?' Appeal to others to respond. If not forthcoming, then respond yourself but keep it brief. A prolonged dialogue may do more harm than good. Make a mental note to have a one-to-one with the individual within the next three days.
- **The oppressed**   'We've had enough. We can't do anymore'. Has full-blown victim complex. Time and energy wholly consumed in worrying. Review workload and agree a customized professional development programme including counselling, if necessary.
- **The Trot**   Wears several hats. Is often engaging in private if menacing in public. Espouses the most radical of political ideologies yet typically practises the most conservative of teaching pedagogies. A revolutionary keen on upholding academic tradition (and preserving their own privileges). Don't let the irony get the better of you. A 'straight bat' is the safest bet.
- **The comedian**   In moderation a terrific aid in facilitating the work of the group; one to cherish. In excess one to muzzle outside the meeting.
- **The old sea dog**   'Been there, seen that, done it and got the t-shirt to prove it.' Often has much to offer – and is willing to – if you can get beneath the world-weariness. Cajole and encourage to give more and do it yet again!
- **The maverick**   A loose cannon in every sense. Nobody's fool, proud and independent and not without influence. Often has much to offer yet too unpredictable. Prime them in advance. Seek out their views beforehand and respect and value their contribution.

- **The barrack-room lawyer** A pedant of the rule-book and champion of 'points of order'. Engage with first time round. Use group members to assert the primacy of the (agreed) process over that of formality and procedure. Don't let them sulk. Bring them back into the fold.
- **The unsung hero** A hidden gem. For whatever reason, too self-effacing by half. Often a fount of wisdom and an invaluable source of new ideas. Sees things others don't, including you. Nurture and encourage at every opportunity.
- **The MBO** 'Master of the Bleedin' Obvious'. Invariably means well but has the irritating habit of reiterating what everyone knows already. Can be an asset when you and others have 'lost the plot'; otherwise interject without giving offence, summarize and move on.
- **The 'tribune of the people'** A class warrior with mono-maniac tendencies. Is only too willing to let you know they've got 'your number'. Don't rise to the bait but do show you're not 'just another suit'. Make a genuine effort to get them to make the valuable contribution of which their commitment shows they are capable.
- **The oracle** A loyal pillar of the institution, touchstone of the department and a fount of stories, gossip and myths about the past. Knows where you've been and how you got there. Respect and value their contribution and they will more often than not be a godsend in times of change.

Unite the group

- Be open, honest and enthusiastic yourself. Genuinely aspire to a win-win outcome.
- Be open about acceptable forms of dissent and negativity.
- Do not, however, resort to gimmicks, unless you and your group jointly agree them. And even then, think again about the consequences. The decision by the BBC, for example – like that of an American HEI – to import football's yellow card system into meetings (encouraging participants to wave a yellow card bearing the words 'Cut the Crap, Make it Happen' at anyone perceived to be blocking a good idea) is more symptomatic of a public corporation desperate to change its bureaucratic culture than it is a considered or viable means of achieving change (Snoddy, 2002). This is not to say that such devices are not effective. On the contrary, they can be a very powerful tool for influencing behaviour. However, the risks associated with them are that much greater, for the device is open to abuse and the likely consequences can be as much negative as positive.
- If there is a disproportionate number of procrastinators in your group, schedule your meetings either prior to lunch or towards the end of the day. The desire to get away will often focus people's attention and curb their natural propensity to verbosity.
- Don't be afraid of 'healthy' aggression. Allow others to let off steam, to 'get things off their chest'.
- Do be wary, however, of 'unhealthy' aggression, which invariably leads to 'a stand-off dialogue between the deaf'. In such instances, do not take sides. Remain impartial. Be aware of those who 'withdraw from the group' and seek to bring in others. Ask value-free questions. Stick to facts, not opinions. Never ask an individual for their opinion if they're aggressive.

If the aggression is aimed at you do not feel obliged to respond to every remonstrance. Keep an even temper, even if provoked (if you lose your temper in public, your credibility will suffer too). Stick to the same approach. Remember not everyone will agree or feel comfortable with the aggrieved parties even if it might seem that way. Agree to meet with the aggrieved parties – but not later that same day. Move on to the next business.

Focus the group
- Stay alert. Keep 'a hand on the wheel'. Steer clear of rogue issues and red herrings.
- Be proactive. Keep asking questions. Test the group's understanding.
- Paraphrase the debate and seek approbation. Modify as appropriate.

Mobilize the group
- Protect and draw out the quieter members of the group.
- Do not jump to 'quick fix' instant solutions. Take time to consider the pros and cons of alternatives.
- Check round the group if two or three individuals are dominating the discussion.
- Record suggestions as they're stated.
- Be open to, and build up, ideas, including those you may initially feel are 'wacky'.

Take 'a leaf out of the book' of others
Just as there are some Chairs who set a poor example, there are others who offer a good one. Like the referee of a football match who has a 'good game', these are conspicuous by their apparent absence. Yet they will invariably have done their homework beforehand: by eliciting support for a particular proposal, having others introduce it rather than themselves, and by gaining the confidence of those who might oppose them. During the meeting they always manage to strike the right balance between direction and consultation, have a cat-like sensitivity for those who may feel excluded, and maintain a brisk pace, sound order and good humour throughout, even in the most difficult circumstance. Most importantly, they 'get the job done' by moving beyond the inevitable divisions of opinion towards an agreed plan of action. It is these role models – those who chair seamlessly with such apparent ease – you should seek out in your own institution. Observe them; learn from them; emulate them.

After the meeting

- Reflect and review whether or not the meeting was successful in achieving the set objectives. What went well? What could have gone better? Test your perceptions against the views of others whose opinion you value.
- Double-check and proofread the 'minutes' and circulate them to all participants as soon as practicable after the meeting and no later than three days afterwards.

Minutes in the literal sense – i.e. a detailed summation of arguments and actions – are not always necessary or indeed desirable. They are usually required nowadays only (and not always even then) in the case of formal academic committees. For the purpose of 'business meetings', however, you should focus on producing a brief set of notes with transparent action points. As this is not always so straightforward – and there is indeed a general tendency within universities to underestimate and undervalue minute taking as a skill – be prepared to take advantage of the professional guidance your minute-taker can offer. Fortunately there is now just such a professional cadre of minute-takers in most universities, a legacy for the most part of the demands made on HEIs by external agencies such as the QAA. If your assistant is not one of them you should ensure they are trained in like manner. This small investment will reap you a great dividend.

Most importantly, check that those who are responsible for taking actions:

- actually receive the notes of the meeting;
- do indeed carry out the actions as agreed: you should not let the process simply slide into abeyance but rather monitor their progress (without 'over-managing' them) in implementing the action(s) in accordance with the agreed timescale.

Team building

The ability to schedule, organize and handle meetings in constructive ways which lead to meaningful action is a critical leadership skill, albeit an under-rated one. No matter. Your success in this regard will make a significant contribution to the way in which your department operates. You will need to develop this momentum, however, if your department is to build and realize its collective 'shared vision'. In particular, you need to examine ways in which you can actively and deliberately promote dialogue, collaboration and team working.

Put another way, you must avoid making the same mistake that has ensnared so many other leaders: i.e. assuming (falsely) that you can achieve everything by yourself. Attractive though this proposition may be – and particularly to those of a very self-confident disposition – its adherents invariably share the same tragic fate: total burn-out to no good effect. The simple reality is that much of what we can achieve as leaders can be done only with the help and consent of others. Hence the necessity for collaboration.

This need is particularly difficult to meet, however, in an academic setting rather than the conventional business one. We are all familiar, for example, with the celebrated practices of the lone researcher and the teacher who proclaim 'I am God in the universe as soon as I close the classroom door', as well as with the contention that universities are characterized by a tribal culture rather than a team one – a condition famously reflected in the observation (now a tired cliché) that managing university academics is akin to 'herding cats'. And yet it is equally the case that the nature of teaching and research is evolving – with a shift towards the facilitating rather than the directing of learning; the external assessment of research on the basis of unit rather than individual contributions, etc. – in ways which will necessitate collaborative effort if they are to be fruitful.

Nor is it nearly so alien as traditionalists would have us believe. At Miami University, Ohio, for instance, teamwork is explicitly acknowledged as one of six core values which make up the university's 'Academic Quality Model': a conceptual framework that is applied to all the institution's units – department, division, college and office (see Figure 4.1). Three values drive unit relationships: leadership, mutual trust and teamwork. Leadership entails 'creating a shared vision of a quality culture and modeling behaviors consistent with that philosophy' while trust refers 'to the positive expectations (openness, reliability, caring and competence) between chair and department members'. And teamwork 'enhances collaboration to create synergistic outcomes that surpass the wisdom of individuals'. An additional three values are recognized as guiding individual actions:

Figure 4.1 Academic Quality
Model: Miami University, Ohio

Source: Shulman, 1998.

Academic Quality Model

learner (faculty–staff) empowerment, the acquisition of process improvement skills and a partnerships orientation. Learner empowerment involves 'giving faculty and staff the permission, power and protection to make decisions so that they become involved, self-sufficient, responsible, committed and intrinsically motivated'. Process improvement uses 'objective and subjective data for analysis of the work system and decision-making'. And finally, a partnerships orientation anticipates 'focusing on satisfying the validated needs of people engaged in professional relationships (i.e. internal and external department constituents)' (Shulman, 1998).

How, then, can you develop teamwork as a means of enhancing the effectiveness of your department?

1 Be aware of the language you use

Talking about 'teamwork' in an abstract sense is more than likely to have the opposite effect to the one you wish – a collective mental 'switching off'. Rather, you should regard your role as that of fostering and nurturing a dialogue with colleagues on the concrete matters that collectively face you. Indeed for Senge (1994) 'the discipline of team learning starts with *dialogue*, the capacity of members of a team to suspend assumptions and enter into a genuine "thinking together"'.

You need to help establish an environment in which colleagues feel confident enough to do just that: to discuss their ideas openly, to articulate their assumptions without ridicule, to disagree in a constructive sense, to discover insights not attainable individually: in other words, a setting in which collegiality can genuinely flourish. Again you will need to lead by personal example in this regard in the way you seek to lay the foundations of such an environment, principally, as indicated in the Miami University model, that of trust and, one might also add, mutual respect. The irony of course – and one you should use – is that, far from being an alien business concept, teamwork in its essence is nothing other than the positive aspect of the collegial spirit writ large.

2 Recognize that:

- *Teams are not the same as groups.* While groups may be little more than a collection of individuals who believe themselves to be a group, teams are special in that they manage to accomplish more than the sum total of their individual members. They evolve from groups who have learned to work together skilfully and achieve, in management jargon, 'synergy' or, as it is sometimes expressed, '1+1=3' (because you count the 'plus', which represents the interaction between different people, the 'ones'). In fact, 'a real team' as Jon Katzenbach (1997) puts it is characterized by a 'discipline of team basics', i.e. it is 'a *small number* of people with *complementary skills* who are committed to a *common purpose, performance goals* and an *approach* for which they hold themselves *mutually accountable*'. In other words they can in practice differ from groups in almost every conceivable way (see Box 4.16).
- *It is the differences rather than the similarities between members that is the critical factor in determining team success*: the interplay of different individuals with different ways of behaving and their willingness to undertake a specific role. Meredith Belbin (2003) has, as is well known, demonstrated that effective teams tend to be comprised of eight such role types (see Box 4.17). Put another way – and this is significant in terms of the HE environment – team success is not simply a function of talent and intelligence. Indeed Belbin discovered that the teams managers were predisposed

Box 4.16 Characteristic differences between teams and groups

Activity	Members of groups tend to be . . .	Members of teams tend to be . . .
Dependence	independent	interdependent
Ownership	'hired hands'	owners of the process
Contribution	directed	encouraged
Climate	divisive	trusting
Communication	cautious 'game players'	open and honest
Training	constrained by dominant supervisors	mutually supportive of development
Involvement	individually uninvolved	collectively engaged

Source: based on Maddix, 1998; Fraser and Neville, 1993.

Box 4.17 Belbin's eight individual types who contribute to effective team performance

Type	Team role	Positive qualities	Allowable weaknesses
Chair/ Coordinator	• Coordinates the way the team moves towards group objectives • Makes the best use of team resources • Recognizes team strengths and weaknesses • Maximizes the potential of each team member	• Welcomes all contributions on their merit • Strong sense of objectives	• Is unlikely to be the most creative member of the team
Shaper	• Shapes the way in which team effort is channelled • Directs attention to the setting of objectives and priorities • Seeks to impose a shape or pattern on group discussions and outcomes	• Drive and a readiness to challenge inertia, ineffectiveness, complacency and self-deception	• Prone to provocation, irritation and impatience
Plant	• Advances new ideas and strategies • Pays special attention to major issues • Creative approach to problem-solving	• Imagination, intellect, knowledge	• Inclined to disregard practical details or protocol
Resource/ Investigate	• Explores and reports on ideas and developments outside the team • Creates external contacts	• Capacity for contacting people and exploring anything new • Ability to respond to challenge	• Loses interest once the initial fascination has passed

Role			
Monitor/ Evaluator	• Analyses problems, evaluates ideas and suggestions • Enables team to take balanced decisions	• Judgement, discretion, hard-headedness	• May lack inspiration and ability to motivate others
Implementer	• Turns concepts and plans into practical working procedures • Carries out agreed plans systematically and efficiently	• Organizing ability, practical common sense • Self-discipline, hard-working	• Lack of flexibility, unresponsive to new or unproven ideas
Team worker	• Supports team members in their strengths • Builds on suggestions • Compensates for team members' shortcomings • Improves communication between members	• Ability to respond to people and situations • Promotes team spirit	• May be indecisive at moments of crisis
Finisher	• Ensures nothing has been overlooked • Checks details • Maintains a sense of urgency	• Capacity for follow-through • Perfectionism	• Tendency to worry about small things • Reluctant to let go

Source: adapted from Belbin, 2003, 2008.

to select (invariably the cleverest and most talented people they could find) were, in fact, the ones most likely to fail in practice!

- *Teams are not static but have their own internal dynamic.* They typically evolve through four different stages of development – forming, storming, norming and performing – each with its own distinctive characteristics which will require you to adapt your leadership style accordingly (see Box 4.18).

Team performance is often hampered by the persistence of a number of enduring myths:

- *Myth: a team should function as a team whenever it meets.* This myth suggests that every task to be tackled, no matter how routine, should automatically qualify as a team opportunity. In practice, routine matters are better handled by meeting as a working group, and teamwork reserved for the tougher, more challenging activities.
- *Myth: teams need to spend more time together building consensus.* This myth assumes that building consensus is synonymous with reducing conflict and that less conflict will somehow lead to more team-like behaviour. In practice, real teams do not avoid (constructive) conflict – they thrive on it. Nor is it always the case that decisions built on consensus are necessarily better than those handed down by individuals.
- *Myth: teamwork will automatically lead to improved team performance.* This myth assumes that by focusing solely on the four Cs of effective teamwork – communication, cooperation, collaboration and compromise – an improvement in team performance is guaranteed to follow. In reality teamwork and team performance are two different things and the latter will only be achieved if team members are equally rigorous in applying the 'discipline of team basics'.
- *Myth: teams composed of the 'brightest and the best' will inevitably outperform any other.* Or, put another way, assuming that those immediately around you have the necessary requisite skills to be an effective top-performing team. This is simply not always the case – not even for senior management teams and so-called 'top teams'. See Belbin (2003, 2008).

3 Consider your options carefully

Whether you are starting from scratch or have inherited an existing group of individuals *you should consider your options carefully.* Teams go by a variety of different names according to their various purposes and goals.

One common way forward is to collectively bring together as a departmental management team those you intend holding one-to-ones with on a regular basis, i.e. those individuals with significant responsibilities.

Another – the optimum size of teams as 6–10 members notwithstanding – is to conceive of your whole department as a team.

And still another is to identify and establish a variety of single-purpose groups organized around the main challenges facing the department – e.g. a strategic issues group, a departmental policy forum, a learner experience set, a commercial development group, a research and innovation body, a quality circle, etc. – and then staff them on the basis of the range of skills individuals will bring to their respective teams, rather than on the basis of their formal title or position.

Box 4.18 Moving through the four stages of team development

Characteristic behaviours:

Stage 1: Forming
- Attempts to define the task and decide how it will be accomplished
- Attempts to determine acceptable group behaviour
- Attempts to determine how to deal with problems
- Decisions on information to be gathered to solve a problem
- Abstract discussions of concepts and issues, and for some, impatience with such discussions and a desire to get on with the task in hand
- Discussions of symptoms or problems not relevant to the task in hand
- Difficulty in identifying relevant problems
- Complaints about the organization and barriers to the task in hand

Stage 2: Storming
- Argument amongst members even when actually agreeing on the real issues
- Defensiveness and competition between team members
- The emergence of factions and 'taking sides'
- Questioning everything: 'why should we do it this way?'
- Establishing unrealistic goals
- Concerns about excessive work
- A perceived 'pecking order', leading to disunity, tension and jealousy

Development actions:

Leader's style: Tell
- Get to know and access one another
- Examine the function and purpose of the team
- Look at the skills, knowledge, cohesiveness and balance already present
- Identify the blocks, frustrations and culture
- Don't jump to conclusions too quickly and impose 'instant' changes

Leader's style: Sell
- Debate risky issues
- Consider wider options
- Encourage openness and feedback
- Handle conflict positively
- Remember it takes time to build trust
- Bring in external help if necessary

Box 4.18 continued

Characteristic behaviours:

Stage 3: Norming
- An attempt to achieve harmony by avoiding conflict
- More friendliness, confiding and a sharing of personal problems
- Better discussions and the development of effective team dynamics
- A sense of team cohesion, with a common spirit and goals
- The establishment and maintenance of team ground rules and
- Clearly defined roles
- The establishment of a framework of formal and informal communication

Stage 4: Reforming
- Humour used in a constructive way to progress the task
- Constructive self-change
- The ability to prevent team problems or work through them
- A close attachment to the team
- Accepting responsibility for themselves and for the achievement

Source: adapted from Fraser and Neville, 1993; Turner, 1998.

Development actions:

Leader's style: Participate
- Maintain openness
- Conduct regular team reviews
- Encourage challenges to established ways of doing things
- Celebrate success
- Focus on individual as well as team developments boundaries

Leader's style: Delegate
- Be wary that established methods do not become an end in themselves
- Remember to look outwards
- Nurture creativity

Each of these ways is equally valid and you should not feel obliged to stick rigidly to one or all three. Indeed you should above all aim to be open-minded and flexible in your approach irrespective of the size of your department.

4 Nurture the four Cs of teamwork

You should indeed attend to the basics of effective teamwork by actively seeking to nurture the four Cs (communication, cooperation, collaboration and compromise).

- Agree a team code of conduct such as to:
  respect each member
  criticize ideas, never people
  listen actively
  seek to understand before being understood
  contribute thoughts, feelings and questions
  keep an open mind
  share responsibility
  attend all meetings.
- Undertake formal team-building activities through away-days, retreats and the like. Away-days should keep to the genuine sense of the term – organized sessions held off-site to 'step back' and explore issues over and above the everyday run-of-the-mill – not as they are too frequently (mis-)used nowadays, elongated meetings (held on-site more often than not) and devoted to matters of immediate concern. See the CIPD's portfolio for an extensive range of authenticated activities that you can use in promoting effective teamwork within your own group.
- Establish peer support networks in:
  research – fortnightly or monthly seminars; grant application syndicates; publications workshops – 'brown bag' luncheons to discuss work in progress; outside speakers forum;
  learning and teaching – a peer review of the teaching scheme; a pedagogical innovation workshop; a learning and teaching research seminar; an employers' liaison forum.

5 Pay attention to the composition of your team

You should seek to encourage and increase individual team members' awareness of their team role by analysing the composition of your new or existing or inherited team. One way of doing this is by asking all your team members to complete the questionnaire Belbin devised to identify own team-role preferences (see Fraser and Neville, 1993). This activity is a relatively low-risk one for both individual members and the team in that it is confined to highlighting strengths and 'allowable weaknesses'. There are thus no winners or losers in the analysis.

More than that, it not only satisfies the inherent curiosity of individual members who want to 'see how I come out and how others score in my team' but also yields a most valuable insight on others' self-perception, which in turn typically generates an animated and usually good-natured discussion on the outcomes. It furthermore enables the team to modify its behaviour to compensate for any obvious omissions in its role make-up highlighted by the questionnaire. Thus, for example, the team which struggled to meet deadlines in the past for want of an obvious 'finisher' could formally assign an individual to undertake this responsibility for each task or project as it arises.

That said, there can, of course, be drawbacks to team-role indicators – they are based on subjective perceptions that can lead to stereotyping (as in, 'What do you expect, Colin is a shaper!') and having them all does not automatically guarantee success. Overall, however, Belbin awareness should enable you to heighten both the sense of expectation and responsibility on the part of your individual members while simultaneously enhancing your collective group consciousness.

6 Identify team development needs

You should seek to identify your team's development needs – and to raise your collective group consciousness still further – by reviewing your team's progress along the 'forming–storming–norming–performing' development continuum. This activity, like the previous one, is based on self-perception and self-assessment. Unlike the one above, however, which your team should find relatively straightforward to handle itself, this activity has a greater likelihood of generating a more authentic and reliable outcome if facilitated by an outside party. Therefore you should enlist the services of your management development adviser, or an experienced colleague respected by all your team members, or an external consultant. Whichever, their role would be to tease out your members' perceptions – both individually and collectively – of the functioning and effectiveness of the team.

One simple yet very illuminating way of doing this is to conceive of the team development process as a 'clock-face' – with the undeveloped (forming) team starting at midnight and evolving through the experimenting (storming) and consolidating (norming) stages to reach maturity (the performing team) within 24 hours.

In essence you and your team members should be aiming to:

- identify which stage of development, or 'time on the clock-face', the team is currently at, and to share your views freely with one another;
- identify and explore any issues of concern around the team's development and the *internal* and *external* perceptions of your team;
- explore and identify strategies which can take your team forward to the next stage;
- identify team development needs and how they can be met.

Put another way, this 'team development clock' activity will help bring out perceptions often striking in their contrast which would otherwise remain hidden: differences of view, that is, which are invariably stimulating in themselves and which you can use to enhance the working of your team.

One UK 'new' university, indeed, used this development tool to good effect when it established a new academic structure based on 'schools of study'. In doing so, it identified the characteristics that typified school management teams as they evolved through different stages (see Box 4.19). Can you identify where your team is in this cycle?

7 Review progress regularly

Finally, you should develop the habit of reviewing your team on a regular basis. This practice is as important for teams as it is for individuals. Use the signifiers listed below

Box 4.19 School management team development at one UK 'new' (post-1992) university: characteristic perceptions and behaviours

Undeveloped team
- Unclear objectives, values and guiding principles
- Bureaucracy and lack of informal communication
- Weaknesses covered up
- Poor listening skills
- Workplace is only for work
- Feelings and stress not dealt with
- Role conflict and lack of recognition of individuals' areas of expertise and accountabilities
- No 'rocking the boat'
- Lack of equality in team
- One or more team members seen as outsiders or scapegoats
- Head of school takes most decisions and seen as a strong leader without vulnerabilities

Experimenting team
- Greater openness
- Experimentation and risk-taking
- Increased listening
- Challenging and confronting each other
- Issues of concern debated and grievances aired
- Failure regarded as learning opportunity
- Questioning of problem-solving and decision-making methods
- Review of team performances begins
- Head of school offers high level of facilitation and begins to share her/his own needs

Mature team
- Experimentation *plus* consolidation *plus* flexibility
- Bridges built with other teams inside and outside the school
- Willingness to learn from other teams
- Team leadership changes with the needs of the task
- Experiments with different forms of leadership
- Insularity and a sense of being better or different are resisted
- Team provides enhanced input into meeting wider needs of university
- Team functioning open to external evaluation
- Maximum use of individual and team energy
- Team and individuals are role models and change agents for other school teams
- High levels of support given to each other
- All members contribute equally to the facilitation of continuing team development

Consolidating team
- Agreed procedures and established ground rules by which the team and individual members operate
- Balance of experimentation and methodical working
- Team problem-solving and decision-making skills develop
- Team develops capacity to compensate for individual weaknesses
- Individuals' skills are developed
- Strengths are shared and successes are celebrated
- Team performance and objectives regularly reviewed and improvements implemented
- Increased levels of support given to each other
- Head of school gives moderate level of facilitation and enables other team members to develop facilitative skills

as a checklist to guide the review of your team's performance every quarter. Regular reviews – when combined with your understanding of team development and your support in helping your team to move through the different stages – can have a significant impact on your team's effectiveness (Moores, 1994).

Checklist for reviewing your team's performance:

- Clarity and understanding of roles
- Achievement of the team's objectives
- Openness and confrontation
- Support and trust
- Cooperation and conflict
- Procedures
- Appropriate leadership
- Development of individuals
- Good relationship with other groups
- Good communications (Woodcock, 1989)

Handling conflict

Team building is neither a smooth nor an uncontested process. Not everyone is prepared to help or to give their consent. On the contrary, since people, psychologists tell us, do not really 'change their spots' between home and work – i.e. they bring their 'unseen baggage' with them to work even if they believe they don't – you should not be surprised if emotions run high. Put another way, you need to recognize that conflict is an inevitable corollary of the team-building process. And you must anticipate and prepare to handle it (Fraser and Neville, 1993).

We have already noted that conflict is not without merit: it can be constructive as much as destructive and good teams thrive on it. This is because conflict is used in such a way – as a source of energy and creativity – as to allow new ideas to surface and to create positive forces for innovation and change. Handled constructively, then, conflict enables individuals to examine their ideas and beliefs and to stretch their imagination, thereby providing the team with a wider range of options and the prospect of a more favourable outcome. Conflict is unhealthy, however, when it is either avoided or approached solely on a win/lose basis. Handled destructively in this way, conflict will manifest itself at best in a breakdown in communication and deterioration in mutual trust and support, and at worst in open hostility and revolt. Either outcome would have a deleterious effect on your department, your institution and your own credibility. How then can you avoid such a scenario? How do you handle conflict constructively?

1 *By not being taken off guard. Conflict does not come out of the blue and you should be alert to the early warning signs – silence and withdrawal, anger, dissent and intransigence, escalating to open dispute and meeting walkouts.*

Put another way, by understanding your departmental environment and knowing that conflict arises from individuals' 'unseen' (but often not unknown emotional) 'baggage' – i.e. their differing needs, objectives, values and beliefs; perceptions and motives;

expectations and levels of commitment – you should be able to anticipate the degree to which prospective changes or issues are likely to be contentious and to monitor them. Thus, by knowing how the conflict is developing you will be better equipped to deal with it.

Conversely, if you have a group in which everyone gets on well together and there are no public disagreements you should not delude yourself into thinking you have an effective team. Very often such teams are inhibited by *groupthink* – the reluctance to discuss individual members' ideas openly for fear of upsetting the group consensus. This condition not only may perpetuate poor decision making and low performance, but also may conceal the cumulative build-up of individual frustrations and resentments.

2 *By recognizing there is no single best way of handling conflict; or that the alternatives are limited solely to fight or flight. There are in fact five different ways in which we can approach conflict*:

Non-confrontational strategies
- Avoiding: 'leave well enough alone'
- Accommodating: 'kill your enemies with kindness'

Control strategies
- Competing: 'might makes right'

Solution-oriented strategies
- Collaborating: 'two heads are better than one'
- Compromising: 'split the difference'

Each of us is capable of all five conflict-handling modes (Thomas and Kilmann, 2002). Their effectiveness, however, is of course dependent both on the circumstances and the skill with which they are applied. You need to ensure therefore that – since all five are useful in some situations – *you select the 'right' mode to fit the particular requirements of the conflict situation* (see Box 4.20).

Knowing *when* and *where* to apply it is one thing. *Doing* it, however, is quite another. Each of us, for example, has our own set of social skills, our different predispositions and our preferred ways of handling discord. You need to recognize that these may lead you to rely upon some approaches more, or less, than you should. You may use them, that is, in situations which do not warrant it while neglecting other approaches which would be better suited. Taken too far, your predisposition could well have adverse consequences. Box 4.21 helps you to identify the potential dangers and the associated risks which you must counter. Again you should take heart; these warning signs and risks are not insurmountable – for they are a legacy of the styles you've learned or failed to learn in the past. There is no reason why you cannot develop new ones.

3 *Through the adoption of an assertive rather than an aggressive or non-confrontational approach in those instances (i.e. the great majority which you will have to contend) in which your goal is conflict resolution.*

You should recognize that while there may be occasions when it is best to let things go (why risk losing the war for the sake of a minor battle?) and others where prudence

Box 4.20 The five ways to handle conflict and when to use them

Style	Conflict management approach you should apply it	Characteristic context: the circumstances in which	Assessment
1 Competing *'I win, you lose'*	• Assertive and uncooperative • Must win at all costs • Entails 'standing up for your rights' • Defending a position which you believe is correct	• When quick, decisive action is vital, e.g. in emergencies • On important issues where unpopular courses of action need implementing; e.g. discipline, cost-cutting, enforcing unpopular rules • On issues vital to the organization's welfare, and when you know you are right • To protect yourself against people who take advantage of non-competitive behaviour	• A power-oriented mode you should be careful in using • Are the benefits worth the cost, possibly in lost goodwill?
2 Accommodating *'I lose, you win'*	• Unassertive and cooperative (the opposite of competing) • Agreeable to others at the expense of oneself • Entails selfless generosity • Yielding to another's point of view when you would prefer not to	• When you realize that you are wrong – to allow a better position to be heard, to learn from others and to show that you are reasonable • When issues are more important to others than to you – to satisfy others and maintain cooperation • To build up social credits for later issues • To minimize loss when you are outmatched and losing • When preserving harmony and avoiding disruption are especially important • To help other develop by learning from mistakes	• Not a good strategy if used out of fear or with reluctance • Good if the issue is more important to the other person than to you and you want to show goodwill
3 Avoiding *'I lose, you lose'*	• Unassertive and uncooperative • Does not address the conflict • Entails sidestepping or postponing an issue, or simply withdrawing	• When an issue is trivial, or more important issues are pressing • When you perceive no chance of satisfying your concerns • When potential disruption outweighs the benefits of resolution	• Fine to use when the issue is unimportant, but wrong if burying it stores up long-term trouble

Style	Characteristics	When to use	Comments
		• To let people cool down and regain perspective • When gathering more information outweighs the advantages of an immediate decision • When others can resolve the conflict more effectively • When the issues seems tangential or symptomatic of another more basic issue	
4 Collaborating *'I win, you win'*	• Assertive and cooperative (the opposite of avoiding) • Working with others for mutual gain • Entails digging into an issue, exploring disagreements, learning from one another and searching for creative solutions	• To find an integrative solution when both sets of concerns are too important to be compromised • When your objective is to learn – e.g. to test your assumptions; understand the views of others • To merge insights from people with different perspectives • To gain commitment by incorporating others' concerns into a consensual decision • To work through hard feelings which have interfered with an interpersonal relationship	• Overcoming hard feelings and assimilating different concerns and perspectives could lead to a superior solution when commitment to that is important • It is not a good approach, however, when time is urgent
5 Compromising *'I win and maybe let you win more'*	• Intermediate in both assertiveness and cooperativeness • A middle ground between competing and accommodating • Entails seeking an expedient, mutually acceptable solution which partially satisfies both parties	• When goals are moderately important, but not worth the effort or potential disruption of more assertive modes • When two opponents with equal power are strongly committed to mutually exclusive goals – as in management–trade union bargaining • To achieve temporary settlements to complex issues • To arrive at expedient solutions under time pressure • As a back-up mode when collaboration or competition fails to be successful	• This is not as good as many would have us believe. Both parties can be unhappy at giving up something • Decisions are fuzzy

Source: adapted from Thomas and Kilmann, 2002.

Box 4.21 Potential risks of your own preferred style of handling conflict

Style	Questions you should ask yourself if you rely on this approach *more or less than you should*	Risk
1 Competing		
If *more:*	Are you surrounded by 'yes' *men*? Do colleagues find it difficult to confess ignorance and uncertainties to you?	You close yourself off from vital information. You fail to help those around you to learn.
If *less:*	Do you often feel impotent in situations? Do you find it hard to take a firm stand, even when you see the need?	You restrict your influence unnecessarily. You exacerbate the suffering and resentment of others.
2 Accommodating		
If *more:*	Do you feel your ideas and concerns do not receive the attention they deserve? Do staff have a casual approach to fulfilling obligations?	You lose influence, respect and recognition within the department. You lose the respect of other stakeholders.
If *less:*	Do you find it difficult to build up goodwill with colleagues? Do colleagues consider you to be unreasonable?	You miss opportunities which are important to others, if not yourself. You will not be able to garner support when you need it most.
3 Avoiding		
If *more:*	Do others complain about getting your inputs on issues? Is your coordination impaired as a consequence? Does it often seem that others are 'walking on eggshells'? Are decisions on important issues made by accident rather than design?	You become a 'lame duck'. You ignore issues that urgently need addressing. You end up with a poor decision and maybe the wrong one.
If *less:*	Do you often find yourself stirring up hostility in others? Do you often feel swamped by a number of competing issues?	You stoke up unnecessary conflict through your lack of discretion. You fail to prioritize what is really important.

4 Collaborating

If *more*:

- Do you devote a disproportionate amount of time and effort to issues that do not warrant it?
- Is your collaborative behaviour failing to elicit a collaborative response from others?

- You waste your most precious resources – time and energy.
- You may be overlooking some cues – defensiveness, impatience, conflict, competition.
- You are being unduly pessimistic.
- You will not establish 'ownership' if their concerns are not addressed.

If *less*:

- Do you find it difficult to see differences as opportunities for mutual gain?
- Are your colleagues uncommitted to departmental decisions and policies?

5 Compromising

If *more*:

- Do you focus so much upon the practicalities and tactics of compromise that you sometimes lose sight of the 'bigger picture' – principles, values, objectives, institutional welfare?
- Is the emphasis on bargaining and negotiating creating a cynical climate of gamesmanship?

- You compromise your own position.

If *less*:

- Are you embarrassed or too sensitive in bargaining situations to be effective?
- Do you find it difficult to make concessions?

- You sacrifice the merits of the issues being discussed.
- You lose an opportunity you can ill afford.
- You make a 'rod for your own back'.

Source: adapted from Thomas and Kilmann, 2002.

is the most appropriate course of action (is the benefit really worth the amount of hassle?) the option that offers the greatest potential is that of facing the conflict rather than avoiding it or diffusing it. How you face it though makes all the difference. Tackling it aggressively – by exaggerating your case, belittling and interrupting the other party, dogmatically refusing to make concessions and so on – may well reap you dividends but the effect will not be lasting, and you are more than likely to alienate your colleagues. Handling it assertively, on the other hand, offers you not only the best prospect of resolving the conflict but also one which may benefit all.

Managing conflict assertively means you should seek to do the following:

Examine the cause
- Work with the other parties.
- Attack the problem, not the people.
- Allow others to 'let off steam'.
- Listen actively, show you understand their views.
- Value openness.

Clarify expectations
- Focus on interests and compatible areas.
- List interests.
- Ask questions, don't make statements.
- Encourage questions.
- Be hard on the problem, not the people.

Develop options for mutual gain
- Divide the problem into smaller and more manageable units.
- Agree on common areas of interest.
- Clarify remaining areas of disagreement.
- Look for new ways or thoughts; brainstorm; generate new ideas.
- Ask for members' preferences.
- Involve other parties (if helpful).

Agree a course of action
- Relate the problem to your work objectives.
- Ask for members' solutions.
- Present your preferred solution.
- Agree joint actions.
- Explore ways of avoiding repetition of conflict.

All this, of course, sounds fine in theory but will be harder to achieve in practice, particularly so since our reasoning is strongly affected by our emotions and most of us find it difficult to be completely rational when dealing with conflict. Nevertheless, provided you have, or are prepared to develop, the necessary advanced interpersonal skills – self-awareness, strong listening and observational skills, empathy and a fundamental belief that the other person's point of view may be right – as well as the ability to 'read situations' – you are, or will be, well equipped to achieve control in conflict situations. Acquiring and maintaining such skills and applying the most appropriate conflict-handling mode will not be easy. And you may well need professional training to help you. Either way, there is no reason why, with practice and growing confidence, you should not succeed, or be denied the satisfaction that conflict resolution can bring – a job well done.

5 Managing for high performance

It is immoral to misuse people, under-use them and abuse them but it is highly moral to call forth and make use of the talents that are in people. It is also certain that people will not use their gifts to the benefit of the organization unless they are treated as people with all the needs that people have.

St Thomas Aquinas, thirteenth century

While Marx wrote of the horrifying intensification of the working day, most university managers are, unfortunately, pre-Marxist – they only know how to flog the horse.

UK regional union official, December 2000

'The University recognizes that its staff are its most valuable resource and the key to the achievement of the Strategic Plan and all its objectives'. 'But for the contribution of our staff the University would not have established the reputation it enjoys today'. 'The staff of the University are our greatest asset.' We have all read or heard these familiar refrains many times over. In many staff, though, they raise a hollow laugh – not simply because such claims have become virtual clichés but rather because of the glaring mismatch these staff perceive in their daily lives between what their institution says and what it does in practice. To them, and they do appear to be in the majority, universities have an enormous credibility gap to fill, for as employers they do not seem to act or behave in a way that suggests they actually believe in what they claim. And for that, staff, quite rightly, hold management directly accountable. Indeed the degree of staff dissatisfaction and alienation is such that one national survey in 2007 found that university staff had the worst perceptions of their managers of any employment sector. More than half of university employees considered their managers were reactive (53 per cent), secretive (52 per cent) and inconsistent (51 per cent) compared with 40 per cent, 42 per cent and 40 per cent respectively in the private sector (Newman, 2008a). This outcome is consistent with a similar survey carried out five years previously, in which more than half of employees considered the management of their institutions to be either 'poor' or 'mostly unreasonable' (NATFHE, 2002).

Only the foolhardy and the unreflective would dismiss this scale of criticism as just so much whingeing. The shame, as well as the irony, of course – as the private sector readily acknowledges – is that it is indeed people who make all the difference. In management parlance, the quality of a company's people is the only significant strategic variable for any enterprise. It is their contribution that most affects bottom-line performance. The surprise is that it has taken the university sector so long, not to acknowledge it, but rather to recognize and act on it. The UK Bett Report (1999) on pay and conditions in HE still felt it necessary – as late as 1999 – to recommend that 'the management of people should be given greater priority at all levels of the HE system'. Not before time, UK universities have finally put in place a strategic framework for enhancing and developing leadership and management in higher education, with the 2003 White Paper paving the way for the creation of the Leadership Foundation for Higher Education. Committed to a vision of world-class practice in leadership, governance and management, the LFHE has sought to develop individual leaders, build institutional capacity, nurture networks and communities of learning, commission applied research and disseminate and champion good practice to burgeoning effect (LFHE, 2003; 2007).

This initiative notwithstanding, you should be under no illusion that managing the staff in your department – motivating them, developing their competence, improving their performance, realizing their potential, and maximizing their contribution – constitutes your biggest challenge. It is at the heart of your responsibilities as head. The challenge is particularly tough not simply because of the degree of internal malaise we noted, which you may well have to overcome, but also because of the peculiar character of the academic world in which you have to operate: the penchant for peer review and collaborative decision making; the autonomy of the individual scholar; the precedence of subject over institutional loyalty; the strength of tradition; the cult of the 'expert' and so on.

More than that, you will be expected, quite rightly, to 'value diversity': to establish an environment based on trust and mutual respect, one in which everyone can, and is encouraged to, play their full part irrespective of their gender, age, background, race, disability or sexual orientation. This is a matter that universities, at least in the UK, have not, to date, grasped – as the enduring pay inequalities and under-representation within the professoriate testify – with the conviction that their stakeholders are entitled to expect.

Finally, as well as the 'equality challenge', you will also have to contend with a setting in which management is at best regarded as inessential or intrusive and at worse discredited, or simply predictable and unimaginative. How then are you to rise to these challenges? The purpose of this chapter and the two that follow is to help you do just that. It seeks to demonstrate how you can establish and sustain high performance within your department. In doing so, it explains how you can and should manage staff performance; motivate staff; develop staff; and recruit staff as well as celebrate and lead for diversity.

Managing staff performance

Managing staff performance is demanding even in the best of circumstances. You could be forgiven for thinking it is doubly so in the unfavourable climate which prevails in so many academic institutions. And it remains one of the most enduring and contentious issues for those working both inside and outside the HE sector. To many academic staff, their experience to date of institutional attempts to guide and support academic work – principally through staff appraisal – has made many of them dismissive, if not contemptuous, of such initiatives. Indeed, staff frequently perceive them (and not always unreasonably) as an unwelcome intrusion on their academic freedom, a barrier to their creativity and freedom, a 'dumbing-down' of their expertise or simply (and maddeningly) as yet another example of bureaucracy at its worst – just so much time-consuming form filling.

To many outsiders, however, academia seems content to remain an unreformed and unaccountable bastion of privilege out of tune with other public sector professional groups, one in which the penchant for form-filling takes precedence over the quest for genuine performance improvement, and in which under-performance is too frequently tolerated by managers who themselves end up under-performing in the process (Kellaway, 2006; Murlis and Hartle, 1996; Tahir, 2008). As far as governments are concerned there is a common consensus that this issue is a priority that must be addressed. In the UK for instance, HEFCE (2001c) – as part of the government's public sector modernization programme – made additional resources available to universities for the first time in summer 2001 specifically to enable them to reward and develop staff. Such funding was contingent on universities developing their own Human Resources strategies. And these strategies in turn were expected to make provision for 'regular reviews of all staff, based on open and objective criteria with rewards connected to the performance of individuals including where appropriate their contribution to teams'. They were further expected to explain how the university intended to tackle instances of poor performance.

It is likely, then, that you will find yourself in a setting where you will be required to both contribute to, as well as implement, your university's HR strategy and more specifically the performance management dimension of it. To meet this challenge you will, as has been suggested, need to prepare yourself for a long and difficult haul ahead. More than that, self-evidently, you will also need to fully understand the principles of performance management and how to apply them. This, however, is not straightforward for the concept in practice has itself been the source of much confusion, misunderstanding and indeed rancour in academic environments. Let us begin by clarifying and specifying what exactly is meant when you're asked to undertake 'performance management'.

What is performance management?

A commonplace practice outside the public sector, performance management is a relatively novel phenomenon within higher education. Simply put, it is basically a method of connecting organizational objectives to the people who are there to carry them out. Or as Michael Armstrong (2001) defines it: 'performance management is a strategic and integrated approach to developing the capabilities of individuals and teams in order to increase organizational effectiveness'. It is, in fact, the latest in a long line of attempts – people approaches, work process approaches, management by objectives (MBO), staff appraisal, etc. – to devise the perfect management technique. Where it differs from its predecessors is in its:

- focus – prospective rather than retrospective;
- scope – holistic rather than limited;
- application – tailored rather than packaged;
- emphasis – support rather than control.

Indeed, performance management has itself evolved over the last decade. Where once it was regarded as a top-down monolithic appraisal system driven by HR departments, it is more likely nowadays to be a flexible supportive process owned by line managers (Armstrong, 2006a; Armstrong and Baron, 1998). Such has been the shift then, it is not surprising that the term has generated so much misunderstanding. In essence, performance management has evolved:

from (an emphasis on)	*to* (an emphasis on)
systems	processes
appraisal	joint review
outputs	outputs and inputs
performance-related pay	development
ratings	fewer ratings
the top-down	360-degree feedback
direction	support
the monolithic	flexibility
ownership by HR	ownership by line managers.

Either way, the concept is perhaps more accurately termed 'performance and development management' (Armstrong, 2001), for it is essentially about:

- personal development;
- continuous improvement;
- dialogue, support and agreement;
- teams as well as individuals;
- managing performance *throughout the year*;
- managing the organization.

Performance management then is most definitely *not* just about:

- pay
- direction and control
- poor performance
- individuals
- form-filling
- going through the motions.

Principles of performance management

Putting the above together, we can identify a number of key principles which characterize effective performance management.

1 Effective organizations need effective performance management

Or, put the other way, organizational effectiveness is not possible without performance management. That is why we have it; among other things to:

- facilitate the integration of individual and organizational objectives and values;
- develop a performance-orientated culture;
- identify and meet individual development needs;
- identify those with potential;
- identify poor performers;
- provide a basis for valuing people;
- improve the quality of management.

2 Performance management is concerned with performance across the entire range from A (poor) to Z (excellent)

It is not – as is often perceived – simply a device to deal with difficult people at point A of the scale. Nor is it something to hit people with when they are down. Rather it is about identifying standards of performance and understanding where your staff are located across the range.

3 Effective performance management is critically dependent on the manager's ability to deliver

Managers should not only have an open and honest management style but should also provide support and direction through:

- having a thorough understanding of their institutional strategy and the 'big picture' and being wary of any assumptions they may hold about their staff's interest in such matters before engaging with them on such issues;
- recognizing that appraisal is not about supervision but is more concerned with helping individuals set strategic goals for themselves that are consistent with those of the organization.

4 Performance management is a cyclical process centred on learning and development – not a fixed one-off event

Performance management does not just happen, as is often – and wrongly – assumed, at an annual event set up for the purpose. Formal appraisal is but a single aspect of the process. At heart, performance management is about learning and development: i.e. a continuous and ongoing activity. And as such it is one which – like all the best learning experiences – is more effective if it is planned in advance, experienced, reviewed and evaluated on a regular basis, thus emulating and reinforcing the 'learning cycle' (Honey and Mumford, 1995). A critical aspect of the learning cycle, of course, is that of feedback on progress and achievement. And in this respect staff are no different from students. We all need high-quality, regular feedback if we are to develop. Indeed conventional wisdom tells us that any feedback – even if it is negative – is better than none at all. Managers, then, not only need to be particularly skilled in this regard, they must also (stop making excuses and) seek every opportunity to provide feedback to staff – to make it in fact an everyday feature of working life.

5 Performance management is about how we manage people

Performance management is a natural process of management – it's not 'a system'. It goes to the heart of how an organization views its employees. This may not necessarily entail following 'best practice' per se but rather 'doing what we deem is best for us'. Either way, the focus will or should invariably be on changing behaviour, not paperwork, and on the process rather than 'the system', to help the organization get to where it wants to be in its performance culture. Performance management works best and succeeds most when it is aligned with the climate, culture, values and aspirations of the organization – when it complements, that is, 'the way we do things round here'. It invariably fails, however, if it is perceived to be (as has so often been the case in many organizations including universities) an artificial implant grafted on to the existing order of things.

6 Good processes alone cannot deliver good performance management – only you can

It may seem perverse but it is not unknown for organizations to have excellent paper systems yet to exhibit no demonstrable improvement in performance, and for those without such systems to demonstrate appreciable achievement in performance management. On the contrary, it is very often the case in practice, and herein lies the danger inherent in HEFCE requirements, that accountability may not only bureaucratize the process but also yield no appreciable gain. You should not, however, let the 'dead hand' of compliance distract you from your goal. You should aim to exceed, and not be confined by, HEFCE guidelines. And your university will, in view of the far greater competitive environment in which we now all operate, certainly want you to do so.

Implementing performance management

Viewed in this way, then, there is no compelling reason why performance management cannot operate in a university environment. Indeed, far from being an alien practice, the principles on which it is based are central to the values that underpin universities as learning communities. How, though, should you proceed in implementing performance management?

Assess and reflect on your own approach

Performance management, as we've noted, is about consistency and about how we manage people. It should not make you behave any differently therefore from the way you normally function day to day. That said, it is important, in the first instance, that you take time to reflect on your own leadership style and on the assumptions you make about people and human nature. For understanding your own personal perceptions is of critical significance to the way you will approach performance management. On the one hand it raises your consciousness of them (and of the need perhaps to modify or adapt them) and on the other it will alert you – as Douglas McGregor (1960) has convincingly shown – to the danger of self-fulfilling prophecies. Thus, for example, if you believe people are lazy, uninterested in work or responsibility and thus must be pushed and cajoled in order to get anything done (assumptions which McGregor dubs Theory X) you will manage them in a way that is consistent with these assumptions – watch over their shoulders all the time and the like. This behaviour in turn could cause staff to feel that they essentially have little responsibility in their job and lead them to work hard only when you are watching them closely. A self-fulfilling prophecy has thus begun and will be continually reinforced.

The questionnaires in Boxes 5.1 and 5.2 are designed to help you probe and better understand your current predisposition. Box 5.1 enables you in a formal way to measure

---

Box 5.1 Are you a traditional or contemporary leader?

Directions
This is designed to help you better understand the assumptions you make about people and human nature. There are 10 pairs of statements. Assign a weight from 0 to 10 to each statement to show the relative strength of your belief in the statements in each pair. Higher points indicate greater belief in the statement. The points assigned for each item pair must total 10. Answer all items.

1 It's only human nature for people to do as little as they can get away with.   ___ (a)

   When people avoid work, it's usually because their work has been
   deprived of its meaning.   ___ (b)   (10)

2 If faculty/staff have access to any information they want, they tend to
   have better attitudes and behave more responsibly.   ___ (c)

   If faculty/staff have access to more information than they need to do
   their immediate tasks, they will usually misuse it.   ___ (d)   (10)

3 One problem in asking for the ideas of faculty/staff is that their
   perspective is too limited for their suggestions to be of much practical use.   ___(e)

   Asking faculty/staff for their ideas broadens their perspective and results
   in the development of useful suggestions.   ___ (f)   (10)

4 If people don't use much imagination and ingenuity on the job, it's
   probably because relatively few people have much of either.   ___ (g)

   Most people are imaginative and creative but may not show it because
   of limitations imposed by supervision and the job.   ___ (h)   (10)

5 People tend to raise their standards if they are accountable for their own
   behaviour and for correcting their own mistakes.   ___ (i)

People tend to lower their standards if they are not punished for their misbehaviour and mistakes. ___ (j) (10)

6 It's better to give people both good and bad news because most want the whole story, no matter how painful. ___ (k)

It's better to withhold unfavourable news about the university because most faculty/staff really want to hear only the good news. ___ (l) (10)

7 Because a leader is entitled to more respect than those below in the organization, it weakens prestige to admit that a subordinate was right and the leader was wrong. ___ (m)

Because people at all levels are entitled to equal respect, a leader's prestige is increased by admitting that a subordinate was right and the leader was wrong. ___ (n) (10)

8 If you give people enough money, they are less likely to be concerned with such intangibles as responsibility and recognition. ___ (o)

If you give people interesting and challenging work, they are less likely to complain about such things as pay and supplementary benefits. ___ (p) (10)

9 If people are allowed to set their own goals and standards of performance, they tend to set them higher than the Chair would. ___ (q)

If people are allowed to set their own goals and standards of performance, they tend to set them lower than the chair would. ___ (r) (10)

10 The more knowledge and freedom a person has regarding his or her job, the more controls are needed to keep him or her in line. ___ (s)

The more knowledge and freedom a person has regarding his or her job, the fewer controls are needed to ensure satisfactory job performance. ___ (t) (10)

Scoring

To get your scores, add up the points you assigned to the following:

Theory X score = sum of:		Theory Y score = sum of:	
(a)	___	(b)	___
(d)	___	(c)	___
(e)	___	(f)	___
(g)	___	(h)	___
(j)	___	(i)	___
(l)	___	(k)	___
(m)	___	(n)	___
(o)	___	(p)	___
(r)	___	(q)	___
(s)	___	(t)	___
X Total	___	Y Total	___

So which are you? To what extent do you have traditional assumptions about people and human nature and to what degree contemporary? Are you surprised? What are the implications? What changes do you need to make?

Source: Shulman, 1998; adapted from Myers, 1991.

your assumptions about human behaviour against McGregor's Theory X–Theory Y dichotomy wherein Theory Y (McGregor's principle of 'management by integration and self-control') assumes the exact opposite of Theory X: that people want to work, that they enjoy achievement, gain satisfaction from responsibility and are naturally inclined to seek ways of making work a positive experience. Box 5.2 enables you in an informal but no less penetrating way to reflect on how you actually behave in relation to others at work. Taking the results together, you will be able to determine not only whether you favour a traditional or contemporary style of leadership, but also the extent to which you are guilty of what is an allegedly common practice in universities (if the education press is to be believed), that of 'mushroom farming'. Hopefully you will not be guilty of the latter but, if you are, you should take immediate steps to remedy it. You should also reflect on the relative merits of Theories X and Y and how Theory Y (surely the more attractive of the two) has provided the framework on which contemporary notions of continuous quality improvement and individual empowerment have been built. More than that, the process

---

Box 5.2 Are you a mushroom farmer?

The old joke about 'mushroom management' (keeping people in the dark and showering them with manure) isn't really funny when you're the mushroom.

Here is a short list designed to sort out the leaders from the mushroom farmers. So which are you? There are no scores, but it's easy – if you're honest with yourself – to draw your conclusions.

- Do you ensure colleagues are given an adequate induction to the university and your department very shortly after they join?
- Can you honestly say you're doing all you can to develop your colleagues 'on the job'?
- Do you give your colleagues credit for good work with:
  - face-to-face congratulations?
  - written notes after exceptionally good results?
  - telling your own line manager about it?
- Do you know how many children your colleagues have, their ages and personal things about them?
- Could you list the current domestic concerns or causes of celebration amongst your colleagues?
- Do you show favouritism? Do the same people in your department tend to get the mundane tasks?
- When did you last get your team together to discuss progress? Was the session a monologue?
- After reproaching someone, do you appear to forget it and start again, or keep the grudge alive?
- Can you say you give someone a fair hearing before turning them down on an idea or request?
- Are you considered a good listener?
- When did you last send a birthday, seasonal or get well card to a colleague?
- When were you last approached for advice on a strictly personal (non-working) matter?
- When did you last send flowers or anything else to say thank you?
- Are the words 'please' and 'thank you' a regular part of your working vocabulary?
- Finally, can you look yourself in the eye and say that in the past year you have never taken credit for someone else's work or good idea?

of completing the questionnaires should not only reveal how McGregor's conceptualization highlights the inherent complexity of human behaviour, but also confirm how essential it is for you as a department head to be similarly flexible and adaptable in your own leadership behaviour.

Foster staff 'ownership' of their own development: encourage a questioning culture

Performance management has become something of a 'dirty word' in universities over the past decade and not without good reason. Often narrowly conceived as a retrospective 'appraisal scheme', such devices have not surprisingly been regarded by staff as an externally imposed mechanism aimed at controlling them rather than developing them. At best such initiatives have tended to breed staff compliance and defensiveness and at worst open hostility and defiance. Either way, staff invariably bemoan the waste of time taken up by such schemes – to so little effect, a complaint often borne out by managers themselves who, in routinely struggling to complete the necessary paperwork on schedule, tacitly acknowledge by their behaviour that the process is of little or no real value.

It is against this kind of backdrop, then, that you are likely to be expected to operate – and just as likely to be given a 'performance management system' by your university to implement in your department. In doing so, you will need to take positive steps if you are to avoid repeating the mistakes of the past. For example:

- You should ensure you do not get bogged down in the trivia and ritual of your particular institutional scheme. If it is a good scheme, i.e. one based on broad consultation with staff, then this shouldn't happen.
- You should not 'allow the tail to wag the dog'. It is the process not the form that is important.

More importantly still, and also more difficult:

- You need to foster an environment in which performance and development are recognized by staff as *something they do and not something which is done to them by management*. Ideally you should be seeking to establish a setting in which a staff member says to you: 'Here's my personal strategic plan for the year. What do you think of it?'

While it is the case, as we noted before, that you may not be able to 'manage culture' per se, your role is a critical one in influencing it through your leadership and management behaviour. In this instance, as before, you should be seeking to establish an 'open' departmental culture: one which, as Gerard Egan (1995) advises, encourages staff to ask questions about themselves, their role, their needs, their work objectives and their career plans (see Box 5.3).

Conversely you can – and should – also assess the degree to which you are being effective in this regard by putting yourself in the place of each of your colleagues, and completing the survey outlined in Box 5.4. You should then test out the accuracy of your perceptions and assumptions against those of your colleagues directly by burying any embarrassment you may have (which in itself may be an indicator of avoidance or lack

Box 5.3 Performance improvement: questions you and your departmental culture should encourage staff to ask

Objectives	What are the key or strategic things I need to accomplish this year?
Delegation	What authority do I have? How far can I go?
Work plans	What are the best routes to my destination?
Initial training	Do I have the skills to implement these plans and achieve these targets?
Facilitation	What can I expect from my head of department in helping me to achieve them?
Feedback	What kind of feedback can I expect from my head of department? What kind of feedback am I expected to give him/her?
Tracking	What is the best way of monitoring my progress?
Recognition	What kind of recognition can I expect for my accomplishments?
Development	How can I prepare myself to do even bigger and better things in the future?

Source: adapted from Egan, 1995; Armstrong 2006b.

Box 5.4 Measuring your effectiveness in performance management

Put yourself in the place of your colleagues or, better still, invite them to answer the following questions.

What do I get?
1   Do I know what is due to me?
2   Do I have the materials and equipment I need to do my work right?

What do I give?
3   Do I have the opportunity at work to do what I do best every day?
4   Have I received recognition or praise for my work in the last month?
5   Does my head of department seem to care about me as a person?
6   Does my head of department encourage my development?

Do I belong here?
7   Are my opinions valued?
8   Does the university mission make me feel my role is important?
9   Are the colleagues in my department committed to doing quality work?
10   Do I have a best friend at work?

How can we all grow?
11   In the last six months, has my Head of Department talked with me about my progress?
12   This year, have I had the opportunities at work to learn and grow?

Scoring
Award one point for every positive response: 12 Outstanding; 10–11 Very Good; 9 Good; 8 Fair; 7 and below Poor.

Source: based on Buckingham and Coffman, 2001; ACAS, 2008a.

of openness on your part) and inviting a representative sample of them to go through the survey with you.

As this is not – or should not be – an exercise grounded in ignorance, the disparity between your perceptions and the reality of your colleagues' experience should not be that great. (If it is, you should address your 'out-of-touchness' urgently by instigating regular 'surgeries' with your colleagues.) More telling is the extent to which you and – each of them – were able to respond positively to each of the questions – ideally all or not far short of all (10–12). Anything less, and there may be a common difference between you and your colleagues which you need to address, or perhaps there is a variety of different perceptions particular to each individual. Either way, you should respond with urgency.

Identify and specify standards of performance for staff: communicate and disseminate these standards

The controversy over performance management in universities – and the difficulties in implementing it – has not just arisen from differences of a theoretical nature, its legitimacy and appropriateness in such a setting. It also stems from concerns that are innately practical: principally the difficulty in unravelling the 'mystery' of academic work and in particular the very 'private' activity of teaching. Put another way, received wisdom had it that even if the theoretical difficulties concerning performance management were overcome, such is the complexity of academic work that it couldn't be effectively applied in universities anyway.

The reality is more prosaic. HEIs have traditionally not been very good at either clarifying or explaining to staff their expectations of them. In truth, they have not, until recent times, needed to be. But it does not follow from this – the contentious and voluminous debate on what constitutes 'good teaching' (as we will see later) notwithstanding – that it cannot or should not be done. Indeed it is essential this is done, for without it how can we expect individuals to perform to their full potential? In this respect, academics are no different from other professional groups and, like them, need help in determining their targets, charting their progress towards them and developing their careers. It is a fallacy – as well as irresponsible – to assume that it could otherwise be the case. Academics may be autonomous professionals, but they are not going to realize their full potential independently of others, particularly if they do not know what is required of them in the first place. It is incumbent on you, then, to address this deficiency. Good practice (Armstrong, 2006b) tells us that in order to maximize their potential individuals need to know – and it is your responsibility as manager to ensure they do – the following:

Staff need to know	*As a manager you must*
• What is my role? Why do I exist?	Develop the job role.
• Who is my immediate line manager?	Establish accountability.
• What is expected of me?	Specify standards of performance.
• What are the priorities?	Establish SMART targets.
• How am I doing?	Measure and give feedback on performance.
• Where can I go from here?	Identify and resource staff
• How can I get there?	development needs.

In the first instance, you should aim to determine and clarify for staff the standard of performance expected of them, and the key to developing that is through an analysis of their particular job role(s).

Your predecessor or your HR representative may already have undertaken a preliminary analysis of this nature, but you should not be surprised if you have to start from scratch. In all likelihood you will inherit a situation in which academics are on 'general contracts' which have relatively loosely worded terms and conditions of employment: the norm for 'old' universities in the UK where the emphasis is on 'research, teaching and administration' (typically in that order) or 'teaching, scholarship and service', as is often preferred in state universities in the USA. Or they may be on a national professional contract (as is the case in 'new' universities in the UK) where staff can be expected to undertake up to a maximum of 550 hours' formal scheduled teaching, as well as participate in 'research and other forms of scholarly activity, examining, curriculum development, administration and related activities'.

Whatever your context, you are also likely to find some staff with job descriptions and others without – including those who work exclusively in academic administration – and of those that have them many will be out-dated. Either way, you too need to be clear about what you have to do. You need to focus on 'job roles' rather than on 'job descriptions' per se, which so often tend to be little more than a shopping-list of different tasks and duties that are neither exhaustive nor eternal. Unlike job descriptions, job roles are competence-based rather than task-based. They articulate the responsibilities of the role, the competencies which the post-holder will need to fulfil them and the standard of performance (or measure of success) the appointee is expected to achieve; i.e. they provide an objective yard-stick for determining whether performance is at an acceptable level (Erban, 2001).

Job roles are also invaluable in that they provide an objective (or at least much less subjective) basis on which to offer feedback, assess development needs or determine rewards. Indeed, when applied in academic settings, they offer an additional particular benefit in that they open up the possibility (by relying on an evidential base to measure success) for universities, *if they so wish*, to recognize and reward effective teaching on an equal footing with research. The role analysis outlined in Appendix I shows how one UK 'new' university has attempted to define the expectations it has of staff, in this instance principal lecturers (the equivalent of senior lecturers in the 'old' university sector, and of associate professors in the US system). The 'role map' sets out the core competences or key responsibilities pertaining to the role, and identifies the skills, styles and qualities (or competencies) needed to fulfil the role and the criteria of success by which individual performance is measured. (On an explanatory note: competence = the 'what', e.g. typing a letter; and competency = the 'how', i.e. the skills and behaviour needed to type a letter well.) The same university also sought to establish a common professional standard which it expected all academic staff to adhere to, irrespective of status – a basic minimum standard of performance, that is, by which to gauge academic conduct and practice (see Box 5.5).

It is this competence-based approach you need to adopt for the staff roles in your department, and while this may seem a daunting task, breaking it down in stages will make it seem far less so. Better still, you are likely to find it much easier if you attempt this undertaking jointly with your peers in similar roles across the university, aided by

Box 5.5 Code of professional conduct for academic staff in one UK 'new' (post-1992) university

Academic staff are expected to commit to:
1　Doing things on time.
2　Being punctual, courteous, caring.
3　Being available.
4　Taking responsibility for supporting and guiding students' learning.
5　Being properly prepared, including knowing how to use teaching and learning facilities.
6　Preparing materials to time and quality.
7　Continuing own learning.
8　Engaging in intellectual work; scholarly activity; research.
9　Evaluating learning as a means of evaluating teaching.
10　The vision and values of the university.

your HR expert. That way, you should not only achieve a more informed and accurate outcome, but, equally important, one that should also guarantee institutional consistency. Either way, you should first identify the number and variety of roles in your department – demonstrator, technician, lecturer, professor, research fellow, administrative assistant, section head, etc. For each role ask yourself: What is my purpose? Why do I exist? Summarize your answer in a succinct statement or short number of bullet points. For instance, if you think of your own role as, say, a Head of an Academic Department or Dean of Faculty, then it might be defined thus:

Role of dean of faculty
- To develop and implement a strategy for the work of the Faculty, provide academic leadership and manage the Faculty's human and other resources.
- To contribute to the overall academic development of the University.
- To represent the Faculty and the University to the wider community.

Role of head of subject
- To provide subject leadership and with the Dean take responsibility for securing the effective deployment and development of academic staff.
- To take line management responsibility for staff in the subject area.

Next you need to identify the five to six key competences or areas of responsibility for each role. Again, if we use your own as an example these may well include: strategy and policy formulation; academic leadership (in teaching and/or research); budget and resource management; managing staff performance; teamwork; career and professional development. You then need to specify, as illustrated in the principal lecturer example shown in Appendix I, the requisite competencies and success criteria for each of these areas of responsibility. Once they have been specified you need to communicate them accurately, clearly, creatively and assertively – in meetings and briefings, as part of induction and appraisal, as well as through MBWA and documentation: the university's mission, the departmental strategic plan, job roles and so on.

Negotiate and agree SMART (not DUMB) goals and targets with individual staff

You now have an established framework within which to agree specific goals with your staff. Goals are different to standards in that they are negotiable – minimum performance standards are *not*. Goals are concerned with priorities: immediate concerns 'over and above the job'. As such, their emphasis is on individual progress and growth in the role rather than simply routine maintenance matters. In practice, therefore, they tend to accommodate both work and developmental objectives and are as likely to be apportioned to teams as they are to individuals (Moores, 1994; Armstrong, 2006b). In either case, as we noted earlier in discussing your departmental strategy, goals should always be SMART – specific, measurable, achievable, realistic and time-related – and not DUMB – defective, unrealistic, misdirected or bureaucratic.

Put another way, you should aim to:

- identify, negotiate and agree a small number of specific goals (typically no more than six) with each individual or team;
- focus on goals that make a difference – *that will improve performance* and are not just a list of routine or ongoing events;
- make them consistent with your department's and your university's strategic aims;
- quantify the goals and specify the actions (targets) needed to achieve them;
- ensure that they are set in areas within the control of the individual or team;
- ensure they challenge and stretch the team or individual concerned: i.e. they are set neither too low, lest they encourage underachievement relative to potential, nor, just as damaging, too high lest they lead to underachievement relative to others' expectations;
- establish, by staggering deadlines, a realistic timescale for completion while recognizing the need for flexibility should circumstances change;
- ensure that the SMART quest for rigid performance objectives does not hinder you from recognizing ongoing accomplishments by staff in realizing your department's and your university's aspirations (see Box 5.6 for examples of good and bad SMART targets).

While you may know what SMART goals are you still have the tricky business of negotiating them: no easy task given the degree of scepticism which prevails over such matters in so many HEIs. Therefore it is vital that you prepare for your one-to-ones with staff by anticipating and rehearsing the arguments which they might raise against this process, including the perennial ones:

- My role doesn't lend itself to target-setting.
- You are wasting my time requiring me to do irrelevant things.
- Why should I work hard for no extra reward?
- I have had responsibilities passed on to me which are rightly management's, and carried the can too. Why should I do more?
- I have enough on my plate as it is.
- Why is management always changing the goalposts?
- What's the point?

Box 5.6 SMART – and not so *smart* targets

SMART	Not so *smart* targets
Develop, negotiate and agree an admissions compact with three local providers by the end of year.	Establish closer liaison with local schools and colleges.
Establish regular meetings of the Course Team on the first Wednesday of each month beginning in September.	Improve communications with Course Team.
Conduct a SWOT analysis of Personal Development Planning Schemes for students and present three alternative models to the Course Committee for their adoption by the end of semester.	Improve student support.
Identify a dozen local employers and arrange a programme of breakfast seminars on work-related learning and employer involvement in curriculum design and validation. Establish an employer register and enrol six by the end of year.	Improve links with local businesses and employers.
Select one module as a pilot and using Blackboard develop and establish an e-learning infrastructure centred on information (Bulletin Board), learning (a discussion forum) and (formative) assessment for next academic year.	Explore the potential for e-learning.
Organize a focus group of ethnic minority students to evaluate their experience; to report to the Course Committee with findings and recommendations by Xmas.	Improve the minority student experience.
Submit a finished article to one refereed journal of international repute and negotiate and agree a monograph contract with an international publisher by the end of year.	Publish my research findings.

In each case you must be prepared to discuss them openly and honestly with the individual concerned. You should not dismiss such claims out of hand or ride roughshod over them. On the contrary, take the trouble to examine them thoroughly. You may not convince every unbeliever, but probing these assertions invariably unearths more substantive, deep-seated concerns: issues which very often prompt a more meaningful dialogue. You must also not forget that the great majority of people prefer to do a good job and want to do so. And while it is the case that you need to remind them that goals and targets are simply a way of setting sights on the future – and yes, we do live in a world of changing goalposts – it is incumbent on you to be positive: to encourage reflection. One proven method that works well is to ask individuals:

- What do you see as your main accomplishments over the last six months or year?
- How do you see them supporting the strategic aims of the department and the university?

Or alternatively:

- What are the four or five points by which you would recognize whether you've had a good semester or a bad semester?

Either way, the responses are almost invariably couched in relation to the aspirations and modus operandi of the department or university – and as such provide both you and them with the raw material on which to build, shape and agree an appropriate set of SMART targets.

Measuring performance and giving feedback to staff on their performance

Performance improvement is, or should be, a matter of everyday concern. Whether it is or not, of course, is dependent to a large extent on the prevailing mindset within your department. If it is a positive one, then – provided that staff do indeed have targets that are authentically SMART – measuring performance should present no real difficulty. Unfortunately this is rarely the case in practice, and not simply because the everyday expectations and standards of professionalism are not as high as perhaps they should be but rather because of the tardiness with which managers very often approach performance monitoring and staff feedback. This condition, historically at least, has been a characteristic feature of so many academic environments. That is to say, university managers have, on the one hand, too often sought to rely on appraisal as the sole means of measuring staff performance when they need not have done (thereby psychologically allowing 'the tail to wag the dog') and, on the other, have been far too grudging in the manner they have given feedback to staff on their performance. In this respect, ironically, managers are guilty of doing unto staff what staff themselves are ritually accused of doing unto students, namely, failing to offer students feedback on their learning which is clear, accurate and consistent as well as comprehensive. These are errors of omission you should aim not to repeat.

Thus you need to recognize, and should utilize, the multiple ways in which you are able to monitor staff performance. For example:

- collecting specific, concrete data;
- 'number crunching';
- management by walking about;
- engaging in a collaborative endeavour with staff;
- team monitoring;
- one-to-one supervision;
- one-to-one appraisal.

If you do so you will ensure that the dynamics of performance management are prospective rather than retrospective: that performance improvement does indeed become an integral aspect of everyday life and that appraisal becomes the creative (rather than the reactive) process it should be, one in which staff take the lead.

Measuring teaching effectiveness

A critical weakness of performance management in universities in the past has, as we noted earlier, been the perennial difficulty of assessing staff effectiveness in teaching. This deficiency has meant that a large aspect of an academic's work has been not only unevaluated, but also unrecognized and consequently unrewarded. More than that, it has institutionalized the position of teaching as the poor relation of research. Put another way, even if a university was minded to reward teaching and research in an equal fashion, it is argued that the difficulties in demonstrating achievement in teaching compared to that in research (where performance indicators such as research grants, published works in academic journals or books and citations by other authors are relatively easy to document) are such as to thwart all but the most persevering of institutions. Some universities have shown, however, that this need not be the case, that the issue can in fact be tackled afresh in innovative ways.

The University of Ballarat, Victoria, Australia, for example, has sought to 'overcome the old staff tension between teaching and research' by adopting a vision of scholarly life derived from the work of Ernest Boyer. A new, small, regional university, Ballarat has even more unusually sought to apply Boyer's theoretical conception of the four interrelated scholarships – those of teaching, integration, application and discovery – to all aspects of its operation. Thus the university's budget, the activities of university-wide services and schools, and the allocation of job titles and roles are all conceived and measured on the contribution they make towards the integration of the four scholarships.

The same is equally the case for academic staff: that is, they are all obliged to demonstrate they are competent in all four of Boyer's categories, and not simply one or two as is usually the case. This they do through the 'personal development portfolio' they are required to maintain. Essentially a record of professional practice and achievements, the portfolio comprises evidence collected by the individual staff member, including that obtained by 360-degree feedback: self, peer, student and supervisor (Kemmis and Maconachie, 1998).

Arizona State University has likewise adopted an integrative approach to this issue (Krahenbuhl *et al.*, 1998). It has done so by constructing a conceptual model that articulates the full range of faculty activities, one that:

- breaks down the arbitrary boundaries that surround teaching, scholarship and service;
- displays the multiple effects of the specific activities that constitute faculty work;
- provides a visual management tool for allocating differential workloads across and within academic units.

Thus it not only recognizes and caters for the fact that faculty interests, skills and motivation may change from year to year and over the course of a faculty member's career; it also provides department heads with a framework with which to assess their department's (collective staff) contribution to the university's mission on the one hand and that of the individual staff member's role in this process on the other (see Appendix II).

The teaching portfolio

A key driver in the initiatives developed by Arizona State University and the Univerity of Ballarat was the institutional desire in each case to broaden the traditional concept of scholarship to reflect more fully and accurately the true range of tutors' work. Not all universities have gone this far but many nevertheless have sought to promote, principally through the 'teaching portfolio', the documentation of individual staff performance in teaching. It is a trend you would do well to emulate, not simply because such portfolios will indeed provide you with the evidential base by which 'to assess how far individual staff members make sense of, engage with and learn from the professional practice of helping students to learn', but also because of the additional and equally important benefits such systematic documentation, observation and critical reflection would bring in facilitating still further improvements in both the learning of students and the learning of staff. They will also, of course, provide a basis for recognizing, celebrating and rewarding staff excellence in this regard, a theme we will return to in Chapter 8.

Nor does the compilation of such teaching portfolios have to be as difficult as some would have us believe. For, unlike academics, students have no doubts as to what constitutes 'good teaching'. While it is the case we certainly need to recognize that teaching is a dynamic, not a static activity, and encompasses a much broader range of tasks beyond classroom performance (assessment, course design, the production of learning materials, the stimulation and supervision of independent learning and so on) we also should remember that students repeatedly emphasize the same qualities:

- *enthusiasm* for and *knowledge* of the subject matter;
- regular and timely *feedback* for students;
- a capacity to engage students with the mystery and importance of key ideas;
- ability to give a *clear explanation* of these ideas (Martin, 1999).

That said, the portfolios that work best, and deliver most, are those which are premised on this basis: that use criteria, in other words, to tap into and bring out evidence of these qualities (see Box 5.7 for an exemplar).

Giving feedback to staff

The teaching portfolio will enable you to assess aspects of academic work that hitherto may have been undocumented. Your obligation does not end there, however, for there is still the matter of giving staff adequate and proper feedback on their performance: a duty which managers have often been either reluctant, or downright negligent, in undertaking in the past. Why this has been so is largely rooted in the erroneous assumptions which managers make about their staff, for example:

- Staff don't need it, don't want it and wouldn't appreciate it.
- As self-motivated and self-evaluating professionals, academics are best left alone to get on with it.
- Positive feedback will only encourage staff to rest on their laurels.

Box 5.7 The teaching portfolio: bespoke criteria for evaluating teaching*

1 Teaching with the university

(i)	Preparation for teaching	• Clarity of aims, objectives and learning outcomes for each module • Preparation of content, learning materials, IT and visual aids • Estimation of student learning effort needed
(ii)	Quality of actual teaching activity	• Evidence of effectiveness and excellence of: lecturing, small-group work, practicals, fieldwork, project supervision, etc.
(iii)	Value and range of teaching	• Amount of time spent on teaching • Experience of a wide range of teaching, e.g. to a variety of students; sizes of groups; content of intrinsic difficulty; service teaching; interdisciplinary teaching
(iv)	Innovation in teaching	• Evidence of innovations in curriculum/programme design and/or teaching methodology, e.g. resource-based learning; learning through work; e-learning; problem-based learning; 'action learning', etc. • Collaboration in teaching: team teaching, etc. • Innovations of national/international repute in the teaching of the specific subject area • Short-course developments; modular programme developments
(v)	Communication with students	• Evidence of effectiveness in student guidance and counselling; motivating students; the quality of marking and feedback on students' work; interpersonal relationships; availability and accessibility
(vi)	Assessment practices	• Evidence of range of methods of assessment used; innovation in assessment techniques • Congruence of assessment and learning outcomes
(vii)	Evaluation of own teaching	• Systematic and regular reflection on all the above practices • Regular use of peer/student evaluation • Continuing reflection on teaching in relationship to: the overall teaching aims and objectives of the department, and the curriculum on offer as a whole
(viii)	Management of teaching	• Programme leadership: chair of programme committees for curriculum development, quality assurance, student experience, etc. • Responsibilities for learning support • Staff–student liaison role • Learning and Teaching Fellow
(ix)	Teaching scholarship and research	• Evidence of scholarship • Effect of scholarship on teaching • Influence of research on teaching
(x)	Teaching and the world of work	• Benefits from employer contact • Involvement of employers in curriculum design and teaching • Placement of students

2 External activity

(xi)	Invitations to teach elsewhere	• National/international conferences, lectures, seminars
		• Regular teaching visits to other university departments
(xii)	Membership of professional groups and bodies	• Subject-based; teaching-based; interest-specific, e.g. assessment, recording achievement, curriculum development
(xiii)	Professional service to other universities and organizations	• As external examiner; consultant; quality auditor/ quality assessor; subject reviewer/institutional auditor
(xiv)	Publications on teaching	• Critical reflection on teaching approaches; scholarly work and textbooks; compilations of teaching materials; publication of one's own pedagogic research and development; editorial work; refereeing for journals, etc.
(xv)	Teaching grants, contracts and fellowships	• Grants for teaching development work; contracts to provide programmes for other organizations; fellowships awarded

Note * The effectiveness of the teaching portfolio is also dependent, of course, on the effort and commitment that staff put into it. You can help them in this by asking them to reflect on their professional practice using the HEA Professional Recognition Scheme, the HERDSA, 'Challenging Conceptions of Teaching: Some prompts for good practice' or simply by posing the following questions:

- What are you particularly good at in teaching?
- What aspects of your teaching do you still need to work on?
- What interests or excites you in teaching?
- What have you discovered about your teaching?
- What is your philosophy of teaching?
- In what ways have you sought to promote and enhance the student experience: in your professional practice; by influencing the professional practice of others within and beyond your department and institution; in continuing to develop your professional practice?

Sources: adapted from the HEA, 2008; University of Western Australia, 1998; Elton and Partington, 1993.

- The annual appraisal interview is sufficient in itself to keep staff on track.
- Staff know managers have competing demands and do not expect them to waste time giving unnecessary feedback.

The reality of course, as we noted earlier, is the exact opposite. We all need quality feedback on a routine basis if we are to develop, let alone excel, and any feedback, even negative, is better than none at all. It helps us learn from our mistakes, encourages reflection, develops persistence and gives us a sense of making progress. Thus you should regard giving feedback as a critical and not marginal aspect of your role. Nor should you underestimate the impact it will have on the recipient. As such it is a key skill you must master. In the first instance you need to recognize that:

- Feedback can be given in a variety of ways: formally as well as informally, orally as well as in writing.
- Feedback is more effective and constructive if given promptly in the most appropriate way, in public or more likely in private.

- Good performance and achievements (book launch, QAA outcomes, etc.) provide you with many opportunities in which to publicly congratulate staff on their success.

Most feedback, however, takes place one to one in private and it is these encounters you will likely find the most demanding. To get the best out of them you will find they are more constructive – for you, your department and the individual concerned – if you adhere to the following good practice guidelines:

- Be clear what you want to say in advance. Practice in advance if necessary.
- Start with the positive.
- Think of it as a two-way conversation in which you expect to talk for approximately 20 per cent of the time and listen for the remaining 80 per cent.
- Put yourself in the other person's shoes.
- Be open and honest and seek a genuine dialogue.
- Invite reflection and prepare to listen actively.
- Ask open-ended questions: What progress do you feel you've made since we last spoke? What things have gone well – less well? What has helped or hindered you in reaching your targets? What do you still need to do to achieve your goal?
- Acknowledge and recognize the individual's contribution and achievements.
- Always remember *goals* – and how these link with the individual, the department and the university's objectives.
- Be tolerant of emotional outbursts (anger, weeping, etc.) and be prepared to empathize.
- Be specific. Always make your message clear and explicit, whether you are criticizing or praising.
- Always try to combine critical feedback with support, organizational and personal: what help would you like me to offer you?
- Own the feedback: use 'I' not 'you' and no 'third parties'.
- Think behaviour, not person. Never criticize personality. For example, never say 'you are aggressive'. Quote examples instead. 'Some of your behaviours mislead others into believing you are – what can we do about it?' (i.e. always use behaviour as evidence of use or non-use of a competency).
- Think about the impact that *you* have on the situation and take responsibility for your own feelings. Think, too, what the feedback says about you.
- Discuss the causes of problems as well as the symptoms.
- Continuously check that your feedback has been accurately received – clarify, clarify, clarify.
- Be flexible – if an approach is not working then can you change tack? Don't impose solutions; develop options for consideration.
- Always be ready to listen as well as to speak.
- Actively reflect afterwards on how accurately your feedback was received (see Box 5.8) (Boutall, 1997).

Box 5.8 How well do you give feedback?

Ideally you should always score 4 rather than 3. If less than 3, you must make a conscious effort to improve on the next occasion.

The 1-2-3-4 feedback model

1 Complete misunderstanding
- Not listening
- Communication unclear
- Other party does not want to listen

2 Inaccurately or only partially reflecting back
- Partial misunderstanding
- Fuller explanation/greater clarity needed
- Details incorrect

3 Accurately reflecting back
- Listening attentively
- Explaining clearly in own words
- Using own words to feedback

4 Reflecting back more
- The meaning behind the facts
- Clarifying the context
- A shared interpretation
- Engaging with the emotion
- Understanding the 'real point'
- Achieving empathy

Source: adapted from Boutall, 1997; ACAS, 2008a.

Tackling poor performance

> Your organization is only as strong as the weakest member in it.
> Sir John Harvey-Jones

You will quickly find that your success – or lack of it – in monitoring performance and giving feedback becomes apparent in the degree of trust that your colleagues are willing to place in you: that and the way in which they respond to the professional challenges you set them. Not everyone will be alike of course. Ideally we would all want every colleague to be a high achiever who exceeded the standard of performance, and in reality you will probably find that there are indeed many in this position. It is equally likely that you will find a small number who are under-performing: i.e. who fall short of the standard of performance. What should you do?

Resolve to take action

The overwhelming temptation may be to do nothing at all. You could persuade yourself, for instance, that given this matter involves only a small minority, and in the absence of any real pressure either from above or from other departmental colleagues, why should you not turn a blind eye. With everything else you have to do, others would surely understand why you would not want to devote a disproportionate amount of your time and energy to a handful of individuals – besides, the benefits are unlikely to outweigh all the hassle that would be involved.

Nothing in fact could be further from the truth. You would be making a colossal error of judgement if you were to follow this path. For there is only one thing more corrosive of departmental morale than staff under-performance, and that is managers who tolerate it. It may well be unspoken, and it may be unwritten, but it is nearly always the case that everyone knows which staff are under-performing and, whenever the issue is addressed, everyone is usually only too keen to ask you afterwards – 'What took you so long to deal with it?'

Such behaviour and depth of feeling indicate just how important staff regard this issue as. It goes to the heart of staff equity. And as such it poses one of the – if not the – most difficult tests you will face as a manager. Shirk it and you risk becoming a lame duck. Embrace it and you have the opportunity to significantly improve staff performance and morale. Resolved to act, you will need both patience and understanding – that and equal measures of tact, imagination and perseverance.

Tackle the issue, not the person

It is essential you recognize that:

Under-performance is not necessarily the individual's fault

There could very likely be an *organizational* explanation for this apparent individual failing – lack of resources, poor management, unbalanced workload, etc. Therefore this matter should be tackled as an issue and not as a means of targeting an individual for punishment. Indeed, it is very unrewarding to think in terms of blame or fault in these situations, unless it really does turn out to be a genuine case of misconduct (which you would need to handle under your university's disciplinary procedure, which we discuss in Chapter 10). Put another way, you need to remember that individuals respond better to encouragement than to punishment, so your focus should be a positive one aimed at improving performance, and not on apportioning blame or identifying 'passengers' for redundancy. You should therefore avoid labelling people as 'under-performers'.

Under-performance is not the same as unsatisfactory performance

Unsatisfactory performance means that an individual is performing at a level below that stipulated in their employment contract (and ought to be dealt with under your disciplinary procedure), whereas under-performance is concerned with individuals who are working below their level of capability. In instances of under-performance your university may have a 'competency procedure' for staff. In either case it is important you consult with your HR adviser and your line manager before initiating any formal procedure. Do not act alone.

Under-performance is not just about the individual staff member concerned

It is also about you – and your performance. Indeed, painful as it may be, you need to remain open to the possibility that you – through your actions, the assumptions you've made, the way you have organized workloads, delegated activities, communicated tasks, etc. – may be the chief factor responsible for the under-performance in the first place. Managing under-performance then involves a scrutiny of *yourself* and *your* actions as well as those of the staff member.

While under-performance may be one of the most difficult challenges you will face, it can also be one of the most rewarding experiences. It may stretch your beliefs and abilities in so many contrasting ways and to a far greater degree than is usually the case: your respect for human values; your capacity to motivate and inspire; your creativity and so on. However, few issues give you such an immediate sense of personal satisfaction as that which you experience in successfully resolving instances of under-performance.

Identify the nature and causes of staff under-performance

You can be alerted to instances of under-performance in very many ways: through letters of complaint or petitions from students and/or staff; through formal expressions of concern from course leaders or subject heads; from a critical report from an external examiner or accredited external body; as a consequence of appraisal; through staff absenteeism; through staff self-admission and so on.

Whichever way you learn about it, you must first investigate the shortfall in performance: i.e. you must avoid jumping to conclusions too quickly. The common assumption is that poor performance happens either because the person can't do it (which makes it a training issue) or because they won't, in which case it becomes a 'rewards' issue. It may not, however, as we've noted, be nearly so straightforward. Incapability and unwillingness are only two of many potential causes of under-performance. You therefore need to focus on issues around:

- problem-solving;
- staff motivation;
- collaboration and consultation;
- fairness and justice.

More specifically, ask yourself: is it because they:

- don't know *why* they are supposed to be doing something?
- don't know *what* to do?

- don't know to *what standard* they have to achieve a particular task? If so, it is a communication issue – about strategic vision, specific objectives, standards of performance, etc. – which you need to put right.
- don't know *how* to do the task? If so, it is a training and development issue and again it is your responsibility to take the initiative.
- simply *cannot* do the task? They don't have and cannot acquire the necessary skills. If so, this is a recruitment and selection, or more likely a delegation, problem and usually the staff member is not responsible.
- are *stopped* from completing tasks by organizational constraints: resources, poor communications, poor management? If so, it is again incumbent on you to take the initiative.
- simply *refuse* and *won't* do the task? If so, this is a discipline issue – *but* only after the above questions have been asked.

Agree a course of action – and review it

Keeping an open mind, therefore, you should:

- act early – don't let the situation escalate until it becomes chronic. If it is one you have inherited do not ignore it, even if your predecessor did;
- gather information to understand what the staff member is doing wrong (and also what s/he is getting right);
- talk with them one to one. Give them a clear outline of the issue and specific feedback on their performance;
- allow them an opportunity to respond;
- listen to their reactions and try to get to the root cause of the problems.

Ask open questions; invite suggestions: 'What do you need to help you become more effective? What can I do to help you?' Check tactfully whether any obstacles – their colleagues or their domestic and personal circumstances – have hindered their performance.

If the staff member is responsible for the under-performance then together come up with ideas for tackling the situation. In doing so you must bear in mind that:

- People do not have unlimited potential: they cannot achieve things simply because they want to enough.
- People don't change that much.

Therefore:

- Do not waste time trying to fix weaknesses, trying to put in what was left out.
- Focus on, capitalize on, strengths – try to draw out what there already is; this is hard enough by itself.
- Decide and agree on a 'training' course of action, starting with a key issue: e.g. assistance in the preparation of lectures; peer review; team teaching; counselling; shadowing; change in workload; change in role; visits to other departments/ institutions; pursuit of a course of study or relevant qualification.

- Consider nominating – and providing for – a mentor.
- Follow up to review progress and give further guidance on a regular basis, fortnightly or monthly depending on the seriousness of the issue.
- Gird yourself to run through several cycles of this process if there are a number of issues to address.
- Anticipate – and expect – a significant improvement in performance over a six-month period. In the event that satisfactory progress is not achieved, however – and it is unfortunately more than likely you will not be able to eliminate all cases of under-performance in this way – you will need to initiate your university's disciplinary procedure under guidance from your HR adviser as a means of securing performance improvement.

Motivating staff

> I feel that no rational person would work in the British higher education system, and that anyone who enters it under present conditions is engaged in a self-destructive act; it is an ill-paid, overworked line of work and has lost almost all the old pleasures.
>
> Alan Ryan, on resigning as Warden
> of New College, Oxford, May 2002

Staff under-performance – albeit restricted to a minority – will severely test your leadership capacity. It is not the only one you have to face, however. You will also be expected to meet the equally demanding challenge of ensuring that all staff members within your department are suitably and appropriately motivated. This is another tall order, particularly given, as we noted earlier, the degree to which alienation, cynicism and demoralization are seemingly rife in so many academic communities. Such is, in fact, the anger of staff about ever more intrusive accountability, their resentment at the increasing demands made upon them, their concern over the decline of collegiality, and their scepticism about the capacity of their institutional leaders, that it is perhaps not as surprising as it may first appear that university academics – undervalued, overlooked and unappreciated, as they undoubtedly perceive themselves – should actually be top of the UK Job Misery Index. What should – and can – you do?

Faced with such unpropitious circumstances – as much externally as internally generated – you may feel that whatever you do the impact would be negligible. You would make little difference. Not so. You need to reflect on the following key proposition: *each individual's line manager is the most important factor in an employee's effectiveness.*

You should not ever underestimate either your ability or potential to make a difference. Consider, in the first instance, what few HEIs apparently seem to have thought about to date: i.e. how to understand and cater to the wants and needs of their staff. This may sound straightforward enough, yet it is surprising how often employers – and not simply those in HE – fail in this regard. For example, Barrow and Davenport (2002) in their survey of the UK private sector found that while staff tended to value (in order of priority) recognition of their work, involvement in change, a job 'that gets the best out of me', role clarity, consultation and 'management that motivates', most organizations scored a satisfactory rating of less than 50 per cent in all six categories. Many private sector companies, like their HEI counterparts, then, are failing either to understand the wants of their staff or to meet them – indeed they are succeeding in neither case. Motivation is, in fact, a complex matter, particular to each individual. It is also one which you can affect dramatically either way, positively or negatively. Therefore it is important you understand motivation theory, to use as a guide to your actions.

Theories of motivation

Motivation is about giving people good reason to want to do things well: to excel. Motivation theory is grounded in the context in – and articulates the basis on – which all motivational effort must be directed. Three influential and well-known theories in particular are worthy of note.

Maslow's hierarchy of needs

According to Abraham Maslow, people's needs are satisfied progressively, beginning with their most basic physiological ones (e.g. the basics of food, warmth, shelter, rest) before rising up a hierarchy that embraces, in sequential order, safety needs (e.g. job security), social needs (e.g. sense of belonging), ego needs (e.g. recognition by others) and self-actualization needs (e.g. the need for self-fulfilment) (see Figure 5.1).

What it says, wholly sensibly, is that people's motivations can only be satisfied if this hierarchy is respected, and conversely that you ignore it at your peril. Thus your efforts

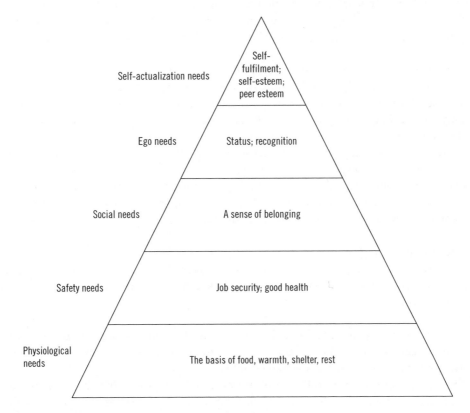

Figure 5.1 Maslow's hierarchy of motivational needs

aimed at engaging colleagues, for example, in the department strategic plan are likely to be blighted if staff feel they have more pressing concerns about their work environment or the security of their jobs. The hierarchy also reminds us that the work environment is very much a social environment and indeed for some individuals it may represent the majority of the people contact in their lives.

Hertzberg's motivator/hygiene factors

Frederick Hertzberg's theory has more immediate practical relevance to the everyday work environment, and certainly offers a more detailed insight on how to develop positive motivation and avoid demotivation. In it, Hertzberg identifies two categories of factor:

- hygiene factors, i.e. those things that switch people off if they cause negative feelings;
- motivators, i.e. those factors that can make people feel good.

The hygiene factors, or dissatisfiers, Hertzberg identifies are all external (environmental) factors that can affect the individual and include such things as: institutional policy and administrative processes; supervision; working conditions; salary; relationship with peers; personal life (and the impact of work on it); status; security.

The motivators, or satisfiers, by contrast all stem from the intrinsic (internalized) qualities of human nature. They are all in varying degrees a force for positive motivation and include in ascending order of power: achievement; recognition; the work itself; responsibility; advancement; growth. The implications for managers, then, are clear.

- Nullify or at least minimize the effect of the hygiene factors: those aspects of work that give rise to gripes and dissatisfaction – everything from pay inequities, workload differences and bureaucratic systems to car parking facilities, smoking policy and access to the photocopier. Get these things right and you will avoid staff demotivation.
- Nurture and accentuate the key factors that create positive motivation within individuals; those aspects of work which give staff a deep sense of satisfaction; everything from professional development, promotion and responsibility to simple acknowledgement of a job 'well done'. Get these things right and you will ensure people will want to perform and to perform well.

Vroom's expectancy theory

Victor Vroom's expectancy theory, like that of Hertzberg, also offers us a practical application. In it, Vroom identifies principles linked to the achievement of goals, chiefly the notions that:

- There is, or can be, a virtuous circle involved in this process: namely, purposeful activity leads to goals and the liking for achieving them acts as a spur to people. The pattern repeats itself as new goals are set.
- The positive effect is multiplied in proportion to the degree to which the goals are regarded as attainable. Thus the higher the probability of success the greater will be the strength of motivational feeling.

Again, the implications for managers are clear. Set goals that are either too easy or hopelessly unrealistic and you will inspire no one. Give people a challenging target on the other hand and they may just surprise themselves, and you, in the process. As in other instances you need to be wary of a blanket approach. Individuals will need to be persuaded in different ways according to their beliefs and aspirations. Timing is also an issue – the most effective interventions are invariably at the outset when the task appears most daunting and the belief in accomplishing it least certain (Forsyth, 2000).

Motivation principles for managers

Motivation, as we've said, and as these theories exemplify, is a complex business: one which is affected by many disparate factors. Nonetheless we can discern a number of guiding principles to help us when we seek to motivate colleagues.

- *There is no magic formula* – no simple lever, least of all money, for maintaining or increasing motivation either specifically in universities or indeed elsewhere.
- *Success, as ever, lies in the details* – in minimizing the dissatisfiers and maximizing the motivators. The motivational climate of your department is literally the sum total of all the pluses and minuses of the various individual factors, on both sides of the equation. As such it is essential you consider *all of them* on either side.
- *Continuity and consistency* – establishing a positive motivational climate takes time. It doesn't just happen overnight. It requires constant attention. Almost everything you do has motivational consequences. You should, therefore, always attempt to anticipate the effects, and equally important the side-effects, of your actions. Thus the introduction of a new system aimed at cost-saving, for example, will not secure the maximum positive effect if the process of complying with it is perceived as bureaucratic and time-consuming. Indeed, the lasting motivational effect may well be a negative one.
- *Differences in timescale* – motivation and performance levels do not rise and fall together. Rather, performance always follows motivation. Thus if you keep your ear to the ground you may be able to prevent a drop in motivation adversely affecting levels of performance. Equally, you need to be patient and avoid over-reacting if initiatives you take do not instantly yield the desired effect.
- *Always keep others in mind* – the things that motivate or concern your colleagues may not be ones you value yourself. Equally, what you believe is important may not be important to them. No matter. It is what they value that counts. You must be careful therefore not to dismiss matters and suggestions out of hand. Resist your internal censor. If not, you will at best be regarded as uncaring, and at worst may miss the opportunity to improve your motivational climate.

Your department's motivational climate

What about the motivational climate within your department? If you are to make a positive difference it is also important you understand the nature of your motivational climate; not least so that you will know the effect of the actions you decide to take. It may well be you feel that you know the atmosphere of your department well enough; indeed you may even feel you know it only too well! Even so, you should still be prepared to acknowledge that not everything may be as it appears; that signs and attitudes may not be what they seem; that departmental meetings, staff appraisals, informal gatherings and MBWA may have given you a sharp insight into the motivational climate, but maybe not a comprehensive picture or, indeed, an accurate one. Why not? This may be due to any number of reasons: openness may not have been encouraged; the belief that no one ever seems to listen; the fear of reprisal; peer pressure; the lack of understanding; a lack of time; 'it is just simply not done around here', etc. Whatever, the point is, no matter how well you feel you know it, you should still be prepared to test your assumptions and allow yourself to be surprised.

Appalachian State University

The simplest way of finding out exactly how people feel is, of course, to ask them. You may not, however, as we've said, get either a frank or an honest opinion in public settings, or indeed in private one-to-one conversations. A more reliable alternative, as many employers have come to recognize, is to survey staff opinion – a trend which is also growing among HEIs. Occupational Stress surveys, for example, carried out institution-wide by external consultants, and often yielding unexpected outcomes, have become increasingly commonplace under new health and safety regulations. Few universities, however, have matched the rigour, depth or honesty with which Appalachian State University, one of 16 institutions that make up the University of North Carolina system, has attempted to assess its 'Faculty Quality of Life' (Durham *et al.*, 1998).

Working to a brief set by the Provost's Office – 'to design and implement a study of faculty to identify personal and institutional factors influencing their perception of the quality of life' – the University's Hubbard Center for Faculty and Staff Support team developed a 90-minute structured interview protocol derived from Senge's *The Fifth Discipline* (2006). Following a pilot study of university administrators, the researchers (in male and female mixed pairs) interviewed a 10 per cent stratified random sample of 48 full-time, tenure track faculty members representing the demographic parameters of the population. The interviewers – with the interviewees' permission – hand-recorded or keyboarded the responses and then analysed their nature, frequency and context. In this way, they were able to identify several major themes: faculty perceptions, that is, which have given a clear direction to the university in its desire to maintain its tradition of strong faculty–student relationships and ensure faculty vitality and well-being. The team found that:

1 'Teaching and interactions with students have the greatest impact overall on faculty life' (teaching excellence is a primary mission of the university).
2 'The department chairperson, departmental climate and relationships with colleagues can make academic life "heaven or hell"'(thereby underlining what we noted earlier).
3 'Most faculty members feel they have difficulty balancing the demands of teaching, research and service as well as difficulty balancing personal and family lives with professional expectations.'
4 'Key incidents can have significant negative impact on overall perceptions of well-being.'

5 'A common faculty perception is that the institution is characterized by a reversal of the state and university motto, *esse quam videri*' ('here to be seen', i.e. staff do not think management 'walk the talk').

The Appalachian study is also remarkable in that it managed to fulfil the two essential preconditions for an effective opinion poll without involving an outside agency: namely, faculty perceived it to be not only a genuine initiative (as opposed to a gimmick), but also one which was organized in such a way they felt free to say what they really thought without fear of any comeback.

These conditions are difficult to replicate when it comes to your own department. The very fact of conducting a survey may be seen as an admission of failure or difficulty; even the sheer novelty may itself be sufficient to arouse suspicion. Nonetheless, even if your HEI does not want to take a leaf from Appalachian State, you can still meet these preconditions in other ways, for example:

- by linking your survey to – and making it part of – a key initiative: e.g. the formulation of your department's strategic plan; the department's annual review; a staff development action plan; a response to an initiative from the university centre;
- by allowing respondents the opportunity to remain anonymous if they wish;
- by explaining how the findings will be used and when you will give feedback to staff.

In this way, you should be able to convince staff that you yourself do not have an ulterior motive (other than the well-being of the department) and that you are serious about eliciting a genuine and candid response. See Box 5.9 for an exemplar of one such survey in a newly created faculty in one UK 'new' university.

There is, of course, one further prerequisite of such surveys, and that is to do with you rather than your colleagues. You've got to be prepared to listen – and to act on – what you might not like or wish to hear. Unless you are prepared to do so, you should not proceed with this idea. An alternative, or indeed an additional, approach – no less reflective even if possibly not capable of generating as incisive an outcome – is to conduct your own self-assessment of your department and your HEI.

1 Department – motivation is based on trust. To what extent do you and your colleagues have mutual trust in – and positive expectations of – one another? See Box 5.10.
2 HEI – what contribution does your institution make to the motivational climate in your department? What functional, economic and psychological benefits does your institution offer staff? In short, is your university a good employer? See Box 5.11.

Think about how your dean or faculty/staff might complete this survey. Remember that it takes time to improve perceptions of trust in ongoing relationships. Work on the dimensions where your scores are the lowest to increase the overall climate of mutual trust. Develop an action plan to improve the climate of trust in your department and university.

Box 5.9 Faculty staff survey questionnaire in one UK 'new' (post-1992) university

Name (optional) _____

1 What three things do you like most about:
   (i)   your current job?
   (ii) the university?

2 What three things concern you most about:
   (i)   your current job?
   (ii) the university?

3 What do you consider to be the three main things you offer in contributing to the work of the university?

4 What do you regard as:
   (i)   your main achievement this year?
   (ii) the university's main achievement this year?

5 Are there any skills you have, which are not fully utilized in your work?

6 What do you believe should be the new faculty's main goals and priorities?

7 What are the values you would most like to see/feel in the faculty on a day-to-day basis?

8 What three things could the faculty do to make a positive difference in your working life?

9 Any other comments you would like to make?

These self-assessments, along with your anonymous staff survey and your own informal observations, should give you a clearer picture of the motivational situation in your department.

Having 'taken the temperature', you now need to *act* on it. It may be that – if you have not already done so – you need to develop a modus operandi based on the leadership strategies highlighted earlier in this book. You will also find that the principles discussed in this chapter – on performance management, target-setting and feedback – can, when applied consistently, make a major positive difference. What else you can and should do will of course depend on your particular circumstances although, given the nature of academic environments in general, it is likely you will find more freedom of manoeuvre with regard to the 'psychological contract' of staff than their 'economic' one. Either way, you should leave no stone unturned. More specifically, you should consider at both macro- and micro-level the following:

1 All staff, and students for that matter, want and need four basic things: challenge, a sense of belonging, support and social space. Do you provide them? If not, what can you do about it?

2 Research tells us, as we noted above, that staff tend to value, in order of priority: recognition of their work; involvement in change; a job 'that gets the best out of me'; role clarity; consultation; 'management that motivates'. Are your actions consistent with these priorities?

Box 5.10 Assess the climate of your department

Trust is the set of expectations that one individual has in another individual, group, or organization unit. Mutual trust is the extent to which two or more individuals share positive expectations of one another. Think about members of your department while completing this questionnaire. The purpose of this self-assessment is to stimulate personal reflection and development.

Directions
The following statements assess various aspects of trust between you (as head) and faculty/staff in your department. Please use the following scale to indicate your level of agreement with each of the statements below:

Strongly disagree	Moderately disagree	Slightly disagree	Neutral	Slightly agree	Moderately agree	Strongly agree
1	2	3	4	5	6	7

Faculty and staff trust that I . . .

____ 1 am completely honest with them.

____ 2 place our department's interests above my own.

____ 3 will keep the promises I make.

____ 4 am competent in performing my job.

____ 5 express my true feelings about important issues.

____ 6 care about their well-being.

____ 7 can contribute to our department's success.

____ 8 take actions that are consistent with my words.

____ 9 share important information with them.

____ 10 care about the future of our department.

____ 11 can help solve important problems in our department.

____ 12 have consistent expectations of them.

____ 13 would make personal sacrifices for our department.

____ 14 would acknowledge my own mistakes.

____ 15 can help our department thrive in the future.

____ 16 can be relied upon.

I trust that faculty and staff . . .

____ 17 are completely honest with me.

____ 18 place our department's interests above their own.

____ 19 will keep the promises they make.

____ 20 are competent in performing their jobs.

____ 21 express their true feelings about important issues.

____ 22 care about my well-being.

____ 23 can contribute to our department's success.

____ 24 take actions that are consistent with their words.

____ 25 share important information with me.

____ 26 care about the future of our department.

____ 27 can help solve important problems in our department.

____ 28 have consistent expectations of me.

____ 29 would make personal sacrifices for our department.

____ 30 would acknowledge their own mistakes.

____ 31 can help our department thrive in the future.

____ 32 can be relied upon.

Definitions
Trust is the set of expectations that one individual has in another individual, group or organizational unit in terms of four dimensions (Openness, Caring, Reliability, and Competence). *Mutual trust* is the extent to which two or more individuals have positive expectations in one another along the four dimensions.

Scoring

Record the scale values for the following questionnaire items. The potential range of subtotal scores is 4–28 and the potential range of total dimension scores is 8–56. Use your relative scores in each of the dimensions to assess the nature of mutual trust in your department. Subtotal scores less than 20 and total scores less than 40 indicate areas for possible improvement.

OPENNESS:
- ___ 1
- ___ 5
- ___ 9
- ___ 14
- ___ Subtotal
- ___ 17
- ___ 21
- ___ 25
- ___ 30
- ___ Subtotal
- ___ TOTAL

RELIABILITY:
- ___ 3
- ___ 8
- ___ 12
- ___ 16
- ___ Subtotal
- ___ 19
- ___ 24
- ___ 28
- ___ 32
- ___ Subtotal
- ___ TOTAL

CARING:
- ___ 2
- ___ 6
- ___ 10
- ___ 13
- ___ Subtotal
- ___ 18
- ___ 22
- ___ 26
- ___ 29
- ___ Subtotal
- ___ TOTAL

COMPETENCE:
- ___ 4
- ___ 7
- ___ 11
- ___ 15
- ___ Subtotal
- ___ 20
- ___ 23
- ___ 27
- ___ 31
- ___ Subtotal
- ___ TOTAL

Source: Shulman, 1998; adapted from Myers, 1991.

Box 5.11 Is your university a good employer?

What messages does your institution give out to your staff? To prospective employees? To the outside world? What is the nature of the motivational situation in your university and how does it affect your department? Listed below are the dozen variables which constitute the 'employer brand' (the perception on which your reputation is based). Consider each in turn and rate them 1–5 (1 being the most negative, 5 the most positive). Identify the shortfalls in your university and department which you need to address to realize your aspirations.

1 Vision and leadership
   - How clear is the existing vision?
   - Is it demonstrated by senior management?

- Is the strategy to achieve the vision clear?
- What is the style of leadership? Is it aligned with the vision?

2 Policies and values
- What is the balance between reality and aspiration?
- Are values implicit or explicit?
- Are policies applied consistently?
- Are values demonstrated in behaviour?
- Are values linked to performance management?

3 Fairness and cooperation
- Are equality and diversity taken seriously?
- How do academic and 'non-academic' staff feel about one another?
- What is the degree of cooperation between faculties/departments and central services?
- What is the level of mutual respect?

4 Corporate personality
- How would you describe your organizational culture (see Chapter 2)?
- How does it manifest itself (language, artefacts)?
- What is the balance between stability and risk-taking?
- How far does the 'corporate culture' extend?

5 External reputation
- To what extent are staff views coloured by their perception of external reputation?
- Who are your key audiences? How do they feel about you?
- Reputation for what? Cutting edge research; academic innovation; care for students; range of offerings; challenge to status quo, etc.?

6 Communication
- Do your people know what you are trying to do?
- Are they engaged with you on this journey?
- Do they feel they are listened to?
- Are good practices and ideas shared across your university?
- Do staff think their individual line managers are good communicators?

7 Recruitment and induction
- Do you attract the best people?
- What is the initial contact like for people who approach your institution?
- Does it match your external reputation?
- Does your recruitment process leave candidates (successful and unsuccessful ones) feeling good about themselves and you and your university?
- How do the 'first 30 days' affect new post-holders?

8 Performance management
- Is there clarity of standards and targets for all staff?
- What happens to those who are 'under-performing'?
- How do you bring out the best in people?
- Is performance management linked with your institution's plans and aspirations?
- Do all managers grasp the importance of performance management?

9 Development
- Is personal and professional development planning a feature for everyone?
- What do you do to encourage continuous improvement?

- Is promised development delivered?
- Is there development for the current job or career, or both?

10 Working environment
  - What is the quality of your working environment?
  - Physical – light, heat, décor, furniture
  - Equipment including IT
  - Amenities – restaurants, meeting places, etc.
  - Do staff have 'social space'?

11 Reward
  - Increments or performance-related pay?
  - Benefits v. salary?
  - Do you pay for scarcity/role of supply and demand?
  - Pay for the job or pay for performance?
  - How well do you see non-financial rewards?

12 Post-employment
  - People die or leave – you hope most of them leave. What will they say when they've gone?
  - How does your university look on their CV?
  - What legendary figures have been members of your staff?
  - Do you breed 'high-fliers'?
  - How sensitive are you to the reasons people leave?

Source: adapted from Barrow and Davenport, 2002.

3 Following Hertzberg, what can you do to minimize the dissatisfiers and maximize the motivators? Examine each one in turn – as outlined in Box 5.12 – and draw up an action plan for your department.

You will only realize your action plan, however, if you are able to maximize the potential of your staff. Staff motivation and staff development are both sides of the same coin. How, then, can you best encourage and facilitate staff development?

Box 5.12 Prompts for improving the motivational climate in your department

Factors	Questions you should consider fully
Motivators	*To maximize satisfaction*
Achievement	• Do all staff have SMART (and not DUMB) targets? • Do staff feel able 'to get the best out of their job'?
Recognition	• Do you recognize staff achievements in departmental meetings – in writing – in the university's newsletter? • Do you celebrate staff achievements?

	• Do you reward staff achievements beyond the norm? • In what ways do you recognize lifetime achievement? • Are 'well done' and 'thank you' a regular part of your vocabulary?
Work itself	• Do staff have the fullest opportunity to do what they do best? • Are all staff allocated to roles that are right for them?
	• Do you foster and encourage self-direction as well as accountability; do you have the balance? • Do you respect and value academic freedom (if not the freedom for academics to do what they like)? • Do staff have manageable workloads? • Do you involve staff in decisions affecting their role? • Do staff enjoy their work? • Do you engender a sense of fun? • Is leadership – from the top – seen as inspirational?
Responsibility	• Do you give staff the opportunity to take on further responsibilities? • Do you encourage staff to 'take ownership' of their roles?
Advancement	• Is your promotional ladder organized to recognize achievement in the optimum way? Do you make full use of it? How do staff feel about it? • Do you give staff regular opportunities to add to their experience? • Do you encourage and support staff in developing their professional networks? • Do you show commitment to their career progression?
Growth	• Do staff leave for positive reasons? • Do leavers go on to do bigger and better things? • Does your department breed 'high fliers'?
Maintenance	*To minimize dissatisfaction*
Institutional policy and administration	• What rules do you have and how do staff regard them (intellectual property rights; workload allocations; consultancy arrangements; scholarly activity; conference expenses; smoking policy, etc.)? • What systems are staff expected to use and how do they regard them (quality assurance; student data; management info; finance; personnel, etc.)?
Supervision	• Is your management style appropriate for your department? • Do you consult properly? • Do you give staff the support they need? • Are you considered a good communicator? • Do you know how staff rate you?
Working conditions	• Are working conditions seen as attractive? Do they meet staff expectations? • Is equipment regarded as suitable? • Are there additional facilities that are regarded as necessary? • Are staff involved in considering proposals for change?
Salary	• Are salaries seen as fair internally? • Is there evidence of pay inequities? • How do salaries compare relative to those HEIs you regard as rivals? • Do you make the most of the salary flexibility available to you? • What benefits do staff have? Do you use them fully? fairly?

Relationship with peers	• Do staff willingly collaborate? • Do you have teams or tribes? • Do you foster and encourage peer group review?
Personal life conditions	• Do staff have social space? How do they rate it? • Do staff work longer hours than they should? • Do you recognize the value of – and support – work–life balance? • Do staff confide in you?
Status	• Do staff feel valued? • Does the way they are described in institutional publications support this? • What recognition is there of long service, special expertise and outstanding performance? • Do staff feel management supports their position within the university as a whole?
Security	• Do all staff have a job role? • Do staff know what is expected of them? • Do staff know how they are performing? • Is corporate communication – internal and external – regarded as good? • Do you hoard information? • Is management seen as fair and robust? • Do you have an adult–adult employment relationship?

6 Developing staff

To discover and to teach are distinct functions: they are also distinct gifts and are not commonly found united in the same person.

Cardinal John Henry Newman, 1852

A mistake is only a mistake if it happens twice.

Merrill Lynch, Investment Bankers, Code of Practice

Staff development in HE has come a long way in a short time. From a cottage industry 20 years ago it is now an established – if not always accepted – feature of institutional life. Almost all UK universities have a staff development unit, or educational development unit, and in many instances both. Where once staff development was narrowly conceived in terms of teaching and learning improvement for individual academics, it is now more broadly identified – and rightly so – with professional development for all staff in line with pre-determined institutional priorities. A recognized priority area itself, it is not uncommon for UK universities to devote 5 per cent of their staffing budget to staff development and training (Blackmore and Blackwell, 2004; Brew, 1995; Webb, 1996).

The learning organization

The debate surrounding the growth and maturation of staff development within HE has, in turn, been influenced by the emergence and popularization of a parallel phenomenon – the concept of the 'learning organization'. Indeed, the book on staff development that doesn't make reference to the idea is the exception rather than the norm. And for good reason, for the concept is transparently an attractive proposition – one that, as we noted in Chapter 3, could give organizations the leading competitive edge they yearn for. More than that, the emphasis on learning, the values it espouses and the practical way forward it envisages all resonate strongly with the way in which HE operates in particular. It should not surprise us then – even if it is rare – to have, on this occasion, a 'managerial concept' that is almost as well known and endorsed across HE as it is in the corporate world beyond. It is surely self-evident, advocates argue, that HEIs as 'institutions of learning' – and latterly as champions of lifelong learning – should want, and seek, to be 'learning organizations' as well (Duke, 1992; Martin, 1999). What could be more logical, natural and desirable?

The reality, however, could not unfortunately be more different. The concept is two decades old and yet there is little evidence that any organization has managed to transform itself into a 'learning organization', either in HE or elsewhere. The view has formed that the goal may, in fact, be an unattainable one, as John Burgoyne has admitted:

> our early thinking on the learning organization had some naivety and was a bit happy-clappy. Because we came from self-development, there was a lot about love, trust and getting teams to share their needs and aspirations. While some of the values were quite appealing, there was a naivety about power relationships.
> (Burgoyne, 2001)

Still others maintain there was nothing new about the concept anyway (Garratt, 1995); that it was derived in large part from the pioneering work of Reg Revans (on action learning) and Chris Argyris and Donald Schon (on single-loop and double-loop learning) and that it is time we should be considering a new model – the 'learning, knowledge-managing, virtual organization'. Senge (1998) himself counsels: 'Never say to staff, "we are going to become a learning organization"' lest you leave yourself open to a hiding for nothing. Lastly, we should remind ourselves that, at one level, there can, in fact, be no such thing as a 'learning organization' for the simple reason it is human communities who learn, not organizations.

That said, it would be wrong to conclude that, because of its failure in practice, the idea does not have merit. On the contrary, it still has value as an aspiration, as a modus operandi, as a guide to what you and your HEI should be doing, and, equally important, what you both should not be doing (see Box 6.1). In following it you will at least make progress towards this elusive goal (see Figure 6.1).

Box 6.1 Learning and non-learning organizations

Learning organization	Non-learning organization
Anticipates future problems	Reacts to current problems
Pays attention to external environment	Pays attention only to internal operations
Continuously seeks improvement	Responds to accumulation of poor performance
Problem-solving is based on conceptual analysis and understanding	Problem-solving is based on trial and error
Problem-solving is organization-wide and problem-centred	Problem-solving is compartmentalized and hierarchical
Rewards for growth, initiative and creativity	Rewards for historical performance
Job definitions encourage exploration, initiative and information-sharing	Jobs are narrowly circumscribed and risk-taking is discouraged

Source: adapted from National Commission on Education, 1995; Senge, 2006.

Figure 6.1 Distinguishing characteristics of the learning organization

Note: *The authors' preference for 'learning company' is an aesthetic choice. They believe it to be a more 'convivial' term than 'learning organization'.

Source: adapted from Pedler *et al.*, 1991.

Valuing staff development

HE has been very tardy about showing a *genuine* commitment to the idea of staff development. Too often the latter has unfairly and mistakenly been given a low priority and with it low status. This has been due in part to:

- perception: its (pejorative) association with low-level 'training';
- self-infliction: the repellent jargon ('staffdevelopmentese') used by some practitioners;
- a clash of cultures: the antipathy between the idea of staff development and the variety of cults prevalent within academic life (the 'gifted amateur', the 'intellectual', etc.).

It is also symptomatic of academic environments in general, in that they tend to be cultures of 'knowers' (the cult of the 'expert') rather than 'learners'; as Chris Argyris (2008) reminds us, 'Why Smart People Have So Much Difficulty Learning' is because they think they know it all already.

Whatever the particular reasons – and no doubt they are difficult obstacles to overcome – it is important you do not succumb to them. You must seek not only to value staff development but *be seen to do so*, by making it one of your key priorities. To do that you first need to be clear about what is meant by staff development and, equally, what your institution means by it.

What is staff development?

One additional reason why staff development has not been accorded the status and priority it merits in HE has been the way it has been conceived – often in a very narrow sense, as a tailored programme of activities aimed at remedying a specific skills deficit. While staff development can be about this type of provision it is by no means restricted to it. Indeed the phrase has sufficient elasticity that it can, and has been taken to, mean anything and everything. And herein lies the problem. To say you favour and value staff development can be seen to be just so many words. That said, we can, in fact, discern a degree of convergence on this issue in the literature.

At the *organizational* level, staff development is usually integrated with the institution's overall human resource strategy and 'is normally considered to include the institutional policies, programmes and procedures which facilitate and support staff so that they may fully serve their own and their institution's needs' (Webb, 1996).

At the *individual* level, staff development is concerned with the acquisition of something that is *new*: a new skill; a new way of seeing things; a new attitude; a new set of feelings; a new level of consciousness. It does not mean more of something that one has already: it is not simply an increase in knowledge or a higher degree of an existing skill. Rather, development implies a *different* state of being or functioning. Operationally, staff development is about learning in all its variety of forms including:

- education: those processes which result in formal awards up to and including postgraduate and professional qualifications;

- training: formal learning activities which may not lead to qualifications but may be undertaken at any time in a working career;
- development: informal learning experiences arising from the job; working with peers; liaising with partners and professional networks, etc. (Pedler *et al.*, 2001).

As one UK 'new' university has succinctly put it:

> **Staff development is defined as a learning opportunity or activity which**
> - enhances the ability of individuals, teams and the institution to deliver the University's Mission and Strategic Plan
> - enables staff to carry out their current and future roles effectively and to adapt to change
> - assures the quality of teaching, learning and research and the services which support them.

Put another way, staff development is about inducting staff into a 'community of practice' at both the institutional and disciplinary levels, a process from which the individual and the institution should derive mutual benefit. Conceived in this way, staff development is, in practice, often guided by a number of working principles of which you need to be aware:

Expectations and responsibilities

It is usually anticipated that individual staff will take an active role in articulating their needs. Heads of department carry the fundamental responsibility for ensuring that staff are enabled to perform their roles effectively and efficiently, and enjoy continuous learning opportunities through which their abilities and potential can be developed.

The principle of subsidiarity

As head of department, you are often granted a large degree of autonomy in fulfilling the responsibility you have been given – in the language you choose to use (or not); the way in which you determine development needs; the discretion you exercise in providing experiences; the way in which you manage resources to support development opportunities.

Emphasis on continuous professional development (CPD)

In keeping with the spirit of the 'learning organization' concept – as well as recognizing that in an age of lifelong learning 'what you learned last year is as important as what you achieved' – the near-universal tendency among HEIs, as elsewhere, has been to promote staff development as *a continuous and ongoing process*. You can anticipate that you will be expected to establish behaviours and practices which actively encourage continuous professional development.

In what ways can and should you promote staff development? In the first instance:

- through understanding the strategic approach (or 'espoused theory') your own institution has towards staff development and using it as a *guide* for your actions;

- through understanding the nature of staff development in practice (or 'theory-in-use') in your institution and using it as a *means* of meeting the expectations your institution has placed on you;
- by exploring, considering and maximizing the discretionary opportunities available to you.

Staff development in your university

Your own university's approach to staff development is, as we've noted, likely to be included in your institution's overall human resource strategy. What does this document tell you about the obligations you have to meet? What policy aims and objectives are laid down? What commitments are expressed? What guiding principles are enunciated? What statements of intent are made? Does it conceive of staff development as:

- passive: a simple reporting mechanism on development activities?
- active: anticipating performance improvement?
- dynamic: establishing quantitative targets?
- radical: establishing ratings and rewards alongside quantitative and operational performance criteria?

Does it commit your university to establishing a 'learning organization'?

It is likely your university will consider adopting one of the following approaches (Harrison, 2005). Which one applies to your institution? What are the implications for you and your particular role?

A total or comprehensive approach
- This involves a systematic, full-scale analysis of all the organization's training and development needs identified through discussion with all relevant stakeholders. It anticipates the establishment of an institution-wide staff development plan.
- It is favoured by institutions which regard their environment as relatively stable and those equipped with a robust specialist staff development function.
- *Risk.* Development is confined solely to filling skills gaps in relation to current roles; it becomes disproportionately individual-led at the expense of institutional drivers.

A problem-centred approach
- This focuses on urgent problems facing the institution which require a training and development response. Development is selective and partial with the emphasis on flexibility rather than planning.
- It is favoured by institutions which regard their environment as highly unpredictable and those suffering severe resource constraint.
- *Risk.* Development becomes preoccupied with responding to immediate needs and loses its long-term focus.

A business strategy approach
- This assumes that needs assessment and development plans must be produced and driven 'from the top' on the basis of the institution's key 'business drivers' (its own

business strategy; operational priorities; the environmental changes it faces, etc.). It gives heads of department primary responsibility for staff development.

- It is favoured by institutions which regard their environment as highly competitive and those that are imbued with self-confidence.
- *Risk*. Development fails to tap innovations 'bottom up'; it becomes disproportionately business-led at the expense of individual professional fulfilment.

Such is the 'espoused theory'. To what extent, however, is this reflected in the way that staff development is actually delivered in practice? Is the practice consistent with the theory? Reflect on your own institution and consider if the 'theory-in-use' matches the 'espoused theory'. You can do this in a number of ways.

Perception and value

How is staff development regarded across your institution – within your department? What value attaches to it?

Organization

How is staff development formally organized in your institution? For example, via a faculty development committee; small support unit; large central unit; a central unit with departmental affiliates; networked faculty development; an institutional 'ginger group'? Or do you have no formal provision?

Delivery

How is staff development 'delivered' in your institution and within your department? Is it on-the-job or off-the-job? Ad hoc or systematic? Process- or event-driven? Remedial or developmental? Voluntaristic or comprehensive? Tolerated or evaluated? Implanted or embedded? A cost or an investment?

Role of staff and/or educational developer

Staff and Educational Developmental Units can – in theory – fulfil a number of roles – as a provider of specialist services; a dispenser of advice; a counsellor; a collaborator; a broker; a controller; a 'change agent' – or indeed a variety of them. How does the unit operate in your institution? Is it consistent – in practice – with what your university is seeking to achieve in terms of staff development?

Model of practice

Staff development in many institutions is typically organized around one of three distinct approaches in practice (Brown and Sommerlad, 1992):

- fragmented: one in which staff development is conducted as a singular ad hoc activity without reference to the needs or goals of the organization;
- formalized: a 'systemic' approach based on an analysis of training needs;
- focused: one which regards training and development as continuous activities which are intrinsic to organizational well-being.

The tendency among organizations has been to evolve from a 'fragmented' approach to a 'focused' one via a more systematic 'formalized' phase. Such a trend is also consistent with the 'learning organization' ideal (see Box 6.2). Which practical approach most closely resembles the staff development provision in your university? Again, is it consistent with your university's strategic staff development aim?

It may well be that in your institution the 'theory-in-use' is indeed consistent with the theory that is 'espoused'. You should not be too surprised, however, if it is not, for implementation naturally lags behind strategic formulation in practice. On the other hand, the mismatch should not be so great either. If it is, you should:

- seek clarification from your line manager;
- seek advice from your staff development officer. Do not wait for them to come to you. They are nearly always only too willing to help;
- maintain good faith in the strategic approach articulated by your university;
- propose a practical way forward.

Remember that staff development is, as we noted earlier, about inducting staff into a 'community of practice' to the joint benefit of them and their institution. Consequently, you would do no harm – and more than likely a great deal of good – if you were to use

---

Box 6.2 Emergent models of staff development

The fragmented approach

Training and development is:

- A cost not an investment
- Not linked to organizational goals
- Perceived as a luxury
- Based in a training department
- Primarily knowledge-based courses

The formalized approach

Training and development is:

- Systemic – part of career development
- Linked to human resource needs
- Linked to appraisal and individual needs
- Knowledge-based courses plus a focus on skills
- Carried out by trainers and line managers

The focused approach

Training and development is:

- A continuous learning process
- Essential for organizational survival
- Linked to organizational strategy and individual goals
- On-the-job plus specialist courses
- Line manager's responsibility
- Tolerant

Source: adapted from Brown and Sommerlad, 1992; Harrison, 2005.

the design principles of the 'learning organization' as your guide in determining staff development provision in your department, i.e.:

- Staff development should be:

  C omprehensive
  A nticipatory
  R esearch-based
  E xemplary
  E mbedded
  R eflective

- And have programme design criteria which are

  L inked and interconnected
  E mpowering and transformative
  A daptable and dynamic
  R eflective and improvement-oriented
  N on-hierarchical
  I nteractive
  N etwork and group-based
  G enerative and knowledge-creating.

(Candy, 1998)

Your university may have adopted these 'learning organization' principles or indeed a similar model of development. Ultimately, however, it will be you who will have to implement it. How can you make the most of this opportunity, for your staff, your department and your institution?

Staff development in your department

Develop, agree and establish your own departmental staff development policy framework

You must first, as we've said, seek to understand the nature of staff development, the 'espoused theory' and the 'theory-in-use', within your institution. Beyond that, you must also seek to establish a similar clarity, as well as consistency, of purpose within your department. And the most effective way to do that is by developing and adopting a formal policy statement which makes this both explicit and transparent.

Departmental staff provision has too often been, and in many instances still is, a hotchpotch of academic tradition (concerning sabbaticals, conference support and the like) and ad hoc initiatives which are seldom coordinated or evaluated and not always understood by those who might benefit from them. The process itself is characterized by a lack of clarity over direction, the distribution of responsibility and the allocation of funding and resources. Departments are increasingly spurning such confusion by formalizing their staff development arrangements. This is a trend you would do well to emulate (Brew, 1995). Put another way, your first priority must be to develop your own *focused* approach at the local level.

It may be that you've inherited a staff development policy framework (in which case you should review it) or that you are starting from scratch. Either way, you should be aiming to develop and seek agreement on a framework appropriate to the needs of your department: a comprehensive framework in which you address each of the following.

Context
- Briefly outline the institutional and external environment within which your department operates.
- Explain how your staff development policy is linked to your departmental and institutional strategy.
- Outline the origins of your policy and how it was created: the process of consultation etc.

Aims
Elaborate the overall intentions of your policy: e.g. to enhance the ability of staff to deliver the department's strategy; to carry out their current and future roles effectively; to adapt to change; to have job satisfaction; to achieve career progression, etc.

Objectives
Specify the needs and priorities your policy will address: e.g. in relation to assessment practice, mode of teaching, learner support, student diversity, commercialization, links to the community, research and innovation, and so on.

Guiding principles
Identify the values and beliefs which underpin your policy: e.g. commitment to individual empowerment; guarantee of equitable access; the establishment of a supportive, enabling framework; the opportunity for regular review.

Plan
Specify the outcomes of your policy. Outline what you expect the department to achieve over the next 2–3 years. Set SMART targets: e.g. x per cent of staff formally qualified in teaching or members of a professional teaching body; x per cent increase in the number of work-based learning opportunities for students; x per cent of the department's courses to be delivered by e-learning; x per cent increase in the number of students successfully completing their programme of study; x per cent of the department's income to be generated from 'third stream' sources.

Delivery
Identify the various ways in which the policy will be delivered – the emphasis being on the plural rather than the singular, i.e. all those mechanisms both on-the-job and off-the-job. See p. 211 below, under the heading 'Assess and determine how you will deliver staff development'.

Monitoring and evaluation

Explain how you will measure the effectiveness of your staff development provision – the quality assurance process: e.g. self-assessment; peer review; stakeholder evaluation; linkage to departmental decision making.

Resources

Specify the resources available to support the policy (e.g. per capita allocation, discretionary allowance, departmental and central provision, the proportion of the staffing budget) and how the allocation will be managed (e.g. staff development committee, line manager, institutional staff development manager, etc.).

Indicate the level of support – or entitlements – which staff can expect to receive, including pro-rata allowances for part-timers: e.g. number of days' study leave (typically 35 for full-time academic staff in UK 'new' universities); number of training days per year; conference expenses; materials allowance; professional membership subsidy, etc.

Identify and analyse staff development needs

The success (or otherwise) of your policy framework is dependent, in the first instance, on your having a sound grasp of the staff development needs in your department. Indeed an accurate and comprehensive needs analysis is a *sine qua non* of such frameworks. It is, however, not always easy to achieve – not least because individuals themselves may not be sure what they need. Faulty methodology, poor application and insensitive communication can exacerbate this situation still further (Harrison, 2005). These are all pitfalls you must seek to avoid.

There are, in theory, a number of possible approaches you can take in determining individual development needs:

- Training needs survey: what training do you think you/they need?
- Competence study: what competences do you think you/they need?
- Task analysis: what tasks are required/do you do on this job?
- Performance analysis: how does this role impact on the performance of the department? What are (or should be) the critical accomplishments and how is each critical?

In practice, the tendency is to rely on an amalgam of these, depending on the context in which you work. Thus training needs surveys, for example, tend to be used as a knee-jerk response to a series of complaints, as in 'how can we fix it?'

In the case of HE, where job roles are not always easy to define, the most fruitful way forward, as suggested earlier, is that based on standards of performance and competency requirements. Having articulated job roles which specify these, you – and your colleagues – can use them as an objective measure in determining shortfalls. Indeed, competency-based job roles provide you – and them – with a rich source of data by which to manage not only performance but also development. As the assessment of needs is (or should be) a collective endeavour – on your part as well as theirs – it also follows that the more sources of information you can tap the greater likelihood there is of getting it right.

In addition to *job roles*, then, you should also consider the outcomes of the following.

Individual and team performance review

If you manage performance in your department in the way that's been suggested, you should find staff, both individually and collectively, becoming more confident in saying: 'Here's my personal (or team) strategic plan for the year. What do you think of it? What can you do for my personal (or team) development plan?' If they do not, then you need to prompt them explicitly: 'In view of the department's strategic plan and your own professional development to date, what competencies do you feel you need to acquire? And what do you think would be the best way of doing so?'

Course monitoring and review

Typically conducted formally on an annual basis, programme monitoring and review are now commonplace in virtually all university academic departments. This process invariably highlights issues or identifies problems and concerns. You need to distil the staff development implications.

Learning and teaching evaluations

The student evaluation of teaching, and that of modules or units, has likewise become increasingly formalized in many academic departments. What are the main areas for improvement?

Student feedback

Feedback from students is now canvassed with almost religious fervour and not solely with regard to learning and teaching. What do your questionnaire surveys, focus groups, student reps and staff–student committees tell you about the degree of student satisfaction? In what ways could staff development enhance the nature of the student experience?

External review

Universities have, as we've noted, had to become more accountable for the way they manage their affairs. To respond and to satisfy not just external examiners (of courses, as heretofore) but also those assessors, reviewers and auditors concerned with assuring quality in teaching (the teaching quality assessment; subject review and 'developmental engagement'), research (the RAE) and overall well-being (the institutional audit). What are your department's strengths and weaknesses? Equally, the QAA publishes extensive documentation on the purposes and processes of these quality assurance mechanisms. Measure your department against these benchmarks or, better still, have a 'critical friend' do so. What gaps do you need to make good?

Staff self-assessment surveys

Not a widespread practice: partly because the outcomes are not always reliable, and partly because staff very often mistrust such devices, regarding them as vehicles for admitting personal weaknesses. They can nevertheless be used to good effect provided you apply them tactfully: i.e. offer staff the opportunity for self-assessment but do not ask for the results of their self-assessment. Respect their desire to keep this information to themselves.

Instead, ask staff for the outcomes of the process – to identify the staff development activities they wish to undertake (see Appendix III).

Assess and determine how you will deliver staff development

Staff development is not just about 'content', it is about 'method' too. Once you have identified your department's development needs you need to consider the various ways in which you can address them, including those which your staff have indicated they would prefer. It is important you are flexible in this regard. Try not to let yourself, and others, be limited by any preconception you or they might have. Instead, think of all the learning opportunities that can arise along the broadest of continuums: individual–collective development; professional–departmental development; and the interstices between them: individual–professional; individual–departmental; collective–professional; collective–departmental (see Figure 6.2). What staff development you identify and how you deliver it will, of course, depend on your needs analysis and it may well be that your assessment leads you to focus heavily on one or two aspects of this schema. You should, however, ensure you do at least have some staff development activity planned for each of the different aspects of the model exemplified in Figure 6.2.

Establish a learning climate in your department

More than that, you should be proactive in seeking to establish a learning climate within your department. How? By:

- being seen to be continuously learning yourself; by setting yourself challenging learning goals;
- continuously providing staff with learning opportunities both on and off the job;
- providing new learning experiences from which colleagues can learn;
- not being afraid to encourage staff to challenge the traditional ways of doing things;
- tolerating mistakes made by colleagues provided they try to learn from them;
- continuously helping staff to review and reach conclusions from their experiences and to decide what to plan next;
- building 'learning into the system' so that it is an integral, not a marginal, departmental activity.

You can do this in a variety of ways, the conventional and not-so-conventional. Take the examples that follow. How many of these activities do you consciously promote? If not, why not? Consider the merits in each case of applying them (if you have not already done so) in your department.

Formal learning opportunities

- Dedicated periods of staff leave: sabbaticals, study leave
- Off-campus workshops, seminars and conferences
- Institutional and departmental workshops, seminars and conferences

Individual
development

Induction
Peer review
Shadowing
Mentoring
Secondments
Exchanges
Job rotation
Workshops
'Offers' and 'requests'

Department focus group
Partnering
External visits
Departmental audit of expertise

Individual
development

Professional
development

Departmental
development

Lunchtime forum
Team reviews
Learning noticeboard
Departmental newsletter

'Away days'
Collaborative workshops
Departmental meetings
Strategic planning conference
Benchmarking
Bringing in consultants

Collective
development

Figure 6.2 'One size doesn't fit all': a comprehensive approach to planning staff development activity

A common weakness of these events is that they fail to attract colleagues beyond a dedicated minority: i.e. they suffer from the 'persistent absentee' and/or the 'not invented here' syndromes. Well-targeted events, however, based on an intimate knowledge of individual learning needs, will help you overcome this problem and reach the parts of your department that other initiatives have failed to do before.

- Departmental 'away days' or retreats

Not an extended departmental meeting, or a protracted information-giving monologue, and not just a different location either, but rather a genuinely *different* interactive session held off-campus. One that has a clear purpose – on, say, a common problem, challenge or issue – is inclusive, nurtures team-building and generates productive outcomes.

- National and institutional funded projects in developing learning and teaching

Learning from one another

Audit of departmental expertise
How well do your colleagues know one another's expertise – in learning and teaching innovation, external examining, quality assessment and review, research applications, refereeing publications, editing journals, handling committees, utilizing new technologies, etc.? Establish a simple departmental database using a common pro forma.

'Offers' and 'requests'
A 'skills-swap' scheme which builds on the department's database of staff expertise. Staff members identify three areas in which they are willing to share their expertise with colleagues (say, using Blackboard or implementing equal opportunities) in return for help in addressing their own particular needs for help in, for example, applying for EU funding or writing up a book proposal. The advantages of such schemes are self-evident. Not only do they bring staff needs out into the open in a non-threatening way, they also recognize that we are often both experts and novices in equal measure.

Shadowing
Shadowing is a time-consuming but simple and very effective means of enabling staff to understand or learn to undertake the role of others – as programme leader, admissions tutor, assessment board chair and the like. It is particularly useful when there is little written guidance yet relatively easy access to experienced practitioners.

Mentoring
Often cited yet not always understood or applied, mentoring is in fact the fastest-growing method of professional development in all kinds of working environments today. Not simply in the conventional sense of helping new staff through their probationary period, but also in terms of career enhancement in general and, as we shall see later, in helping those disadvantaged in employment (such as women and ethnic minorities) overcome barriers to their progression in particular.

At its heart mentoring is a cooperative and nurturing relationship between a more experienced staff member and one who is less so. It is not a line management relationship. Or, put another way, when line managers attempt to act as mentors they invariably find the more formal aspects of their role (probationary review, workload allocation, performance appraisal, etc.) ultimately clash with the cooperative ethos on which the mentoring agreement is based.

Peer observation and review of teaching

Typically regarded with deep mistrust and suspicion not so long ago (and still in some quarters), peer observation and review has become the norm, rather than the exception, in most university departments. And for good reason too, for despite what the 'naysayers' may claim, by enabling staff to share their professional experience and expertise in confidence, peer observation is in fact one of the best ways in which staff can improve their teaching performance. To be fair, in those instances where peer review has not worked well, it is very often because the scheme has been operated with a very different purpose in mind – as a basis for appraisal or promotion, or simply for making judgements about staff. To avoid this fate, you need to ensure your scheme offers staff the guarantee of confidentiality. That way you are most likely to gain their confidence, if not always their consent. More than that, you will need to have clear ground rules for the process, as well as guidance on how participants should conduct each of the different aspects – the pre-meeting, the observation itself, and the post-observation feedback. Equally important, you should ensure staff are explicitly prompted to identify their professional development needs, on the one hand, and disseminate their own examples of good practice to the rest of their colleagues in the department, on the other.

Team reviews

Ensure your course teams and administrative teams get into the habit of reviewing their work – not in a passive, reactive way on an annual basis, as is so often the norm, but in a regular, systematic and ongoing fashion at every opportunity. Build reviews into the calendar in the first instance, though ideally they should become a normal part of the daily routine.

Job rotation

Not always practicable, and potentially disruptive, planned job rotation can be a powerful means not only of developing new ideas, skills and expertise but also of generating different perspectives, cross-fertilization and very often a new and improved way of doing things.

Departmental meetings

Learning and development may not be the primary business of meetings but are too often a neglected aspect of such gatherings. Increase awareness and reflection by including:

- staff report-backs on workshops and conferences they have attended as a brief agenda item (literally five minutes). Reports should take the form of one side of A4, outlining in bullet point format the key learning points for the department;

- an appendix to the meeting minutes outlining in summary form the development activities of staff: papers published, grants secured, conferences attended and so on.

Departmental focus groups

Much maligned and not always fairly, focus groups are under-rated and under-used in HE as a means of enhancing collective learning. Such groups, diverse in character, can often be a useful resource in helping your department to address particular concerns (such as student retention, assessment workload, the integration of part-time staff and so on) or indeed to develop new initiatives: the production of a development handbook for staff, the creation of a 'good practice' guide on assessment, etc.

Departmental newsletter

This works best, of course, if it is published on a regular basis. It is easier to maintain continuity – as well as interest – if you share the responsibility. Alternate the editors and use it to celebrate learning achievements as well as to inform staff of forthcoming events.

Learning noticeboard

Get each of your teams to take it in turn to highlight and celebrate 'a learning theme of the month': one, that is, which can be work- or indeed non-work-related.

Lunchtime forums

Identify your main organizational group (or groups): course leaders, subject heads, research coordinators or simply all departmental staff. Establish a regular meeting time – say the second Wednesday of each month, 12–2pm – and stick to it.

You supply the refreshments and help – or better still ask one of your colleagues – to develop a programme of activities based on what the participants themselves have said they would like to do. Such forums typically choose to focus on an array of issues: ranging from the topical (the implications of the planned fees review) to the local (a SWOT analysis of the department), the global (the New Academic Scholar), the theoretical (the multiple meanings of mass HE) and the practical (the institutional costing model for new courses). Either way, the participants in these informal gatherings nearly always derive far greater benefit in terms of knowledge, understanding and a sense of belonging than they had originally expected.

Learning from others

Staff secondments and exchanges

A staple of staff development, typically with other universities and usually with an international partner institution. You should also consider secondment opportunities for staff with partner employers. Indeed seconding staff into industry on a short-term basis (as opposed to bringing employers into academia) would arguably have a greater impact on your departmental culture than any other single factor.

Combined workshops with other departments

Too often an underestimated and underused practice. Departments all face common problems and issues, yet nearly always have varying levels of expertise. Combined workshops and joint events with other departments can be extremely valuable, then, in increasing learning through the sharing of ideas and expertise; in generating new and different perspectives on shared concerns and in addressing deficiencies (or 'skills gaps') particular to each. More than that, they are also likely – since individuals are inclined to behave better in the company of others – to do so in less time, and with less rancour, than would be the case if these events were confined solely to the members of your department.

Partnering

A 'blind date' scheme aimed at increasing awareness and understanding of working practices and improving working relationships institution-wide. Strike up an agreement with central services (or if a central service with departments), arrange reciprocal 'open-days' and pair off staff who then have to explain what they do.

Visits to other institutions

Don't waste time 'reinventing the wheel' if it already exists elsewhere. In such instances, it is far more cost-effective to have staff visit other institutions than it is to bring 'outsiders' in to tell them how something is done. Not only that, such visits often deepen staff understanding as well as influence their attitude to change, a shift in developmental learning that would be unlikely to occur if they had attended an 'in-house' seminar instead.

Bringing in consultants

Often misused and occasionally maligned, consultants can, nevertheless, in the right circumstances, still give you considerable 'added-value'. They come in all shapes and sizes and willingly perform any number of roles, most notably as 'doctor', 'detective', 'salesperson' or 'travel agent'. And herein lies the dilemma. On the one hand, you can use them in almost any circumstance, yet, on the other, you need to avoid using them in the wrong circumstances. The cardinal principle to remember is that *consultants are there as 'outsiders' to help you do what you can't do alone.* As such, you should use them as and when these instances arise – and only then.

To get the most out of them, you need to be honest, both with them and with staff, about the nature and purpose of their role, whether it be that of 'critical friend', impartial facilitator, advocate of new ideas, project manager or systems analyst, etc. That way, you should at least avoid the pitfalls that can so often stall a consultancy relationship when it is barely under way.

Benchmarking

The penchant for performance indicators, itself a consequence of the governmental drive for greater accountability, has become a commonplace activity both among, and within, many institutions. Try to ensure, however, that you do not rely solely on indicators from like-minded departments, or QAA guidelines, as your only comparators. Consciously assess yourself – or invite others to assess you – against other third-party instruments: the European Foundation Quality Model (EFQM) for business excellence, the Cabinet

Office Charter-Mark, Customer First, Investors in People, the Institute of Advice and Guidance and the like. Success in this regard, and all else, is likely to follow too.

Learning from you

Coaching

Training is specific, pre-planned and can take place on the job or off the job. It is about instructing, demonstrating, testing and applying in practice. Coaching is not like this at all – indeed it is just the opposite. Coaching is about helping others to help themselves through discussion, guidance, encouragement, observation and assessment. Or, as the Work Foundation (2006) puts it, coaching is 'the art of facilitating the performance, learning and development of others'. Widely regarded as the elusive key to success in managing today's business organization, it is ironically, by its very nature, a practice more ideally suited perhaps to academic environments than almost any other. As such, it is a golden opportunity you ought not to spurn. Indeed, you should regard coaching as one of the principal aspects of your role. Not everyone finds this easy, however, and those who do are not always effective. Some believe they simply can't do it or think it not worth the effort, while others find it goes against the grain of their natural belief system – particularly those with a propensity towards a 'command and control' or parenting style of management. There is no single right way to coach – different people and different situations require different approaches.

All that said, you will begin to overcome the doubts you may have, or alternatively improve your effectiveness, if you follow these two steps:

1 Follow the basic ground-rules of coaching (see Box 6.3).
2 Have, or be prepared to acquire, the essential key competencies for effective coaching, i.e. the ability to be an active listener, ask open questions, establish trust and rapport, remain non-judgemental and offer constructive feedback and evaluation (see Box 6.4).

If you succeed in mastering these two steps – in learning, that is, the art of coaching – you will be well placed to avoid the pitfalls that so often blight coaching relationships (see Box 6.5). Put another way, you will have helped colleagues to uncover strengths and abilities they never knew they had and also learned something about yourself in the process.

Delegation

Delegation is one of those principles often widely admired in theory, yet rarely implemented to the same extent in practice. HE is no exception. If anything, delegation is less likely to occur in academic settings than in others. Why this is so is not difficult to discern. The strong belief in individual autonomy, intrinsic motivation and independence which characterizes these settings often leads to situations in which heads of department become reluctant to assign particular tasks and duties, and even if they do, the implication is that academic staff wouldn't want them – or have the time to do them – anyway. When combined with the other reasons often given for not promoting delegation – that it is too risky, it takes too much time and effort, that 'nobody can do the job as well or as quickly as I can' (along with the unexpressed anxiety that maybe they can), etc. – then it is not surprising that delegation should have met with such stiff resistance in practice. Even

Box 6.3 The ground rules for effective coaching

1 Planning: agree the topic or issue

Opportunities for coaching often arise from performance reviews and the regular one-to-one meetings you hold. They can, too, present themselves naturally at very short notice (as when changes occur) in day-to-day work. Either way, the activity must still be a planned one and mutually agreed to, by you and the individual concerned.

2 Identify the goals

The goals must be:

- achievable
- measurable through quality, quantity, cost and time.

Maybe you are contemplating a proposal for external funding, a new academic programme, or changes to the system of support and guidance for students. Or – and perhaps more likely – you are seeking to persuade individuals to become more flexible in their views about the 'right' way to do a job, about how they manage their time, their order of priorities, the ways in which they channel their energies, etc. Either way, the objective is to agree the goal and the skill development to be achieved, ideally volunteered by the individual. Avoid imposing the goal yourself.

3 Promote discovery

Coaching is non-directive. You are there to encourage individuals to find their own solutions, not tell them how to solve their problems. There will of course be a tendency for pre-judgements to exist on either side and false information may well have been gathered from others. Your role is to help your coachee explore a situation, identify options and select a way forward – to discover, that is, the constraints, demands and full implications of the task they are undertaking. In doing so, you must ensure they pursue all lines of enquiry, draw out all the consequences for each and evaluate the likely outcomes of adopting particular courses of action.

4 Set the parameters

Having set the goals and discussed options, now set the parameters: i.e. establish clearly what has to be done and by when. You can then both monitor progress and control any risk which may be involved.

5 Authorize and empower

It is essential that the individual does not charge ahead and find blockages in every direction. Make sure they have right of access to information, attendance on courses and other colleagues as well as clerical support and expenses as appropriate. Inform other people who need to know what is happening.

6 Recap and review

At the end of each session, make sure everything is clear. Ask the individual to recap the points discussed and agreed and note down the action points. Review these at the start of the next session.

Source: adapted from Work Foundation, 2006; Adair and Thomas, 2008.

Box 6.4 Key skills for effective coaching

1 Active listening
Good listening requires discipline and commitment to show people you value and respect their contribution. You can demonstrate this in a number of ways:

- Stop talking. You can't listen if you are talking.
- Put the person at ease. Be attentive – look interested.
- Allow air space – give the person room to talk.
- Remove distractions – don't doodle or shuffle papers. Maintain eye contact.
- Show empathy – try to see their point of view from their position.
- Be patient, do not interrupt and restrain emotions.
- Avoid confrontation through criticism.
- Ask questions and encourage the talker to respond.
- Cut your mental chatter and concentrate.

Be wary of the barriers to effective listening. Ensure your listening is not of the following kind:

- 'On-off' – cut out the distraction.
- 'Red flag' – try not to get irritated.
- 'Open ears – Closed mind' – avoid jumping to conclusions too quickly.
- 'Glassy-eyed' – fools no one. Save the day-dreaming for later.
- 'Too-deep-for-me' – concentrate harder, don't shut off.
- 'Matter-over-mind' – be magnanimous. You can always make your point later.
- 'Subject-centred not speaker-centred' – don't forget empathy.
- 'Fact-driven' – keep with the flow, you can always check the facts later.
- 'Pencil-driven' – ditto and make sure your maintain eye contact.
- 'Hubbub' – switch off the noise and focus.

2 Asking questions
Questions guide and help the individual to establish understanding. Use different types as required:

- Open – the question that avoids a yes or no answer and encourages the individual to open up.
- Fact seeking – ask for information by invitation but beware becoming interrogative.
- Probing – asking for examples or direct specific instructions.
- Reflective – use to respond to signals of feeling about what is being said. Identify strong feelings such as anger, frustration, worry, uncertainty and reflect these back.
- Summarize – at intervals, summarize the discussion, the key learning points and action points. Focus information which shows you have been listening.
- Suspend judgement – listen to information with an open mind. If you close your mind you will start asking closed questions and not gather useful information.

Feedback
Feedback is essential to the process of coaching so that progress can be evaluated. To be successful the key elements are:

- Give recognition for efforts made.
- Ask what has happened – use probes.
- Ask how things could have been done differently.
- Ask what has been learned.
- Ask what further actions are now necessary.

- Suggest or explore other options.
- Encourage the individual to implement agreed actions.
- Be flexible to adjust your approach as needed – stay positive.

Evaluation
Evaluation should be based on an analysis of agreed measurements of progress. You must therefore have clear objectives from the outset. Ensure too that you monitor actual progress through regular contact with the coachee. Ask for stakeholder evaluation as well as self-assessment. Determine and agree conclusions and key learning and development outcomes.

Source: adapted from Work Foundation, 2006; Adair and Thomas, 2008.

Box 6.5 Coaching pitfalls you must avoid

- Unclear objectives
- Not agreeing goals
- Not assessing a situation
- Losing objectivity
- Not agreeing next steps
- Hidden agenda(s)

- Solving their problems
- Being judgemental
- Trying to prove a point
- Imposing your view
- Not listening

---

so, you must not allow yourself to fall into the same trap – otherwise your department will begin to exhibit the characteristics of those working environments in which delegation is conspicuous by its absence: namely, under-development, plateau performance, a climate of mistrust, silo thinking and a head constantly engaged in a losing struggle to stay on top of things.

You need to set aside your fears and reservations whatever their origin.

- If you have concerns about 'letting go', remember you can't possibly do everything yourself nor is it your job to; and besides, the rewards – in time saved and people developed – are potentially as great as the risk incurred.
- If you feel insecure about staff making a better fist of it than you, remember you will gain credit as well as them.
- If you simply don't trust staff, then remember that trust is a two-way street. You have to show trust yourself in order to earn the trust of others; i.e. it is down to you to take the first step to break the cycle of mistrust.
- If you think staff won't do it, you will never know unless you ask. Don't underestimate people's desire to take on a new responsibility – to feel valued and to have challenge in their work.

You need to recognize, in other words, the critical significance of delegation. It goes to the very heart of your capability as an academic leader for it is about enabling, developing, recognizing and utilizing the value of all those colleagues around you. Not only that – it is equally good for you, your department and your institution. It is in short, like coaching, yet another essential art you must learn to master (see Box 6.6).

Box 6.6 Principles of effective delegation

What is delegation?

Delegation is the practice of giving one of your colleagues the authority to take decisions within defined areas of responsibility; in essence, to authorize someone to do a job on your behalf. It does not mean, however, that you abdicate responsibility for it. You still continue to be accountable – to 'carry the can' – if things go wrong.

(Then again, risks can be minimized so long as you carry out the planning and timing in a proper fashion.)

The benefits of delegation

For you: it will provide more time and energy to focus on what you're supposed to be doing, leading and managing (i.e. not doing yourself every single job for which you are responsible); it will also demonstrate to others you have confidence in yourself and your colleagues and that you are capable of being an effective leader.

For staff: it can enhance their self-esteem, job satisfaction and professional development as well as their sense of being valued, of being in control.

For your department: it brings a fresh perspective (and maybe a better one) to the task at hand, provides for cover in your absence and identifies a feasible future replacement.

For your institution: it helps in developing future leaders (or 'succession planning'); increases the levels of commitment and morale, and improves efficiency, effectiveness and productivity.

Planning for delegation

Before beginning, brainstorm your role:

* What do I do? Make a list of 20 or so different aspects of your job.
* Why do I do it? Should I keep it and why?
* Identify those tasks which you cannot delegate (matters of discipline, confidentiality, financial jurisdiction and the like) and approx 6–7 that you can – such as for example staff development coordination, pastoral support for students, new courses, liaison with external examiners, etc.
* To whom could I give the job now?
* Have a one-to-one to assess their willingness. Don't assume that staff won't want to. Don't underestimate the impact of your willingness to assign authority to them. There is no surer way of demonstrating the trust and confidence you have in them.
* Who else should I be developing to do it and how?

Implementing delegation

* Clarify the objectives and identify the task and constraints with the individual.
* Brief them in a genuine, open and enthusiastic manner.
* Establish priorities, check resources and identify any training requirements.
* Agree a target handover date and inform all relevant parties.
* Monitor and evaluate progress through regular one-to-one support.

Pitfalls to avoid

* Underselling – don't trivialize the task or duty you're handing over, or it will be perceived as a boring chore.
* Overselling – don't over-hype it either – otherwise you may give the delegate a conflicting sense of priorities or worse still imbue them with self-doubt.
* Supervising too closely – resist the temptation to intrude on the delegate the whole time.
* Supervising not nearly enough – don't let the delegate flounder. Offer help and guidance to support them through their learning curve. Learn when to step in and when not.
* Usurping their authority – don't under-cut or over-rule the delegate.

Source: adapted from Work Foundation, 2006; Adair and Thomas, 2008.

Learning for all

Inducting new staff

Deemed a high priority in theory, staff induction in practice is not always taken seriously in some university departments, and is occasionally overlooked altogether in others. This is a huge mistake on their part. In such instances newcomers are needlessly forced to put more time and energy (and expense) into 'settling in' (if indeed they ever do) than would ordinarily be the case. Equally, the department heads will have forgone a golden opportunity to guide the newcomers' future contribution and behaviour at the very moment when the latter are most receptive to such influence. Put another way, induction is not simply an act of kindness, but is also a sound business practice and universally recognized as such within and beyond HE.

Most universities do, however, offer induction programmes to new staff. Such programmes usually focus – quite rightly – on introducing staff to the institution itself: its character and ethos (the history, mission, structure and organization of the university, etc.) as well as the way it operates in practice, typically with regard to generic matters such as health and safety, personnel, library and computing services, telecommunications and voicemail, reprographics and so on. The more adventurous programmes do not rely solely on information packs and presentations, but also seek to include tours (virtual as well as guided), treasure hunts, quizzes and receptions too.

Whichever way your programme is structured, your role as head of department is to ensure your newcomers – whether experienced or probationary – are given the time and opportunity to attend it. More than that, you also need to make arrangements to cover all those epiphenomenal matters peculiar to your department (access to stationery, clarification on course development, conditions of service, etc.) which are not dealt with in your general institutional programme. You can do this in a number of ways:

- through developing your own departmental guide for new staff: one, that is, which complements, not duplicates, your central induction programme. And do not forget, as so many do, to include a visit to your Students Union as part of the itinerary;
- by appointing a mentor – or, if the circumstances warrant a less formal approach, a 'buddy' – for each new member of staff, to help them through their first six months;
- by taking an active part yourself in their induction.

This will ensure that the induction process is, as it should be – *a planned and systematic one*, and not one left to the vagaries of circumstance. The most critical aspect in the effective induction of new staff, however, is – as with so many other things – that of *attitude*. If you take it seriously it is more likely they will, and the reverse holds equally true. It is essential therefore that you start as you mean to carry on, otherwise you will be facing an uphill struggle from the outset. Remember, too, that induction is about initiating newcomers to your department's culture. If you are satisfied with 'the way we do things around here', then all well and good; if not you should use induction for what it is – an opportunity to begin again, to start afresh. Put another way, you can take advantage of the fact that new staff are not yet inculcated in the behavioural norms of your department as a means of changing how it operates. After all, new staff – like students – have a *tabula rasa* when they first arrive. You need to do your utmost, then, to ensure that what they learn about your department is what you want them to learn.

Part-time staff

If universities were judged as employers solely on the basis of the experience of their part-time staff, it is likely that few would emerge with their reputation intact, let alone enhanced. Routinely neglected, casual staff, it seems – if reports are to be believed – occupy some nether world in which they are expected to meet the everyday demands of academic work – the development of schemes of work, the completion of module specifications, the marking of assessments and attendance at meetings – often without support, and occasionally without pay of any kind. Worse still, it appears that this shabby treatment is often justified on the basis that part-time staff have lower capabilities: a mistaken assumption which in itself is discriminatory, and which, in effect, has a disproportionate impact on those (and women in particular) who do not always follow a conventional career path. Not surprisingly, teaching unions have accused universities of cultivating managers whose dominant mindset is one that views people as readily dispensable (Baty, 2006; Jaques, 1998; Marcus, 2009; NATFHE 2001; UCEA, 2000).

This is of course a path you should not follow. Or put another way, you need to recognize that there is nothing inherently wrong with casualization. Indeed so long as you do not come to over-rely on it (a staffing ratio of 80 per cent full time to 20 per cent part time is around the norm), casualization, like induction, is another sound business practice. In this case it offers you flexibility in planning staff workload allocations and managing your departmental budget. Not only that, it invariably brings in fresh ideas, new perspectives and expertise and very often a great deal of enthusiasm. Indeed, one of the enduring myths about relying on part-time teaching support is that it will have an adverse impact on quality. This is patent nonsense – as well as dismissive of the energy, enthusiasm and talent which the great majority of part-timers bring to their work. When issues of quality do arise it is usually because part-timers have not been supported in the way they should have been, not because they lack capability. If you are to avoid falling into this trap, you must make sure you respond to the needs of your part-time staff with the same consistency and resolution as you do those of your full-time staff. Not because you're legally obliged to (under European Union law part-time staff are entitled to the same employment rights as full-time staff; to do otherwise is to discriminate unlawfully) but because it is self-evidently the right thing to do – for them, for you and for your department. More specifically, you need to address the specific concerns that so often blight the part-time staff experience: the lack of access to accommodation, telephone, email, printing, car parking, ID and so on and, most especially, their sense of isolation. You can do this in a number of ways – by:

- organizing a proper induction programme for part-time staff;
- establishing a policy for the development and support of part-timers, one that specifies explicitly the pro-rata entitlements they can expect (initial training, desk space, access to library and computing facilities, invitations to 'away-days', etc.);
- ensuring all part-timers are included on your department and email circulation lists so that they routinely receive the same information as full-time staff;
- including part-timers in your peer review of teaching schemes;

- fostering a part-time teaching network; bringing part-timers together socially and publishing a part-timers' directory listing contact details;
- appointing a mentor or 'buddy' for their period of employment;
- offering review and development opportunities in the same way you would to full-time staff.

In this way, you should at least be able to ensure that your part-time staff will feel valued sufficiently to want to make the 'full' contribution they may have been prevented from, or felt unable to do, hitherto. This situation, in itself, will put your department one up on very many others – and rightly so.

Recruiting and selecting staff

> I was gifted at an early age – the minute I saw a person I could see the flaw in that person. It was like a curse.
>
> V.S. Naipaul, 2002

> How can I possibly know what other members of the faculty promotions committee were thinking and on what basis they arrived at the different statements they made in the committee meeting?
>
> Cambridge professor giving feedback
> to a failed professorial candidate, May 2000

Induction, like staff development, derives from a common starting point: the recruitment and selection of new staff. Induction we have covered, but not as yet recruitment. The appointment of new staff is a process with which many will not only be familiar but also feel comfortable. And *prima facie* it has a chronological symmetry – from job analysis and job design through to advertisement, interview and selection – which makes it appear a relatively straightforward process.

Yet therein lies its main weakness. It is precisely because we approach this activity with such certainty – after all, who doesn't like to think they are the best judge of character and ability? – that the probability of making mistakes also becomes that much greater: the temptation to 'cut corners' in determining the nature of the appointment and in specifying the job criteria; the over-reliance on a single selection method; the propensity to appoint those in your own self-image and so on. Indeed, it is hard to identify another process quite so prone to flaws in practice as that of appointing staff. There is a very real danger, then, if you are not careful, that you may end up, however unwittingly, not only appointing someone who is unsuitable (which happens more often than many care to admit) but also falling foul of the discrimination laws in the process. As most of us now operate in a climate of ever-increasing resource constraint you will, moreover, have squandered a golden opportunity to improve your staffing resource.

The purpose of this final section is to show how you can avoid these pitfalls, or, more positively, what you can do to give yourself the best opportunity of both promoting diversity and making the 'right' appointment for you and your department. To demonstrate that, indeed, you do have the attributes of a good employer.

To appoint or not? Making the business case

The first rule in making the right appointment is *to think through precisely what you're looking for*. Seems obvious – and it is – yet it is still surprising how many fail to do this adequately in practice. Why it is not always given the full attention it deserves is usually because the recruiters have fallen into the classic trap of making one if not two false assumptions. One – since vacancies arise as and when people leave or retire, the case for filling them is self-evident. And the other – if the last person who did the job was really good it is assumed they must have a clone to replace them. To avoid this trap, it is important you keep an 'open mind' on both the need for an appointment and its nature. For all vacancies – whether arising from expansion or from staff who have left – you should ask yourself:

- Is there really a staffing gap in our provision? In the case of growth, is it more imagined than real? What is the hard evidence, as opposed to speculation? If a member of staff is leaving, what specialist (not generic) expertise has the department lost? What is the nature of the staff workload you have to make good – its size, breadth, distinguishing features?
- If there is a gap, what is the most *appropriate* way of filling it? By reorganizing the workloads of remaining staff members? By hiring one or more part-timer(s)? By making overtime payments? By sub-contracting the work? Or by recruiting a full-blown replacement?
- What other staffing shortages do you have in your department? Are they similar in size or nature to this new one? How do these relate to your department's strategic objectives and your long-term staffing requirements: the different skills mix, the age profile of your staff and so on? What area should take priority? Why?
- If you require a new appointment, how will that person's role be similar to and different from the previous incumbent's?

Don't rush these questions; the more you reflect the more value you are likely to get from trying to view the vacancy in a different and broader light. You may ultimately decide on one of the above options and not appoint at all, or alternatively you may use the vacancy (or 'saving') to fund a new appointment in another aspect of your department's work altogether. Then again, after due consideration, you may decide you do indeed need a full-blown replacement. Either way, you will more than likely have to present an appointment 'business case' (or rationale) to your HR department, or university, or faculty staffing group for their approval before you can proceed.

From their perspective this exercise is very much strictly a business one and rightly so: i.e. a matter of budgetary numbers. How many students do you have? How many staff members? What is your staff–student ratio? What is the average staff workload? What proportion is your part-time staffing complement? How much and how many are your sources of research and enterprise income? What are your department's mid-term priorities? What and where is the market demand?

As such you need to understand their orientation and respond to them on that basis; do not feel obliged – as so many do – to write a lengthy narrative extolling the virtues of your department. Such non-quantified commentaries clog up the work of staffing committees with regular monotony, are never appreciated by its members, and leave them second-guessing the author's intention. Instead, save your time and theirs by outlining your rationale in a short concise statement (no more than one side of A4) that includes the pertinent facts and numbers.

Preparing the job description and person specification

Your business case approved, you then need to draw up a job description and a person specification. These HR tools are, of course, a well-known staple of the recruitment process and – as in the first instance of determining the nature of the appointment – are just as easily overlooked precisely for that reason. While this may not be so much an instance of familiarity breeding contempt, there is often a tendency in practice to treat them far less seriously than they deserve. This is a fatal mistake. Indeed the difficulties that often arise during the final stages of selection can invariably be traced back to misunderstandings and flaws in the original design of these two documents. In the worst instances some selection panels even manage to confuse the two.

To avoid this outcome you will need to make sure you not only differentiate the two, but that you consider each of them with due regard to accuracy and detail as well as diversity. Your HR department will be able to advise on these matters and it is very likely that your institution may well have developed its own 'in-house' style. Either way, there are common ground rules you can – and should – follow.

The job description

A job description or job purpose or role definition is a summary report of information relating to a particular job. It can, as we noted earlier, come in a variety of forms – ranging from the competence-based one illustrated in Appendix I to more conventional ones which list a range of duties. Whichever you prefer, you should ensure that your job role:

- is written in a style that is clear, concise and gender neutral;
- keeps words to a minimum, avoids duplication, yet gives prospective candidates sufficient information to decide whether to proceed with an application;
- identifies the 'principal accountabilities' (or duties) attached to the post;
- explains where the post is located in the organizational structure.

In other words, it should specify, in a way that is precise and accurate as well as non-discriminatory, all the critical determinants of the post (as exemplified in the specimen outline in Box 6.7): namely the job title, location, line management relationship, job purpose, main tasks and employment terms and conditions (Torrington *et al.*, 2007).

The person specification

The person specification, by contrast, outlines the characteristics that an individual would need to possess in order to fulfil the requirements of a job. Typically expressed in terms of the qualifications, experience, skills and abilities required of applicants, the person specification is based on – and derived from – the job description. It is not drawn up – nor should it ever be (despite the temptation in practice to do so) – either parallel with or in isolation from the job description. That way, you risk jeopardizing the entire appointment process for it is the person specification which forms the basis for the next stages.

Box 6.7 Job role for a learning and teaching fellow

Job title	Faculty Learning and Teaching Fellow
Job purpose	To provide leadership in learning and teaching innovation across the Faculty. To contribute to the realization of the University's learning and teaching strategy. To act as a role model for continuous professional development in learning and teaching.
Reports to	Faculty director of learning support and development.
Campus base	City Campus.
Key responsibilities	<ul><li>Take the lead in at least one of the Faculty's prioritized areas of development: e.g. assessment of learning; e-learning and e-tutoring; problem-based learning; progress files; student-centred learning; work-based learning.</li><li>Provide individual expertise in relation to an aspect of learning and teaching.</li><li>Work collaboratively with subject groups, programme teams and individual tutors to enhance the student learning experience, e.g. subject reviews, programme validation.</li><li>Proactively disseminate best practice in learning and teaching innovation across the Faculty.</li><li>Contribute to the development and implementation of strategies to embed new approaches to learning and teaching across the Faculty.</li><li>Work with other members of the team of Fellows to enhance and develop learning and teaching across the Faculty.</li><li>Participate actively in regional, national and international forums on learning and teaching innovation.</li><li>Act as a role model for continuous professional development.</li></ul>

Terms and conditions		
	Job title:	Title retained beyond term of office
	Length of office:	3 years (subject to annual review)
	Appointment:	0.5 FTE
	Responsibility allowance:	£2,500 per year (throughout duration of office)
	Number of Appointments:	3
	Date of Appointment:	Start of academic year
	Eligibility:	All staff engaged in teaching and/or the support of learning.

In devising your person specification you should do the following, as in the specimen outlined in Box 6.8:

- Avoid overestimating the characteristics of the person required to do the job, otherwise you risk restricting your potential pool of applicants or alternatively appointing someone who is overqualified. Thus in the case of educational

Box 6.8 Person specification for a learning and teaching fellow

Criteria	Priority (1, 2)	Method of assessment
1 Qualifications		
(a) Education to first degree level	1	Application Form
(b) Recognized teacher training qualification	2	Application Form
(c) Achieving or seeking accreditation from The Academy for the Advancement of Learning and Teaching in HE	1	Letter of Application
2 Skills/Knowledge		
(a) Knowledge of contemporary approaches to learning and teaching in HE	1	Presentation, interview
(b) Ability to communicate ideas clearly, in writing and orally	1	Presentation, teaching portfolio
(c) Ability to empathize with staff from a wide variety of academic backgrounds	1	Interview
(d) Ability to use a variety of means to support staff development in learning and teaching	1	Letter of application, interview
3 Experience		
(a) Successful track record in teaching and/or support for learning	1	Letter of application
(b) Awareness of changes in HE curriculum	1	Presentation, interview
(c) Experience in one of the specified priority areas with demonstrable achievement	1	Application form, interview
4 Personal qualities		
(a) Innovative	1	Letter of application
(b) Resilient, self-confident and credible	1	Presentation, interview
(c) Energy, enthusiasm and good humour	1	Presentation, interview

1 **Priority 1** indicates *essential* criteria – extremely unlikely that a candidate would be successful if unable to satisfy any one of these.

2 **Priority 2** indicates *desirable* criteria – candidates failing to satisfy a number of these are unlikely to be successful.

requirements, for example, you should stipulate the minimum necessary for satisfactory performance.

- Do not assume (as is a common in HE) that qualifications guarantee skills such as organizational ability, oral and written communication and team working.
- Consider the importance of potential. Skills can always be learned but deep-seated personality traits may never alter. Thus someone with the potential to be able to learn a task may be an acceptable substitute for a person who has already obtained those skills, particularly if the latter is not as suitable as the former for appointment. Remember, too, some skills may have been developed from work experience which under-represented groups may have been unable to obtain.
- Take care to avoid unlawful indirect or direct discrimination such as length of experience (which indirectly discriminates against women who have had career breaks to raise a family); specific qualifications (which may exclude people who

have gained the required knowledge or skills in other ways or who may have equivalent qualifications from another country); size or physical strength of candidates (instead, specify the capability needed and request evidence during the selection process) (ECU, 2004; CUCO, 1997).

- Distinguish between those characteristics which are essential and those which are desirable, thereby avoiding being unnecessarily restrictive.
- Write (as in the case of the job description) in a style that is not only gender neutral but also clear, concise and accurate. For example, you should avoid using terms such as 'a good/sound educational background': what do you mean by 'good' or 'sound'? 'Relevant experience in a related field' is another: what do you consider 'relevant' or 'related'? Likewise 'previous experience required' – it is possible to have had 10 years' bad experience. Stipulate the type, level and quality of experience you require.
- Reflect on, and determine, how best you will 'evidence' these characteristics: through the application form, personal portfolio, interview, presentation, psychometric test, CV, etc.

Advertising, short-listing and selection

Advertising

When you advertise you ought to have two main aims: to reach as many potential applicants as possible, and to enhance the image of your department and institution in the process. It is important you do not lose sight of either aim. To reach potential candidates you should advertise in the appropriate newspapers (the national education press etc.) journals (professional, specialist) and electronic networks in a way that secures an optimum balance between coverage and cost and is also most likely to produce a reasonable field of candidates to do the job. In doing so, you should also consider both the local and ethnic community press, as well as taking 'positive action' to encourage job applications by explicitly stating you would welcome them from women or men or minority groups in those instances where few, or no, members of that sex or group have been employed in your organization in the previous year.

Every recruitment exercise is also a marketing opportunity. You therefore need to give careful consideration to the impression your advertisement conveys. UK universities have traditionally been slower than their counterparts in the USA to acknowledge this reality. While American universities have in many instances articulated distinctive 'positioning statements', some UK institutions, by contrast, have still not moved beyond proclaiming to the outside world that they are a 'No Smoking Employer' or that they are not yet equipped to handle online applications. The absurdity inherent in such notions – the idea that of all the things they could tell strangers about themselves they should choose these in particular – beggars belief. It is likely to disappear, however, as the new competitive environment forces institutions to take their 'brand-image' and target markets far more seriously than ever before. The danger then, of course, is that universities may veer to the other extreme – to that of hype and spin (HEPI, 2009).

From your perspective you need to ensure that your advertisement is not only accurate, logical and non-discriminatory in language, but that it also conveys the 'right message': the one that intuitively reflects your core purpose and values, your key strengths and aspirations, etc. If it does not, you risk putting off those who may be ideally suited, and attracting others who may not be. The same holds true of the further information pack you send prospective applicants. Don't opt for the lazy way out, as others sometimes do, and rely on 'a glossy' and the standard institutional application form. It is just not good enough. In both cases:

- Think of the lasting impression you are giving to those who do not proceed with an application, as well as those who do.
- Give your advert and further information the 'personal touch' and customize them in the same way you expect prospective candidates to do with their applications.

Your HR and marketing departments have the specialist expertise to help get your message across. Make sure you use them.

Short-listing

If your advertisement, job description and person specification are equally consistent, as well as accurate, then the short-listing of applicants should, in theory, be relatively straightforward. You can also make the task easier by asking prospective applicants to explicitly address the individual criteria laid down in the person specification in a 'letter of application' or 'supporting statement'. That said, practical difficulties arise in some instances simply from the sheer volume of applications (particularly in subjects where market supply outstrips demand) as well as from the potential for discrimination. Either way, you can best overcome such difficulties by sticking to the following short-listing conventions:

- Operate on the principle of inclusion rather than exclusion so that the process is positive; look for strengths rather than shortcomings.
- Use only the original agreed criteria on the person specification. In other words, do not allow the introduction of any new criteria or the use of any criteria that may lead to discrimination (i.e. age, gender, race, marital status, religion, disability or sexual orientation).
- Consider only the facts and do not make any assumptions; you will thus avoid the risk of stereotyping and at the same time ensure that internal and external applications are treated alike.
- Prepare your shortlist with at least one other person, if not the whole selection panel.
- Use only desirable criteria when a large number of applicants appear to meet the essential criteria. In such instances, you and your selectors should each compile a personal list of, say, 10 candidates. Reveal them to one another and seek agreement. There should be a high degree of consensus if you have each followed the process properly. If not, seek to reduce the areas of disagreement by classifying candidates as 'strong', 'possible' or 'maverick'. Continue the discussion until you all agree a final shortlist or, as some tend to favour nowadays, an initial 'long-list'. In either case take care to guard against including compromise candidates: those not strong but offensive to no one.
- Record, for feedback purposes, the reasons, in each case, for short-listing or not short-listing individual applicants.

Selection

Interviewing, of course, is the most common method of selection. Yet it is not always the most appropriate, or the most accurate, of devices. Indeed, its critics claim that not only are interview panels invariably flawed, but that, at worst, unstructured interviews are little better than using astrology to assess candidates. What is clear, as most now recognize, is that, used on their own, interviews are not a reliable predictor of future performance. Consequently, most organizations now use a variety of selection methods in appointing staff, not so much as an alternative to interviews, but rather as a complement to them. HE is no exception. It is as commonplace now, for example, to ask prospective tutors to give a presentation, or submit a teaching portfolio, as it is to ask managers to take psychometric tests or attend an assessment centre (Torrington *et al.*, 2007).

You, too, need to give this matter due consideration when making your own appointment. To what extent would it help your decision-making to ask candidates to deliver a mini-lecture, lead a research seminar, give a presentation, offer a SWOT analysis on your department or the future of HE, take a personality test, etc. Equally, you need to remember that *selection is a two-way process* and that you should give candidates both the opportunity to visit your department, and to meet informally with staff members. As for the interview itself, there are a number of simple, yet important, steps you can – and should – take to address the flaws in the process and make it a more reliable one:

Arrange recruitment and selection training for all panel members

It is common practice nowadays to ensure that all interviewers are trained in awareness of equal opportunities. You only have to reflect on your own personal experience as an interviewee, however, to realize that this is not nearly enough. Too often a cosy assumption is made – and here academia is conspicuously more guilty than others – that any reasonably educated individual can interview effectively at the drop of a hat. More than that, interviewers are often unaware of the very things that bring the process into disrepute – namely their own predisposition to bias. Research, for example, tells us that interviewers very often decide to accept or reject a candidate within the first three or four minutes ('the first impression' syndrome) and then spend the remainder of the interview seeking to confirm that their initial impression was right. Evidence also suggests that we all tend to approach interviews with a mental model of a 'typical' interviewee and are therefore susceptible to the 'contrast tendency': i.e. we over-react either positively or negatively when a highly qualified or very weak candidate is preceded by an average one. Indeed as interviewers we are prone to committing – as Box 6.10 illustrates – a whole host of errors in the process (ACAS, 2008a; Hanscombe, 1998). A professional development programme will not of course eliminate all these errors but, in helping to raise the level of awareness and consciousness of such flaws among members, it should at least enable them to avoid the most obvious pitfalls in making their final selection.

Make sure everyone knows in advance what to expect

In the case of:

- candidates: where, when and to whom they should report; the activities and tasks they are expected to undertake; the time and place of interview;

- panel members: who they are; where and when they should gather (typically 30 minutes before the first interview).

There are no hard and fast rules on the size and composition of interview panels. Nevertheless you should always aim to interview with at least one other person (of the opposite sex) and ideally with a small representative group of 3–4 (anything bigger becomes progressively more unwieldy) which should also include your HR staff relations adviser. Although the panel has a collective responsibility, it is also a good idea to have one member specifically designated to act as the group's monitor with regard to equal opportunities. Check, too, that your HR representative circulates interviewers with a candidate information pack – containing the interview schedule, job description, person specification, advertisement and individual applications – at least three days prior to the interview.

- Support staff and facilities.

Confirm that candidates have been asked if they need any prior assistance in attending the interview; that arrangements have been made for hotels, transport, car parking and refreshments and that reception staff know who is expected, when and for what purpose.

Develop and agree a structured interview plan – and stick to it

There are – despite what some of your colleagues might argue to the contrary – a number of compelling reasons why interviews should be structured, which you ignore at your peril:

- A structure makes sure you cover all the relevant areas (as well as avoid the irrelevant ones).
- The candidate will expect a structure within which to operate.
- It looks professional. Structure lends the process a sense of coherence and direction.
- It makes the most effective use of the time available.
- It can act as a memory aid for panel members when making and comparing notes on candidates.
- It makes it easier to compare candidates.
- It is the most reliable guarantor of eliminating discriminatory practice.

Rehearse these arguments with any of your panel members who may beg to differ. Then seek to agree a structure based on:

- the specific criteria which will be used for assessing the candidates, i.e. those articulated in the person specification;
- the areas of questioning to be put to *all* candidates by each member of the panel related to these criteria;
- the order in which each panel member will ask their particular set of questions. You need to ensure the process is systematic and not one in which panel members 'jump about', posing questions of the candidates simultaneously. Make the sequence a logical one so that conversation flows naturally;

- a standard length of time, typically no more than 45 minutes followed by 5–10 minutes in which members can write up their notes immediately after each candidate has been interviewed;
- the number of candidates to be interviewed. You ought not to exceed four in any one session and allow for comfort breaks in between.

Seek to ensure each interviewee has the opportunity to give of their best

Once agreed, it ought not to be too difficult, hopefully, to get your colleagues to stick to the plan. You still have the problem of how to get what you want from each of the candidates. There are, of course, as is well known, a number of interview strategies you can deploy – the 'sweet and sour' strategy, the 'stress' strategy, the 'problem-solving' strategy and so on. The one typically used in both HE and elsewhere, and rightly so, is the so-called 'frank and friendly' approach for the very practical reason that the less interviewees feels threatened and are relaxed, the more likely it is they will be forthcoming in the information they offer (Torrington *et al.*, 2007). You have a critical role to play, then – in ensuring that both the tone and the style of the interview is such that candidates feel able to do just that. You can do this in a variety of ways:

- Arrange the seating as informally as possible by having a low table or nothing between the interviewers and candidates. Barriers like large tables and use of telephones during an interview can be threatening and can get in the way of effective communication.
- Attempt to put the candidate at their ease. Adopt a friendly, easy manner. Be attentive. Project a sense of peacefulness and quiet. Smile and make eye contact without being overbearing or relentless. Introduce the panel and yourself. Explain the interview format.
- Seek to establish rapport. Try to find something non-controversial that genuinely interests you about each of the candidates: 'I noticed with interest that you mentioned . . . on your application form. Can you fill me in on some of the details?' Show empathy: 'I would have found the situation you're describing very frustrating/demanding. How did you feel about it? So what did you do as a result/how did you deal with that?'
- Take care with the range and type of questions you and your colleagues use; choose the right type of question that fits the particular circumstance (see Box 6.9).
- Rule out questions that imply the candidate is going to be treated differently in the interview or job because of their race, gender, disability or sexual orientation. For example, do not allow questions like: 'How will you cope as the only woman/ disabled/black person in the department?' 'Do you think people will take you seriously as a female manager?'
- Prepare your questions for the candidates. Your questioning technique is extremely important but so, of course, is the subject matter you choose to talk about. Research tells us, for example, that *past behaviour in a given situation is very often the best predictor of future performance* (Torrington *et al.*, 2007). As such, it makes far more sense for you to spend time probing candidates on this aspect of their previous experience than it does in canvassing their opinion on the various matters at hand. Again you

Box 6.9 Questioning techniques to employ

Type of question	Nature of question	Purpose
Open	What, when, why, how 'Tell me about . . .'	• To get the candidates to open up • To establish rapport • To explore opinions, attitudes and feelings
Probing or 'follow through'	Concentrates on specific points: • 'What exactly . . .' • 'Describe to me step by step . . .' • 'Can you give me an example to help me understand?'	• To get under surface of initial answer • To clarify uncertainties • To test validity of a more general response
Closed	Prompts short or yes/ no response	• To confirm basic facts • To avoid strain at the start of a discussion or to bring discussion back on the rails (Use sparingly and always follow up with an 'open' question. Do not misuse either. For example, do not ask 'Was your last job challenging?' Instead rephrase as: 'What did you find challenging about your last job?')

Avoid: Leading, multiple and hypothetical questions.

should do this by asking 'behavioural questions' related to the specific competencies in the person specification, for example: Can you think of a time when . . .
- you had to organize others in the completion of a major project?
- you changed your style of teaching or delivery of the course in response to student feedback?
- you had to make a decision about two conflicting priorities?
- a member of your course team was not 'pulling their weight'?
- you identified a potential problem which you successfully averted?
- you had to make a difficult decision concerning the allocation of resources?
- 'Walk me through the situation.'
- 'Tell me your part in it.'
- 'What happened as a result of what you did/said?'
- 'What was the outcome?'
• Remember to leave time for the candidates to ask their questions.

Rating bias

Watch out for rating bias in yourself and your panel members when making your final selection. You should not judge candidates – nor allow your panel members to – until all the interviews have been completed and all available information (including that of feedback from presentations, tests, etc. has been gathered together. Your panel should then review each candidate's performance in turn – not initially against one another but rather against the demands of the job.

- Systematically use a common rating system (strong–average–weak; 1–10, etc.) based on the selection criteria – easier said than done. Enlist your colleagues' support in ensuring you all avoid the classic interview errors listed in Box 6.10.
- Do not make any assumptions. Be especially wary of members expressing unease about candidates if their feelings cannot be substantiated by reference to the agreed selection criteria.
- Keep all the information in context; don't focus only on one or two issues.
- Make assessments based on the answers given and the behaviour demonstrated.

Compare candidates

With interviewing completed you are now in a position to compare candidates and reach a final decision. If there is disagreement you should seek to resolve it by reference to the selection criteria. In making your decision you should also consider a second-choice candidate, in case your preferred candidate declines the offer.

References

Finally, you should check that the candidate's references do not contain any negative or unexpected information. (As references can be subjective and open to abuse and error, consulting them prior to interview can often prejudice panel members for or against candidates.) If doubt is expressed then check the matter with the referee and if necessary recall the candidate for a second interview. If not, then offer the appointment to the candidate. Once accepted, remember that staff development begins with the interview. Make arrangements for their induction and offer them the opportunity to identify their professional development needs.

Box 6.10 Interview rating errors to avoid

Rating error	Consequence
Halo	Impressive performance in one area leads to a good rating in all areas
Horn	Poor performance in one area taints rating in all areas
First impression	Forming opinion (good or bad) early; first impression influences all later perceptions
Recency	Opinion based on recent observation influences rating for the whole period
Leniency	Consistently rating higher than deserved
Severity	Consistently rating lower than deserved
Central tendency	Avoiding extremes; rating everybody in the centre categories
Clone	Giving better ratings to individuals who are perceived to be similar to oneself
Spillover	Continued downgrading for poor performance in past rating areas

7 Leading and celebrating diversity

> Everyone is different. Unique. Achieving diversity is about bringing together a rich mix of people, with differing perspectives and from different backgrounds, and creating an environment in which their differences are valued. A vibrant, open and creative culture. A culture in which ideas flourish. Where people thrive, grow and have fun. A culture where energy is unleashed. A winning culture for the 21st century.
>
> Unilever UK (Schneider, 2001)

Few issues are guaranteed to generate as much heat within higher education as that of equal opportunities. Our record of handling equal opportunities has, indeed, not been a good one, but we cannot put this down simply to the controversy associated with the issue – 'quotas versus targets', 'affirmative action versus reverse discrimination' and so on – even if, for many, it is a totem of political correctness. Truth to tell, our performance has been poor because it has, until recently, been accorded a fairly low priority in the sector. It was not until the turn of the millennium, for example, that all UK universities managed to develop their own individual human resource strategies, and even then only at the insistence of the funding councils in some cases.

To claim their share of the £330 million HEFCE initiative on *Rewarding and Developing Staff in HE* (HEFCE, 2002a), each HEI was required to submit not just an HR strategy but one which addressed six priority areas, including, in particular, equal opportunities (the others being recruitment and retention, staff development and training, equal pay and job evaluation, staffing needs review, and performance management). It was not until 2002–3, then, that all universities finally agreed to establish quantitative as well as qualitative targets in equal opportunities. Meantime the rest of the world had moved on – beyond 'the numbers' issue. Although historically deeply sceptical of 'equal opportunities' ('organization man', you will recall, was meant not only to look alike but also to think alike: Whyte, 1956), the private sector nowadays has not only embraced minority representation but has also sought to create working cultures which celebrate individual diversity, as in the case of Unilever UK (Schneider, 2001), not for the most part, admittedly, for altruistic reasons (that they believe it is socially or morally the right thing to do), but simply because diversity makes good business sense; it boosts 'the bottom line'. Either way, private sector performance in equal opportunities far outstrips that of HEIs, even among traditionally conservative businesses such as Ford Europe (also known as the 'multilocal multinational'), which is an irony in itself, given the principled stance that so many academics have taken for so long on this particular issue. It does us no favours then – and certainly none for our credibility in the world at large – if we do not seem capable of putting our own house in order.

We cannot, in our defence, certainly in the UK at least, claim that we have been ignorant of the matter either. The 1999 report into ethnicity and employment in higher education (Modood Report, 1999), for example, pointed out that only a third of universities had separate racial equality policies, while the Bett Report of the same year drew attention to gender inequalities in HE, and countless surveys have since confirmed what many already suspected, namely that, inter alia, all vice chancellors and principals, bar one, are white, and fewer than 30 of them are women; female professors account for just above 10 per cent of the professoriate; and the proportion of women in senior lecturer and researcher grades is little better than 1 in 5, while that of male and female British nationals from ethnic minorities is much lower still, 1 in 20; and so on (Finch, 2001; Oxford, 2008). Nor can we claim to have had no support in the matter. The Commission on University Career Opportunity established by the Committee of Vice Chancellors and Principals (CVCP) in the mid-1990s, for instance, developed a full range of (detailed and still useful) guides to equal opportunities – on everything from setting out strategies and implementing them to explaining harassment and advice on avoiding age discrimination. Its successor, the Equality Challenge Unit (2008) set up in 2001, is likewise committed to working in partnership with HEIs to establish 'a higher education sector that promotes diversity and where equality of opportunity is a reality for all'.

A similar support structure has emerged in the USA – through the Compact for Faculty Diversity, AAUP and the Association of American Colleges and Universities (see, for example, *Diversifying the Faculty: A guidebook for search committees* (2002) in particular) – where colleges and universities are enrolling far more minority students than ever before but are still failing to diversify their faculty (Moody, 2004).

We are all likely to need such support more than ever, for the legislative pace has quickened in recent years, most notably through the proposed Single Equality Bill which, *inter alia*, will:

- replace the current race, disability and gender duties with a new 'Equality Duty' covering not only the three latter areas but also those of gender reassignment, age, sexual orientation and religion and belief – this will place a new and enforceable positive duty on British universities to take proactive steps to eliminate any unlawful discrimination against both staff and students on the new grounds, as well as to promote good relations for these groups and between these groups;
- extend the scope of 'positive action' to allow universities to take under-representation into account (as is now the case in Scandinavian universities) when selecting between two equally qualified candidates in recruiting staff;
- require universities to conduct equal pay job evaluation audits, publish the percentage difference in the average pay of men and women and work towards achieving equal pay practices – itself an integral part of the National Framework Agreement process (ECU, 2008).

The 'equality challenge', then, is a very tall order indeed for all universities and all university managers. The purpose of this chapter is to help you, your department and your university to meet this challenge. It explains why diversity matters and the differences between it and equal opportunity. It outlines the practical steps you can take to generate momentum towards achieving diversity, as well as the ways in which universities are responding to widening participation, reconnecting with their local communities and reaching out to new international ones. In doing so, it shows how you can use *your difference* to make a significant difference in leading for diversity.

Why does diversity matter?

> Affirmative action is not about getting minorities in the door that can't compete – rather it's about making sure that organizations allow *in* the door those who most certainly can compete, if given the chance.
>
> Jo Ann Moody, diversity consultant, 2004

Diversity is a relatively new concept that emerged in the mid-1990s precisely because of the negative connotations that many felt were associated with equal opportunities. Following the lead of the private sector and early pioneers like Tufts University and Carnegie Mellon University, many universities are now seeking 'to mainstream diversity' within their institutions.

Diversity is about 'respect for the individual'. It recognizes, indeed celebrates, the fact that each of us is different and unique, and that uniqueness is made up of a mix of visible characteristics (gender, ethnicity and some disabilities) and others that are not immediately evident (sexual orientation, nationality, functional background, personality and so forth). Unlike equal opportunities, then, which is often perceived as little more than complying with the legal framework (see Box 7.1), diversity is about:

- valuing people as individuals;
- respecting people's differences;

Box 7.1 Differences between equal opportunities and diversity

Equal opportunities
- Reactive
- Concerned with legal compliance
- Focused on treating everyone alike
- About 'doing the right thing for disadvantaged groups'
- About helping 'them' join 'us'

Diversity
- Proactive
- Looking beyond legal compliance
- About treating everyone fairly but not necessarily in the same way
- About critically looking at 'us' ourselves and eliminating aspects of our culture that stop us from being inclusive
- About preventing 'us' excluding them

- making the best use of these differences for the benefit of both the individual and the organization;
- celebrating our individual differences and uniqueness.

Diversity matters, then, for a number of reasons.

Ethical

At heart diversity is, of course, an issue about social justice. It's about creating an environment that is fair and equitable for all. In this respect it speaks to universities in particular, and their historic role as emancipator institutions in striving for an open and just society; that is – it's the right thing to do.

Social

Diversity is more than just 'doing the right thing for historically disadvantaged groups'. Diversity is wholly inclusive. The focus is on all of us – every single individual.

Business

Diversity boosts institutional performance. It mobilizes a wider range of individual strengths, experiences and perspectives, yields substantial educational benefit to staff and students of all backgrounds and enhances institutional reputation (Moody, 2004; Worman, 2008).

Legal

Institutions must meet statutory requirements.
   Or, put another way, diversity is important because it is about:

- using people's talents to the full;
- ensuring that selection decisions and policies are based on objective criteria and not on unlawful discrimination, prejudice or unfair assumptions;
- making your university more attractive to prospective applicants: becoming an 'employer of choice' for staff and a 'university of choice' for students;
- improving retention, making recruitment easier;
- generating greater staff commitment, loyalty and productivity;
- getting closer to students, clients, partners and other stakeholders;
- operating internationally with success;
- sustaining a healthy society;
- avoiding the costs of discrimination.

To 'manage diversity', then, is to value individual differences and seek to harness them to establish a vibrant working culture. In doing so you need to remember that good management is not about giving a minority preferential treatment – far from it. We need to acknowledge a critical difference here, one that is often misunderstood. That is, equal opportunity is invariably about *treating everyone the same way* while the focus of diversity is on *treating everyone fairly but not necessarily in the same way*.

You will find that while many of your colleagues understand this distinction in theory, it is very often the case they do not internalize it. And when you do seek to implement it in practice you may come under inordinate pressure from colleagues to revert to 'treating everyone the same way'. It is one you must strive to resist and uphold the distinction in respecting people's differences.

Diversity in your university

> What do I think of quotas? Well, universities could do with a quota of people who understand that discrimination damages the quality of education. Maybe a small quota of people who recognize that publicly funded bodies have a responsibility to their locality. Perhaps another quota of people who can see that scholarship belongs to all kinds of body shapes and skin tones and that you cannot judge the quality of the thought by looking at the package.
>
> (Gargi Bhattacharyya, UK university lecturer,
> in Bhattacharyya, 2000)

So much for the theory, what about the practice? How well do your university, your department – and you – measure up? As with so many other things, there is no single right approach to managing diversity. All institutions will quite properly seek to do what seems best for them according to their particular circumstances and environment. That said, to manage diversity successfully we all, in the first instance, need to understand where we are now, what progress we've made, and what problems we still have to overcome. Without such understanding we cannot plan where we want to go in an informed manner. And, more particularly, as head of department you need to understand how your university is managing diversity, both as a guide to your actions at the local level (to ensure consistency, address deficiencies, and so on), and also as an advocate for change across your institution. The diagnostic model outlined in Box 7.2 is designed to help you do just that. Use it to assess your university's performance. Ask one of your colleagues to complete it too, and compare your findings.

More specifically, how does your university rate (1–5) on the diversity 'ladder of success' in Box 7.2? To what extent has your institution:

- met the statutory requirements?
- 'done the right thing for disadvantaged groups'?
- articulated a vision for diversity and developed initiatives to positive intent?
- internalized diversity as a core institutional value?
- achieved an internal vision of equity for all and fostered diversity among partners and the local community?

Do not be too surprised or disheartened if you rate your university no higher than 1–2. The fact is most organizations tend to fall into this category. To achieve a rate of 3 and above calls for a significant organizational stretch or cultural shift, which many organizations, understandably, find difficult despite their positive intent. There are,

Box 7.2 How well does your university measure up on diversity?

Consider the eight elements listed below; weigh up the positive and negative indicators in each case and rate how effective you think your university has been in that area.

Scale: 1 – Poor (all negative indicators) 2 – Marginal 3 – Satisfactory 4 – Good 5 – Excellent (all positive indicators)

Strategic implementation element	Positive indicators	Negative indicators	Ratings
Organizational vision	• Vision of the university incorporates diversity • Clear diversity policy/statement • Policy outlines main areas of attention/objectives • Clear responsibilities indicated • Clear how it is to be used by different parts of the university • Linked to educational mission and values	• No vision • No policy • Vaguely worded • No objectives • No accountabilities • No statement of why necessary • Not linked to mission or values	
Senior management commitment	• Positive, visible support given by management team • Message communicated directly to staff • Managers practise what they preach • Preparedness to allocate resources • Clear understanding about what they want to achieve • Staff agree that management are committed	• Behaviour and words don't agree • Message rarely, if ever, discussed in public forums • No preparedness to allocate resources • Uncertainty about what should be achieved • Staff would say management are not committed, that they are an obstacle	

Auditing and assessment of needs	• Key HR processes are audited and re-audited for fairness
	 • Staff are surveyed on their perceptions re diversity
	 • Monitoring data are kept on:
	   – ethnic origin
	   – sex
	   – disability
	   – age
		• Processes are never audited
		 • Staff are not encouraged to give their views
		 • No data, or only poor data are available
		 • Data are not kept up to date
		 • Data are not reviewed regularly
		 • Very little action takes place on the basis of the analysis	

Strategic implementation element	Positive indicators	Negative indicators	Ratings
	• Data are regularly reviewed • Diversity successes/disasters are recorded and communicated • Action is taken on basis of analysis		
Clarity of objectives	• Clear, quantifiable objectives are set • Timescale for achieving objectives are realistic • Objectives fit in with strategic objectives • A programme for action has been developed • Actions have been prioritized within the programme • Only targets/quotas and no objectives are set	• Unclear goals • Unclear or no timescales • Objectives and timescales are too ambitious, or are extremely conservative • Objectives do not fit in with strategic objectives	
Clear accountability	• All staff are made aware of their responsibilities • Managers are made accountable for the way they select and manage their staff • Specific and diversity-achievable objectives are set for key staff • Staff are informed and trained in how they can meet their objectives	• Key staff are not given responsibilities • Managers have no accountability for diversity issues • Little or no training is provided • Personal objectives set are unrealistic and are ignored • Objectives are not understood	
Effective communication	• Vision/policy is communicated to everybody • Policy is communicated to public • Variety of media is used in raising awareness of the issues • Information on progress is regularly fed back to staff • The views of staff are sought on how to proceed • Awareness training is available for all	• Vision/policy is poorly communicated to staff • Policy is poorly communicated to public • There is limited use of different media • Messages are treated as one-off, not reinforced • No follow-up on actions is planned	
Co-ordination of activity	• Champions for diversity have been established in different areas/departments	• No one person or group has been given overall responsibility	

- Clear who has overall coordinating responsibility for diversity
- Role of the champions has been communicated
- Regular contact is maintained with other parts of the university to share experience
- Contact has been made with outside organizations in order to learn from them

- Lack of contact with other parts of the organization; 'reinventing the wheel'
- No clear role for the champions has been established
- Lack of direction for individuals or groups

Evaluation
- All actions taken are reviewed
- Evaluation is linked to strategic and diversity objectives
- Data are taken from a variety of sources
- Evaluation is an ongoing process
- Results are fed back to everyone

- Actions taken are not reviewed
- Evaluation is not linked to strategic and diversity objectives
- Data focus on one or two areas – e.g. numbers employed
- Information is not communicated

Scoring and interpretation:

Add your rating scores together and divide by 8 to determine your overall institutional average.
Universities rated as:

1 are motivated by legal compliance. They focus on equality (treating everyone in the same way), rather than diversity (respecting people's differences). They are primarily reactive in implementing equal opportunities.

2 recognize the value in going beyond simple compliance. They aim to support groups that have been historically disadvantaged, recognizing the benefits to their internal and public image. Equity means being seen to 'do the right thing for disadvantaged groups'. Initiatives are ad hoc, without any integrated plan.

3 understand that certain diversity initiatives can improve recruitment and retention as well as efficiency. They evaluate diversity initiatives to identify programmes that will positively affect institutional life and view equality targets as a means to an end rather than the focus of the diversity strategy. They use an inclusive definition of diversity with the vision of creating an environment that is equitable for all.

4 have internalized diversity as a core organizational value. Diversity is viewed as an essential element of continued growth and is integrated into all aspects of the institution and all staff consider themselves responsible for creating an environment that is fair and equitable for all.

5 have achieved their internal vision of equity for all and now seek to foster diversity beyond their own boundaries – for their partners and in the local and regional community. Diversity needs no special internal consideration as its value, importance and necessity are firmly integrated into all aspects of institutional life.

Source: adapted from Kandola and Fullerton, 1998. Reproduced with permission.

though, a number of tried and tested initiatives which have been used in prompting just such a shift. Such institution-wide interventions 'breathe life into diversity' beyond the data analysis and the formal committee structure, and can generate a momentum towards change. You may wish to consider them for your university.

Articulating your university values and associated behaviours afresh

Let us not forget that a value is only a value if it is chosen voluntarily – values cannot be imposed. What are your university's values? When were they developed? How? By whom? Are your university's values widely understood? Are they 'owned' by your staff? If not, why not?

You may find it fruitful to look afresh at your university's values even if you do have a consensus. Doing so would enable you to confirm or revise your institutional values on the basis of a genuine university-wide consultation. It would also provide you with the opportunity – in the spirit of a learning community in which we have obligations to, and expectations of, one another – to articulate 'what we mean by them': that is, the associated behaviours by which your staff and students will 'live the values' of your university, and for which you want your university to be known.

You would then be able to develop a Staff (and Student) Code of Professional Conduct organized – as at Northwest Missouri State University – around a series of reciprocal commitments between the university and staff:

- 'As a member of staff you are expected to . . .'
- 'As a member of staff you can expect the university to . . .'

In setting a practical standard that everyone is expected to live up to, and demonstrating that you intend 'to practise what we preach', such a code can provide the basis for creating a fairer working environment for all.

Extend your staff award scheme to include diversity

Staff awards for excellence in research, enterprise and learning and teaching are commonplace nowadays. It follows that if you've established behaviours relative to your values then you can go one step further and recognize, celebrate and reward those staff who excel in 'living the values' of your university.

Such a diversity award could be on the basis of peer nomination. Either way, your consistency in aligning your actions with your rhetoric will send a powerful message to colleagues on the importance you place on your institutional values, behaviours and dignity at work.

Foster the creation of staff affinity networks

Also commonplace in many private and public sector organizations, affinity networks comprise members who may be disproportionately 'at risk' from discrimination and other forms of unacceptable behaviour: for example, black and ethnic minority colleagues; women; disabled; lesbian, gay, bisexual and transgender (LGBT); carers;

junior staff, and so on. Such networks provide support, advice and development for their members as well as acting as a specialist 'think-tank' in helping their organization address diversity issues.

Supporting their creation in your university requires confidence, and a little bravery, for there is a risk that these networks will take you in a direction you may not want to go! Not to do so, however, carries arguably an even greater risk. To be an 'employer of choice' you must acknowledge and support the culturally diverse realities of your staff and harness their experiences to make your organization more inclusive. Affinity networks are a terrific enabler in this regard. As the University of Manchester found, 'staff network input transformed the development of our policies from words written on paper to a process where they felt ownership and became stakeholders' (Gaule and Box, 2008).

You will need to provide a modest resource to 'kick-start' your networks, but the quid pro quo here is that you will also be entitled to challenge them, in much the same way they will challenge you. Your maxim should be: how can we work together in helping our university become a truly inclusive organization consistent with our values?

Establish a diversity task force

Similar in intent to affinity networks, and based on the same principles as the EFQM business model, a diversity task force is comprised of a representative group of staff operating at a range of levels across the organization (Brown, 2004; Thackwray *et al.*, 2007): a 'diagonal slice', if you will, of your institution, determined by length of service, functional background, age, gender, ethnicity, sexual orientation and so on.

Selected by self-nomination and peer-nomination – along with volunteers you may need to canvass to ensure an appropriate balance – task force members are expected to be champions of diversity in their respective departments.

More than that, they can be extremely effective as a sounding board, and think-tank, in helping you to prioritize your particular diversity agenda, and mobilizing support for and engagement with it.

Develop a university mentoring programme for diversity

Using your wider management group as a pilot, develop a university mentoring programme for diversity aimed at meeting the needs of those groups who are currently under-represented in your senior management team. Mentoring, as is well known, can be a very powerful tool for mentors, mentees and organizations alike. Such programmes can raise the profile of women and black and ethnic minority managers on the cusp of leadership positions, for example by enhancing their development, and enabling them to realize their potential – through critical self-appraisal and career planning, greater networking opportunities, increased self-confidence and reduced feelings of isolation in a predominantly white male management group (Farrar, 2008).

Equally, they can benefit the university by motivating managers and others to contribute more fully to the institution by providing a formal link with succession planning, and by facilitating further collaboration and partnerships, as well as helping to retain new talent.

Programmes can take various forms, with mentors drawn from external public and private sector organizations, or, as in the case of Bradford University, internally in a mutual learning partnership (Marshall, 2007).

The important consideration is that this is not a 'deficit model' approach – or an apprentice, line manager or PhD supervisor one for that matter – but rather a developmental relationship, which recognizes that both mentor and mentee each 'bring something with them to the table' in learning together.

Set quantitative diversity targets and develop an action plan to deliver them

We noted earlier that many organizations have moved beyond the 'numbers issue'. Even so, the development of quantitative equality targets can be extremely useful in mobilizing institutional will, particularly if you've not set them before.

To be successful, you need to remember that your targets must be genuinely SMART and you will need to develop an action plan on how you will deliver them. Why organizations have failed in the past with such targets is often because they did not have a delivery strategy, and their targets were not really targets at all – merely, an aspiration to take a leap in the dark.

Conduct a university staff experience survey and develop an appropriate action plan to address the findings

A bold step – and one taken by only a handful of universities to date – but, arguably, an essential one. How else are you going to be sure that what your institution is doing is appropriate, accessible and inclusive – that barriers do not exist? How are you going to know the reality of the everyday experience of your staff – as opposed to the smoke and mirrors and prevailing myths of institutional life – if you do not ask them?

A staff survey, conducted by a credible independent third party, provides an excellent opportunity not only for staff to inform us about their experiences but also for learning – in the fullest sense – as an organization. Such surveys (typically a 20–30-minute questionnaire available online over a period of a month) will provide you with a very detailed insight into staff opinion on a whole host of issues: not just diversity and inclusion, but also leadership, line management, organizational values and effectiveness, physical infrastructure, teamwork and communication, workload and security, performance evaluation and reward and so on – as well as a measure of staff engagement within your institution, and how this compares with other public and private sector organizations.

Such is the degree of granularity indeed (an analysis can be generated provided 10 questionnaires are submitted in any given category, thereby assuring staff confidentiality) that you will be able to discern quite clearly the similarities and the differences across a whole range of staff indices: by age group, job role, campus location, department, full and part time, ethnic group, religion, gender, sexuality and so on. In short, it will provide you with a clear guide to which issues you need to focus and act upon.

You will also gain greater staff buy-in if you involve them in drawing up an appropriate action plan and making a commitment to repeat the survey on a biennial basis, thereby allowing yourself sufficient time to be judged on your actions. Your initial survey has, after all, given you the baseline trend data by which you can measure your future progress.

Provide diversity awareness training with a difference

'Serious issues tackled with imagination and good humour'; 'I challenge everyone to watch and participate and then tell me they haven't learnt something'.

Not the feedback you might expect from your Powerpoint briefing on the latest equalities legislation or force-field analysis of the barriers to diversity. Then again it wasn't. This feedback came from a theatre-based workshop aimed at challenging stereotypes, evoking debate and positively influencing staff attitudes and behaviours.

If you have not already done so, why not rethink your best approach to diversity awareness training? Take a cue from Loughborough University, for example, which uses an osteoarthritic simulation suit which allows participants to experience limited mobility.

Keep up your dialogue on diversity

Beyond formal diversity awareness training, seek to maintain the momentum through leadership round-table events and 'Lunch and Learn' sessions: 'Diversity@ my university – it's debatable'.

Select and customize themes that are relevant and topical to you: for example, 'Religion and Faith in a Secular University'; 'Race Equality: Building Bridges, not Barriers'.

Move beyond the boiler-plate statements in your job advertisements

'This university is an equal opportunity employer'; 'this university is positive about disabled people'. We are all familiar with these generic statements and we've all used them.

Why not reframe your use of language in job advertisements to reflect your desire for diversity? 'This university and department are committed to student and staff diversity and value the educational benefits flowing from such diversity. Candidates should make known their experience and leadership in this area' (Moody, 2004).

Take a cue from Michigan State University and Colorado College in this regard (Moody, 2004).

Make all your managers accountable for diversity

Finally, but most importantly, let us not forget that diversity is first and foremost a leadership issue. 'What have you done to enhance diversity in your department over the last year?' is a key question in the annual performance review for every head of a government department in Whitehall. And to ensure there is no room for doubt, 360-degree feedback is garnered through an equally key follow-up question to all departmental staff: 'How do you think your department has enhanced diversity over the last year?'

This approach is also common in the private sector and is now making headway in higher education too, as in the case of Rensselaer Polytechnic Institute (Moody, 2004). Such accountability will ensure – in the spirit of 'what's logged, evaluated and rewarded gets done' – that diversity will be taken seriously as a leadership issue in your university, as it should be.

The university and community engagement

> To be a great university we must be a great local university.
> Shirley Strum Kenny, President,
> State University of New York, Stony Brook, 1999

Commitment to diversity is measured in terms of what universities are doing not just within their own community but also beyond it. And here there is evidence, all around the world, of universities revisiting old ground – their relationship with their 'natural constituency', their local community – and re-assessing their civic and social roles, not because governments have driven them to do so, but from an enlightened recognition that it is in their own self-interest.

In 2004, for instance, the Association of Commonwealth Universities developed an international benchmarking tool to support universities in assessing their civic engagement. Likewise, the Talloires movement grew out of the international conference Tufts University hosted in September 2005 at its European centre in France. In June 2006, a 'Declaration of Participatory Democracy' was approved by 150 university and government leaders (from Australia, Europe, North America, South Africa and South Korea) in Strasbourg, under the aegis of the Council of Europe Forum on Higher Education and Democratic Culture. Drawing on the work previously undertaken by the International Consortium for Higher Education, Civic Responsibility and Democracy (a peer network pioneered by the University of Pennsylvania), the Declaration seeks to 'document, understand and advance the contributions of higher education to democracy on the campus, in the local community and the wider society' (Benson and Harkavy, 2000; Maurrasse, 2001; Watson, 2007b).

From an institutional perspective, civic engagement essentially 'presents a challenge to universities to be of and not just in the community; not simply to engage in knowledge-transfer but to establish a dialogue across the boundary between the university and its community which is open-ended, fluid and experimental' (Watson, 2007b) (see Figure 7.1 and Box 7.3). Universities in the USA have been particularly conspicuous in meeting this challenge. Here, the environment has been especially propitious in facilitating university-community interaction in three distinctive ways:

1 Many mission-specific, often faith-based, institutions regard 'service learning' as a prime strategic goal: Tufts, for example, has sought 'to establish civic engagement as a Tufts signature'. Collectively, the Association of American Colleges and Universities has established a Center for Liberal Education and Civic Engagement and called for a new understanding of 'civic learning', while almost 1,000 college presidents have signed up for a new Campus Compact.
2 The concept of 'active citizenship' – which regards political engagement as a worthy and non-contentious outcome – is one which is more readily accepted in the USA than by universities in Europe and Australasia.

Figure 7.1 The potential and scope for community engagement

New companies	Business competitiveness	Skills and enterprise	Infrastructure/ environment	Cultural enrichment	Healthy society	Social inclusion
Incubator unit	Food science and technology	Employer engagement	Sustainability	Visual arts	Mental and physical well-being	Educational aspiration and achievement
Spin outs	Digital media	Enterprise in schools	New energy	Music	Lifestyle management	Community networks and development
Start ups	Clothing/textiles	Business enterprise	Regeneration	Performing arts	Nutrition and diet	Values and behaviours
Social enterprises	ICT	Enterprise in the community	Architecture	Sport	Living conditions	Diversity and equality
Intellectual property	Sports and leisure	Enterprise in HE	Landscape design	Literature, philosophy and history	Self-identity and development ('i-branding')	Flexible working; work-life balance
Patents and licences	Creative industries	Self-enterprise	Transport	Fashion	Environments and pollution control	Neet: Not in education, employment or training

Wealth creation
Business facing
(Business–private sector)

Quality of life
Community engagement
(Voluntary–public services)

A virtuous cycle of regeneration and growth

Source: adapted from Wedgewood, 2006; Watson, 2007b.

Box 7.3 University pioneers in community engagement

Universities are not just path-breaking as entrepreneurial (or 'business-facing') institutions. They are also, world-wide, reviewing their role with regard to their own local communities – as organizations in the community, of the community and for the community. Three universities in particular exemplify this trend.

University of Pennsylvania, USA

Prima facie, Penn (1740) is an unlikely pioneer in this regard. A leading private research university and Ivy League member, sandwiched between centre city and greater West Philadelphia (an area of marked deprivation), its University City on the banks of the Schuylkill appears to resemble more the archetypal 'ivory tower' or 'castle in the swamp' than it does a community institution. Conscious of its privileged position and location, Penn has made a deliberate attempt to play an active role to effect positive change in its immediate locality notably through the development of university-assisted community schools – an initiative now widely emulated elsewhere.

Taking their cue from John Dewey's twin notions of active learning and participatory democracy, Penn historians Lee Benson and Ira Harkavy initiated the Center for Community Partnerships in 1992 and built a network of support, commitment and intellectual interest across the university and out into the community.

- By 2005, 62 academically based community service courses were being taught across 19 departments and eight schools (including 16 graduate courses), embracing 1,650 students earning credit this way and over 60 faculty staff.
- Especially innovative is Penn's Urban Nutrition Initiative which takes in everything from school gardens and meals planning, nutrition-monitoring and health interventions through to direct advocacy and lobbying with city and local government.
- Penn also coordinates a higher education network for neighbourhood development within Philadelphia (with 42 partners) as well as a state-wide, service learning alliance which seeks to roll out its community school programme in other locations (currently 23).

The most intractable issue, however, that of increasing the tiny proportion of local residents able to enrol at the university, still remains (as it does with other universities of like characteristics) an outstanding priority (Benson and Harkavy, 2000; Maurrasse, 2001; Watson, 2007b).

University of Queensland, Australia

In Australia, 'the rush to community' has also been a rapid if recent phenomenon but nonetheless a significant one, as evidenced by the strength of the Australian Consortium on Higher Education, Community Engagement and Social Responsibility. A national alliance moreover – the Australian Universities' Community Engagement Alliance Inc – was incorporated in 2004 (with 25 institutional members) under the leadership of the University of Western Sydney with support from the federal Department of Education, Science and Training.

Also prominent here has been the University of Queensland, particularly the way in which this research-intensive university (one of the 'Sandstone Eight') has developed its new Ipswich campus in the heart of a community marked by economic deprivation and political extremism. Prompted by the murder in 1999 of an elderly local resident by seven youths in 'public care', leaders of the local community, government and university joined together to see what they could do to prevent a reoccurrence of such a tragedy. The result was the creation of the UQ Community Service and Research (or 'Boilerhouse') Centre whose goal is 'to facilitate just and sustainable community outcomes' grounded in an emphatically collaborative approach.

To date the Boilerhouse project has delivered a series of accredited and short course programmes in community and inter-professional leadership for over 200 community leaders and is seeking to implement a variety of access and social equity initiatives for students from culturally and linguistically diverse groups in the Ipswich/Inala corridor, alongside 'a collaborative approach to ageing well in the community' (Watson, 2007b).

University of Brighton, UK

In the UK, institutional activity has been encouraged by a series of special initiatives launched by the funding councils: for example, Higher Education Resources for Business and Community (HEROBAC); Higher Education Innovation Fund (HEIF) and Higher Education Active Community Fund (HEACF). These so-called 'third leg' (business and enterprise) initiatives – while creating a complexity of funding streams that institutions have had to manage within their own individual accountability frameworks – have nevertheless all comprised elements 'for engagement with non-commercial (including social and civic) organisations'. HEFCE (2009) has also added 'securing the public interest' as a new priority in its latest strategic plan.

A former polytechnic that is essentially a federation of professional schools (from art and design, health and medicine through to science and technology), the University of Brighton launched a Community–University Partnership Programme (CUPP) in 2003 with financial support from Atlantic Philanthropies. Working with a variety of local communities – including the University of Sussex through the Brighton and Sussex Community Knowledge Exchange – the CUPP has developed an array of projects that draws upon the full range of the university's disciplinary resources: from Football 4 Unity (addressing social inclusion), a Box of Tricks (to build resilience in disadvantaged children) and Well-Being, Health and Occupation for Older People (WHOOP) to knowledge transfer partnerships (with community organizations), the establishment of a community research help-desk and the development with Sussex of a new foundation degree in community service (Watson, 2007b).

3 Since professional education is largely at postgraduate level, the undergraduate curriculum in US universities offers more opportunities (than in UK and Australian universities) to use credit-bearing time for community-based activity – almost half of all students in four-year colleges now spend time volunteering (Watson, 2007b).

So what about community engagement in your university? Consider the assessment tool in Box 7.4 and map out the current state of your institution's community relations.

- What effort does your department make in developing community relations?
- What is unique or distinctive about your institution and department that could make a difference to your local community?
- What could you do – that you don't do now – that would bring mutual benefit to both your institution and your local community?
- How will you do it? What steps do you need to take to move from passive coexistence to active partnerships that will actually advance your institution's mission and improve society?

Widening participation

> I'm a statistical oddity. A black girl brought up on the South Side of Chicago . . . I'm certainly not supposed to be standing here.
> Michelle Obama, Democratic Party rally, Pittsburgh, May 2008

Box 7.4 Understanding and enhancing your university's community relations

1 The nature and scope of your institution's community relations
   - What do you regard as your local community – its geographic boundaries?
   - How are projects between your institution and the community generally initiated?
   - What do community groups tend to say about your institution? The good and the not so good?
   - In what ways is your institution accessible to the community?
   - How do you elicit feedback from your community?
   - What is your institution's role in community relations with respect to learning and teaching? To research?
   - What proportion of your employees is from the local community? In which categories do they tend to work?
   - What proportion of your student body comes from the local community and does your institution recruit locally?
   - What proportion of your contractors are local businesses and in which industries?
   - Do you know the social and economic impact of your institution in the local community? Has this been measured? Is this research available?
   - Which departments and faculties would you say make the most effort in community relations? The least effort?
   - In what ways do the Vice Chancellor/President, Senior Management Team and Governors/ Trustees demonstrate that community relations and partnerships are a priority?
   - Where do you think your institution can most improve its community relations?

2 The characteristics of your community
   - What would you say are the three greatest assets in your local community?
   - What would you say are the three greatest challenges confronting your local community?
   - What is the racial, ethnic, cultural, age and economic profile of your community?
   - In what ways do the needs of these various communities converge? And diverge?
   - Who (individuals or organizations) makes most of the major decisions in your community?

3 The distinctiveness of your institution
   - Overall, what are the five greatest strengths of your institution?
   - For what is your institution best known?
   - For what would you like it to be best known in the future?
   - What distinguishing qualities set your institution apart from other HEIs in your region?
   - Through which aspect of your institution have local residents and organizations made the most use of your institution?

4 Approaching and embracing diversity
   - What is the demographic profile of your staff and student body? How does it compare with five years ago? And with the demographic profile of your local community?
   - In what ways do your curriculum and programmes help prepare students to function in diverse settings? How can these be extended and improved still further?
   - What would you say is the relationship between your institution's ability to address issues of diversity and its ability to be a good community partner? Congruent or not? If not, why not?

5 Action planning
   - Taking into account 1, 2, 3 and 4:
   - Where do you see the 'best fit' between the assets and needs of your institution and the assets and needs of your community?

- Review your existing partnerships: Which of these should you build upon – expand – improve – dissolve – merge?
- Identify two particular efforts that your institution could begin to work on that mutually benefit your institution and your community.

Consider how best to take these forward:
- With which community groups do you wish to work?
- What is the most effective means of communication and collaboration?
- What steps does your institution need to take in order to make it as culturally competent (with the variety of cultures in your community) as possible?
- Which programmes and departments in your institution should play a role in the development of these partnerships?
- What hindrances in the community or in your institution do you need to address?

Source: adapted from Maurrasse, 2001.

> No matter how liberal and open-minded some of my White professors and classmates try to be towards me, I sometimes feel like a visitor on campus; as if I really don't belong. Regardless of the circumstances under which I interact with Whites at Princeton, it often seems as if, to them, I will always be Black first and a student second.
>
> Michelle Obama, 1985

For many universities the local community is also, of course, an important source in helping them to realize public expectations to broaden their student profile. Either way, widening participation is integral to diversity and important for the same reason – it is an issue of social justice which can promote greater social cohesion and, equally, is capable, as in the Laura Spence affair, of sparking a 'moral panic'.

In aggregate the UK, if not as diverse as the USA, is doing relatively well compared with mainland Europe – and while the long-standing target of 50 per cent participation of young people (18–30) in higher education by 2010 may have proved beyond the sector's reach, the rate the UK has achieved (42–3 per cent) is well in excess of the criteria (40 per cent plus) in Martin Trow's (1973) model to qualify as a universal system of higher education (NAO, 2007; Eastwood, 2008). Aggregate figures, however, mask some intractable problems at both ends of the higher education spectrum:

1 Universities that have been very successful in recruiting working-class students, for example, have been much less so in retaining them. While it is the case, as we noted in the last chapter, that retention has held up nationally as participation has increased, in 10 universities more than one-third of undergraduate students are expected to drop out before finishing their degree courses (NAO, 2007).
2 Russell Group universities, by contrast – including Oxford and Cambridge in particular – have made little progress in recruiting more working-class students. In 2006–7 fewer than 10 per cent of Oxford entrants were from the lowest socio-economic groups, compared with a national average of 18 per cent at other universities for students with the same entry grades. At Cambridge the proportion of state school students (57 per cent) – like that at Oxford (53 per cent) – has been

relatively static, and well below its official benchmark, or aspiration target, of 75 per cent (Frean, 2008b).

3 Commonly, across all institutions, students from every minority group dispro-portionately underachieve in comparison to their white counterparts (15 per cent of whom achieved first-class degrees in 2005–6), with the attainment gap being largest for Black Caribbean (3 per cent), Black African (4 per cent) and Chinese (7 per cent) students. They are also less likely to be satisfied and much more likely to be unemployed on graduation (Tahir, 2007; HEA, 2008a).

These outcomes are not that dissimilar from the USA where participation 'has largely stalled at around 60 per cent since the late 1990s' and 'college completion has remained largely stagnant'. One-third of Whites obtain a bachelor's degree by age 25–29 compared with just 18 per cent of Blacks and 10 per cent of Latinos, and 'access is unduly limited by the complex interplay of inadequate preparation, lack of information about college opportunities and persistent financial barriers' (Spellings, 2006).

The approach to widening participation in the USA, however, is quite different from that in the UK. In the USA, elite universities compete for excellent students from minorities and disadvantaged communities because they want to create a 'class' which is representative of the best and brightest that American society can offer. And while the battle-lines are drawn within elite institutions – as to how far their financial aid resources should be awarded on the basis of (scholarly and athletic) merit versus need – the imperative in society at large is to streamline the extremely complex and confusing support systems 'to direct aid to those students who truly need it' (Spellings, 2006).

Financial support is of course also an issue in the UK – and the planned review on variable tuition fees makes it certain it will remain so – but the widening participation debate is structured far more around a deficit model, with much public agonizing over the under-representation of lower socio-economic groups in the system as a whole, especially in the most prestigious institutions, as well as 'the failure' to curb student drop-out rates.

There is, however, no simple quick fix for the UK, though this has not stopped the sector from searching for one, and it is clear that this issue will not be satisfactorily resolved unless there is effective action beyond higher education (see Box 7.5). Even so, this does not mean that the sector can abrogate its responsibilities in this regard. What, then, can you do to increase widening participation in your institution? It will, of course, vary according to where you are on the spectrum.

1 If you are in one of those universities that have been successful in recruiting socially disadvantaged students, then your greatest challenge is retaining them – ensuring your 'open door' is not a revolving one. And in this respect you need to consider the recommendations proposed in the next chapter as a means of enhancing the progression and achievement of your students.

2 If you are in one of the highly selective, prestigious institutions, and particularly if you are a long way from achieving your benchmark target, then you need to reflect yet again on the two fundamental questions:
   • What is it about 'us' – our institutional culture – which is inappropriately excluding students and preventing us from being inclusive?

Box 7.5 Proposed solutions for widening participation in UK higher education

There is no magic silver bullet for widening participation but various options have been proposed. We would improve widening participation if only we could:

Solutions

- Get the supply-side right by providing more accelerated two-year degree programmes, extending foundation degrees and learning through work. That way we could still reach the 50 per cent (of 18–30-year-olds in HE) target.

- Assuage debt aversion by reassuring students particularly from low-income households of the readily available financial support.

- Get our admissions procedures in order by ensuring consistency across admissions tutors and introducing a post-qualification admissions (PQA) system to give applicants more time to consider their options on the basis of their actual – rather than predicted – achievements.

- Persuade well-qualified students from poorer or minority backgrounds to choose the most selective and prestigious universities.

- Raise levels of aspiration among young people particularly state-educated pupils from low-income households.

Assumption

- Employers and students want the 'full package' that HE can offer rather than 'bite-sized' provision.

- This SMART target is, in fact, smart. The UK has an ageing population – average age 35 plus – and the political commitment is to lifelong learning.

- Debt aversion is indeed a disincentive in the absence of any real evidence. Attitudes to debt, particularly among the young, may be more problematic than we think – a case of debt joy rather than debt fear.

- The work of admissions tutors has not improved when the evidence suggests it has – there is greater distributional fairness in university admissions than hitherto.

- The main beneficiaries of a PQA would be well-qualified, socially disadvantaged students. It is unclear if this would indeed be the case.

- Students are irrational in their choice of institution. They may well have very sound reasons for making their particular choice. Besides, the research tells them 'you won't necessarily learn more by going to a posh place'.

- There are indeed significant numbers of such high-achieving applicants. The evidence suggests the contrary – a very strong correlation between high educational achievements and family prosperity.

Persuade others beyond higher education to:

- Improve the quality of school-based experience for all students and particularly those from under-represented groups.

  - The reform of qualifications for 14–19-year-olds (the introduction of the new diplomas alongside A levels) is successful. Though again, as with Curriculum 2000, this is not certain given the lack of political consensus and ambiguity of employer support.

- Empower parents and raise their expectations.

  - The system can supply all parents with genuine choice yet is rarely the case in practice. Giving more 'power to parents' is likely to increase rather than reduce polarization, though evidence suggests this may well have a positive effect on some groups of minority ethnic students.

- 'Walk the talk' – for employers to genuinely support both younger and older workers in their personal and professional development.

  - Employers will behave differently in the future from how they have done in the past. Currently one-quarter of all English 16–18-year-olds receive no education or training at all even when in work.

- Build on the belated recognition by government and employers that Level 3 (university matriculation or high school graduation) is the real gateway to creating a learning society. That raising the school-leaving age to 18 creates an opportunity to re-engage those who ordinarily would have been classed as 'post-16 failures'.

  - Formal education 16–18 is the best way to arrest levels of disaffection. Not all students and employers accept this proposition – not unless there is also significant opportunity to learn through work.

Source: adapted from Watson, 2007b.

- What else can we, should we, be doing outside the university to attract socially disadvantaged students?

Cambridge, for example, has taken a lead in this regard by easing its entry requirements and dropping the insistence on a GCSE in a foreign language, not because it eschews languages but because it recognizes that the opportunities for studying one in the state school sector are far more limited. Also, by inviting state school teachers to spend time at the university it can encourage more of them to persuade their pupils to apply to Cambridge (Frean, 2008b).

Other selecting universities – like Bristol – have endured 'trial by media' in rethinking their recruitment strategy so as not to fall prey to the 'header-tank' problem of admissions: i.e. recruit first the students whom it is easiest to recruit and then go looking for the rest (Watson, 2007b). Either way, the bottom line is that if there is a significant disparity between your performance and other universities in recruiting students of the same calibre, then you must endeavour to resolve this uncomfortable truth as follows.

- Establish the facts. What differences are there in degree attainment by ethnicity in your university – your department? To what extent is there variation in attainment between courses – within courses? Is there a pattern? Can you account for these differences? (See also Box 7.7.)
- Research your 'minority' student experience. Examine those courses where degree attainment is more equal and investigate why this is the case. Interview BME students who have achieved a good degree. Set up a series of focus groups of students who may be excluded from the dominant culture.
- Examine the student complaints and academic appeals (including plagiarism) you have received by ethnicity. Determine if there are any dominant themes or patterns you can address.
- Seek to ensure that the 'attainment gap' is taken seriously by formally requesting your examination boards to monitor and evaluate performance across different groups, and by including it in your training and development programme for both new and established staff.
- Review your assessment practices to ensure there is genuine diversity in your approach and not an over-reliance on a particular single method: e.g. one-off, high stakes, unseen examinations.
- Review the provision of your pre-entry and post-entry learning support and consider how you might customize it further to meet BME student needs: e.g. through diagnostic testing; specialized writing workshops; extended induction; career management and 'i-branding' (personal capacity building).
- Develop a multi-level mentoring scheme for your BME students which can support them throughout the student life-cycle, linking them with:
  - student peers;
  - role models – staff members who belong to your BME affinity network;
  - external employers – with a focus on career planning.
- Ensure your BME students are fully represented on course boards and staff–student committees.
- Ensure – and this is critically important – that your actions are presented within a model of promoting educational enhancement for *all*. Otherwise there is a real danger you may inadvertently increase stigmatization still further, through what is perceived to be a stereotypical deficit-model approach.

Internationalization

> We felt a more holistic approach to internationalization was necessary.
> Standing on a British Council stall is no longer enough.
> Royal Holloway International Director, April 2008

Participation in higher education has extended to include not only greater numbers of local students and socially disadvantaged students but also those from much further afield. The flow of students across national boundaries is nothing new, of course. It has long been regarded as beneficial – for the students and their career prospects, for the universities, and for the economic and democratic well-being of nations. What has changed, however, in recent years, is both the volume of this flow and the financial dependency of universities on it.

In its *Vision 2020* the British Council forecast that the global demand for international places is likely to grow from 2.1 million in 2004 to 5.8 million in 2020. In the UK overseas students contributed £1.5 billion to the national economy in 2005–6, including (through tuition fees) 8 per cent of the total income earned by universities (Cemmell and Bekhradnia, 2008; Woolcock, 2008).

Such is the dependency on this income stream (it accounts for up to 20 per cent of all revenue at some individual institutions) that when a temporary downturn occurred in 2005–6, the President of UUK declared, 'If this trend continues many universities will face real difficulties . . . it could mean serious cutbacks in capital investment and in staff numbers' (Luker, 2006). As the significance of these numbers has increased, so universities – with encouragement from the Prime Minister's Initiative for International Education – now recognize that 'the international dimension is no longer marginal to their real activities' (Marginson, 2004).

Many universities, indeed, have developed, or are in the process of developing, their own elaborate system of transnational provision:

- as a provider institution in a foreign country through 'twinning' arrangements, 'franchise' agreements or, as in the case of the University of Nottingham, for example, by opening up their own branch campus;
- through cross-border online learning, e.g. Western Governors University;
- through cross-border partnerships and consortia, e.g. World University Network, *Universitas 21*;
- as a provider institution in their country to international students: the original approach.

Such has been the growth of these off-shore developments, indeed, that overseas delivery now accounts for 50 per cent of international enrolments to UK programmes (Luker, 2006).

This development of course has had major implications, not least for governance arrangements and quality assurance processes as well as for the ability (or lack of it) to retain market share, which for the UK fell from 16 per cent in 1997 to 12 per cent in 2007 (Cemmell and Bekhradnia, 2008) (see Box 7.6). It also begs the questions: What are the implications of internationalization for diversity in your university – your department? What can and should you do?

You should recognize the following.

- Internationalization is more than simply the recruitment and teaching of international students. As Jane Knight puts it, internationalization is 'the process of integrating an international, intercultural or global dimension into the purpose, functions or delivery of post-secondary education' (Middlehurst, 2006).

Box 7.6 Guiding principles for effective overseas collaboration

Reasons to be careful:

1 Your responsibility to others
   - Your national HE brand is very strong. Don't be the one who gives it a bad name.
   - Your graduates are the living embodiment of the standards of your awards. Be consistent in the awards you confer at home and overseas.

2 Resources and investment
   - Collaboration does not come cheap. Be prepared for the cost, particularly up-front investment.

3 Due diligence
   - Don't lose money by failing to appreciate the terms and conditions of the partnership on offer, particular with regard to for-profit organizations. Hire professional advisers, if necessary, to conduct a thorough due diligence review.

4 Taking the decision
   - It must be taken by the proper body, typically the sovereign academic authority, e.g. University Senate, Academic Board.

5 Obey the local law
   - But don't assume your local partner also does so.

6 Your partner's resources
   - Check that they are up to the mark and can be delivered as promised.

7 Collectivity of interest
   - If you pull out of a partnership you should tell other universities why, if it is to do with the quality of standards or facilities.

8 Propriety
   - You must keep to your own institutional and national regulations even if the local culture has a different set of norms, e.g. the giving and taking of bribes.

9 Agents
   - Ensure you both fully understand the ground rules. Always retain control of the use of your logo. Never delegate it.

10 Award certificate
   - Should always include the language of instruction and the location of study.

11 Contact
   - Maintain regular contact through informal as well as formal means.

Source: adapted from QAA, 2004; Williams, 2007.

It is, in essence – like the 'student experience' we will discuss in the next chapter – a cross-cutting theme that potentially touches all aspects of the university's functioning, from catering and the Careers Service to research and the recruitment of staff and students. It is 'everybody's business' and has to be addressed in the same way as the 'student experience' has to be customized to the particular needs of international students both on-campus and off-campus.

Again this will be no easy task. It is claimed, indeed, that 'a new and radically different generation of international students' is upon us who are 'far more demanding, more sceptical, more inclined to complain, more experimental and with better access to information' (Gill, 2008a). And evidence suggests that international students are increasingly dissatisfied with universities which 'over-promise and under-deliver', do not live up to the claims in their prospectuses or on their websites, do not offer value for money, and whose degrees may not be the premier credentials promised if they are 'study light': requiring less private preparation and offering a relatively low amount of teaching (Cemmell and Bekhradnia, 2008).

- Internationalism is for all our students – home students as well as international students. It's about developing them to be global citizens, to prepare them for living and working in a society where cross-cultural capability will be a premium asset (Shiel, 2006). This means we need to:
  - integrate home and international students far better than we have done hitherto, teaching them together, and not apart, for as we know the greater the diversity in the group, the better the learning (Newman, 2007);
  - review our curriculum – often the most contested issue (Ritchie, 2006) – to ensure internationalization is valued and assessed, while allowing each discipline the freedom to embed the concept in its own way, as at, for example, Royal Melbourne Institute of Technology and Macquarie University;
  - recognize that while students may 'stay at home' in disproportionate numbers (for example, 7,500 UK students participate in the Erasmus student exchange programme each year compared with 20,000 apiece from France, Germany and Spain (Reilly, 2006)), we should still endeavour to increase the mobility of our home students through our own institutional international partnerships.
- Internationalism is ultimately about developing your own concept which is most relevant to your circumstances. At the University of Bristol, for example, 'the internationalization agenda isn't around increasing markets for students. It is about maximizing the potential knowledge generation from collaboration – the additional insight, additional intellectual capital from universities which may also be important geographically' (Gill, 2008c). At Leeds Metropolitan University internationalization is about developing graduates with 'world-wide horizons' and a university where 'an international and multicultural ethos pervades the campus' (Killick, 2006; Jones and Brown, 2007).

Using your difference to make a difference

> With opportunities comes responsibility.
> Winston Churchill

There are many ways, then, as we've seen, in which you could make a significant contribution towards diversity – by taking the lead in supporting the development of your institution's response to it, and by pioneering initiatives within your department with regard to community relations, widening participation and internationalization. What else can you – should you – do in your department to meet the equality challenge?

Recognize that equal opportunity is a key component of good management

You can expect your institution to require you to 'mainstream' equal opportunities in your own department. This means you will in effect be held responsible, and rightly so, for the pursuit of equality goals. For many this will be a novelty, if not an issue. Others, however, may feel less comfortable with this notion. If so, you need to remember and to recognize, as others beyond HE have done, that equal opportunity is not only socially desirable and a moral right, as well as a legal requirement, it is also, at heart, a key component of good management.

Commit to making diversity one of your department's core values

Universities, as we've noted, are inherently intensely individualistic and as such ideally placed to meet this challenge. Indeed the diversity aspiration is not only achievable, it goes to the very essence of the university's *raison d'être*. You therefore need have no qualms about – and should indeed take pride in – proposing diversity as one of the core values of your department.

Assess your department's performance and draw up a diversity action plan

As a prelude to developing your own action plan, you need to determine how well you are managing diversity within your own department. You can, of course, do this on your own but since, as the model outlined in Box 7.7 illustrates, it involves gauging the perceptions of others both within and outside your department, in addition to monitoring statistical information, you should consider setting up a small representative working group to help you reach a more objective, as well as a more accurate, assessment. It will also give reassurance to others and demonstrate your transparency in this matter. With the group, work your way systematically through each of the questions set out in Box 7.7 and log your conclusions.

How well are you doing? Do you have all the necessary statistical information to hand? If not, what gaps do you have to make good? Is the analysis and evaluation of this information a routine activity within your department? Do you act on this information? How thorough is your understanding of the internal and external perceptions of your department? What does this picture tell you? What actions do you need to take to increase your understanding, or to address the perceptions others have of your department?

In developing your action plan, you need to bear in mind (if you have not already done so) that it is precisely this sort of proactivity, in this instance the monitoring, review and revision of departmental practices, which in the cases of disability and race are now a legal obligation. Under SENDA, for example, it is illegal to treat staff or students, current and prospective, 'less favourably' if they have a disability and HEIs are duty-bound to make 'reasonable adjustment' to ensure they do not place anyone at a 'substantial disadvantage'. Similarly the RRA bestows a 'new enforceable positive duty' on HEIs not only to monitor their staff by ethnicity, but also to assess the impact on racial equality of proposed, as well as existing, policies and practices, and to consult on them.

Box 7.7 How well does your department measure up on diversity?

Staff statistics

1 Do you monitor staff profiles by (a) age (b) gender (c) ethnicity (d) disability?
2 Do you then benchmark these figures against (a) other departments in your university (b) equivalent departments in other regional, national or international universities?
3 Do you also monitor (a) recruitment (b) promotion (c) appraisals (d) salary (e) leavers by these same groups?
4 Do you benchmark recruitment against the relevant external labour market? And do you review success ratios (the number of applications per appointee and number of applications for posts available) for different groups?
5 Do you review and compare promotion, salary and leavers across these different groups?

Internal perceptions

6 Have you ever run a focus group for (a) staff who may feel excluded from the dominant culture (b) staff drawn from the dominant culture?
7 Have you ever commissioned or conducted a specific diversity survey within your department? Did you analyse the results by each different group?
8 Have you ever included diversity-related questions in any of your departmental staff surveys?
9 Do you ever benchmark any of these staff diversity questions?
10 Do you know what the level of understanding and commitment to diversity is among your university's senior management group?
11 Do you know if your staff feels different about diversity from staff in other departments?

Student statistics (or customer/client statistics in the case of support departments)

12 Do you monitor student entry by (a) age (b) gender (c) ethnicity and (d) disability as well as by social class, educational qualifications and previous learning experience?
13 Do you then benchmark these figures against course intakes in (a) other departments in your university (b) equivalent departments in universities within your region and nationally?
14 Do your course teams also monitor student withdrawals by these same groups?
15 Do you benchmark recruitment against the relevant student market? And do you review the success ratios (numbers of applications per capita population; numbers of enrolments per number of applications) for different groups?
16 Do your exam boards monitor the number of (a) first-class honours graduates (b) student failures by these different groups?
17 Do your exam boards review and compare performance across these different groups?

External perceptions

18 Do you genuinely cater to the needs of a diverse student body in your learning and teaching strategy and curriculum design? Is diversity covered in your surveys and measures of student satisfaction?
19 What proportion of your student market share is drawn from different groups? Is this in or out of line relative to the nature and size of your portfolio market?
20 Do you analyse student feedback by (a) age (b) ethnicity (c) disability (d) religion?
21 In your market research do you identify the potential and diverse needs of different groups as a matter of course?
22 Have you ever run focus groups with (a) female students (b) minority ethnic students (c) disabled students (d) younger or older students?
23 Do you know how the local community and local educational providers regard your department?
24 Do you know how the senior management group, the board of governors and other departments regard your performance on diversity?

25 Does your appraisal of external partners include an assessment of their own equal opportunities policies and procedures? Do your external partners feel that their different ideas and ways of operating are welcomed?

26 What do your stakeholders think about your performance on diversity?

Source: adapted from Schneider, 2001.

Make sure you practise what you preach

Diversity, however, involves more than simply ensuring that appropriate mechanisms are in place. It is also about making sure that they do their job – of capturing and analysing data and acting upon it. More than that, it is about effecting cultural change in the way your department behaves. It is incumbent on you to take the initiative, otherwise you run the risk that your action plan may fall short of the mark or, worse still, suffer the fate of so many other well-intentioned initiatives before it and be dismissed as just another passing fad. Put the other way, you are more likely to establish diversity as a meaningful concept within your department if you are yourself seen to take it seriously, to give expression to your commitment: in short, to put into practice what you preach. You can do this in a number of ways.

Your style of management

Do not confuse the relationship between equality and effective management. Good management is not about giving a minority preferential treatment over others. On the contrary, it is about treating everyone fairly but not necessarily in the same way. In other words, it is first and foremost about recognizing, respecting and valuing people as individuals each with their own unique characteristics, and responding to them on that basis 'to create a productive environment in which organizational goals are met efficiently and effectively by making the best use of everyone's talents and potential' (CIPD, 2008).

In practical terms, this is yet another instance in which you must consider whether your style of management is the most effective one to achieve this outcome. Are you, for example, receptive to staff proposals for flexible working patterns (a statutory requirement since April 2003 in the case of parents with children under 6 and those with disabled children under 18)? Would you be willing to extend the same right to those of your staff with responsibilities for caring for the elderly, even if it isn't a statutory requirement? More tellingly, do staff feel comfortable in approaching you about their personal welfare – about matters not immediately related to their work? If not, why not? Are you as committed to a work–life balance and 'family-friendly' arrangements as you should be (DfEE, 2000; CIPD 2002; ECU 2009)? Are you always open to fresh ideas on job enrichment? Check with others to confirm this is so even if you feel it in indeed the case.

'Walking the talk', not just 'talking the talk'

Getting others to understand the significance and value of diversity is an important first step. Staff will not be fully convinced, however, and understandably so, until they see by your actions that you are sincere in your commitment to it. You must, therefore 'walk the talk' as well as 'talk the talk' if you want diversity to mean more to staff than merely so many fine words (Mulholland *et al.*, 2006). Your style of management, as we've noted, is important in this respect. You need to go further, however, if you want to make diversity a living reality.

- Establish your own department steering group to coordinate and review your monitoring and data collection activity; the deliberations of your exam boards, programme teams and focus groups; the outcomes of your market research surveys; and the implementation of your action plan.
- Commit a proportion of your annual budget to support and advance equal opportunities within your department.
- Integrate diversity into your performance review discussions.
- Run awareness-raising and skills-building workshops for all your staff.
- Hold regular 'surgeries' – at least three times a year – with 'minority' staff.
- Invite visiting scholars from under-represented groups to your department, and include non-majority speakers in every lecture and seminar series.
- Do not rely on passive advertising to fill job vacancies. Recruit year-round, like a talent scout, not just when an actual job vacancy is at hand. Designate one of your colleagues to cultivate relationships with prospective candidates, for example through particular professional networks, doctoral departments in other universities, or by starting a visiting (PhD) dissertation scholars-in-residence in your department.
- Diversify within each of your appointment and promotion panels. Make sure that every committee itself is diverse and invite a senior academic to serve as an advocate for diversity on each of your panels.
- Develop a retention plan for new staff even before recruitment begins. A retention plan (including, for example, an assigned mentor, professional development sessions and community-building events) is essential for all new staff, but especially for non-majority staff.
- Develop a genuinely effective staff induction programme – supply newcomers with essential information well in advance; prime your colleagues for the arrival of new staff; introduce and promote new staff to students and colleagues immediately on their arrival; ask your senior colleagues to persistently reach out to new arrivals, etc.
- Celebrate your department as a *living* community as well as a *learning* community: recognize the major festivals of the principal religions; organize a Christmas party for your staff's children; establish a 'keep in touch' scheme to support women on maternity leave; host 'open days' for the local community (not just prospective applicants); invite one of the major disabled societies, or the local race equality council, to nominate a representative to sit on your equal opportunities steering group, etc.
- Volunteer your department as a pilot for your institutional job evaluation scheme (typically, higher education role analysis (HERA) addressing inequalities in pay.
- Sign up to join one of your central bodies with institution-wide responsibilities for equal opportunities. Under the RRA, for example, your university will have, or should be establishing, equality teams in: student admissions, support and employment; student assessment, teaching and achievement; student learning support and development; staff employment, welfare and discipline, etc. These will

be headed by lead officers and supported by data controllers overseen by your racial equality or equal opportunities action group. Similar mechanisms may also be in place with regard to policy formulation and implementation on 'joining up disability', 'work–life balance', 'measuring diversity', and 'promoting dignity at work' (by tackling harassment), etc.

- Lobby your HR department or your central equal opportunities body to draw up your own institutional staff 'charter for diversity' based on 'respect for people' if your university has not already done so. If support is not forthcoming then hire a consultant and draw up your own departmental one.
- Make a formal commitment, and ask others to follow suit, to sign up for the leadership challenge initiated and organized by the Equality and Human Rights Commission.

Understanding the legal principles and how to apply them

As you will be judged by your actions, and given that the pace and degree of legislative change in equal opportunities is probably greater than in any other area of your managerial responsibilities, it is imperative that you keep abreast of such changes, however daunting this may seem. This is not only so that you know what you will, or are supposed to, be doing, and what you will be legally bound to comply with, but also because you will be in an *informal* position to counter the lack of awareness and misunderstanding which, surprisingly, still prevails on these matters, despite all the attendant publicity. Such ignorance can often lead staff to draw the wrong conclusion (as in 'I don't want to have to short-list someone from an ethnic minority as a makeweight'), which in turn can make them feel vulnerable and threatened, and ultimately resistant to the notion of diversity, even though the premise on which their opposition is based is an erroneous one. It is a trap you must make sure you do not fall into yourself. You can best avoid doing so through developing an understanding of the key basic principles of equalities legislation, as outlined in Box 7.8, and how they are applied in practice.

For example, you should know the following.

- In the case of recruitment and selection, the law demands you treat all applicants with fair and equal respect, whatever their background. You cannot, however, seek to increase the number of female or ethnic minority staff by only short-listing female or ethnic minority candidates. This is positive discrimination and is illegal in Britain under the Race Relations and Sex Discrimination Acts. It is perfectly legal, however, to take 'positive action' to elicit applications from such disadvantaged groups or to meet the needs of such staff currently in post who, because they are dispro-portionately fewer in number, may feel isolated and ultimately prohibited from achieving their full potential. The successful Athena Project, for example, which offered mentoring support to women in science, engineering and technology in UK HEIs is just one instance of this type of initiative (Athena Guide, 2003; Athena Swan, 2008).
- You cannot impose quotas such as 'The X department must have two members of ethnic minority academic staff by 2013' for your department. Such quotas are unlawful and must be avoided. On the other hand, it is perfectly legitimate for you to set a target such as 'The department of X wishes to initiate representation by staff

Box 7.8 The basic legal principles of equalities legislation

Principle	Theory	Practical implications
Employers are free to decide on the skills, knowledge and qualities that they want from employees.	• Employment decisions should be based on merit but all aspects of the recruitment and selection process must be free from bias and unlawful discrimination. • The law demands you give fair and equal respect to all applicants. • The law does not demand that you give preference to individuals because they are from an under-represented section of society.	• Positive discrimination: i.e. the policy or practice of positively favouring an individual from an under-represented group – as in, for example, seeking to increase the number of female or ethnic minority job candidates – is illegal in the UK under the Race Relations and Sex Discrimination Acts. • Quotas: i.e. the practice of suggesting that minimum levels or numbers of people from certain groups should be employed – for example, that a university should have at least 50 per cent female employees – is illegal in the UK. • Targets: i.e. where a workforce is skewed towards or away from certain groups: it is perfectly legal to set targets that indicate how the numbers might be changed. For example, a university in an area where 10 per cent of the population is black but whose workforce is only 2 per cent black may set a target – in those areas where recruitment is primarily local – to try to make the percentage of black people employed more representative by encouraging more to apply. To avoid discrimination against white people, however, decisions to appoint must still be based solely on merit.
		Targets are: • guidelines to illustrate imbalances within the workforce; • about helping people ensure they do not accidentally discriminate when they are employing; • about trying to encourage different people to consider particular jobs when they are seeking employment.
Organizations are more likely to stay within the law if they have their own clear policies,	Internal guidelines on good practice will ensure organizations adhere to the law	The risk is that the organization does not follow its own guidelines in practice. If it has a written policy and does not follow it then its actions are automatically unfair. The rule: 'failure to follow procedure is automatically unfair', applies. For example, a male employee who harasses a female

procedures and practices that support diversity and equality.

Employers are legally responsible for the actions of their employees except where the employer has taken clear steps to ensure discrimination does not take place.

'Clear steps' means that the employer has provided guidelines on how to treat people equally, together with the necessary training.

If the guidelines and the training are ignored, the employee could be held personally liable for their actions. In many instances both the employer and employee may be held liable for discrimination.

colleague may warrant instant dismissal, but if you do not invoke the written disciplinary procedure and follow its requirements you may find a counter-claim for unfair dismissal from the male employee.

All employees are treated equally.

This includes direct discrimination which occurs when an individual is treated less favourably than someone else in similar circumstances because of their gender, marital status, ethnicity, nationality, disability or sexual orientation.

Instances of direct discrimination are typically obvious and easy to identify.

A provision, criterion or practice which may have a disproportionate effect on men or women is indirect sex discrimination.

Derives from rules which *prima facie* may appear to apply equally to everyone; however, closer examination suggests they are likely to discriminate.

Not as transparent as direct discrimination but nevertheless discriminatory in its effects. For example, working patterns and hours which adversely affect staff with childcare responsibilities; dress codes and health and safety requirements which do not respect religious custom; etc.

Source: adapted from The Grass Roots Group, 2003.

from visible ethnic minorities in its senior staff (principal lecturer upward) within two years, and to increase this representation by the year 2013'. Such targets are different from quotas in that they are aspirational in character, and signal your intention to address an imbalance you have recognized in your staffing profile, relative perhaps to local or national population norms. They do not imply, however, that you intend to discriminate against white people. That said, you should ensure that your aspirational target is reflective of the relevant recruitment pool, i.e. it is realistic and achievable, otherwise it could lead to de-motivation and discouragement in the event that it is not met.

How thorough is your understanding then? Use the quiz in Box 7.9 to make a preliminary assessment. Whether you did well or not (and hopefully you did manage

---

Box 7.9 How do you measure up on knowledge about diversity?

1 Age: What proportion of the UK is now aged over 40?
   (a) 1 in 10
   (b) 1 in 5
   (c) 1 in 3

2 Gender: What percentage of the UK workforce do women represent?
   (a) Under 25%
   (b) 35%
   (c) Over 40%

3 Ethnicity: What percentage of new start-up businesses are opened by Asian businessmen and women each year?
   (a) 2%
   (b) 9%
   (c) 15%

4 Sexual orientation: What percentage of gay, lesbian and bisexual men and women conceal their sexuality because of fear of intimidation?
   (a) None
   (b) 22%
   (c) 64%

5 Disability: How many disabled people are there in the UK?
   (a) Fewer than 1 million
   (b) Up to 5 million
   (c) Over 8 million

6 Discrimination is estimated to account for what percentage of the pay gap between men and women?
   (a) Less than 10%
   (b) 25% to 50%
   (c) Around 75%

7 What percentage of British doctors were born overseas?
   (a) 25%
   (b) 7%
   (c) 15%

8   What percentage of disabled people in the UK use wheelchairs?
    (a)   Less than 5%
    (b)   More than 10%
    (c)   Almost 50%

9   What is the number of students over the age of 25?
    (a)   43%
    (b)   25%
    (c)   19%

10 What proportion of gay men experienced at least one violent attack over the last five years?
    (a)   1 in 3
    (b)   1 in 5
    (c)   1 in 20

11 When evaluated, a marking system for exam papers is shown to produce results for male students that are lower than comparable papers from female students. This might be evidence of:
    (a)   Discrimination
    (b)   Bad behaviour
    (c)   Not discrimination

12 A student who is a wheelchair user is offered a university place on condition that she finds her own accommodation. No other student has this condition placed upon them. This is:
    (a)   Lawful
    (b)   Inconvenient
    (c)   Unlawful

13 A lecturer refuses to stop writing on the white board in order to turn around and speak directly to students to enable a person who lip reads to access the lecture. This is:
    (a)   Unlawful
    (b)   Rude
    (c)   Lawful

14 Monitoring reveals that black students are less likely to secure work placements for a vocational course. This is likely to be:
    (a)   Discrimination
    (b)   Coincidence
    (c)   Not discrimination

15 More African-Caribbean than Chinese students are disciplined for persistently playing very loud music in halls of residence after 02.00am. This is likely to be:
    (a)   Discrimination
    (b)   Coincidence
    (c)   Not discrimination

How did you do? Answers: 1 – c; 2 – c; 3 – b; 4 – c; 5 – c; 6 – b; 7 – a; 8 – a; 9 – a; 10 – a; 11 – a; 12 – c; 13 – a; 14 – a; 15 – b.
Scores:

15 – Excellent
13–14 – Very Good
12 – Good
10 – Fair

Source: adapted from Grass Roots Diversity Group, 2003.

to answer 12 or more questions correctly), the important point is that you are, as in the other aspects of diversity, proactive in this regard. That is, do not wait for, or rely on, others such as your HR department to provide you details of the latest initiatives. Seek them out yourself. The Equality Challenge Unit, for instance, has published guidelines on action planning and monitoring covering all aspects of diversity. Immerse yourself in them, know them, and apply them. Put another way, knowing the pitfalls is half the battle; knowing what to do, the other. When combined with the other initiatives outlined above, you will be well on your way to internalizing diversity as a core value. Indeed, you will know you have reached that point when your department, and your university, accept that in embracing diversity, they stand a much better chance of success than those departments and institutions that don't.

8 Enhancing the student experience

> The most important misconception is that higher education is about satisfying students' wishes as customers rather than about changing them as people.
>
> Roger Brown, former Chief Executive,
> UK Higher Education Quality Council, 2006

'Universities are just another service industry and must respond to the market' (Waterhouse, 2002); 'a higher education experience is not a commodity, it is a participatory experience' (Harvey, 2008); 'a therapy culture pervading universities is creating a generation of hapless students and lecturers' (Newman, 2008b); 'trying to serve students and society puts academe under unbearable strain' (Mills, 2007). Seldom in higher education has the role of students – their relationship with the university, to their study and to society – been so sharply contested, and misunderstood, as it is today. Invoked by politicians, funding providers and governing bodies alike, the so-called 'student experience' – a relatively new concept borrowed from the commercial sector – has been used to chivvy, justify and extol to such an extent that it 'has begun to take on a life of its own relatively removed from reality' (Watson, 2007b).

The reality is, of course, that the students' experience 'is what the whole process is supposed to be about ... the *raison d'être* of both individual staff and institutions' (Haselgrove, 1994). Reminding ourselves of this obligation is one thing; addressing it is quite another. The aim of this chapter is to help you do just that. It seeks to clarify what the student experience is and how we can enhance it. In doing so, it explains the sources of misunderstanding between 'students as learners' and 'students as customers'; examines the relationship between students and university services and the role of students in learning and teaching; and identifies the practical ways in which you and your institution can enhance your students' experience.

What is 'the student experience'?

> The student experience is such a wide-ranging term, influenced by such a complex variety of factors that it is fruitless to attempt to define it as a single 'thing'.
>
> 1994 Group Policy Statement, November, 2007

> The student experience is one of those things which can sound better than it is . . . like 'low-cost mortgages', 'English middle-order batting', 'gastro-pub' and 'sun-dried tomatoes' or in higher education terms, 'the lighter touch' and 'the single conversation'.
>
> David Watson, Institute of Education, 2007

A common expression, used in multiple and unexamined ways, it is not difficult to understand why the term has generated so much confusion. It is, in essence, a compound concept and, as the 1994 Group has rightly pointed out, it is no longer a singular thing as it may have been when Michael Oakeshott called it 'the gift of an interval' (Watson, 2007b). Thus when we consider questions such as: Is the student experience about satisfying student needs and meeting their expectations as consumers of higher education? Or is it about changing their understanding, engaging with them in imaginative intellectual discourse and challenging them to question accepted truths? Or is it about teaching and supervision as much as services, facilities, sports and social life? Or is it about helping students to learn how to earn a living as well as learning how to live? (Ramsden, 2006), the answer in each and every case is a resounding . . . yes. Put simply, the student experience is everything the student says it is, whatever else we may want or consider it to be. Nor can it ever be an unchanging one, for it varies according to the personal expectations and perceptions of each and every individual student.

That said, these many different student 'experiences' have multiplied even further over the last generation. For example, in the UK we now have (like the USA heretofore) a mass system of higher education for the first time, with a far more diverse student profile than ever before. There are also far greater opportunities for study, off-campus as well as on-campus, home-based as well as in the workplace. The introduction of variable fees has also accelerated a trend whereby students are much more likely to work during term-time (while studying full-time) yet still face greater debt on completion.

Put another way, where once the student experience entailed packing a trunk and setting off to read for a degree with like-minded peers in an intensive residential community, nowadays it is as likely to be just a single activity which students fit into their already crowded lifestyles. And here is the crux, for such has been the transformation that it brings into sharp focus the very nature of the relationship between student and university.

Students or customers?

> Students . . .
> - Are the most important people in our business
> - Do not depend on us, we depend on them
> - Never interrupt our work, they are our work

- Do us a favor when they call, we don't do them favors by letting them in
- Are part of our business, not outsiders
- Are flesh-and-blood human beings, not cold statistics
- Bring us their wants, we fulfill them
- Are not to be argued with
- Deserve courteous attention
- Are who we are.

The Systematic Education Group of Colleges, Malaysia

To some it is a simple proposition: students as fee-paying clients have every right to expect to be treated as 'consumers', for higher education is no different to any other service industry (Waterhouse, 2002). While others, such as the 1994 Group (2007), argue that this 'consumer notion should be tempered with the recognition of students' and universities' roles as mutual partners in the development of people's knowledge, skills and experience in order to shape their contribution to society'.

Then there are still others – like Allan Bloom, Frank Furedi, Robert Stevens and Mary Evans – who, stung by the extent of student instrumentalism (or the degree to which students have shifted from being members of an academic community to simple consumers of an academic product), believe that the whole higher education enterprise itself is compromised, irretrievably lost. And what is particularly depressing here is that these professional dystopians take out their disappointment with contemporary academic life on those they are supposed to serve, as in Bloom's *The Closing of the American Mind* (1998) with its view of a self-serving, introverted generation: 'Students these days are not particularly moral or noble. . . . [they] . . . are pleasant, friendly and if not great-souled, at least not particularly mean-spirited. Their primary preoccupation is themselves, understood in the narrowest sense.'

Not only have attitudes towards students, as well as those of students, changed, there has also been a collective endeavour to measure the student experience . . . not least by politicians and funding providers keen on securing another insight into institutional performance. In the UK, for instance, the National Student Survey (NSS) (modelled on the Course Evaluation Questionnaire (CEQ) developed in Australia over a decade earlier) was introduced in 2005 to elicit feedback from final-year undergraduates as a means of helping institutions to improve the experience of their own students and informing prospective student choice. While not intended to be used as a comparator, the NSS has, just as in so many other instances, been widely interpreted as such: yet another national league table ranking programmes and institutions, in this case by 'student satisfaction'. And with it has come all the attendant external and internal pressures on programmes and institutions to respond although some critics have dismissed the NSS as 'shallow, costly, widely manipulated and methodologically worthless' (Harvey, 2008).

Taken together, these changes constitute a formidable challenge to institutions in addressing the student experience. In doing so it is important, in the first instance, to clarify the role of the student and their relationship with the institution. Much of the confusion that has arisen here is because of the failure to recognize that students do not interact with their institutions solely and exclusively on the basis of being 'learners'. As the 1994 Group (2007) points out, the multiple roles of the modern student include not only 'Learner' but also 'Citizen, Colleague, Consumer, Scholar, Ambassador and perhaps most important of all, Partner'. From a student perspective gaining access to the library, the faculty office, the refectory, the fees office, their hall of residence, their IT account and so on is very much a service relationship. And we should recognize it as such and strive to provide service excellence to students as customers, and not shy away from it or 'temper the notion of students as consumers'.

The difficulty arises when we apply the same principle to learning and teaching. Here again, students are indeed consumers in that they will expect lecturers to turn up on time and be available to give help when needed; they will want to know when and how they will be assessed and receive feedback on their work, and so on. They are not solely customers, however, in this regard, far from it. Learning, as we all know, is neither simply a product nor an outcome but also a series of activities and processes . . . and how students approach a subject is as important as what they end up knowing.

The role of teaching therefore is critical. The teacher does not simply impart knowledge but also seeks to cultivate a positive attitude in their students towards skills, clarity, honesty, analysis, responsiveness to evidence and a curiosity for truth; in essence to support them in becoming independent and confident learners. They do this, of course, by suggesting arguments, pointing to facts, evidence and resources and raising questions for students. Additionally, however, students themselves – and this is the critical difference – must also take responsibility for their own learning in the spirit of 'education is something that you do, not something that is done to you' (through 'spoon-feeding' and the like). In this sense then, and here I suggest an additional role to the ones put forward by the 1994 Group, students are not only 'consumers' but are also 'producers' of learning and teaching. With this in mind, how can you and your institution enhance the experience of your students?

Enhancing your students' experience

> One of the foundation stones is management by fact. . . . If you start with a vision and core values and then you manage by fact, you're way down the road . . . we would have cut years off our experience had we started there.
> Dean Hubbard, President, Northwest Missouri State University, 2003, reflecting on meeting the US government's highest standards for excellence in higher education

Conceptualize the student experience in a holistic, 'joined-up' way from the perspective of your own students (see Figure 8.1)

Elementary you might think, but it is in fact one of the most difficult and challenging things to achieve in any institution, not least because responsibility for the student experience is typically dispersed across a number of university services and departments, and requires project management skills of a high order, particularly if there is an endemic 'silo mentality' to overcome.

Consider, then, the experience of your students and reflect on their journey from pre-entry through graduation to alumni. Complete the questions in Table 8.1 first from a university perspective and then with regard to students and staff in your own department.

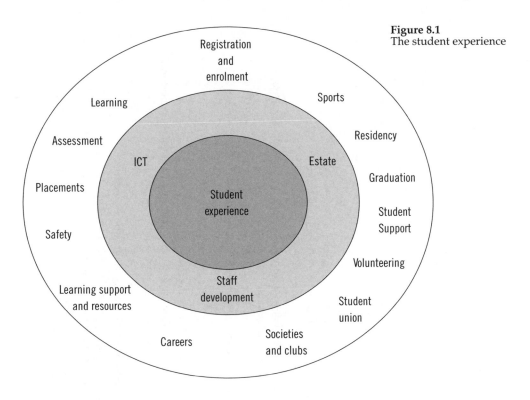

Figure 8.1
The student experience

What are the strengths and weaknesses of the current arrangements in your institution and your department for enhancing the student experience? What are the critical gaps in your provision? What are the areas you need to work on? Is it an issue of structure, culture or people? Should you establish a high-level project working group to coordinate this area either wholly or in part (e.g. student retention; student progression and achievement; student well-being) within your university, or locally within your department?

Align your student services in a student-centred fashion that mirrors the student life-cycle and fosters a culture of professional informality

The increasing heterogeneity of the student body (in terms of entry level qualifications, prior learning and prior working experience, age and ethnic mix, etc.), along with the heightened expectations of students as fee-payers, has generated, and will continue to do so, a concomitant demand for customized and personalized service, not one that is, or has been based on, a standardized 'one size fits all' approach.

Converged student services are now widely perceived, recognized and celebrated as the least 'imperfect' means of meeting this demand (UUK 2002; NAO, 2007). Organized according to the student life-cycle, these 'student centres' typically comprise a recruitment and admissions team and a specialist student services team flanked by a front-office (or 'first-stop shop'), which operates a triage system for handling all initial inquiries and a back-office (or student administration) which ensures that essential administrative requirements are met with regard to student records, examinations and awards, invoicing, funding council returns and so on.

Table 8.1 Enhancing the student experience through 'joined-up' practice

Strategies	Student journey	What your university and department can do
Sorting strategies	How do you deal with your students pre-entry?	Improve student decision-making by making • as much information as possible available • your information welcoming to the full range of potential students Recruit students who have a realistic chance of succeeding Advise students according to their best interests; ensure the 'open door' is not a revolving door Engage with students before they actually arrive
Connecting strategies	How do you help students integrate with one another at your university	Adopt a welcoming attitude to students; acknowledge that higher education is, at heart, a social process Make the induction process welcoming and effective Encourage students to feel that they belong in the institution Help students to become 'streetwise' in their environment through a buddy or peer-mentoring scheme
Supporting strategies	How do you support students inside and outside your university?	Have, as far as possible, a 'first-stop shop' or a portal for support services Provide properly resourced tutoring support and facilities for students Appreciate the complexity of pressures on contemporary students and respond sympathetically to unforeseen circumstances Invite potential withdrawers to an exit interview

| Transforming (student) strategies | How do you help students become confident and capable independent learners? | Provide a culture supportive of student learning based on 'professional informality'
Respond to students' pre-existing level of knowledge
Ensure the programme structures are conducive to student success
Ensure that students know what is expected of them
Ensure that teaching approaches adopted are conducive to student success
Make good use of formative assessment
Disproportionate the allocation of resources in favour of the first-year experience
Treat academic failure as a developmental opportunity |
| Transforming (staff) strategies | How do you best support staff in this process? | Support the development of expertise in teaching
Establish a learning climate and build a community of practice (see Chapter 6)
Recognize, celebrate and reward excellence in teaching |

Source: adapted from Yorke and Longden, 2004; 2008.

By establishing an inter-dependent team-based service in place of independent, discrete service units, these converged student centres have a number of advantages over the traditional organizational model of student services. Most importantly, their holistic approach, grounded in three levels of service (reception, specialized and strategic), enables them to tailor support to meet individual need by placing the student at the centre of all activities and processes: to provide a service, in other words, which is proactive and issues-focused rather than a reactive and referral one (see Figure 8.2).

Additionally, student centres offer flexibility in the deployment of staff at particular pressure-points in the year (e.g. enrolment, graduation), as well as providing staff with greater opportunities for professional development and career progression. Ideally, they should also have, as in the case of academic departments, a culture of professional informality: namely high standards combined with approachability, availability and

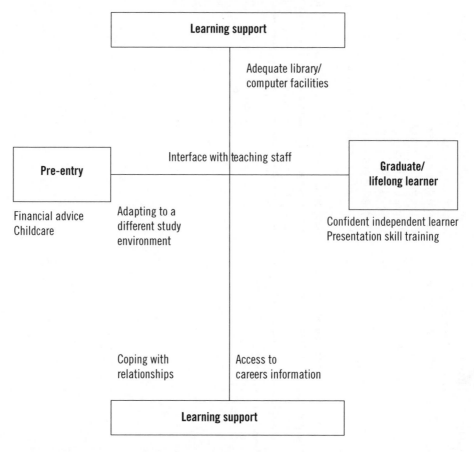

**Support services proactive model
(Issues-focused service)**

Quality cycle: Survey–Evaluate–Review–Change / Improve

Figure 8.2 Aligning student services with the student life-cycle a can-do mentality. Are your university student services and your departmental administration equally fit for purpose?

Recruit students who have a realistic chance of succeeding

Ensure your 'open door' is not a revolving door. This may not be an issue if you are a 'selecting' university or department, but certainly is one if you are a 'recruiting' university or department. There is an inherent tension, as we know, between widening participation and educational opportunity, on the one hand, and institutions' requirement to meet contracted student numbers and the likelihood of student progression and achievement, on the other: a conundrum which the sector has yet to satisfactorily resolve.

While the retention of students in UK higher education is in fact a success story (despite media often reporting the contrary) – the proportion of full-time students in English HEIs continuing from year one to year two grew from 90.3 per cent to 91.6 per cent between 2000 and 2005, and the proportion predicted to complete increased from 77.3 per cent to 78.1 per cent, making the UK fifth in the OECD world table of 'survival rates' (with only Korea above it with as high a participation rate) – it is also the case, as the parliamentary Public Accounts Committee noted, that the drop-out rate has remained virtually unchanged at 22 per cent of full-time students, and 45 per cent of part-time students, despite an additional government investment of £800 million (NAO, 2007; Eastwood, 2008).

A disproportionate number of the students most likely to suspend or withdraw from their studies tend, as we know, to have a modest academic record, or come from families with no experience of higher education, or neighbourhoods with low participation rates, or low-income households, or indeed a combination of all these factors. Likewise in the USA, for example, only 36 per cent of college-qualified students complete bachelor's degrees within 8½ years, compared with 81 per cent of high-income students (Spellings, 2006).

The challenge for the 'recruiting' university, then, is to curb this propensity from becoming a self-fulfilling prophecy by ensuring their 'open door' is not a revolving one. How?

Conventional wisdom tells us that there are four broad categories of influence which prompt students to withdraw (Yorke and Longden, 2004):

1 flawed decision-making about entering the programme;
2 students' experience of the programme and the institution generally;
3 failure to cope with the demands of the programme;
4 events that impact on students' lives outside the institution.

Universities have a direct impact on the first three of these categories and can help in ameliorating the effects of the fourth. It is the first category which lends itself to easier resolution than the others, and while making a good choice is primarily the responsibility of the intending student (in undertaking a significant level of personal research including institutional visits prior to application), it is also the case that this process may well be a hurried rather than a considered one. More than that, peer pressure to enter higher education, fear of 'drift' and an uncritical acquiescence in the message of A-level grades (or equivalent qualifications), as well as that of so-called 'league table' guidance on institutions, may well lead to ill-considered choices (Yorke and Longden, 2008).

Put another way, it is our responsibility as well to advise students according to their best interests – *'What can this course offer me?'* *'Is this course right for me?'* – with regard to their preparation and likelihood of success in higher education. To do otherwise, and enrol students on your programme because of the institutional imperative to recruit contracted student numbers is a flawed approach, and does the university, as well as the student, a disservice. It is not only wasteful of resources but will also have a negative impact on your institutional reputation and may well incur a financial penalty anyway.

Bridge the expectations and skills 'gap'

Like poor choice-making, failure to cope with the demands of the programme is one of the key factors in student withdrawals, the source of which, of course, may lie in underpreparation. As the Spellings Commission (2006) in the USA put it, 'substandard high school preparation is compounded by poor alignment between high schools and colleges, which often creates an "expectations gap" between what colleges require and what high schools produce'. In the UK this 'skills deficit' is manifest in, for example, the Engineering Professors Conference which complains every year about the calculus that first-year students could do 20 years ago, but cannot do now.

While it may well be that students do indeed require both pre-entry and post-entry learning support in numeracy, English for academic purposes, study skills and so on, it is also the case that we can do much to ensure student success. The received wisdom tells us there are three things we can provide which would make a positive difference to student progression in the first year: a high-quality induction experience; a genuinely introductory academic programme and regular access to an academic adviser (Yorke and Longden, 2008; NAO, 2007).

Induction, as exemplified by the Student Transition and Retention (STAR) project at the University of Ulster, is a process, not a fixed one-off event in which students are overloaded with information at the very time (immediately on arrival) they are least likely to absorb it. More than that, it should be a 'big welcoming academic hug' to your learning community which extends arguably from initial contact with the student, right through their first year of study. The most effective induction schemes draw on existing students as sources of local knowledge acting essentially as buddies or mentors who can also provide a slant on provision and the environment not found in the official sources of information.

Increased heterogeneity also has implications for programme design. As students enter from an ever-increasing variety of backgrounds in terms of entry qualifications, learning experiences and learning styles, not only is it more difficult to be sure about students' pre-existing level of knowledge, the pitching of the level of material becomes ever more problematic too. One way of developing a common platform of understanding can be, as we've noted, through diagnostic assessment and pre-entry workshops supported by learning materials to help students fill in their gaps. Another is to customize in a much more deliberate fashion than hitherto the introductory first-year programme: to provide students with an 'intellectual map' on which to build.

Purdue University, Indianapolis, for example has developed 'a core set of Principles of Undergraduate Learning that guide the development of program curriculum, the evaluation of program effectiveness and the development of student proficiencies'. Likewise, many universities are developing 'progression pathways' (or 'curriculum maps') with their local education partners, often in liaison with employer groups.

In so doing, we should be wary about notions of 'skills deficits'. There is much publicity about what new and graduating students cannot do, and about the so-called 'information age mind-set' which, as Jason Frand claims, is characterized by 'ten attributes reflecting values and behaviors' (see Box 8.1). While this may help explain how approaches to study and learning styles may have changed, it fails to recognize what this new generation can do – the skills they bring with them that their predecessors did not. Much of this has to do with information and communication technologies. Disparagingly caricatured as 'toys', ICT will soon be less a marginal than an integral and embedded aspect of all subjects (Watson, 2007a).

Finally, students are far more likely to prosper if they have access to and regular contact with one or more trusted individuals: an assigned academic adviser or personal tutor who is trained and proactive in managing the relationship.

Use pedagogic practices that promote student engagement and adopt approaches to assessment that enhance learning

It is not just programme structures we must ensure are conducive to student success by providing students with coherence in their studies (not simply a packaged set of disconnected modules) but also the way we deliver it. Received wisdom again tells us many students experience difficulties in adjusting to higher education. They can have a tendency to overestimate their knowledge and abilities which, when combined with an approach to teaching and learning that is markedly different from their previous experience, can make for an unwelcome surprise when they receive feedback on their first assignments (Yorke and Longden, 2008).

To enhance student progression, then, we need to reflect on whether our teaching is indeed organized to best effect. Ideally, this implies having a mode of teaching in which students are quickly engaged in academic work and are given formative assessment at an early stage so that they can begin to understand the standards expected in a way that cannot be achieved simply by exhortation or referring them to statements of intended learning outcomes. Many institutions, of course, have begun to re-engineer their first-

---

Box 8.1 The information-age mindset

- Computers aren't technology
- Internet better than TV
- Reality no longer real
- Doing rather than knowing
- Nintendo over logic

- Multi-tasking a way of life
- Typing rather than handwriting
- Staying connected
- Zero tolerance for delays
- Consumer/creator blurring

Source: adapted from Frand, 2000.

year delivery in just such a way, often abandoning summative assessment in the first semester altogether.

Carnegie-Mellon University, Northern Arizona University and Tallahassee Community College, for example, have all redesigned their large introductory courses. They have abandoned the traditional lecture format in favour of active learning strategies to engage students in course material in innovative ways, at an early stage, through online access to web-based tutorials, on-demand feedback and support from student peer mentors. Likewise Neumont University, Salt Lake City, has also developed its computer science programme on a project-based, experiential foundation that incorporates the tools and technologies important to the industry. Students learn the theory of computer science and then apply that theory in real-world projects, initially mentored by staff and, ultimately, by senior students in peer-to-peer relationships.

Assessment is critical here, too, and not simply in terms of formative and summative. It is still the case that assessment is too often seen as an after-thought, a process typically 'bolted on' to courses in an unreflective way, rather than being recognized for what it can be: a primary vehicle for effective learning and teaching. That is to say, since students get qualifications not by taking courses but by passing assessments, it follows that assessment is a crucial way for students to organize their learning and for students and teachers to evaluate it.

Inverting 'teaching, learning and assessment', then, to read 'assessment, learning and teaching', in that order of importance, not only makes the links between the three more explicit, but assessment itself becomes much more than a simple evaluation and grading activity. Indeed it becomes central to the teaching process as well as that of student learning. Examination boards then can also use assessment outcomes as a legitimate means for evaluating the effectiveness of teaching as well as that of student learning.

Are your arrangements for assessment, learning and teaching constructed in the most effective way for promoting student learning and progression?

Be clear about 'the deal' for students

With mass participation the student body will, in time, come to resemble the population at large, and the likelihood that those who enter higher education may have mis-perceptions about what is expected of them will also increase still further. Given that students now almost invariably work for money too (typically in excess of the 12 hours a week endorsed by the House of Commons Select Committee) as much to sustain lifestyles as a response to changes in fees and student support, and that they are indeed fee-payers, it is more important than ever that universities make clear what is expected of them.

Typically, this expectation was articulated some years ago through the introduction of Student Charters, though there was more emphasis here on formal rights and responsibilities. Managing student expectations nowadays is more akin to a 'service-level agreement' than a 'rights charter'. The 'service-level agreement' most likely to be effective in practice is that which mirrors the life-cycle of the student ('Before you arrive'; 'When you arrive'; 'Your course of study'; etc.), is based on reciprocal commitments and associated behaviours ('As a student you are expected to'; 'As a student you can expect') and is grounded ideally in the values of your university. That is to say, the agreement is integral to the values your university and department want to work by and for which you want to be known. Again this will depend on the extent to which your institutional values have been articulated and developed and are 'owned' by your colleagues.

Student feedback – its timeliness, quality and quantity – is a recurring issue and there is an opportunity here to give a commitment to publishing a 'hand back' date as well as a 'hand in' one for assignments, or providing written feedback to students on their formal assessments (within 15 working days for example). That said, this issue is less about coercing staff into giving more feedback more quickly than it is about supporting staff and students in recognizing *and using* the full range of opportunities (informal as well as formal; formative as well as summative; in-class and online) that are available for promoting two-way feedback.

Capture the student voice and establish the facts

Capturing the student voice is, of course, essential if we are to distinguish the reality of the student experience from the imagined one. This need has now been recognized at a sector level, as we noted earlier, with the introduction of the NSS in the UK based on Australia's CEQ. And while the validity of these initiatives may have been questioned – the claim, for example, that the range of scores used to rank institutions and programmes is so narrow that it may be explained by sampling error, and not necessarily by student satisfaction or dissatisfaction (Harvey, 2008) – nevertheless the outcomes for individual institutions and programmes do provide us with 'a window into how our designs for learning are experienced by students' (Ramsden, 2007).

Either way, the outcomes of the NSS, CEQ or any other external independent survey with which you are involved (for example, the growing I-Graduate survey into international student expectations and experiences) should not really be a surprise to you. If they are, then you need to reflect more critically on the internal mechanisms you have for assessing your students' experience, for example: module evaluations; programme monitoring; the election, training and support of your programme student representatives; your relationship with the Students' Union or Student Society and the extent to which your students are involved in course planning committees and review processes, or used as collaborative evaluators of innovations, or even as tutors in implementing new pedagogies. Ultimately, what counts is that you have a rich source of information whose consistency is such as to allow you to focus on particular areas which will make a positive difference to your students' experience.

Enhance the employability of your graduates

If graduates are to benefit in the best way possible from their higher education experience, to take their place in the world of work and society at large as mature well-rounded individuals, it follows that we must recognize the importance of developing and accrediting the transferable skills they acquire outside, as well as within, the academic curriculum. We are also expected to meet the challenge in the Leitch Review (2006) which anticipates the UK workforce in 2020 having 'world-class high skills, exceeding 40 per cent of the adult population qualified to level 4 and above'.

One way forward is to develop, if you have not already done so, mechanisms to accredit non-academic activities such as volunteering and also (given the need for students to support themselves financially while at university) those skills obtained during paid employment, perhaps delivered through an arrangement between your university job shop and employers. Another way is to consider systematically what your approach is, or should be, towards nurturing the employability of your students. Knight and Yorke (2003) have identified five 'ideal types' or ways of incorporating employability into the student experience:

1   employability through the whole curriculum
2   employability in the core curriculum
3   work-related learning incorporated as one or more components
4   employability-related module(s) within the curriculum
5   work-related learning in parallel with the curriculum

Or you could go one step further and employ your students yourself, like Northwest Missouri State University, which hires 20 per cent of its students on-campus during term-time, including five who work in the President's office (Hubbard and Sullivan, 2006) (see Box 8.2).

Either way, it is equally important that you also consider, in a holistic sense, the various ways in which you are seeking to create and sustain capable and confident independent learners in all your programmes, through 'learning-to-learn' provision, personal development planning, career management, emotional skills development and so on: interventions which have all been shown to increase both persistence and performance.

All of this also begs the question – What does 'graduateness' mean for your department, your university and your alumni? What is the 'higher' in 'higher education' for your students? It may well be advanced subject knowledge, higher-order skills and capabilities, employability, the unlocking of meta-cognition (in becoming confident and independent learners) and a curriculum that embodies both education and training. What else is also special and distinctive about your graduates – entrepreneurial savvy; a capacity for leadership; a can-do mentality; original thinking; a compass for life, etc? Is this explicit to your prospective students and employers? Be clear what it means to be a graduate of your university.

One institution that has set out boldly to 'Rethink undergraduate education for the twenty-first century' is the University of Melbourne. Recognizing that many of its undergraduate courses had 'become too narrow and over-specialized', the university initiated the most comprehensive review in its 150-year history under its latest strategic plan 'Growing Esteem' (2005). Under the 'Melbourne Model' launched in April 2007, the university's 96 undergraduate courses are being replaced by just six 'new generation undergraduate courses' (or generalist degrees) in the Arts, Science, Commerce, Environments, Music and Biomedicine, while all professional courses (including medicine, dentistry and veterinary sciences) will change from undergraduate to graduate entry by 2011.

While both the length and cost of study will increase for many of the university's students (with a two-year postgraduate professional programme building on the three-year generalist degree), the university believes that the model will have 'distinctive benefits' for students which will outweigh these consequences: 'a more mature understanding of interests and career ambitions in the transition to postgraduate study';

Box 8.2 An exemplar: Northwest Missouri State University

Successful in meeting the US government's highest standards for excellence in higher education (the Malcolm Baldridge National Quality Award) and three-time winner of the Missouri Quality Award, Northwest Missouri State University has established an enviable reputation for student retention and quality enhancement.

A state-assisted, four-year regional university that also offers graduate degree programs, NWMSU was the first public university in the USA to establish an electronic campus (1984) for its 5,500 undergraduate and 2,000 graduate students. More than that, it has also realized its vision to be 'an internationally recognized innovator in continuously improving higher education'.

Driven by a 'Culture of Quality' with an emphasis on:

- Customer focus, high expectations, involvement, assessment and feedback and continuous improvement informed by Student Comment Cards to the President's office.
- 'Management by fact' using university-wide meaningful performance indicators including the President's dashboard of key quality indicators.
- Shared university values – 'we are a learning organization'; 'we master the details of what we do'; 'we are open and ethical; 'we are leaders in our field'.
- Trust and empowerment – 'there's great tolerance for failure, but there is no tolerance for not trying'.
- Key decision drivers – enrolment; satisfaction (students, faculty and staff); student success; financial performance.

And a willingness to innovate:

- As an employer – 20 per cent of students work for the university on-campus during term-time.
- Talent Development Center – accredits student employees to coach other students in study skills and course material.

NWMSU has achieved one of the highest retention rates among its peer group of 41 universities and colleges, underpinned by a very distinctive organizational culture:

1 We fix processes, not people.
2 We have driven out fear. Assessment and evaluation is good. Data is welcome. Transparency is foundational.
3 We manage by fact in order to focus on prevention.
4 We focus on short cycles of evaluation and improvement to identify leading indicators.
5 We follow the Socratic method. We ask those closest to the action to interpret and make meaning of the data.
6 We promote the use of comparisons and stretch goals. Stretch goals are not target goals. Stretch goals require that the process be re-engineered in order to achieve even better results.
7 We involve everyone in the evaluation, interpretation and planning.
8 We operate as a team without organizational silos, largely disregard rank, and openly discuss and establish operating norms.

Source: Hubbard and Sullivan, 2006.

'external experiences such as community work or international study'; 'generic and interdisciplinary skills suitable for both postgraduate programs and employment in the diverse and changing workplaces of the twenty-first century' and so on.

Recognize that students' priority is top-quality teaching

Important though they are, it is not so much programme design, assessment, feedback and learning resources which are the key determinants of the student experience. On the contrary, they are much less important than the students' experience of the *quality of teaching*. It is top-quality teaching which is of main concern to students. Or, put another way, it is inspiration, not consumerization, which is the key to their experience. 'That's what they remember', as Paul Ramsden (2007), HE Academy Chief Executive, rightly puts it, 'the inspirational lecturers, the knowledge they gained, the sense of empowerment it gave them'.

The formidable challenge facing heads of department therefore is one of inspiring academics to inspire their students in turn to greater things. We addressed this issue earlier in Chapters 4 and 5 and we noted that there is no magic formula for doing so; that it will vary according to the context and the academic discipline, as well as the leadership approach taken. That said, leadership research on fostering excellent teaching in 19 departments within an international network of 11 world-class research-intensive universities has found that the most common characteristics 'were not those concerned with the strategic management of change but with the establishment of credibility and trust and the involvement of students'. Additionally, the general consensus among the department heads was that leadership in this area was primarily about having 'a focus on teaching' that 'emphasizes the students' experience of studying in a continually changing and developing curriculum' (Gibbs *et al.*, 2007).

So what is the distinguishing feature of your learning and teaching context: steady state; seeking to change; maintaining excellence; facing up to a quality problem; or other? What is your department's philosophy and strategy for learning and teaching? (See Box 8.3.) Consider the leadership activities identified in Box 8.4. Which ones do you use most in your department? Which others could you use to enhance the culture of quality in teaching in your department?

Particularly germane here is practising what we preach. Put simply, if we maintain that teaching is important, then we must demonstrate how much we value it by recognizing, celebrating and rewarding excellence. This can be done in a variety of ways:

1 By making teaching excellence a formal requirement in all your appointment, tenure and promotion decisions, including performance-related pay if you have such a scheme.
2 By making it explicit in various initiatives you might adopt to foster a culture of teaching quality, particularly those based around encouraging innovation among academics working in teams; for example, a Learning and Teaching Innovation Projects scheme aimed at fostering collaboration both within and across subject groups.
3 By developing an awards programme specifically for teaching excellence for both individuals – e.g. a Learning and Teaching Fellowship scheme – and for teams. The

Box 8.3 Assessing learning and teaching in your department

Reflect on the existing practices you have for ensuring good-quality teaching in your department and consider the questions below.

Are your existing practices sufficient? What are the strengths and weaknesses of learning and teaching in your department? What key features of your department's activity are maintaining or improving the quality of teaching? What areas do you still need to work on?

1 Promotion of learning and teaching in your department

Outline the main points of your departmental philosophy on learning and teaching objectives and processes.

Outline how your department encourages research into either generic or discipline aspects of its teaching.

What incentives exist at the departmental level to encourage and recognize good teaching?

2 Programme design

Outline the processes used in your department when designing new programmes/modules or revising existing programmes/modules. What steps does your department take to ensure the quality of its courses with respect to:

- the diverse learning needs of students;
- balance of theoretical and practical content (praxis);
- the broader context in which it will be developed;
- course content being up to date;
- the incorporation of relevant research findings of departmental colleagues;
- the university strategic plan.

3 Delivery of programmes

Outline how your department reflects on current methods of delivery of learning opportunities for students and explores and implements, where appropriate, alternative modes of delivery (including those related to e-learning and the workplace).

Outline the processes in your department to ensure quality in programme documentation (programme and module handbook; recruitment literature, etc.).

What strategies are used by colleagues in your department to actively involve students in the learning process and to encourage independent learners?

4 Student assessment

How are assessment activities matched against the desired learning outcomes and teaching methodologies?

What are the common assessment practices operating in your department?

How are assessment activities and the timing of assessment (including the provision of feedback to students) used explicitly to enhance student learning?

How are issues of fairness and equity in assessment, including the provision of clear statements of the criteria and conditions for assessment, dealt with in your department?

5 The management and support of teaching within your department

How is the quality of departmental teaching monitored? How is feedback provided to individual academics?

What departmental support is provided to colleagues to enable them to deliver good-quality teaching?

Box 8.4 Leading learning and teaching in your department

Consider the leadership activities and behaviours below. Given the context for learning and teaching in your department, consider the following questions: Which ones have you found most effective? Why have they worked so well? Can you build on them further? Which others could you use more fully to enhance the quality of teaching in your department?

Leadership activity	Leadership behaviour
Establishing personal credibility and trust	• Acting as a role model in teaching and scholarship and in pioneering new practices • Being open and accessible and willing to listen to all viewpoints
Maintaining a disciplinary focus	• Working with 'the grain' of the particular academic discipline
Identifying problems, turning them into opportunities	• Facing up to problems, not denying them • Using dissent as a lever for change
Articulating a rationale for change	• Learning from others beyond the department • Articulating and championing a pedagogic vision of the future
Devolving leadership	• Recruiting other colleagues to help you • Harnessing the strengths of your colleagues • Encouraging individual initiative
Building a community of practice	• Reaching out to all members of the department • Appointing academics who will bring added value • Promoting professional development and reflection
Rewarding and recognizing teaching	• Retaining and promoting excellent and committed teachers • Supporting individuals in securing external recognition for teaching
Setting teaching expectations	• Identifying the particular teaching methods and setting explicit standards • Ensuring colleagues use feedback to reflect on how they can improve their teaching
Marketing the department as a success	• Ambassador and publicist for the department both within and beyond the university
Supporting change and innovation	• Resource navigator: securing the necessary resources to support change • Using outside expertise as appropriate • Striving for consensus • Perseverance
Involving students	• Securing active engagement of students in decision-making and innovation

Source: adapted from Gibbs et al., 2007.

University of Western Australia, for example, has introduced the Distinguished Subject Teaching and Learning Award: an annual award with a difference, in that the selection criteria are determined by the university community as a whole according to 'What constitutes good teaching?' in their view. A more conventional approach would be, perhaps, to have a university or department Learning and Teaching Team Excellence Award inviting applications or nominations according to three selection criteria: namely, the extent to which the team has sought to enhance the student learning experience in their professional practice; by influencing the professional practice of others; and by continuing to develop their professional practice.

Whichever approach you adopt, the important thing is that you demonstrate by your *actions*, and *not* just your words, how highly you value teaching.

Recognize that students do care, and celebrate their success

Finally, let us not forget that as 'producers of learning' students' success is down to them as much as to us. Judged by the key indicators of matriculation, persistence, graduation and employment, this generation of students has been extremely successful, particularly so since they have also had to support themselves financially to a far greater degree than their predecessors. For all that, too, the vast majority emphatically still see themselves as students, not customers, including even, interestingly, those involved in work-based learning who invariably welcome the opportunity to escape from the workplace and redefine themselves as students (Ramsden, 2007).

They also care as strongly as their predecessors about issues of justice and fairness. They simply have a different focus in expressing it, more likely in terms of environmental sustainability and global responsibility than through party politics (Watson, 2007a). Nor have we infantilized students in the process. We should not regard confidence-building – sustaining students' confidence to grow, confidence to dream dreams and realize aspirations as capable independent learners – as somehow indicative of a 'therapy culture'. Far from carping about students, then, as some do, we should take pride in their success and our role in realizing it. And let us not forget: today's graduates are tomorrow's donors.

9 Managing change

There is nothing constant except change.

Heraclitus, *c.* 500 BC

There is nothing more difficult to take in hand, more perilous to conduct, or more uncertain in its success, than to take the lead in the introduction of a new order of things.

Machiavelli, 1513

Habit is habit and not to be flung out of the window by any man but coaxed down-stairs a step at a time.

Mark Twain, *Pudd'nhead Wilson's Calendar*, 1894

'University damned as incompetent'; 'University in £8 million crisis faces break up'; 'Blairite Vice Chancellor brought low by high ambitions quits as University fails inspection'; 'A Radical Mission that ended in Failure'. Such were the screaming broadsheet headlines in November 1998 which hailed the 'naming and shaming' of Thames Valley University (TVU) as the UK's first 'failing' university: an unprecedented event which many believed had 'profound implications' in the questions it raised 'into the way HE is run' and 'academic quality and standards assured', not only for the institution itself, 'but for the entire HE sector' (Alderman, 1999).

The size, scale and nature of the failure sets TVU apart from other HEIs, but it is not, of course, the only institution to have experienced difficulty in managing change. Indeed, instances where change has faltered in universities are at least as commonplace as those where change has been successful. The University of Cambridge's 'botched attempt' to introduce a new computerized accounting system, for example, is yet another illustration of this tendency. Not only that but, as with TVU, it stands as a salutary warning to other institutions of the inherent dangers in managing change and of the dire consequences that can result when things go awry. In this instance, an independent inquiry found that Cambridge's implementation of the new Capsa system in 2000–1 had proved to be an 'unmitigated disaster' characterized by moments of 'high farce', 'hard to credit naiveté' and 'fallacious' financial reports. So much so, indeed, that it not only 'wasted £10 million of public money' but had also – in the way that the new system hampered and delayed access to research grants, invoices, salaries and expenses – 'almost brought the University to its knees' in the process (Baty, 2001; Owen, 2001; Shattock, 2006).

Knowing these risks, you could be forgiven for wanting to avoid change altogether. As a head of department, however, you do not have the luxury of this option, for change – the commitment to it and the management of it – is a *sine qua non* of the role. Every generation likes to believe that it lives in an age of change, and our own is no exception. Indeed one of the most *unchanging* articles of human faith, as Heraclitus reminds us, is the conviction of every generation that the world is changing faster than ever. And while this may be an erroneous belief, as we noted earlier, on the part of our own generation, it does hold true in the case of higher education. For again, as we saw in Chapter 2, universities have experienced changes in their role and function over the past quarter-century that are unprecedented in their history. Such changes, we noted, were more externally imposed than internally generated. Either way, the implications for you are the same. Others, above and below, will be looking to you to articulate, to implement and to model change; sometimes in circumstances in which change is planned, and likewise in those when it is not. More than that, you will be expected, and should want, to secure the genuine *commitment* of staff to change, as opposed to their mere *compliance* with change. How though should you approach this most difficult of tasks?

The purpose of this chapter is to help you succeed in managing this process: namely, in securing staff commitment to, as well as managing the implementation of, change. The chapter does so in the spirit that we learn as much, if not more, from when things go wrong, as we do when they go right. It contrasts the experience of TVU's attempt to implement change with that of university innovators in the USA and Australia. In doing so, it explains the nature of change, the approaches to change and how to manage change, as well as identifying the distinguishing characteristics of the university innovators.

TVU: an insider's perspective

'No one in the rest of higher education', said the new Deputy Vice Chancellor, 'has undergone the degree of change you've been expected to undertake here'. 'He doesn't know the bleedin' half-of-it', muttered the Head of Student Services who sat alongside me.

'TVU is unlike the score or so of other universities I have been involved with', the hard-faced consultant trouble-shooter explained to the Academic Board, 'in that its difficulties do not appear to be confined solely to issues of finance or of quality but to a unique combination of both. The University is now losing a quarter-million pounds a month.' He thereby confirmed what everyone already knew. For the main teaching building which once used to groan under the weight of student numbers now stood eerily quiet.

'The thing is,' the lecturer in European Studies pointed out, body shaking and voice racked with emotion as he stared redundancy in the face, 'what you've got to understand is that none of this is our fault'.

And yet it had once been all so different. An amalgamation of four very different institutions – Ealing College of Higher Education, Thames Valley College, Queen Charlotte's College of Health Care and the London College of Music – formed in 1992, TVU sought to build on the tradition of its antecedents. At a time when many university mission statements were largely indistinguishable, invariably seeking to be 'all things to all people' or simply plain anaemic, TVU had no ambiguity about its sense of purpose. It was committed to 'supporting mass participation in HE as a contribution to equality and social justice' and aimed 'to become a student-driven institution, committed primarily to teaching and learning and playing a major part in the educational, cultural and economic life of the region'. 'We were constantly struck', the QAA Special Review team later reported, 'by the way in which this [laudable mission] permeated many of our meetings with staff at all levels from the Vice-Chancellor to the most junior support staff'. This sense of mission produced a student body of 'remarkable variety': one in which nearly two-thirds of the university's 28,000 students in 1996–97 were part-timers, 59 per cent were over 25, 48 per cent were from ethnic minorities and one-third were from abroad (QAA, 1998). As the local paper put it, TVU was not 'a university of dry academics, teaching well-off middle class youths', but rather 'a place of learning for single parents, people with jobs, and ethnic minorities, teaching them things they wanted to learn and would find useful' (Tear, 1998).

The university, however, did not confine itself solely to promoting access per se. Building on established strengths in hospitality, nursing, business studies and languages (indeed linguistics achieved the same rating (5) as Cambridge in the 1996 RAE), the university sought to carve a distinctive niche in catering to the needs of the creative and cultural industries in west London and the Thames Valley. Not an unrealistic ambition in view of the university's location, or for an institution that could count Pete Townshend from the Who, Ronnie Wood from the Rolling Stones and the late Freddie Mercury from Queen among its alumni. That the ambition was later realized was also due in no small part to a number of honorary professors, including, among others, David Frost, Jeremy Isaacs, Michael Grade, Howard Goodall and Jenny Abramsky, who all very much wanted to help, and indeed made a generous contribution, towards TVU's development.

TVU, furthermore, also sought to pioneer what were then relatively new ways of learning – electronic-, media- and resource-based – as a substitute for, rather than an addition to, traditional teaching and learning strategies. It sought to move away, that is, from a very narrow teaching and learning environment (in which students attend lectures at a set time and place, complete assessments that are often 'bolt-on' courses and learn passively under the tutor's control) to one that would be holistic and much broader in scope. An environment in which students could tap a wide range of learning resources (their student peers, the most under-used resource in HE, library, computing and multiple media facilities, etc.) and organize their learning around assessment that would be central to their courses, and in which, above all, they would be active participants in the process under the tutor's guardianship. Central to this new environment were the Learning Resource Centres (LRCs), which both integrated and housed multiple learning technologies and were established on the two main campuses in Ealing and Slough. The latter, named after the university's first Chancellor, Paul Hamlyn, was an award-winning design conceived by the architect, Richard Rogers. Not dissimilar to the original Eurostar terminal at London's Waterloo station, the new LRC, in marked contrast to the faded campus buildings (*c*. 1960s) that surrounded it, was and indeed is a stunning learning showcase. So much so in fact that when Tony Blair and David Blunkett came to open it the former enthused: 'What is so remarkable about what I have seen here today is that this could form the benchmark for what could be done right throughout the country. Why

I wonder can't every university be like TVU'. 'Things then' were 'only supposed to get better' . . . but they didn't; they fell apart in spectacular fashion. What went wrong then and why?

Many universities have had to wrestle with the common dilemma of how to do 'more' (teach more students) with 'less' (resources) and still maintain quality in an environment which has become increasingly competitive and in which the pressure for and to change is unremitting. TVU was no different, although since it had no significant financial resources or any realizable assets (other than building stock) and was operating within 40 per cent of the space norms recommended by the HEFCE its problems were relatively more acute than most. Even so, it is difficult to fault the case the Vice Chancellor made for change or the vision of the 'new learning environment' he articulated. On the contrary, if one accepts (and one ought to) the argument that 'radical external changes call for radical internal changes' then it not only offered a far more appealing prospect than 'death by a thousand (funding) cuts' but also a genuinely attractive alternative environment for learning: one indeed that met the challenge facing all of us, of turning 'mass time' into 'quality time' for students. This was no reckless or foolhardy venture, then, but rather an imaginative aspiration ahead of its time, a proposition that has indeed stood the test of time.

And yet herein lay the source of the university's problems. For like almost every other change initiative that fails to achieve its original promise, the rationale very often still makes sense on paper. The mismatch between theory and reality happens because such analyses invariably pay too much attention to what is 'above the waterline' (where any inconsistencies are transparent) and too little to what is going on 'below the waterline' (where inconsistencies are often hidden: Scott-Morgan, 1999). Such was the case at TVU, or as the QAA put it:

> For its success [change] needed very careful and comprehensive planning, effective leadership, prior infrastructural development, good communications, fail-safe contingency plans, fully tested information systems, a realistic timetable and goodwill on the part of all staff. We believe that these were all pre-requisites, not merely desirable options, the absence or failure of any one of which would be likely to jeopardize seriously a successful outcome.
>
> (QAA, 1998)

Put another way, making sense on paper is one thing, putting it into practice quite another. The university failed, in essence, not because its aspirations were unsound, but because it attempted to do too much too quickly in an internal environment that was ill-prepared for change, and came unstuck. This experience warrants closer inspection not least because, in comparing it with the successful innovators I visited as a Churchill Fellow, it is possible to identify the particular reasons for TVU's failure and more importantly, the lessons we can learn from it.

There were in fact a number of reasons why TVU failed in its attempt to manage large-scale change.

The very nature of the change itself . . . and its consequences

The implementation of the 'new learning environment' anticipated a change in the traditional role of the tutor from that of 'director of learning' (or information deliverer) to that of 'facilitator of learning' (or curriculum designer). And yet the fundamental change that this represented – and in some instances it would require tutors to alter their deep-seated habits of a lifetime – did not attract anything like the opprobrium that was directed towards related changes that were made to the curriculum: changes, that is, whose impact in practice had the opposite effect to what staff and students might reasonably have expected. Namely, they weakened rather than strengthened the university's curriculum offer.

For example, the university offered prospective undergraduates an *à la carte* selection of 269 different pathway (or course) combinations. But, in restricting modules to a single pathway, it simultaneously confined students – much to their chagrin – to a set menu of study. Thus the Jean Monnet Professor of Politics, who regularly attracted more than 50 students to her module on the politics of the European Union when it was offered university-wide, found it was rendered unviable when its intake was restricted solely to the small cohort of students majoring in politics. Languages, too, once a mainstay of the institution, became a marginal activity: an outcome as unnecessary as it was damaging.

The inadequacy of the consultation process

Consultation, and the participation and commitment that go with it, is an essential prerequisite for any change process that seeks to be an effective one, and at TVU an extensive and lengthy consultation did indeed take place over a period of nine months. Such was the 'general lack of trust' among staff, however, that this process was never perceived to be anything other than, as the QAA put it, 'a hollow exercise'. Or as one senior academic put it: 'If you ask a question you are deemed to be either mad or bad and when you don't you are accused of not being engaged'.

This modus operandi contrasts sharply with the model of best practice (noted earlier in Chapter 3) that was used by George Mason University, Virginia, in determining its visionary guide, 'Engaging the Future'. Their plan was produced by a faculty group task force working to a brief set by the Provost's office and was the outcome of a process that embraced alumni, the local round table organizations and legislators. So successful was this initiative in championing 'university citizenship' that the Commonwealth of Virginia adopted it as mandatory practice for all its universities.

The failure to predict the full extent of the changes

The phenomenon of unintended negative consequences – where the secondary effects of change nullify those of the primary – is not an unusual one. On the contrary, it has been such a common occurrence as to prompt the formulation of a law in its name. Tutt's (1985) law of unintended consequences states that: 'Social systems frequently respond to change in the opposite way to that intended by those who initiated the change'. This is not a variation of Murphy's famous law that 'anything that can go wrong will go wrong', but rather an acknowledgement of the inherent risks involved if we rely on an over-simplistic cause and effect relationship when designing change. It is a law we too often ignore to our cost.

The 2003 White Paper, for example, necessarily and quite properly, focused on the *domestic* UK audience, many of whom supported the aspirations (if not the means) it set out with regard to world-class research, teaching excellence, wider access and so on. In articulating how this was to be achieved, however – through the creation of 70 (departmental) Centres of Teaching Excellence, the introduction of a six-star research rating, etc. – the impact of such changes from an *international* perspective did not appear to have been considered. For the perception drawn, unintended though it may have been, was that UK universities had only 70 departments where teaching was excellent, and that research outside Oxford and Cambridge, say in a subject like physics, was of minor consequence.

TVU fell victim to the same tendency when it sought to establish an internal market in which 'colleges' ('comprising a small management group') commissioned courses and 'schools' (or 'repositories of staff') ran them. The intention was to incentivize schools and staff to develop, in line with the university's (legitimate and pressing) aspirations, profitable new income sources. In practice this artificial internal division – one in which the colleges sought to exercise a supervisory role over schools, which in turn regarded them as supernumerary – had the effect of reducing the status of tutors, as the QAA put it, to that of a 'hired hand'.

This conception of the tutor's role is strikingly at odds with practice elsewhere. Australia's University of Ballarat, for example, has sought to broaden, not narrow, the traditional concept of scholarship by putting the late Ernest Boyer's theoretical model into practice, an initiative it believes will more accurately reflect the tutor's range of work. Similarly, the University of Western Australia and Queensland University of Technology both encourage competition as a means of promoting change but do so in a way – through departmental awards for excellence in teaching and learning – that fosters, not fractures, academic teamwork.

Opting for the 'big bang' approach and piling one fundamental change on top of another

Again, good practice tells us that when planning change which is both significant in scope and fundamental in character, i.e. the very sort TVU was contemplating, it is prudent to undertake a trial implementation (usually centred on a 'piloting programme') in the first instance. Then if all goes well, and with lessons learned, implement the change in a measured (usually phased) way. The 'new learning environment' went ahead without any such 'trial and error' planning, and was implemented simultaneously across all three levels of undergraduate programmes in one fell swoop in September 1997. This, in spite of the fact, as the QAA put it, that it was 'a very ambitious attempt to restructure the academic organization and culture of the university at its most basic level' and even though 'some staff had warned' of the recklessness of such a 'big bang' approach.

Not only that. This change was introduced on the back of another innovation of equally far-reaching significance that had been set in motion the previous year: i.e. the 'root and branch' restructuring and centralization of all the university's academic-related administration (or ARA). This initiative was designed to replace, as explained to the senior management group, 'the current individuated craft-style system of administration with a post-industrial one to cater for mass student numbers'. Its ramifications in practice, however, were extraordinary: misplaced assignments, missing exam marks, unregistered students and unknown class sizes. Indeed the chaos that was to envelop the university and set in train the sequence of events that led to the newspaper allegations of 'dumbing down', the QAA Special Review, the resignation of the Vice Chancellor and the 'naming' and 'shaming' of TVU, all stem from this common source. Put another way, the first phase of the ARA introduced in September 1996 – an administrative reorganization that involved the transfer of local and specialist staff from schools into a central registry, just as re-sit boards were due to sit that year – was a spectacular own goal from which the university spent much of the next two years trying to recover. This human error was compounded still further by an inadequate examination IT software system (it could not cope with either the volume or complexity of the university's patterns of assessment), which meant that the errors, inaccuracies and omissions outstanding from the re-sit boards of September 1996 rolled over into, and were indeed added to by, those exam boards of the following year. The consequences of this were dire and the university's reputation suffered as a result, and deservedly so. TVU became 'the university that's hip, that's cool, and loses its degree results', and one mother's well-publicized 'run-around nightmare' trying to obtain her son's course results served to underline the point (Wynne-Jones, 1997; Reid, 1997). And yet this situation was by no means irretrievable and the university, as the Vice Chancellor rightly pointed out later, made significant progress in unravelling this assessment imbroglio.

Less publicized, yet infinitely more intractable, were the contemporaneous difficulties encountered in student timetabling and rooming. The introduction of a new student support system meant that each student was supposed to be allocated a director of studies and a named pathway. In practice, however, this system proved impossible to establish using the new timetabling software system, for it was programmed in such a way as to print an individual student timetable based on either a director of studies or a pathway, but not both: i.e. a student could not be allocated a director of studies unless they were registered on a pathway but they couldn't register on a pathway unless they also had a director of studies. This was a devilish 'Catch 22' that had hellish consequences and brought the university to the brink of paralysis. Literally thousands upon thousands of individual student timetables were published centrally of which more than two-thirds were erroneous because of the technical shortcomings. From a student perspective it was akin to going to the bank knowing you have money in your account but not being able to access the cash-point machine for want of a PIN code, or having a valid ticket for the football match but not being allowed through the turnstile. Not surprisingly, student bewilderment and puzzlement soon gave way to frustration and irritation and ultimately anger and full-blown rage. A terminal breakdown was avoided only by forsaking technology in favour of establishing local emergency 'paper systems', or through the 'Herculean and ad hoc efforts of dedicated individuals', as the QAA expressed it.

Again university innovators such as George Mason demonstrate that there are alternative ways of realizing similar aspirations, without necessarily entailing fundamental restructuring. The award-winning New Century College, for instance, was set up to offer students 'the finest small college education within the context of a large state university'. It is one – underpinned, ironically, by an individuated craft-style system – in which students learn actively and collaboratively to design their own 'intellectual map'. In other words, it is one that could not only have diminished the 'long tail' of students which the QAA identified at TVU, but would also have motivated administrators, not demoralized them.

The failure to recognize that change imposed from above cannot, and does not, work

The idea that change will only occur and can only occur if it is 'driven from the top' is, as Senge (1995) reminds us, a deeply entrenched popular belief. It is almost uniformly an unquestioned assumption that persists in spite of abundant evidence to the contrary: evidence that top management in universities, as well as in business, have largely been impotent in transforming their organizations. It is also a very wrong-headed notion, one that is – ironically, in an 'age of empowerment' and 'flatter organizations' – not only deeply disempowering (in that it implies that the way to empowerment can only be achieved by recourse to hierarchical authority) but even more importantly overlooks the crucial fact that *values are only values if they are chosen voluntarily* and as such cannot be imposed from the top. Thus initiatives that are solely top-down are at best likely to evoke *compliance* with change rather than a genuine *commitment to it*, and in some instances actually move an organization backward, rather than forward.

This is essentially what happened at TVU. Taken together, the anticipated changes to the university's organization, system, processes and culture were of such magnitude that they needed, as the QAA noted, 'goodwill on the part of all staff' if they were to stand any chance of success. This prerequisite was conspicuous by its absence at TVU. Indeed, the very period during which many of the above changes were being introduced (November 1996 to May 1997) was itself overshadowed by industrial action on the part of the lecturer's union NATFHE, action, that is, of a nature (such as the withholding of student assessment marks) which was consciously aimed at undermining their implementation. This nadir in the relationship between management and staff was, of course, not inevitable, but it was also no surprise either, and stemmed from a number of different sources.

First, there was the notion of the 'student-driven' university: a novel and indeed revolutionary concept in what has traditionally (if not rightly) been a 'supply-led business'. It became an issue from the outset precisely for that reason. For while many staff, like their counterparts in other 'new' universities, were by inclination, and in practice, 'student-centred' in their teaching and learning and always keen to support students, at TVU they felt threatened by the idea of being 'student-driven'. And with good reason. The initial estate rebuilding programme, centred on an extensive refurbishment of the Students' Union, served to confirm their suspicion. But it was the way the concept was used in a coercive sense rather than, as it should have been, as a guiding aspiration that convinced many staff that their interests and concerns were being over-ridden . . . that they were not just secondary but of minor importance.

Second, there was, as the QAA observed, the 'very poor' industrial relations within the university, the legacy of a long-standing dispute over the contractual terms under which academic staff were employed. In essence, the Ealing NATFHE branch took the view that management should honour the local employment agreement that pre-dated the new national professional contract, while the directorate maintained that the former had been superseded by the latter, and besides staff were not being required to do anything other than was asked of their counterparts at other 'new' universities. This initial disagreement grew over five years into an increasingly bitter and acrimonious dispute that became ideological and personal as well as industrial in character. The dispute was protracted: in the directorate's view because some branch officials (i.e. those known to be active within the Socialist Workers' Party) were bent on making it so for their own ends, over and above the interests of their members (that the latter were in essence 'sheep' led by 'wolves'); and in the union's view because management persistently refused to recognize their grievances over staff workloads. Neither side covered itself in glory and the dispute had knock-on self-defeating consequences, not least the exclusion of academic staff from the recruitment and admissions process over the critical summer period, which in turn undermined staff commitment still further.

Lastly there was the leadership, and in particular the Vice Chancellor's approach to the management of change. We noted in Chapter 2 that although leadership and management are not mutually exclusive, a critical difference between the two emerges in the way that leaders and managers are perceived by their staff. A management relationship, for example, can be perfectly satisfactory, and often is a very productive one when both sides approach it in a cool, calm and purposeful manner. A leadership relationship, on the other hand, will not succeed in this way; it must involve emotion, passion and a stirring of the blood. Vice Chancellor Mike Fitzgerald certainly did that, not least through the well-documented unorthodoxy of his 'image' – the spiky peroxide hair, the dangling ear-ring, the zany ties, the Armani suits, the Cuban cigarillos, the office jukebox, the chauffeur-minder, etc. To his followers he was universally known as 'Mike' and to his detractors as 'The Celestial Ear-Ring', 'The Anti-Christ' or simply 'that man'; only the eccentric ever referred to him as 'Dr Fitzgerald' or 'Vice Chancellor'. These epithets, of course, grew out of more than a simple assessment of image. There were other far more substantive aspects too. No one, for example, doubted his passionate commitment to the values he espoused, his visionary capabilities, or indeed his intellectual agility. Where scepticism did arise and grow, however, was in the way this vision was to be realized.

Taking his cue from management writer Gareth Morgan, the Vice Chancellor, in his very first paper on the university's academic organization, for example, explained that the management philosophy would be more 'hands-off' than 'hands-on' within an institution that would be 'more human and value-based' and centred on 'networks' rather than 'hierarchies' (Fitzgerald, 1992). The reality, however, in the eyes of many staff, never lived up to this expectation. Indeed it seemed to be the very opposite of what had been intended: 'to build up rather than devolve down', 'to empower staff and students', 'to maximize flexibility and simplicity', 'to create a learning organization', etc. This perception was compounded further by the overtly hierarchical 'top-down' approach that the Vice Chancellor took in managing change. As a visionary, and as a putative transformational leader, the Vice Chancellor's approach, based on Richard Beckhard's (1992) 'model for the executive management of transformational change' – may have seemed to be both a logical and a natural one. It was ultimately, however, an ill-judged one, because by their very nature such approaches render staff invisible, as if they are not 'to act' but to be 'acted upon' (Trowler, 1998). For all these reasons, then, it is no surprise that staff were 'seriously disaffected' and felt 'a sense of estrangement' from the institution, as the QAA put it. Nor is it any wonder TVU was unable either to implement the planned changes or to generate a genuine commitment on the part of staff to the proposed changes.

The myth of 'dumbing down'

That said, a myth developed from this failure of leadership and management, linking it to an alleged 'dumbing down' of academic standards which in turn led to the unwarranted demonization of the university both in the media and across the HE sector. It is a canard that ought to be set right:

The central charge of the *Sunday Times* (26 October 1997) that the university 'deliberately lowered standards in order to pass students' was, the QAA concluded, 'without foundation'. What had happened and what had led to the initial allegation is that the initiatives described above – chiefly the ARA and the inadequate IT exam software system, combined with the localized NATFHE industrial action – produced a chaotic situation in the summer of 1997; one in which students identified as needing to re-sit had not been given proper notice of this requirement. Rather than delay the re-sits (as should have happened) the Pro-Vice Chancellor, in the Vice Chancellor's absence, instructed the re-sit assessment boards to pass students who had achieved 30–39 per cent. The well-intentioned impulse behind this instruction was that students should not have to suffer through no fault of their own. The unintended and unforeseen consequence, of course, would be to allow students to pass who might otherwise have failed. As such, this instruction, as the QAA pointed out, was 'almost immediately countermanded by the vice chancellor and not implemented'; and its perpetrator, the Pro-Vice Chancellor, paid the price for her error of judgement.

The failure of any assessment management system is, of course, not only deplorable but also indefensible if it means that students obtain better awards than those to which they are entitled. Even so, as one independent quality assessor has noted, we 'need to put this into perspective'. For although the QAA found TVU's assessment regime 'inherently unstable', the number of students who actually did receive a degree class higher than they should have done (and which was later rescinded) did not exceed the number of fingers on one hand.

Nor is the QAA itself without blemish in this regard. For despite the damning indictment of the special review, the report is itself, as the independent assessor pointed out, 'short on hard evidence'. Not only that but even more remarkable was the fact that the reviewers chose not to derive any of their judgements from the QAA's own teaching inspection reports: namely the four QAA subject reviews – Sociology, Linguistics, Modern Languages and American Studies – which TVU underwent between 1995 and 1997, ones in which the university not only scored around the average (19.25) for TQAs in 'new' universities during this period, but were, in fact, *above* the average specifically for 'Quality Assurance and Enhancement' (3.25v.3.19). Put another way, the special review and the (four) TQAs can't both be right . . . which begs the question: who quality assures the QAA and how?

The partiality of the review was underscored further by the three paragraphs devoted to TVU's international partnerships which the QAA found to be 'less than fully rigorous'. But, again, the independent assessor claimed to 'have read far worse overseas audit reports and continuation audit reports, all relating to "old" universities that paint pictures at least as depressing as that painted in the review of TVU' without, however, attracting 'the clamouring for blood' as happened with TVU.

The focus on personalities and institutions (the former Vice Chancellor v. the former head of the QAA; the QAA v. UUK) and on sector-wide issues (the quest for a quality assurance mechanism acceptable to all stakeholders, the failure of governance, the desire to avoid 'another TVU', etc.) has meant that those who suffered most from the demonization have been overlooked, not least:

- those large areas of TVU (professional, post-graduate, FE and health sciences) which were relatively unaffected by all the changes yet whose reputation was impugned as a consequence;
- the hundreds of students who had their initial learning experience of higher education so unnecessarily blighted;
- the scores of staff who lost their livelihood.

These were the true victims and the real tragedy of TVU: an outcome not fatal in consequence, but one that was as unnecessary, as it was wasteful, and a salutary lesson to all who seek to implement large-scale change in HE.

The university innovators

TVU is a very good example of what *not* to do in implementing change, one that stands in sharp contrast to the university innovators – George Mason, Virginia, University of Ballarat, University of Western Australia, Queensland University of Technology and the University of Phoenix – we identified earlier. This begs the question: what is it that distinguishes successful university innovators from less successful institutions? The innovators themselves are, in fact, very different types of HEIs, each with contrasting cultures, structures, traditions and orientations. It is nevertheless possible to discern a number of significant distinguishing characteristics which these successful innovators have in common (see Box 9.1).

These similarities, indeed, are not restricted solely to these distinguishing traits but also extend further to include the actual processes or change levers which the innovators used in implementing change: specific 'soft' and 'hard' processes, that is, which they all consciously harnessed to telling effect (see Box 9.2). From collective experience – as well as that drawn from TVU – we can identify a number of key principles that can help you in your own efforts to successfully implement change (see Box 9.3).

The innovators show that it is possible for institutions of learning to become more like 'learning organizations'. That smart people don't just know, they can learn too! It is, in short, an example we would all do well to follow. How, though, can and should you put it into practice?

Managing change in your department

> We trained hard, but it seemed that every time we were beginning to form up into teams, we would be reorganized. I was to learn later in life that we tend to meet any new situation by reorganizing, and a wonderful method it

Box 9.1 The distinguishing characteristics of university innovators

1 'Liberated' leadership
Innovators have a well-developed consciousness concerning the importance and significance of leadership both in the manner in which it is practised and the way it is developed.

Their approach to leadership is invariably non-hierarchical and often genuinely transformational (Kouzes and Posner, 2003), i.e. it rests on the exercise of consensual rather than top-down power. Put another way, university presidents and provosts do not dictate change or a vision, but seek rather to nurture others through the transparency of their own individual actions and the use of informal as well as formal networks and forums.

More than that, they view leadership as a distributive phenomenon and have sought to cultivate leadership qualities at all levels (course leader, head of department, dean of faculty, senior general staff) and across different groups (minorities and women in particular). Their intention is to 'liberate' leadership – 'by enabling those closest to the job to take their own decisions'.

Significantly, the various 'cults' which Middlehurst (1993) identified as acting as a brake on leadership development in UK universities (the 'gifted amateur', the 'intellectual', etc.) are conspicuous by their absence among innovators.

2 Champions of 'university citizenship'
Innovators are proactive in attempting to give 'meaning' to membership of their respective communities. They are also 'listening organizations', with a common aspiration to reach out to all their eligible members on an equitable basis.

3 'Learners' as well as 'knowers'
Innovators are self-conscious about their limitations. And though they conspicuously avoid faddism and jargon, they are to all intents and purposes 'learning organizations' even if none of them explicitly claims to be one!

4 Client-focused
Innovators have an acute sense of self-identity. One which does not recognize 'stakeholders' as such, but highlights rather the transactional nature of the relationship between the institution (as an entity in its own right) and a diverse range of clients.

5 Masters of technology
Innovators recognize that IT is a means to an end and not an end in itself; that the key variable in teaching and learning is not computing provision per se, but rather the quality of the interaction between student and teacher. In consequence they integrate IT as appropriate to their needs. Technology is the servant to the innovators, not the master.

can be for creating the illusion of progress while producing confusion, inefficiency and demoralization.

Petronius Arbiter, *c.* AD 66

Make your department a 'pocket of good practice'

Effective leadership, as we noted in Chapter 3, is about nurturing others in a quiet subtle way. It is about developing informal networks to get people 'on board' and establishing a climate in which initiatives can flourish. It is definitely not about dictating change or a vision. These guidelines apply just as much to all leaders as they do to those at the top. In fact when it comes to change even more so, for it is the departments which are the key

Box 9.2 Change levers used by university innovators

'Soft' processes

1 Tapping collegiality as an aspiration

Collegiality, as Ramsden (1998) reminds us, is one of those models which is fine in theory but rarely found in practice. Inward-looking, unwieldy, self-interested and occasionally destructive, Ramsden argues that collegiality has had a rather better press than it deserves. On the other hand, in an age of mass higher education and 'new managerialism', collegiality – and, with it, the virtues of unselfish collaboration and shared decision-making – have acquired meaning of iconic proportion. And it is this sentiment which the innovators have successfully harnessed in fresh and pioneering ways.

2 Working with – and not against – the organizational culture

Of the three broad approaches that tend to be used in managing change – power-coercive; normative-re-educative; and rational-empirical – the innovators employed a mix of the latter two, but rarely the former (Quinn *et al.*, 2007). Put another way, they accepted that culture is a 'process' and not an 'entity' that can be moulded; that universities don't have cultures per se but rather that they *are* cultures.

3 Focus on groups rather than individuals

While accepting that universities are intensely individualistic organizations, the innovators recognize that substantive change can only be secured in a collective fashion. Hence they shifted the focus of their interest – and their resources – away from the 'lone teacher/scholar' to that of the group: the course team, subject group, research unit, department and faculty.

'Hard' processes

4 Questioning of sacred cows

The innovators were also proactive in encouraging the questioning of established customs and practices. Whether it was the status of academic tenure, the efficacy of the directorate, the notion of the 'academic year' or the outsourcing of halls of residence, no aspect of university work was beyond scrutiny.

5 Reframing the academic staff 'contract'

As the task of innovation has become more complex universities have been driven to harness specialist expertise – sometimes in-house but often outside the institution – for aspects of academic work (the design and development of learning resources, delivering instruction, mentoring students, etc.) that conventionally were always undertaken by academic staff.

This being the case, the innovators all attempted to modify their contractual relationship with academic staff in such a way as to reflect more accurately the precise nature of work tutors actually do. In some instances by ignoring tenure, as at Phoenix, in others by establishing 'research professorships' and 'teaching-only' appointments, as at QUT, or by hiring 'senior contract' professors in partnership with private enterprise, as at GMU.

6 Performance management

The innovators have likewise also initiated and established processes of performance management (or more accurately 'performance and development management') in much the same way as outlined in Chapter 5.

Indeed their processes mirror contemporary best practice in this area as outlined by Armstrong and Baron (1998): viz the innovators' approach is developmental rather than judgemental, flexible rather than monolithic, based on 360-degree feedback rather than top-down appraisal, and owned by departments and subject groups rather than the personnel or HR function. In short, they have all sought to link individual staff development with institutional goals in an innovative way.

Box 9.3 Lessons we can learn from university innovators in managing change

1 No magic pill
There is no exact method or prescribed formula for managing change; no pill which will guarantee success.

2 The 'art of conversation': a core process
Significant change depends on dialogue and commitment as much as imagination and perseverance. What is conventionally regarded as the 'soft stuff' of the process (i.e., how we talk to one another; when we do it; the way in which we do it and most critically how we value it) is ironically the 'hard stuff' in managing change successfully.

3 Top-down change cannot – and does not – work
Top-down change, we noted earlier, can only evoke at best compliance with change rather than a genuine commitment to it.
    The experience of the innovators, on the other hand, suggests that the role of people at the top of organizations is to create the climate in which initiatives can flourish. Not so much a case of 'top-down' or 'bottom-up' as 'anywhere up'.

4 Leadership qualities can – and should – be tapped at all levels
A corollary of effective leadership from the top is the recognition by the innovators that leadership is an attribute which is not confined to a particular position in a hierarchy. On the contrary, they harnessed the skills of leadership at all levels within their institution. In essence, they understood something which others have been slow to recognize: namely, that our traditional conception of leadership – 'the captain-of-the-ship' image – stands in need of revision.

organizational units in taking change forward. As such you need to recognize your responsibility, accept it and make the most of it.

You should not underestimate your scope for local discretion in matters of change. We have noted how change that is solely 'top-down' will not lead to a change in values. Nor for that matter, as Petronius Arbiter reminds us, will the penchant for internal restructuring so prevalent in many HEIs. You will find that individuals carry on much as they did before once the initial reorganization is over (Shattock, 2006). We have also seen at TVU how, when faced with chaos, individuals will quite naturally self-organize. It follows then that you should never – nor indeed allow any of your colleagues to – consider change as a matter beyond their influence: an activity in which, as 'passive victims' or jaded cynics, they have no real part to play. On the contrary, you and they have the opportunity to take charge of your own destiny in this regard and that is so *no matter the particular circumstances in the rest of your institution*. Whether you are surrounded by upheaval or inertia you can and should aim to make a real difference by being an agent of 'good practice' within your department, in effect by seeking to establish your department as 'a pocket of good practice' within your university (Butcher and Atkinson, 1999).

Your leadership style is very important in this respect, as too is the need for common sense. Relying on these alone, however, will not suffice. Commonsense approaches, such as those based on rational linear understandings of change, often prevent us from recognizing the true and full complexity of change, for example that:

- the notion that top-down change, as we've seen, does not always work as antici-pated; the law of unintended consequences;
- change begets change; i.e. the process of change is a dynamic one and changes themselves change as they are implemented and adopted;
- any 'implementation gap' (the difference between planned change and reality) may be due to nothing other than the working out of either one or another of the two above;
- a change approach which works in one setting may not do so in another; i.e. approaches need to be customized according to the purpose, audience and context of change;
- the well-known axiom 'If it ain't broke, don't fix it' is often a wrong-headed one since it only applies in the unlikely event of a stable environment.

We have also seen in the case of TVU the folly of not following a textbook approach to the management of change. It is an error you can seek to avoid by familiarizing yourself with the theory as well as the practice of change (Trowler, 1998; Fullan, 1991; 1993; 1999). This chapter is based on the theory and models of change, but this is no substitute for first-hand understanding of the different perspectives (structural, political, symbolic and human resource) (Armstrong, 2000; Trowler *et al.*, 2003) on change, or analytical approaches (systemic conflict versus strategic choice versus complexity) (Cameron and Quinn, 2007; Pettigrew *et al.*, 1992; Seel, 2000) to change, or indeed the various ways (technical, political, cultural: Tichy, 1983; Leandro, 2008) of managing change. There is too, as Kurt Lewin (1951) reminds us, 'nothing so practical as a good theory'. Therefore the more your practice is informed by change theory and evidence, the less likely it is that you will fall foul of these commonsense approaches and the better prepared you will be for change in all its nuances. That said, there are certain fundamentals – 10 aspects, if you will, of successful change management – tenets which you should adhere to (see Box 9.4).

Understand and recognize the different approaches to managing change . . . their strengths and limitations

You should also be aware that there are, in fact, three broad approaches you can take in managing change: power-coercive; normative re-educative and rational-empirical (Quinn *et al.*, 2007). Each has its particular strengths and limitations (see Box 9.5). In practice most tend to rely on a blended approach, drawing on two if not all three of these different strategies.

In developing your own approach you will, of course, need to consider the nature of anticipated change (fundamental or incremental); the likely degree of resistance; the culture of your department and the motivation of your staff. That said, in developing it, you also need to remember too that the nature of HE environments are such that:

- Power-coercive strategies rarely if ever work, nor should you have to rely on them. They can too, as we saw at TVU, backfire.
- Incremental changes are more likely to be successful in the longer term than a 'big bang' approach.

Box 9.4 The 10 fundamentals of successful change management

1   Change invariably stems from changes in the environment, both internal and external.
2   Change must presage a new model for the future.
3   Change will not succeed unless there is dissatisfaction with the old and genuine belief in the new. People must have a reason.
4   Major change is always painful and requires different ways of behaving, thinking and perceiving. People must be involved – resistance is normal.
5   Change is 'lumpy' – people, systems, and processes change at different rates in different ways.
6   As line manager, you must drive it and support it too – as 'designer', 'teacher' and 'steward' (Senge 1990).
7   'Play the ball where it lies': work with the good practice you've got. Avoid deficit models of current practice. Avoid importing models from elsewhere (those 'not invented here').
8   Change is an ongoing process, not an event.
9   Change is unique to each organization. Celebrate your individual landmarks of success.
10 Change is contingent on effective communication, listening to feedback and acting on it – on you 'walking the talk', not just 'taking the talk'.

- The autonomy of individual scholars notwithstanding, you should have due regard for the nature and strength of the existing *group* cultures (the course teams, subject groups and research centres) in which individuals operate.

Reflect on your own experience of change and use that in helping others to understand the nature of the change process

Think about your own psychological contract . . . the key things you valued about a job you had in the past or indeed your current role. All those aspects that were not part of your formal contract: your sense of autonomy and self-responsibility; the respect and esteem of your peers; your reputation; the comfort of your surroundings and so on.

Next, think how you felt when a change impinged on or permanently removed any of these things. What was that experience like: confusing, messy, hurtful, a necessary evil, no bad thing . . . ?

Now consider how a change you have to implement will affect those things your colleagues might value: namely, not whether you would be concerned if you were doing that job but whether *they* are likely to be concerned.

Empathy is an essential skill you must have if you are to successfully implement change; that and an understanding of the contours of the change process. Even on reflection change rarely seems to have the appearance of symmetry, yet we can at least discern three different stages, each with its own needs and demands that you must master: the pre-adoption, adoption and implementation phases. Or what Kurt Lewin has dubbed the process of 'unfreezing-changing-refreezing'. The work of psychologist William Bridges (1991; Bridges and Mitchell 2000) on loss and grieving is particularly useful here, both in explaining the nature of these various stages and in identifying practical strategies we can apply that will help individuals overcome them (see Box 9.6). Two aspects of this process merit further explanation.

Box 9.5 Approaches to managing change

Approach	Assumption	Strength	Weakness
Rational–empirical (or 'Systems–thinking')	• People are rational • Once a proposal is clearly explained individuals see it is in their best interest and subscribe	• Based on the logical and rational analysis of the evidence • Individuals respond more positively to change when the process and details are explained	• Individuals don't always embrace change even if it is in their best interests (e.g. smoking, in spite of health warnings) • Encourages an instrumental attitude • Emphasizes bureaucracy and control over emotional commitment
Normative–re-educative (or individualistic)	• Individuals are affected emotionally and personally by their work experiences • Recognizes the importance of organizational culture as a force for or against change	• Most effective in overcoming individual resistances to change • A 'bottom-up' approach that focuses on 'winning hearts and minds'	• It is slow • Not everyone will 'buy-in' to the change • Underestimates the power of alternative cultures (e.g. subject groups)
Power–coercive (or authoritarian)	• The individual desiring the change has more power than the individual who is expected to comply with it	• Upholds the legitimacy of the hierarchy • Can yield short-term benefits	• Essentially manipulative • Creates resentment and is ineffective in the long term

Source: adapted from Quinn *et al.*, 2007.

Box 9.6 Practical strategies for managing change

The three-stage process of change What you should do

1 *Attending to endings*
- Involves letting go of existing practices
- Marked by feelings of loss and resentment and maybe even emotional outbreaks, illogical claims and threatening behaviour

- Accept and expect emotional behaviour
- Acknowledge the quality of what is lost; treat the past with respect
- Share information. Relate change to the larger environment, internal and external ('the bigger picture')

2 *Managing the transition zone*
- Involves seeking out and giving support during the transition time; i.e. the period of waiting before the new situation has emerged
- Marked by frustration, tension and polarization among staff

- See the change as an opportunity
- Get staff involved in working on changes
- Identify scenarios. Develop a shared purpose and vision, a plan and a part to play for all staff

3 *Launching a new beginning*
- Involves making beginnings as positive as possible
- Marked by individual acceptance and understanding of change

- Ensure that each individual staff member knows the answer to:
- What is the new shared vision – what will it look like?
- What is the new purpose – what is it for?
- What is the plan – how will we get there?
- What part will each individual play?

Source: adapted from Bridges, 1991; Bridges and Mitchell, 2000.

Identifying and presenting your case for change

You may initiate change, or have change imposed upon you, either internally or externally. Either way, you still have to convince others (and maybe even yourself) of the need for change. Kurt Lewin developed a model of *force field* (or *equilibrium*) *analysis* which helps us do just that. Lewin postulates that in any given situation there are forces within organizations that are (driving) 'pressures' for change, and forces that are 'resistances' to change. Thus when the forces for change are stronger than the resistant forces the 'tipping-point' for change will be reached; likewise when the forces against change are stronger than the pressures for change, change will not occur (Gladwell, 2000).

Consider, then, your own particular circumstances and instance of change:

- List all the driving forces, for example: the negative economic imperative (to do 'more' with 'less'); the positive pedagogic imperative (the consensus between employers and educationalists on graduate transferable skills); new learning technologies; student diversity; legislative compliance, etc.

- List all the resisting forces, for example: resource limitations; perceived threat to autonomy; the perception of imposition; the loss of status and esteem; the preference for tradition; the lack of faith in those proposing the change; the belief that something has been overlooked; new skill requirements; risk aversion; the 'not-invented-here' syndrome, etc.
- Examine each force and assess its strengths. Consider the possible consequence of each force and assign each one a numerical value.
- Identify those forces over which you have some influence or control and those over which you do not.
- Analyse the list to determine the efficacy of the proposed change and, assuming the balance is in favour, how you can implement it.

In theory, you have several natural courses of action: to increase the strength of the drivers or to add new drivers. In practice, however, conventional wisdom tells us it is far more effective to focus on diminishing the effect of resisting forces (reducing their strength, removing them or, best of all, turning them into drivers) than it is to emphasize the strength of the drivers.

Put another way, people want a *positive* reason to change (e.g. 'It will bring benefits both to myself and to our students') not a negative one (e.g. 'My job will be on the line if I don't go along with it'). Other than in the immediate short term the latter is never – despite what many seem to believe – a key motivator for change. Identifying the areas over which you have some influence will also tell you where to focus your efforts when implementing the changes.

That said, you must first prepare a 'situational analysis' – a story or picture of 'where we are now' – which explains to your colleagues the circumstances which have prompted the need for change. Again, in doing so, conventional wisdom tells us it is helpful if you identify two dimensions of the 'prompt' for change (Trowler *et al.*, 2003; Pennington, 2006):

- *Chronic* features: i.e. those long-term concerns you may have about particular aspects of professional practice such as over-reliance on a singular mode of assessment; an ethos that is 'knowledge-centred', not 'learner-centred'; a pedagogy that is too traditional; techno-phobia, etc.
- *Conjunctural* features: i.e. new circumstances such as a government or institutional policy change; a new source of funding; the appointment of new staff, etc.

Use the latter to create an immediate impetus for change; to stimulate action, that is, on the former.

Put another way, you should use your analysis as an opportunity not only to depict the present scenario, but also to identify and challenge your department's blind spots: to get leverage, that is, in taking change forward.

Reducing the resistance to change

Rationality will get you so far, but the real challenge in managing change lies in supporting and guiding people through this painful process. You need to have not only empathy as we've said, but also sincerity and genuine respect too, if you are to succeed.

You should also focus, as we've indicated, on reducing resistance (as opposed to increasing the strength of the driving forces) to change. How?

First, by recognizing the notion 'No one likes change' for what it is – yet another popular myth. Humans have always been the most adaptable of species and many not only embrace change but enjoy it too. Seek out those around you who support the proposed changes and get them to articulate and share with others new (and better) scenarios which the changes could bring.

And next take your cue from Senge (1994, 1998, 2006) and seek to build a shared vision of the change with staff – to surface and test the 'mental models' held by staff.

We discussed in Chapter 3 how to build shared vision in strategic planning (see Box 3.4) and the same principles apply here; the second 'discipline', however, requires further explanation.

'Mental models' are the premise on which we base our understanding of the world around us, the assumptions (and prejudices) which underpin our knowing and doing. Unearthing and recognizing your own, as well as those of your colleagues, is of course vital if you are to reduce resistance and work towards a shared goal. This is no easy thing, however, for as noted by Argyris and Shon (on whose work Senge's concept is based), people, and professionals in particular, quite naturally tend to construct 'defensive routines' which help them disguise their vulnerability in the workplace (Argyris, 1999; Argyris and Shon, 1978, 1996). So strong is this motivation, indeed, that, despite what we may think, our basic human tendency is to act according to four basic values:

- to remain in control;
- to maximize winning and minimize losing;
- to suppress negative feelings;
- to be as 'rational' as possible: that is, to define objectives and to evaluate behaviours in terms of whether or not the objectives are achieved.

The consequence of this shared concern to save face, not surprisingly, is that we spurn listening, stifle debate and block learning, what's more without ever even realizing we're doing so. The task of defusing 'defensive routines' is, in fact, even more demanding in the case of HE. For these activities – the questioning of assumptions, the weighing of evidence and the analysis of reasoning – are, by their very nature, at the heart of academic work. And while academics themselves are invariably quick to dissect the research of their colleagues, they are far less inclined to turn the spotlight on to their own reasoning and ways of analysis. Even so it is a task you cannot baulk. You must get your colleagues to consider their own assumptions: if you will, to walk up and down their own 'mental ladder of inference'; i.e. examine their own actions and beliefs about their environment as they see it. You can do this in a number of ways:

- Lead by example: hold off on your own assumptions and be open about your own defensiveness, e.g. 'I am feeling uneasy about this because . . .'; 'I don't quite understand it. Can you help me see this better?'; 'It is threatening to me too . . .'.
- Get staff involved in working on the changes through one-to-ones, small groups and departmental workshops. Collaborative inquiry, in particular, is increasingly

recognized as an effective means of facilitating change by helping organizations 'move to a state of self-organized criticality'. Appreciative Inquiry, Open Space meetings, Future Search conferences, Viral Change networks and the World Café are all techniques which have been successfully employed 'to increase connectivity, improve information flows, increase diversity, help deal with inhibitors, offer clear and energizing goals and provide some clear boundaries' (Seel, 2004; Senge, 2006). Hire an experienced practitioner and experiment with one of these techniques with your colleagues.

- Identify and showcase examples of good practice already in place in your department.
- Bring in an external consultant to run a creative thinking workshop to identify and develop alternative scenarios – the ordinary, the extraordinary, the feasible and the transformative. Develop your own 'rich picture' as well as written scenarios.
- Use 'management-by-walking-about': regularly cited, often under-estimated, and too rarely practised. More than that, take a lead from Leandro's (2008) theory of viral change and begin to build a putative network of committed individuals like yourself who will champion and disseminate the changes as a 'positive contagion' throughout your department and beyond.
- Recognize and be sensitive to the fact that staff respond to and deal with change in different ways at different rates:
  - those who thrive on it: the 'swimmers' who enjoy it; i.e. those you should encourage and leave to get on with it;
  - those who have problems with it: the 'strugglers' who have difficulties staying afloat; i.e. those for whom you should arrange appropriate training and support;
  - those who retreat from it: the 'copers' who withdraw from other professional activities; they are the most taxing and the ones often overlooked and are best dealt with through a searching one-to-one;
  - those who shun it: the 'naysayers' and the 'mossbacks' who work around it or seek to change it, often in creative ways, i.e. those for whom you should gird yourself for the long haul. Try to negotiate and be tolerant unless the change is mandatory.

A final point. Consensus is always desirable, though rarely found in practice. Fortunately it is not essential either. It is, though, as you know, a value close to the heart of many academic communities. Following the guidelines above will bring you closer still to the realization of this elusive aspiration.

10 Managing up and managing the 'down-side'

> In war, resolution; in defeat, defiance; in victory, magnanimity; in peace, goodwill.
>
> Winston Churchill, 1946

We all crave satisfaction in our work. Yet for many it is a desire that remains unfulfilled. Job satisfaction scores in America, Britain and Europe have, in fact, dropped successively in each of the past three decades – today less than half (47 per cent) profess to be 'extremely satisfied at work' (Oswald, 2003b; Watson and Amoah, 2007). In HE, as we noted in the Introduction, this trend is even more marked, an outcome that has been attributed to, among other things, the adverse impact of university management. We have, however, seen how you can use your role – in the way you lead by example, formulate strategy, manage performance, develop staff, celebrate diversity, handle change and so on – to make a *real* and *positive* difference to the working lives of those around you. This, though, begs the question of your own sense of satisfaction. For the same sources of dissatisfaction that affect staff apply equally to you. In both cases it is not so much the long hours of work, the relatively low pay or job insecurity. It is, tellingly, the very nature of the work itself, the relationship you have with your line manager, and the capacity you have to work self-directed which are the real indicators and shapers of professional well-being.

What, though, can you do to overcome or alleviate the adverse effects that these sources of dissatisfaction can bring? How can you manage these less attractive and more difficult – though no less important – aspects of your role? This chapter seeks to demonstrate how you can sustain your sense of self-worth, as well as your belief in the intrinsic value of what you do, and what you contribute. In doing so, it explains how you can – and should – work with your line manager; maximize your political resources; make effective presentations; manage your budget; handle complaints, discipline and grievances; and also how to manage redundancies, sustain your reputation and manage a crisis.

I MANAGING UP

Working with your line manager

The relationship between you as manager and those who you manage is, quite properly, at the heart of any text on management. It is, though, not the only management relationship you must master. You do in fact need to be effective in managing five different ways: 'managing yourself', 'managing across the organization', 'managing outwards' (beyond your organization) and 'managing upwards' as well as 'managing downwards' (Forrest, 1997). Of these, 'managing up' is often the most neglected – to the detriment of both parties. This is a very grave error. For, in the same way that you are the most important factor in your own staff's effectiveness, so too is your line manager with regard to you. Simply because you may have had no choice in deciding who your line manager is, you should not behave as if the relationship was somehow predetermined.

On the contrary, you must be *proactive* in this regard. You should, indeed, make a deliberate and conscious effort to reach both a mutual understanding with your line manager (there are no 'bosses' in a 'learning organization', simply co-learners) and an effective working relationship. And you should attempt this no matter how inauspicious or difficult your own particular circumstances may seem. For it is not just in your interest that you have a good working relationship, but also in your line manager's and – more critically – your university's interest too. How?

Understand the organizational world from your line manager's perspective

What does your line manager want? Put yourself in their shoes and attempt to understand both the theory and the reality of their job. (You can of course also do this literally by 'shadowing' them in their work over a short period.)

Consider, in the first instance, the nature of their job on paper – where it lies in the institutional structure and the particular job role. It is always revealing to read your line manager's job description, for it invariably describes their role in relatively straightforward terms. Make a point of doing so if you haven't already. If you are denied access, then seek an explanation.

Try to gauge the day-to-day reality of their work: the external and internal pressures; the competing interests; the political overtones; the demands on time; the institutional objectives to meet; the traumas; the satisfactions, etc. Remember, too, that organizations always look different at different levels and, as a rule, perceptions of stability, order and predictability typically diminish the further up the institutional hierarchy you climb.

Consider the 'added-value' they bring to their role. Think about your manager's contribution to the university. What are the particular individual, and maybe even unique, skills, experience and abilities that your manager brings to the role? How do they choose to carry out the role? What is their management style? What aspects of the job do they seem to enjoy most – or spend more time on? What aspects of the role are easier for them to carry out than you might have expected? In answering these questions you will distil the personal 'added-value' which your manager contributes: i.e. those qualities which your institution would lose if he or she were run over by a bus tomorrow; ones indeed which might not ever (even if the duties of the post remain unchanged) be replaced, for their successor might have a totally different profile.

Either way, it is in this 'added-value' area you should focus. For it is here you have the best opportunity of reaching a mutual understanding. You will also gain a better insight of their likely reaction to proposals and recommendations. That said, remember, too, that you are not required to like or admire your manager (though it helps) nor do you need to be similar in personality. Indeed, you may be completely different in personality, yet still make an ideal partnership.

Try to look at yourself through their lens. What do they want from you? They will, of course, have quite specific demands depending on the particular nature of your role. As a general rule, though, your manager will want you to help them in the following ways:

- Keep them informed on an on-going basis. Avoid springing last-minute surprises on them. Line managers really resent this, so, no matter how great your immediate difficulty, talk it through with them before it reaches crisis point. Don't conceal it. This way you will at least both have time to deal with it and may even manage to keep a level temperature between the two of you.
- Put forward solutions – not problems. Their world is full of people telling them why something can't be done. Don't add yourself to this list. Take the initiative. Instead of presenting them with a problem to handle, show them how the problem can be resolved. This way you may also avoid having solutions imposed upon you.
- View issues from their perspective. Not only does this show your understanding but it will also lead to better decision-making.
- Be able to cover for them in their absence, which may in turn lead to your own promotion.

If you have a good manager they should also be seeking to raise your pro-file, by providing you with opportunities – through delegating responsibilities, sponsoring management development activities, etc. – to broaden your experience and understanding so that you can be even more effective in your role.

Consider your own expectations of your line manager

What do I want? Reflecting on your own expectations can help you in two ways.

- It allows you to examine whether or not your expectations are, in fact, reasonable – and not wholly unrealistic – ones.
- It provides a basis on which you can negotiate the 'ground-rules' by which you and your manager agree to work together.

Again, individual expectations will vary. Even so, you should be able to expect your manager to commit themselves to helping you by willingly agreeing to:

- keep you informed on an on-going basis;
- have a sound understanding of your role;
- be supportive while respecting your autonomy;

- act as an adviser on how to sort out specific problems;
- openly support your decisions (unless they're truly misguided);
- be prepared to listen to new ideas;
- give you regular feedback on the good things and the 'not so good';
- give you opportunities for professional development;
- recognize your achievements;
- maintain honesty, exercise patience and practise consistency.

The last one may be an ideal and difficult to sustain in practice but there is no reason why it cannot be a shared aspiration.

Negotiate and establish a working agreement with your manager

Having an appreciation of your manager – of their personal contribution as well as their role – and having clarified your own expectations, you now have a sound basis on which to reach a mutual understanding that will benefit you both: one, that is, which ideally plays to each of your strengths. You should – in the first instance, at least – aim to agree and divide your duties and responsibilities on this 'horses for courses' basis. This initial allocation can, of course, be revised as you develop in your role. Whatever the specifics of your particular circumstances you should also aim to ensure that you and your manager agree:

- a set of 'ground rules' for working together, and that you review them – consciously – on a periodic basis and at least once a year;
- to have regular one-to-one meetings (typically one hour, every other week) on the same basis – and conducted on similar lines – as those which you have with colleagues in your own department.

The benefits of establishing a good working relationship with your manager are exponential: mutual support leads to mutual trust and respect, which in turn leads to greater autonomy and increased responsibility – the very things we identified at the outset which nurture professional well-being.

If however you are unfortunate enough to have a bad manager . . .

You should do the following:

- Recognize that – in the short term – this too can have advantages in that you can learn from them what *not* to do. Observe what they fail to do, or do in the wrong way, and vow never to make the same mistakes yourself in the future.
- Try and create, if you don't already have one, a group network of your peers inside and/or outside your institution. Such groups are extremely helpful not only as a source of support but also of ideas.
- Know that – in the long term – bad managers always come undone as a result of their actions one way or another.

And if you are unfortunate enough to have a truly noxious manager . . .

- Recruit a mentor to help you work out ways of coping and managing the situation. Mentors, of course, are not limited to this 'defensive' role but they can be an invaluable safety valve for your frustrations.
- Seek advice and support from your HR department through your staff relations adviser or directly from your Head of Personnel.

If neither of these works then you should consider – but only as a last resort:

- going over your manager's head and appealing direct to their line manager;
- taking out a grievance against your manager. If it is not commonplace you can depend that such action will stall, at least temporarily, the most insensitive and obdurate of bullies;
- invoke the Public Interest Disclosure Act 1998 (or 'Whistleblowers' Act') and appeal directly to your Board of Governors if the concerns you have about your manager are ones of malpractice which threaten not just your own interests but also those of the institution (HEFCE, 2001b).

If you decide that it is not appropriate to take any of the last three steps then resolve to:

- stand your ground; dig in and keep the faith (or)
- work out an exit strategy (or indeed do both).

Building and maintaining a power base

> I seen my opportunities and I took 'em.
> G.W. Plunkitt, Tammany Hall ward boss, New York City, 1905

One effective way of managing up – whether or not your relationship is good or bad – is to help yourself make the most of your political resources. We are all familiar with the phrase: 'power corrupts and absolute power corrupts absolutely'. Power, however, is an inescapable feature of organizational life and one you will have to come to terms with if you are to be a truly effective manager. This does not mean, though, that you have to be manipulative or coercive, or seek personal advantage, at the expense of others. People, of course, can and do use power in this way – and that is the point. Power in itself is not inherently evil; like energy, it is neither good nor bad. Its moral or immoral use stems from the actions of individuals in pursuit of their own agendas (Morgan, 2006). What you should be aiming to do – and will indeed be expected to do by your colleagues – is to maximize your power to advance the interests of the department. You should also be seeking to promote those of your institution as well as your own. How?

Make an inventory of your political resources

There are more than a dozen important sources of power within organizations, ranging from the formal (such as control over resources and information, etc.) to the informal (like interpersonal networks) and from the concrete (control over technology) to the abstract (the management of meaning and symbolism). In broad terms these can be categorized under four main types of power base: authority, expertise, resource control and interpersonal skill (see Figure 10.1). Or, put the other way, from an individual perspective power comes from:

- your formal position: your role;
- your personal authority: the personal characteristics you have (articulacy, empathy, humour, intelligence, dynamism, physical appearance, etc.) that others find attractive or influential or persuasive;
- your expertise: both real and imagined (by others);
- your access to information;
- your ability to recognize and seize an opportunity: to be 'in the right place at the right time'.

Box 10.1 is designed to help you explore and to recognize your political potential. Complete the questionnaire and determine your political profile.

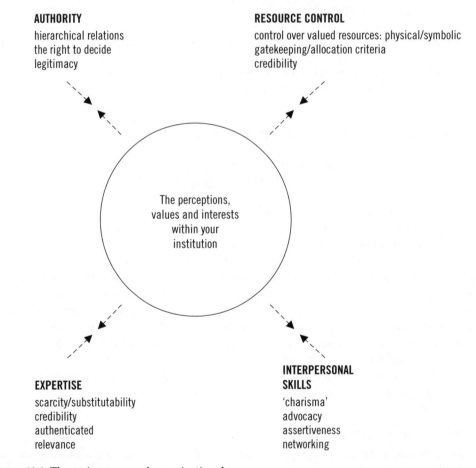

AUTHORITY
hierarchical relations
the right to decide
legitimacy

RESOURCE CONTROL
control over valued resources: physical/symbolic
gatekeeping/allocation criteria
credibility

The perceptions, values and interests within your institution

EXPERTISE
scarcity/substitutability
credibility
authenticated
relevance

INTERPERSONAL SKILLS
'charisma'
advocacy
assertiveness
networking

Figure 10.1 The main sources of organizational power

Source: based on Morgan, 2006.

Box 10.1 Make an inventory of your political resources

The following questions are designed to help you think about the political resources you have. They are divided between the four types of power-base: authority, expertise, resources control and interpersonal skill. The questions help to identify whether you have the particular type of power in each section, but there is space for you to insert additional indicators of your own. The more positive indicators you have, the greater your power.

1 Do you have formal authority?
(a) Do you have the formal right (say, in your job description) to make decisions, other than trivial ones?
(b) Do other people need your approval before they take action?
(c) Do you supervise someone else's work?
(d) Do your decisions significantly affect important aspects of your institution's work long term?
(e) Does your manager typically support your decisions and not over-rule them?
(f) Do you encounter any resistance to your right to make decisions, supervise others, give approval, from colleagues, peers, more senior managers?
(g) _____
(h) _____
(i) _____

'Yes' answers to any of (a)–(e) indicate your possession of authority.

'Yes' to (d) indicates a high level of power based on authority.

'Yes' to (f) suggests a reduction of your political resources which you may need to do something about.

2 Do you have the power of expertise?
(a) Does it take a year or longer to learn to do your job adequately?
(b) Do you need a qualification to do your job?
(c) What is the highest qualification in your field – do you have it?
(d) Are you the only person in your institution who can do your job?
(e) If you were to leave your institution would it have difficulty in replacing you?
(f) Do your knowledge and skill relate to a major aspect of the institution's work?
(g) Do people frequently consult you and follow your advice?
(h) Do more senior managers clearly show that they value your contribution?
(i) _____
(j) _____
(k) _____

'Yes' to any of (a)–(h) indicates your possession of expert power, but 'no' to (g) and (h) suggests a lack of perception of your expertise by others, and you may need to do something about this if this political resource is to be fully used.

3 Do you control resources?
(a) Can you give or withhold access to the following resources of your organization:
    (i) money
    (ii) information (non-trivial)
    (iii) promotion
    (iv) training and development
    (v) senior managers and other powerful people
    (vi) computers and other operational or administrative facilities

    (vii)   'perks'
    (viii) _____
    (ix)   _____
    (x)   _____

(b)   Are others aware that you can give or withhold access to these things, perhaps because you have on occasion refused them?

(c)   Do others have alternative sources of access to these resources?

'Yes' to any of the items in (a) indicates that you have power based on resource control.

'No' to (b) suggests that you may need to do something about this in order to fully use this political resource, but 'yes' to (c) in reference to any resource indicates a low level of power in relation to that resource, to which you may not wish to draw attention.

4 Do you have interpersonal power?

(a)   Are you on good terms with a number of people in the institution across different departments and hierarchical levels?

(b)   Do you know who the powerful people are, and are you on good terms with them?

(c)   Do people confide in you?

(d)   Do you usually speak at meetings?

(e)   Are you an 'active listener' – you make sure you have understood the other person's point of view?

(f)   Do you make sure that other people take your views seriously when it matters to you?

(g)   Do you avoid being either passive or aggressive in formal or informal discussion with others in the institution?

(h)   Can you hold the attention of a group or larger audience?

'Yes' to any of these questions indicates your power based on interpersonal skills.

'No' to any of (d)–(h) suggests that training and development would help you increase your political potential.

Looking back over your answers to these questions, you will probably have found that you have in some degree each of the types of power-base. If you give yourself a rating for each of the four types on the chart below, you will have a profile of your political resources.

Profile of political resources					
High	5				
	4				
Medium	3				
	2				
Low	1				
		Authority	Expertise	Resource Control	Interpersonal Skill

Conducting a power/dependency analysis of your position

As well as making an assessment of your political resources, you also need to go further and examine your position in relation to that of others; in particular those with whom you have the most interaction. Think of your own immediate power network – those individuals in positions upon whom you depend – and begin mapping them out as suggested in Figure 10.2. You will probably find that on the surface your network of dependencies is in fact a fairly simple one. This is quite normal. You must make a real effort to answer the questions set. If you do so it is more likely that you will identify the true complexity of the network of power and influence in which you operate. Enlist the support if you can of a trusted colleague or peer – as indeed you should in the case of Box 10.1, too. It will not only make the task easier but also ensure a more accurate outcome than if you rely solely on your own self-assessment.

Drawing up an action plan to realize your political potential

How, then, did you get on? Is the analysis of your 'power net' consistent with the inventory of your political resources? What are the differences? Can you account for

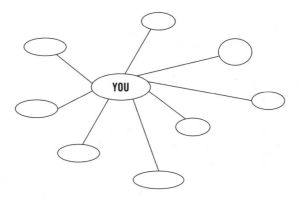

This diagram represents the network of contacts you have in carrying out your role. Use it to identify the people with whom you have the more important interactions, regardless of their position in the hierarchy. Then consider the following questions:

(a) What kinds of power do they have in relation to you?

(b) What kinds of power do you have in relation to them?

(c) What interests are they pursuing (both pragmatic and psychological)?

(d) What interests are you pursuing?

Consider in particular what evidence there is for (c) and alternative interpretations of it.

Figure 10.2 Analysing your network of power

them? What does your political profile tell you? What areas do you need to work on? What are you going to do about it?

- Consider those individuals at the top of your institution – do they have any characteristic(s) in common?
- Consider too where your institution is headed and what characteristics might be needed in the future.
- Commit then to 'making your own luck' and draw up an action plan that will realize your full political potential.

Making effective presentations

> What puzzles me is how anyone can write sentences such as 'The act of approval integrates considerations of not only academic integrity but resource efficiency and fitness for purpose as measured against university strategic direction and culture paradigm' without their face crashing onto their keyboard with boredom. For management speak is not only depersonalized, it is clanking, repetitive, ungrammatical and full of non-sequiturs.
>
> Gary Day, UK university lecturer, 11 October 2002

One simple and common way of trying to exercise influence is through the presentation of ideas or analyses to your manager or peers orally or, more typically, in writing. As this is the *raison d'être* of HE you could be forgiven for thinking that we are as incisive in the way we communicate within our institutions as we are in our research or our teaching. The sad truth is that you could not be more wrong. For much of what passes for internal communication often has the hallmarks of a poor student essay: ill prepared, ill thought out, long-winded and sloppily executed. Either that, or just as depressing, it bears the imprint of the bureaucratic 'dead hand'. Or, worse still, it is littered with the pseudo-jargon (pretentious words that are neither definite nor fixed in meaning: 'synergy', 'holistic', 'end-product', 'problematize', 'actioned', 'joined-up thinking' and so on) that has come to dominate subject disciplines and academic life in much the same way as it has business, the professions and government.

This is not a path you should follow if your aim is to be understood (indeed many use jargon precisely to avoid such transparency) and, contrary to what many academics believe, it is also very unlikely to persuade your manager into supporting your idea or proposal. Put another way – and as many institutions have increasingly begun to recognize, including even the funding councils – there is no substitute for plain English, plus brevity and precision.

More specifically, you should observe the following when preparing your proposal – or executive summary, if it is a report:

- It should be no more than one to two sides of A4. Lengthy tomes are as off-putting to your manager as they are to you, and they are likely to receive more of them than you. You risk your proposal being given short shrift if you are not considerate in this regard.

- It should be written in a simple clear style and structured in a bullet point or short paragraph format: i.e. it should be 'easy on the eye'.
- It should be written from the perspective of the reader and not your own. If your first words are 'This paper . . .', your proposal will not stand out from the pack, and your audience will be entitled to conclude that you – like the lazy reviewer who begins 'This book . . .' – has not expended much thought on enlisting their attention. Think instead of an arresting opening that takes them from where they stand, in point of knowledge, to the proposal you are setting out before them.
- It should be organized around a basic framework in which you:
  - state the problem, the issue or idea;
  - identify the causes and effects, the pros and cons, etc.;
  - list the possible solutions, alternatives, options;
  - make a recommendation – i.e. you make it easier for them by cutting down what they have to do to either agreeing or disagreeing; conversely you also make it more difficult for them to procrastinate.

It should be consistent with the virtues of a good research paper: one that is based on a love of order, accuracy, logic, honesty, self-awareness and imagination (Barzun and Graff, 2003).

Similar principles apply when it comes to oral presentations.

- Ascertain how long you are expected to speak and who and how many are expected to attend. The first question will help you determine the amount and kind of material to present; the second, the vocabulary, tone, and degree of complexity that are appropriate. Knowing the characteristics of your audience, you can pitch your remarks at the right level.
- Write your script 'for the ear' and not 'the eye' as any good lecturer does. Do not write long sentences or begin with qualifiers. Do not go from one main point to another without a break. Use more signposts than are necessary for print etc. In the past lecturers used 'overheads' to *complement* what they had to say; nowadays presenters are too often led by the all-pervasive PowerPoint technology into confining what they say to what is literally on the screen. Do not fall into the same trap. Concentrate on your message, not the technology.
- Focus on getting across your main key points (issues, ideas, conclusions) – six at most – and only them. Remember the longer and quicker you speak, the less likely you are to be heard.
- Believe in what you are saying, and believe it matters how you say it. Your audience is not there to attend a reading. Practise your delivery so that it adds value to the printed word and maintain a good pace too, *c.* 125 words a minute (Barzun and Graff, 2003; Siddons, 1998; Grant, 1997).
- Recognize that – as with the written word – the key to an effective presentation is thorough preparation. As Churchill himself put it, after one long rambling oration: 'I am sorry to have made such a long speech but I did not have time to write a shorter one'.

Managing your budget

One of the very first demands your manager will make is that you deliver your budget; that you, in effect, not only break even on your budget – by keeping your expenditure within limits and achieving your income targets – but also (ideally) generate a surplus too. This responsibility can be an unnerving one for even the most experienced head of department, let alone the newly appointed head for whom it is very often a novelty. It is also an activity that traditionally at least – and efficiency gains notwithstanding – we have not managed that well either. Whether for their own reasons, or because of the particular budget-setting arrangements within their institutions, heads of department have too often been *reactive* rather than proactive in managing their budgets. This again is not an example you should copy. For the competitive and straitened circumstances in which your department operates (let alone your institution) make it imperative you take the initiative in this regard. How?

- Recognize and understand the basic principles of what budgets are and why we have them (see Box 10.2).
- Recognize and understand the principles underpinning your own budget.

The nature of your budget

Are you head of:

- a 'profit centre'– a centre that has revenue as well as costs attributed to it?
- an 'investment centre' – a centre in which not only profit but the investment required to generate the profit is measured (or more likely)?
- a 'cost centre'– a centre in which only costs are measured?

Box 10.2 Budgets and their purposes

What is a budget?
A budget is 'a plan quantified in monetary terms, prepared and approved prior to a defined period of time, usually showing planning income to be generated and/or expenditure to be incurred during that period and the capital to be employed to attain a given objective' (Chartered Institute of Management Accountants).

Why do we have budgets?
- To define the objectives of the organization and thus provide a framework for the individual departments to operate within.
- To provide a system whereby the resources of the organization are used most efficiently.
- To indicate the efficiency and effectiveness with which the activities of the organization have been coordinated.
- To identify and quantify areas that have exceeded or fallen short of the targets.
- To allow management to rectify adverse variances and capitalize on favourable variances.
- To provide a basis for revising the current budget and preparation of future budgets (forecasting).
- To provide some centralized control over diverse activities and responsibilities.
- To provide a stabilizing influence in seasonal or cyclical activities (profiling).
- To provide a means of focusing on the important issues and highlighting areas where individuals can make a contribution.

The sources of your budget

- The proportion of your income that is funding council grant, tuition fee income, research grants and contracts, commercial activity, endowments and investments, etc.
- The proportion of your expenditure that is: (a) staffing costs (academic, administrative, technical, part-time, over-time, etc.); (b) general costs (consumables, staff development, equipment, travel and subsistence, telephone, postage, etc).

The basis of your budget

Know the way in which it was (or could be) formulated, for example:

- the incremental budget: this is the traditional 'base + adjustment' approach where the budget is based on what has happened in the past with any forecast changes built into the plan;
- the rolling or continuous budget: this reduces the level of uncertainty by allowing money to flow from one year to the next;
- the three-level or probabilistic budget: this analyses the degree of future uncertainty and projects three possible outcomes (the most likely, the best and the worst), thereby setting the parameters within which the actual budget out-turn is expected to fall;
- the zero-based budget: this budget is built up 'from scratch' by estimating the resources needed to deliver (and assure the quality of) the level of forecasted activity;
- the activity-based budget: in this budget overheads (i.e. all costs that are not direct) are allocated in line with the cost drivers (student numbers, staffing and building) that actually (and not speculatively) influence the way overheads operate within the institution: that is to say, overheads are not apportioned indiscriminately, as in the case of the traditional 'top-slice' approach, but in line with the way in which resources are actually consumed, as determined by the institution's particular 'resource allocation model'.

The institutional framework within which your budget is set

What are the key objectives of your institution's financial strategy and the implications for your budget and your department? For example, they could be: to establish a central Strategic Priorities Investment Fund; to fund specific capital projects; to build up a financial reserve; to obtain 50 per cent of income from non-funding council sources, etc. (HEFCE, 2002b). More fundamental, how healthy are your institution's finances? (See Box 10.3.)

Knowing your budget in this way is the first step towards establishing control over it. It will mean you will never be fazed or paralysed by any set of 'dead' figures that is put before you. It will give you the confidence, for example to:

- challenge both the accuracy of your budget and the assumptions on which it is based;

Box 10.3 How healthy are your institution's finances?

Key principles

University financial strategies typically seek to address five key issues.

1   The setting of financial performance objectives to ensure long-term viability and matching resources with objectives. Examining the financial implications – and value for money – of the current academic positioning; ensuring the appropriate balance between objectives, resources and infrastructure.

2   Identifying the investment needs to maintain productive capacity and to meet current objectives. Sustaining the value and contribution of human resources, physical assets, intellectual assets and information and systems critical to the institution's mission.

3   Identifying the appropriate levels of financing for capital development and other investments, including the business case for the use of borrowing and other external sources of finance.

4   Establishing a framework for evaluating strategic alternatives and managing risks to support and prioritize strategic opportunities; to minimize the impact of unexpected downturns.

5   Integration of the financial strategy with other corporate strategies ensuring the coherence and alignment across all key strategies with provision for monitoring and review.

The litmus test in each case is the firmness of the planning ground – the thoroughness and the degree to which these key principles have been formulated, developed and implemented.

To what extent does your HEI address these key principles?

Key financial performance indicators

1   Surplus or deficit as a percentage of income?
    A simple but fundamental measure of your institution's ability to pay its way, year on year
       Is it covering operating costs with operating income and by how much?
       Is it generating an annual surplus of 3 per cent in line with funding council expectations?

2   Discretionary reserves (or institutional equity) as percentage of income
    A long-term indicator of institutional health
       What would be left if your institution's assets were realized and all debts settled?
       Are the number of days of recurrent expenditure for your HEI consistent with the sector median (105)?

3   External borrowing as a percentage of income (also known as 'gearing')
    A measure of the burden of institutional debt
       Is your institution's total long-term borrowing as a percentage of income consistent with the sector median (14 per cent)?

4   Ratio of current assets falling due in one year
    A short-term test of financial strength
       The ratio of what you are owed by others to what you owe to others (<1 or >1)
       How does your HEI compare with the sector median of 1.23?

5   Liquidity (cash plus investments less overdrafts) against expenditure
    The hard test of short-term survival
       What cash can your HEI lay its hands on quickly either by access to cash reserves or arrangements for overdraft facilities on demand?
       How safe are your institution's bank deposits?
       Are the number of 'survival days' for your HEI consistent with the sector median (61)?

Source: adapted from Pearson, 2009.

- monitor whether your university's policy on matters of institution-wide interest (e.g. on internal recharging, overhead allocation) is being fairly and consistently applied across all budget centres in keeping with the government's requirement that all HEIs establish a 'transparent approach to costing' (JCPSG, 2005).

You should also take comfort in the knowledge that whatever your budget, people are your biggest asset and so long as you've adhered to the principles of performance management set out earlier, you will be close to maximizing the potential of what is typically your department's most expensive resource.

If you have not, however, you are likely to have a shortfall which cannot be made good through savings from the general (or non-pay) costs of your budget. Nor should you attempt to do so. The de-motivational consequences of cuts to – say – your travel and conference budget would far outweigh any savings they may generate. You should instead go back and review your initial staff workload allocations and part-time teaching budget.

Beyond that, you need to go further and recognize that the three most important things in budgetary management are *planning*, *planning* and *planning*!

For your budget is (or should be) in essence no more than your strategic plan translated into another language. The pity is not all institutions or heads of department (to their mutual detriment) appear to recognize this is the case. Indeed, it too often happens that heads of department – by choice or force of circumstance – get caught up, as we've noted, in a reactive cycle; one in which they are given an operating budget – see how much they can spend – passively monitor it – then hope for the best at the end of the financial year (see Figure 10.3).

To avoid this trap, or to break out of this cycle, you need to do as follows:

- Go back to the first principles of your department's strategic plan. What are your department's objectives: the targets; the critical milestones? Are they quantifiable? For example: to decrease reliance on Treasury funding by 10 per cent; to reduce part-time staffing costs by 10 per cent; to increase the proportion of income from CPD short courses by 25 per cent, etc. Do you anticipate the cessation of existing activities; the development of new ones? Is your course portfolio planning sensitive to 'product life-cycles'?
- Conceive of your plan and your budget as *dynamic* and not static. Take a leaf from the military strategic planners who determine their objectives, and then work backwards. What do you need to do to achieve your objectives? What do you need to do in the next three hours – never mind the next three years – to make it a reality? Review both your plan and your budget in the light of your actions. If they are dynamic you ought never to move beyond Year I of your plan (see Figure 10.4).
- Recognize that the approach on which your budget is based may not be conducive to forward planning: e.g. the traditional 'base + adjustment' budgets may be fairly simple to manage and make it relatively easy to draw comparisons (with previous years' results and current forecasts), but they do not highlight any inefficiencies in the existing order of things, nor do they reflect any risks or opportunities either. Therefore you should enlist the support and expertise of your management accountant to apply the budgeting techniques noted above (the activity-based, the

Proactive: how to do it?

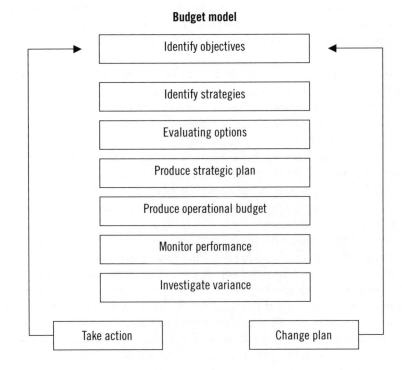

Reactive: how *not* to do it?

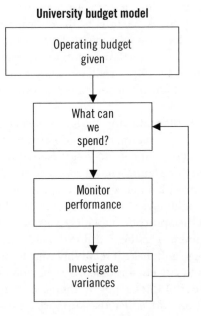

Figure 10.3 Managing your budget

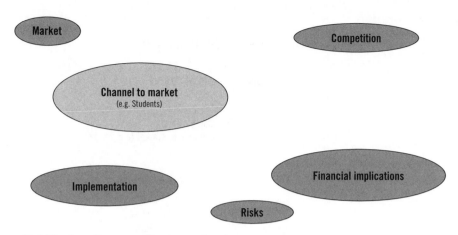

Figure 10.4 The key elements of business planning

zero-based and the three-level) to your own budget, as a means of bringing these to the fore – and act on them.
- Work with your management accountant in actively managing your budget, for example:
  - divide your general cost items by 12, plot in the expenditure and monitor them;
  - identify expenditure items that are 'lumpy'; e.g. one-off capital projects, the part-time staffing budget;
  - profile your budget by plotting when and how you will spend it;
  - prepare a budget forecast over three months, six months and nine months. Try and match expenditure with planning. As with everything else, your accuracy will improve with practice.

None of this is rocket science but all put together it will ensure that your future is not left to chance – that it is one you can manage and control.

Preparing a business plan

As government has successively levied greater fiscal accountability on HEIs, so too have institutions themselves within their own domains. And it is increasingly the case that if you wish to develop a new course or research proposal, or apply for a public grant, you will only be permitted to do so on the basis that you have a sound business plan. How best can you meet this requirement?

View the business plan as tool to help, not hinder

Business planning is simply:

- the structured management of business ideas from concept to delivery through agreed stages (see Figure 10.5);

Figure 10.5
Preparing a business plan

Overview and SWOT analysis

Environmental review

- The market
- Competitors
- Channel to market (e.g. students)

Implementation

- Who
- How
- By when

Financial implications

- Cost
- Income

Risk assessment

- a tool to help you capitalize on strengths, pioneer opportunities, redefine weaknesses and minimize threats.

It also:

- provides a means of targeting and measuring commercial activity;
- provides an accurate indication of costs and implications;
- avoids wasted effort and duplication;
- operates as an 'early warning' system should things go wrong.

Or put another way, it turns conventional academic planning on its head by ensuring that any development activities are market-driven, not supply-driven (Luffman *et al.*, 1996).

Present your proposal on the basis of systematic planning

Your proposal should be based on a systematic examination of the various stages of the business planning process outlined in Figure 10.5. It should include the following.

A swot analysis of your proposal
- Strengths – What does your department have that others don't? What are your unique selling points (USPs)?
- Weaknesses – What are the risks? What could you lose? How much will it cost?

- Opportunities – What is the target market? Why will they buy it? What is the market size? What market share are you expecting? How is this divided up over time? What is the build up?
- Threats – Who are the known competitors with similar offerings? How strong are they? How long have they been in the market? What is the size of their market share – their turnover? What do you know about their offer (e.g. pricing information)?

The logistics of implementation

- How will you sell to this market? Who will carry out this activity? What are their targets?
- What marketing support is needed (brochures, advertising, attendance at exhibitions)? Who needs to be involved to make the project work: directly and indirectly (e.g. support services)?
- What timelines are you working to and why?
- What are the key delivery stages in the process?
- Are there any special requirements (e.g. weekend provision only)?

A breakdown of costs and income

- What are your investment costs – your forecast of up-front development costs?
- What are the costs of your recruitment and marketing activity?
- What are the costs associated to delivery?

In all three cases make sure you allow for full cost recovery and include all direct costs (e.g. salary, consumables), indirect costs (e.g. library, premises) and overhead costs (i.e. those costs incurred whether the activity runs or not, e.g. fuel, rates, lighting, maintenance).

How has your pricing been based? What is your market intelligence? Are you seeking to:

- grab the market? – penetration pricing;
- make a fast return? – skimming the price;
- offer a quality product? – premium pricing;
- look for economies of scale? – economy pricing;
- exploit different perceptions? – differential pricing.

What are your income forecasts (pricing x student nos)? How much activity does it represent? Is it genuinely realistic?

An assessment of risk

Outline the risks which may cause changes to the plan: e.g. delays in course development; difficulty in targeting the market; rival activity; quality issues.

- Financial sensitivity: What are the implications of changes in costs and income over time? What would be the financial impact of an increase in the cost of development or a shortfall in student recruitment?
- Cost-benefits: What impact (high–medium–low) would the development have on the overall activity of the department? What is the likelihood (high–medium–low)

of this development not succeeding? What are the risks for the department in *not* pursuing this development: i.e. the cost of forgoing the opportunity (HEFCE, 2001d)?

II MANAGING THE 'DOWN-SIDE'

Handling complaints, discipline and grievances

> At the heart of our political system is a culture which cares more about the right process than the best outcome.
>
> James Strachan, Chair, UK Audit Commission, May 2003

Tricky, demanding and unpleasant are all accurate ways of describing this 'shadow side' of your role. It can, however, be an illuminating, instructive and enhancing experience too. In the popular imagination complaints, discipline and grievances are about apportioning blame, seeking retribution, meting out punishment or scoring points: a belief unwittingly given substance by the necessary, if formal and elaborate, way in which almost all HEIs have introduced procedures (adversarial in character) to deal with them. This is not the place to rehearse the efficacy of your institution's procedures; suffice it to say that this is not their intended purpose. Nor should it be yours. On the contrary your focus in all three instances should be on *seeking to bring about improvement*:

- in the provision of service (complaints);
- in the performance levels or conduct of staff (discipline);
- in the nature of working relationships (grievance).

Put another way, you should be seeking to turn each of these 'negatives' into a 'positive'. How? Simply, but critically, in the way you approach them, and the manner in which you handle them:

- *Recognize the complaint, the grievance or the discipline issue as an opportunity to enhance quality.* This may seem perverse as a guiding principle in these instances, but – given quality is one of those curious features which is visible only in its absence – they do, in fact, present you with the best opportunity you're likely to have to make a real difference in this regard. For they offer you the rare chance 'to take the lid off' your surface reality: to probe the 'back-stage' and 'under-the-stage' of your department (Becher, 2001) – to unearth it, learn from it, to influence it and to improve it.

  Such instances also constitute a reminder – as well as a test – of your commitment to quality. Quality of course is not conceived in any singular way in HE. Some institutions purport to offer 'value for money', others 'fitness for purpose' and still others 'service excellence' (see Box 10.4). Either way, complaints, grievances and disciplinary matters are, by their very nature, likely to breach such commitments. It is incumbent on you to meet this challenge.
- *Be prepared to engage in critical self-reflection on your own role in these matters.* Complaints, grievances and matters of discipline are rarely cut and dried. They

Box 10.4 Quality in higher education

1 The 'exceptional' view
   – synonymous with excellence
   e.g. student services

2 the 'perfection' view
   – consistent with flawless outcomes
   e.g. the world-class university

3 the 'fitness for purpose' view
   – fulfilling a customer need
   e.g. the QAA

4 the 'value for money' view
   – a return on investment
   e.g. the Funding Council

5 The 'transformation' view
   – a change from one state to another
   e.g. learning and teaching

Source: based on Harvey, 1995; 2007.

often raise other issues to do with working practices, or the involvement of other parties, or may, indeed, be symptomatic of a more fundamental problem. They are as likely to be about you, too, if not directly then indirectly: about what you may or may not have done. You must, therefore, be prepared to put your own self-justification to one side and critically reflect on your own role as a contributory factor in these matters (Moores, 1994).

- *Take responsibility for the issue; accept the buck and do not pass it.* In all these cases the procedures governing them invariably – and quite properly – lay down very specific guidelines on how they should be handled: the various stages, the conduct of the hearing, the right of appeal and so on. As such they can be very protracted, for they each usually have a 'built-in escalator' whereby – if the issue remains unresolved – it can be referred ever upward. To the extent, indeed, that at the final stage there is usually provision for some form of independent or external arbitration – through the Board of Governors, a Visitor or ombudsman. It is also the case that the portent of such matters often grows exponentially – as if 'it takes on a life of its own' – and what may have started as a simple misunderstanding between a student and a lecturer has developed into a full-blown disciplinary concern. It is down to you to ensure this does *not* happen. You should always endeavour to reconcile such differences – to nip them in the bud – before they get out of hand. Or, if they are out of hand, take responsibility for dealing with them under the requisite procedure. Do not hide behind the procedure or make a fetish of it either. The 'letter of the law' is important and you should follow it, but keep your eye on your overall objective – the 'best outcome'.

- *Remember you have 'a duty of care' to staff as well as to students and other stakeholders.* And while it is the case the majority of complaints are likely to raise legitimate concerns there will be some – a vexatious minority – that do not. Again, it will be up to you to weed these out in timely fashion.

How then should you handle these matters?

Complaints

Identify the nature of the complaint

This may seem – and may well be – straightforward. But it is not always so. Indeed it can often take time, patience and skilled questioning to 'get to the bottom' of a complainant's concern. As a first step ask them – if they have not already done so – to submit their complaint in writing on one side of A4.

Appraise the significance of the complaint

    (a) Does it arise, for example, from a misunderstanding on the complainant's part, a difference of expectation or a failing on the part of your department for which there is collective culpability?

    (b) Or is it about the (alleged) conduct or incompetence of a member of your staff and therefore (potentially) serious?

Determine how to proceed

- If (a) telephone the complainant and explain your position or send them a letter of apology. Resolve to investigate your department's collective failing and aim to avoid a repeat.
- If (b) formally write to them inviting them to a meeting to discuss their complaint. Offer them the opportunity to bring a friend, or Student Union (or legal) adviser with them if they wish.
- If you receive a student petition agree to meet with two student representatives. Do not be cajoled into meeting the whole group. It may jeopardize any subsequent investigation and, if unwarranted, totally undermine your colleague and leave you looking you unprofessional too.
- If the complaint was an anonymous one do not ignore it. Have an informal word with the staff member concerned. It may be you have a mischievous complainant in your midst. On the other hand it may be symptomatic of a problem brewing. Seek to both reassure and help your colleague resolve any difficulty.
- At the meeting seek to clarify and thoroughly understand the nub of the complaint. Summarize it to the complainant and get them to confirm it.
- Write to the member outlining the complaint and invite them to a meeting to discuss the matter. Offer them the same rights as the complainant. Indicate too that the nature of the meeting is an informal one. Unless it is an issue of gross misconduct (e.g. theft, assault, aggravated harassment, etc.) you should *never* invoke the disciplinary procedure before a staff member has been given the opportunity to answer any charges that have been made against them (ACAS, 2008b).
- In the interim complete any further investigation that may be necessary, including the interview of any third parties.

Determine how to act

Having interviewed both parties and considered the case, you must determine what to do next. You can choose to:

- uphold the complaint;
- reject the complaint as unfounded, unproven or vexatious;

- take no action;
- take informal action, e.g. counselling and development;
- invoke the competence procedure if it is a matter of poor performance;
- invoke the disciplinary procedure if it is a matter of conduct.

Whatever you decide, you should summarize your findings in a short report and inform both parties of the outcome accordingly.

Discipline

Handling cases of discipline is – or should – not be so different in practice from the way you deal with complaints. For the same principles and processes – keeping an open mind, gathering the facts, the interview, the written record, etc. – apply in both instances. The main difference, of course, lies in the formality of the procedure and its potential consequences – up to and including dismissal. For these reasons, then, you need to be absolutely certain it is the correct path to follow; or, put another way, that you are invoking it:

- as a 'last resort' and not as your 'first port of call';
- because you have given informal oral warnings or reprimands in the past that have had no effect and you've now exhausted the limits of your authority;
- because the nature of the case merits it.

A complaints procedure must follow in cases of:

- *misconduct*, e.g. abusive or threatening behaviour including bullying, and sexual, social or racial harassment; regular unauthorized absence; constant unsatisfactory timekeeping; wilful refusal to carry out a reasonable request; negligence which causes unacceptable loss, damage or injury; the deliberate breach of health and safety regulations, etc.;
- *gross misconduct*, e.g. theft, fraud, arson, physical assault, aggravated harassment, total incapacity due to the influence of alcohol or illegal drugs (having already exhausted the existing procedures in place for health-related abuse), etc.;
- *incompetence*, having already exhausted the competence procedure for tackling poor performance.

If any of the above do not apply then you should not proceed. Indeed it is unlikely your HR department will allow you to because your actions will not have satisfied 'the test of reasonableness', i.e. one of the three critical factors (the others being the grounds for dismissal and the veracity of the procedure itself) which Employment Tribunals take into account in their adjudication of appeals (ACAS, 2008b).

If this test is also satisfied then you should proceed but do so with the support of your manager and your HR adviser. In the preliminary investigation make sure you always have someone else in attendance with you when meeting the other party. And remember that, when it comes to the formal hearing, you – and you alone – will be acting as 'chief prosecutor', while the Director of HR takes on the role of chair.

Your aim is, and must remain, one of seeking improvement in conduct or performance, and not one of retribution.

Grievances

Grievances, too, are no different, in the sense that, like discipline, every effort should be made to resolve them in an informal way. They typically arise out of long-standing differences, or may be sparked by a single incident, but they should be the exception not the rule. (If they are the norm in your department then there is something seriously amiss with your management style, or the motivation and performance of your staff; issues which you should address with urgency.)

Either way, the grievance procedure does allow individuals to exercise their right to raise matters of concern or to have problems addressed – issues which you may have under-estimated or been unaware of – and by the same token it offers you the opportunity to put things right. Therefore you should act promptly and fairly, as indeed you are required to, and with due regard to natural justice.

If a grievance is taken out against you
- Take it seriously without being defensive.
- Do not take offence.
- Focus on the complaint, not the individual.
- Consider the complaint through their lens, not yours. Is it symptomatic of another issue?
- Prepare to defend – or apologize for – your actions.
- And, most importantly, explore ways you can move forward in resolving these differences to each other's benefit.

Managing redundancies

> Even people who are unhappy about the outcome of a process will have less dissatisfaction and fewer dysfunctions than they might otherwise have if they understand the process through open communications and see that it was fair . . .
>
> (De Nisi, 2000)

If you are lucky you may avoid having to manage redundancies. If not, you should prepare yourself for what is one of the most challenging – and unpleasant – duties you will ever have as a manager. Like discipline, redundancy is, or should be, the very last resort. The process, too, is subject, if not to an agreed internal procedure, then to external statutory requirements. And again, like discipline, it has common misconceptions attached to it. Redundancy is not about dismissal – it is the job, not the individual, that is redundant. It is also, in practice, far more often voluntary than it is compulsory. And while it can be a brutal process it doesn't have to be. And that's the point. For, no matter how inauspicious the circumstances, all staff who leave should be able to do so with their dignity and respect intact. And it is your responsibility – once a redundancy programme has been agreed – to help ensure this is the case (Rothwell, 2000). Put another way, redundancy is nearly always a painful process for everyone involved – for leavers, stayers and you alike. Even so, you should realize – and accept – that you can still make a real and positive difference, despite how unpropitious your situation may seem; that you can, in fact, by seeking to minimize the stress on those who leave – while upholding the morale of those who remain – render the process far less traumatic than it would otherwise be. How?

Do all you can to avoid a redundancy situation in the first place

You should do this principally through your institution's human resource strategy. A 'redundancy' arises when the employer ceases 'to carry on the business for the purpose of which the employee was employed' or 'in the place where the employee was employed' or where 'the requirements of the business for employees to carry out work of a particular kind has ceased or diminished' (ACAS, 2008c). Your HR strategy – if it is an effective one – will have taken just such scenarios into account. And more particularly it will have been based on a planned forecast of existing and future staffing needs institution-wide. This way, if a redundancy situation arises then at least job losses should be minimized. Careful HR planning will also help to improve job security among staff as well as avoid knee-jerk reactions to immediate problems at the expense of longer-term staffing needs.

Additionally, use specific practical initiatives that may minimize or avoid a redundancy situation: e.g. natural wastage; restricting the recruitment of permanent staff; reducing (or curtailing) the use of temporary staff; filling vacancies from among existing staff; reducing (or curtailing) overtime; retiring all staff at the normal retirement age and (if permissible) seeking applicants for early retirement; retraining and deploying staff elsewhere in the institution.

Use full proper and early consultation on the redundancy proposals

In the UK employers are legally obliged to have a consultation period of at least 30 days if the intention is to make 20–99 employees redundant and at least 90 days in cases where more than 100 employees are affected. Your institution may also have a formal policy, or a formal agreement indeed, with trade union or employee representatives setting out the procedure to be followed. Either way, the golden rule is that consultation should take place as early as practicable in order to provide an opportunity for all parties to share the problem and explore the options. Also:

- Remember to consult beyond those immediately at risk and with individual staff, not just their representatives. Failure to do so could result in an Employment Tribunal granting a 'Protective Award' to any – and every – individual who complained you did not fulfil this requirement (ACAS, 2008c).
- Remember that 'notice of consultation' is not 'notice of redundancy' and it is possible that more acceptable alternative ways of tackling the problem or of minimizing hardship may emerge during this period.

Have a compelling business case for the proposed redundancies

The process is one thing and should be relatively unproblematic. Where the contention invariably lies is, of course, in the substance of your proposals: the reasons for the redundancies; the number and categories of staff involved; the selection procedure and the method for calculating redundancy payments (over and above the statutory entitlement).

First and foremost is your rationale. Your business case must be a compelling one and, more importantly, must be equally convincing to others: staff, their representatives, managers and governors alike. If not, you will encounter serious opposition – and rightly so. Put another way, a legitimate business reason – e.g. a sustained shortfall in student numbers and recruitment – is by itself not sufficient. You must *demonstrate* it. That is, you must offer a thorough and systematic analysis of all the factors that have given rise to the particular circumstance (based, for example, on market research, sector norms, etc.) as well as an explanation of why you believe the area (e.g. course, subject, service) is no longer viable, and in view of why institutional needs and requirements, likely to remain so: a redundancy programme would in essence be in the best overall interests (or 'greater good') of the institution. Your business case then is akin to drawing up a business plan, the difference being in the outcome usually associated with it: retrenchment rather than growth.

In determining the number of jobs lost, you will ironically find it easier to start from the opposite premise. How many staff do you need – and will you need – to 'roll through' and 'roll out' the provision of your course, subject or service while still maintaining quality? This figure subtracted from your overall staffing complement will give you the number of jobs surplus to requirements. Implicit in this 'zero-based' approach – in building up your budget from scratch on the basis of the number of staff needed to provide for the number of registered students – is a consensus on the level of provision needed to maintain quality: the requisite staff–student ratio, the level of service and so on. As there is no such consensus, your safest option is to draw up your contingency plans based on published sector norms. Either way, you should anticipate having to produce and reproduce successive resource plans – outlining the best case, worst case and most likely case scenarios, etc. – many times over as the consultation develops and the process gets under way. The other unacknowledged aspect of this approach is that it often shows in stark relief just how little contribution – in business terms – research makes to institutional viability. Contrary to the popular belief that research is often the critical factor in keeping institutions afloat, it is in fact a luxury that only a few HEIs can afford.

Agree and establish selection criteria that are objective and transparent, and are applied consistently

The method of selection is typically just as contentious as the number and category of staff involved – and for good reason. For the less objectively and the less precisely criteria are defined, the greater is the risk that staff are liable to discrimination or unfair selection for redundancy. The desirability of avoiding such an outcome – and indeed the legal imperative to do so – is rarely disputed. Where the real difficulty often lies, however, is not so much in the commitment to establishing objective and transparent criteria but in agreeing the very nature of the criteria in the first place – and typically even more so when it comes to prioritizing and weighting the individual criteria once they are agreed.

The number, nature and weighting of the specific criteria that are finally agreed will of course depend on your local circumstances. Even so, they should not only be objective but also – if they are to be perceived as legitimate – consistent with the strategic direction of your institution and department. And again – as in the case of the recruitment of staff – you need to take particular care to ensure that they are not directly or indirectly discriminatory on the grounds of sex, race or disability (see Box 10.5). Finally – should your 'notice of redundancy' not yield a sufficient number of volunteers (and you should make every effort to ensure that it does, given the far more demoralizing effect of compulsory severance) you need to ensure that the criteria are *applied* with as much care as they were drawn up. As a fail-safe best practice, suggest that an appeals process is also set up internally. This not only has the advantage of bringing a speedy resolution to legitimate individual grievances but also reduces the likelihood of any future complaint to an employment tribunal.

Box 10.5 Specimen selection criteria for redundancy of academic staff

Criteria		Scoring (0–5 points)
Qualifications	• Higher degree; teaching; professional body	

Teaching and learning	• Competence in delivery of subject – as evidenced by external examiners' comments, teaching materials, etc.
	• Contribution to scholarship:
	  – evidence of scholarship integrated in practice of teaching and learning;
	  – application of IT in the curriculum;
	  – willingness to gain experience of commercial application of the subject;
	  – specific module/programme development;
	  – evidence of innovation in the curriculum.	

Breadth and depth of experience	• Spread of subject specialisms • Spread of levels taught • Programme leadership and management • External examining • Competence in personal tutoring	
Research	• Refereed publications eligible for the RAE • Number of research students	
Workload	• Number of teaching contact hours • Amount of funded research work	

Offer staff help and assistance in finding alternative employment

Employers have a statutory obligation to allow staff who are under notice of redundancy 'a reasonable amount of paid time off' to look for another job or to arrange training. Good employers of course can – and do – offer a whole lot more: typically, access to an outplacement service which usually provides workshops on financial planning, job searching and self-marketing as well as one-to-one specialist sessions on careers guidance (ACAS, 2008c).

Understand the effects of the change on staff and support them throughout this process

Textbook theories will tell you that people go through four different stages before coming to terms with redundancy: negation – self-justification – exploration – and ultimately, resolution. And it is indeed the case that some staff – a minority – will pass imperceptibly through these stages and move on (De Nisi, 2000). What they do not prepare you for, however, is the way in which many people go backwards and forwards through these stages (as they work through their feelings) before finally coming to resolution. And still others – another sizeable minority – can go through all these different stages on the same day, every single day of the week. You can best help staff through this by the following:

- Resist the natural tendency to withdraw; deal *visibly* with the reality of the situation by talking to staff and being with staff. This is not the time for hiding. Communication, communication and communication are the watchwords. Counsel them. You do not have to be a professional counsellor, nor are you expected to be. Counselling – in a management sense – is a way of responding and relating to someone so that they feel clearer about what is concerning them and are then better able to help themselves and make their own decisions. It means in practice you should:
  - be non-directive, non-judgemental;
  - have empathy;
  - respect confidentiality;
  - help to release tension;
  - help to release creative energy;
  - recognize the individual wants counselling and ensure ownership of the problem stays with them.

  Put another way, there are, in this context, three stages to the counselling process:

1 getting the story: listening, interpreting and responding;
2 understanding the situation: exploring, focusing and giving feedback;
3 moving on: developing strategies, gaining acceptance.

All this, of course, is a lot easier said than done. Nor should you underestimate the task, for it is an emotional roller-coaster of epic proportion for them – and also for you. And in that sense it is important that you recognize – as should your manager and HR department – that you too will need support and maybe counselling during this process.

If you are made redundant

It may also transpire that you, too, are to be made redundant, and if so:

- Remember and recognize that the same cycle of stages – negation, self-justification, exploration and resolution – that staff go through applies equally to you too.
- Probe the legitimacy of the business rationale. Suggest alternative courses of action. Be realistic, not fanciful. And stick to business reasons, not appeals based on emotion.
- Play the accountants at their own game. Think of all the extraneous factors they may have missed. Take them beyond the zero-based approach. Present them with the 'Doomsday scenario'. Make them rethink.

After you have accepted the business case for the decision, then:

- Resolve to be as professional and as responsible as you always have been until you leave.
- Don't waste time beating yourself up or seeking to blame others.
- Don't be coy either about trying to secure the best severance package you can. Ask your employer to pay for outplacement counselling and for any legal costs. Try to negotiate salary in lieu of notice and to keep any non-pay allowances you may have been given in your role: e.g. your mobile phone number, laptop computer, etc.
- Recognize, too, that even redundancy can have 'a silver lining'. For although it may be traumatic it forces you, in the same way as with staff, to hold a mirror up to yourself; to look inwards, to reflect and re-evaluate your priorities; to realize indeed the genuine qualities and marketable skills you have; and to understand that it is not the end of the world, that it is a job, not life; that you always have choices and there are always opportunities.

Managing your reputation

> All is fair in love and war and in getting the story out.
>
> Juliet Alexander, media consultant

Like quality, reputation is a virtue that only really becomes visible in its absence – we can see, and we all know, when we've lost it. A poor quality rating, an unexpected drop in research rankings, the failings of an overseas partner or the public airing of student and staff grievances can undermine your institutional, departmental and personal reputation in an instant.

Even more disconcerting, the increasingly market-driven nature of HE and the internal and external pressures to be 'excellent', 'world class' and 'top of the league' have also ensured that the importance of your reputation is now greater than ever – and with it more at risk as media scrutiny has likewise become ever more intrusive. The blaze of publicity the handful of lecturers attracted, for example, for lobbying their students to provide a positive response to the 2008 UK National Student Survey demonstrates just how quickly the unsuspecting can find themselves the subject of unwelcome headlines (Harvey, 2008).

However much we might rail against such matters – 'excellence has become a meaningless term for higher education'; 'league tables are pernicious, in the way they present "information" about the sector as if it were "knowledge" of the sector'; they are 'ludicrous, insidious, prejudicial, flawed, corrosive, banal, inane,' and so on (Kelly, 2008) – they are not going to go away. League tables, media interest and the demand for greater transparency and accountability are here to stay. What then can, and should, you do to manage and enhance your reputation?

Be clear what league tables mean to you, your department and your university

For some, like the small number of elite business schools all chasing the international 'sponsored executive' market, the 'Top Business School rankings' represent the only game in town. Almost the same can be said of the Russell Group and 1994 Group of research-intensive universities, which often use league tables as key performance indicators and set desired ranking positions as strategic targets – and they have good reason for doing so. We know, for example, that it is high-achieving students rather than others who typically consult league rankings and that the tables are invariably compiled in a way that favours these institutions. By placing greater emphasis on research assessment scores, on entry qualifications and good degrees, on reputation rather than actual performance, on a traditional rather than a diverse model of HE, and so on, the league tables give powerful public credence to their aspirations to be considered 'world class' (HEFCE, 2008b; Morris, 2008; Bekhradnia, 2007).

For others, like many post-1992 universities, league tables are not really their game at all. Compilers invariably make no allowance for institutions with disproportionate numbers of mature students and part-time students, or for the 'added value' which institutions bestow on their students, or indeed the differential level of public subsidy enjoyed by universities (even though the latter is a criterion used in governing EU market competition). Even so, these universities cannot ignore league tables, not least because they occupy the lower rankings which has implications for staff and student morale, governing body expectations as well as public perception. Still others, such as small specialist institutions, are excluded from league tables altogether (Attwood, 2008).

You need to be clear, then, how the various league tables are compiled; what they say about your institution or subject department; what they mean to you; and most importantly what you can do to influence them. In essence, all league tables broadly subscribe to one of two different approaches:

1 the objective scorecard approach – which attempts to find and apply as neutral and consistent a set of statistics about performance as possible, as, for example, the Shanghai Jiao Tong University (Academic Ranking of World Universities) list of the 'top 500';
2 the subjective beauty contest approach – which typically acknowledges the importance of some vital statistics, but is heavily reliant on insider opinion: academic peer review, employer preference and so on; *The Times Higher Education* (THE/QS World University Rankings) has rapidly become the brand leader here, with 50 per cent of its ranking accounted for in this way.

It is also the case that national league tables rarely offer many surprises. The geological strata of the UK's *Times* league table, for example, is roughly the same as it was a decade ago with Oxbridge at the top, and in descending order, the majority of pre-1992 universities, followed by the majority of post-1992 institutions and a few former polytechnics always near the bottom – an outcome that can just as easily be replicated using a single measure (that of dividing student enrolments by total income) not included in any of the league tables (Watson, 2007b; HEFCE, 2008b).

This situation is in sharp contrast to international rankings, where there has been considerable variation. Between rounds one and two of the THE/QS world rankings, for example, Duke University rose to eleventh from outside the top 50, while Sussex University, which had devised a promotional strategy around being '58th in the world', dropped to 100; again between rounds four and five Washington University in St Louis jumped over 100 places to 60, while Cardiff University dropped out of the top 100 to 133 (Ince, 2008).

The contrasting outcomes, of course, are attributable to the different measures compilers use in drawing up the league tables and the variable weighting they place upon them. And while compilers may claim they are simply responding to increasing public demand for information from students and their parents, and that their rankings help drive up institutions' performance, the message to institutions is a clear one:

- You need to determine if you are entering one competition, or several, and tactically you need to prepare for more than one set of rules.
- Given that league tables include some factors and omit others (the Shanghai Jiao Tong table, for example, does not include any 'common-sense' criteria for teaching quality, widening participation, social mobility or services to business and the community), you need to consider the risks to your own institutional agenda if you make league table rankings your critical key driver (Schmidt, 2008).

If you are a casualty of 'the serious methodological limitations' (Attwood, 2008) of the rankings, the onus is on you:

- to challenge – individually and collectively – the basis on which compilers have drawn up their particular table, and lobby them to include those aspects you believe would provide a more accurate and valid outcome;
- to ensure that all your institutional data submissions are (without over-engineering) both comprehensive and accurate as well as 'joined up';
- to explain to your critical audiences the reasons why you occupy a particular ranking;
- to aspire to be ranked above those institutions with similar characteristics to your own, and develop the necessary action plan to realize it. (Or alternatively follow the lead of one or two others and withdraw from the league tables, though this may well be interpreted in an even more negative light, particularly if you happen to have university values centred on 'transparency', 'openness', 'inclusivity' and the like.)

Safeguard yourself and undertake what many institutions now do as a matter of course. That is, benchmark your performance against other universities (entirely independently of the league tables) and according to the criteria which are important to you and the realization of your own institutional agenda.

Be wary about over-claiming your prowess

The term 'excellence' is common currency in universities today, so much so that many argue it has become meaningless as a concept. And given that at least one university purports to have 'Excellent Awards for Excellence at one Excellent University', this contention may not be far off the mark (Bekhradnia, 2007). The reason for this is in part because excellence is a *relative* concept and there is a question whether it means excellent relative *to everyone else* (as in top of a league table) or excellent relative *to a set of standards* (which in theory we could all meet). It is also, of course, bound up with the politically inspired drive (in a proxy competition for resources) to be recognized as 'world class', which, like excellence, is another relative concept. There has also been the growth of professional marketing within universities and with it a concerted effort to develop institutional branding. Finally, there is the understandable desire to assuage the nagging concern: if everyone else is claiming to be excellent and you're not, what is wrong with you?

Either way, lazy over-claiming is one of the first things we teach our students to guard against, and you need to be careful not to allow yourself to fall into the same trap. Indeed, as we noted earlier, students, particularly international ones, are increasingly dissatisfied with the value-for-money of what is provided, and equally disparaging about the claims made in many university prospectuses. Then there are the self-proclaimed 'leading research-intensive universities' of the *Universitas* 21 network, several of which didn't make the top 500 universities in the initial Shanghai rankings list (Bekhradnia, 2007; Watson, 2007b).

'Excellence' and 'world class' are too often casually claimed, then, without proof, and can readily backfire, diminishing your reputation rather than enhancing it. You should not overuse these terms to describe yourself. Better still, leave it to others to do so.

Strategic communication: recognize that managing your reputation is a year-round activity

In the same way that we said recruitment was far more than simply relying on passive advertising to fill job vacancies – it entailed year-round talent scouting – this is equally the case in managing your reputation. That is to say, it is not about reacting after the fact to the bad news story, it's about being proactive and having a working media plan in place – above all, it's about being strategic in your communication.

Strategic communication is about:

- getting key messages across proactively
- to important target-groups
- over a defined period of time
- in a systematic, coordinated and creative manner.

It is the opposite of communication which is

- defensive
- ad hoc
- unconsidered.

Consider the principles and design of strategic communication outlined in Box 10.6. Your university will have many of these arrangements in place – are there any omissions? Reflect on your own department. What can you do to enhance the perception of your area to both internal and external audiences?

Box 10.6 Strategic communication in practice

Principles

Strategic	Based on your university's overall strategy
	Audiences understand your university/department goals and can participate in their achievement.
Coordinated	All communication activities support and build on one another.
Relationship-building	Long-term relationships are built with key audiences inside and outside the university.
Inspired	'The medium is the message' too – radio, television, print, electronic. Be creative. Do not rely on boiler-plate statements.
Proactive	Don't wait until others communicate with you.
	You determine when, where, how and with whom you communicate.
Thematic	Centred on a set of consistent themes. Three subprinciples: repetition, repetition, repetition.
Topical	Focused on the here and now.
Access	Ultimate responsibility lies with senior management. Be available, be straight and don't lie. Never say 'no comment' and remember there is no such thing as 'off the record'.

Plan

The design and implementation of your Strategic Communication Plan should aim to:

- Support and advance the strategic goals of your university. What are the key messages you want to get across?
- Reach and address the concerns of all key audiences. Who are your key audiences?
- Coordinate communications in all areas:

Media relations	Are you able to clearly communicate your message to the media? Do you need media training? Do your staff know what to do if approached by the media?
Public relations	Do you clearly define who you are and where you are going in your communications? Do your audiences understand you? How do you

	know? Are you working to build a relationship with the people you really want to talk to?
Internal communications	Do you effectively communicate your message to internal audiences, in a way they take on board? How do you know?
Crisis communications (see also next section, p. 346)	Do you have a plan for worst-case scenarios? Do you have an appointed spokesperson with an emergency call-out list?
Editorial	Are you clearly communicating who you are in written communications?
Issue management	Are you prepared for the predictable issues? Do you have arrangements in place for the unpredictable?
Advertising	Do you consistently define who and what you are and your goals in your advertisements?

Source: adapted from Cabinet Office, 2001.

Develop your own positioning statement

At its simplest, and also its best, effective strategic communication is about creating a clear, honest and positive message about your university, or your department, which is reflected in all your dealings with internal and external audiences. Getting this right is critical in making a positive impact on the way in which you are regarded and understood both internally and externally. And for this reason many universities now have professional marketers, a trend which in itself has caused much disquiet in the sector. Even so, we should not blame the marketers, when it is the responsibility of senior managers to take the lead.

Many universities' initial attempts at sector positioning attracted criticism (and rightly so) because they were too often introspective, self-referential and undistinguished (see Box 10.7). We also know that so-called Unique Selling Points 'are rarely such; there are in fact only six of them and everybody claims to have four!' (Watson, 2007a). This does not mean we should simply give up. What you can do (with or without the help of marketing expertise) is develop your own positioning statement for your department.

What is distinctive, if not unique, about your department? What are the six 'killer facts' about your department?

Imagine the government minister is arriving to deliver a guest lecture, or to officially open one of your new buildings. You have literally one minute to brief the minister about your department. What three key messages would you get across?

Follow the steps in Box 10.8 and draw up a positioning statement for your department. It is the series of propositions you develop here which will provide you with the necessary foundations on which to build and enhance your reputation. You will also be able to use them to inform your institutional marketing strategy, and brand development perhaps, in a more meaningful way than hitherto.

Box 10.7 University positioning statements

Common pitfalls Desirable traits

Overly traditional
- interchangeable statements
- lack of differentiation
- 'tick box' purpose: we have to have one

Break the mould
- we aim to do what it says on the tin
- 'this is what we live and breathe'

Wallpaper effect
- i.e. research, quality, etc.

What you see is what you get
- 'we know where we're going'
- 'we mean what we say . . . look: here's the evidence in all that we do'

Arrogant and bureaucratic, not character or personality

Aspiration and inspiration
- 'journey with us', 'we will help you fulfil your dreams'
- 'know us by our attitude'

'We're the best, so there!'
- navel inspection: peer measurement

Stand up and be counted
- proud and confident, assertive

Little identity with clients and partners
- it's all about 'me, me, ME'

There's a bigger world out there
- 'we are part of it and know our role in it'

'We're in it for US'
- 'this is about our successes and aspirations, not yours'
- 'don't expect us to meet you half way! (we're much too busy)'

'We're in it for you, you, YOU'
- 'our measure of success is your success; being able to better serve you'
- 'we will be the catalyst for your fulfilment'

Counterproductive to marketing effort: useless as a marketing tool

Natural marketing source material

Source: adapted from Stamp (2002).

Box 10.8 Developing a positioning statement for your department

A positioning statement is not a marketing strategy nor is it brand development. It can, though, inform both these processes.*

1	Strategic intent	What vision do you have for your department?
2	Objectives	Why do you do what you do? What courses and services do you offer?
3	Market definition	Who are you seeking to attract and why? (Students, researchers, funders, etc.)
4	Guiding principles	What are the (genuinely shared) core values of your department?
5	Distinctive competencies	What attributes do you have that others do not?

6 Competitive positioning	What is distinctive about what you do or how you do it? What would be missed if you did not exist?
7 Added value	What do you really contribute to the greater good? How have you helped others to succeed? What do others say about you?

Note *Marketing is about getting the right goods and services to the right people at the right place at the right price with the right communication and promotion.

Conventionally, a brand is a product or service made distinctive by its positioning relative to the competition and by its personality (both functional and symbolic). Latterly it is typically characterized as being imbued with emotion.

Source: adapted from Stamp, 2002.

Managing in a crisis

> If I said there are 1,001 things we could plan for, I would probably be under-estimating it.
> Emergency planning officer, University of Birmingham, April 2008

The single biggest risk to your reputation is, of course, during a time of crisis. Instances which can arise from any number of sources – from fire, flood and flu pandemic, through data and structural collapse and electricity blackouts, to terrorist bombings, and tragic incidents such as the shooting sprees which resulted in the death of 33 people, including the gunman, at Virginia Tech in April 2007 (the deadliest such rampage in American history), and six people, again including the gunman, at Northern Illinois University in February 2008.

Crisis response is increasingly de rigueur in higher education, as reflected in the recruitment surge of a new breed of university personnel in recent years – the business continuity manager and the emergency planning officer (Stothart, 2008). Most institutions have developed their own crisis management plans, typically based on a risk or threat assessment, with the response centred on a dedicated major incident management team. Essential and reassuring as these innovations have been, it is just not possible to plan for every single conceivable contingency – in part because they are so numerous and in part because we do not know them all. Nor can we always anticipate every eventuality even when we think we've planned exhaustively for them. The collapse and shutdown of the mobile telephone network in London, for instance, during the terrorist incidents of July 2005, created major unanticipated problems for institutional teams grappling to ensure the safety and security of their students and staff.

Equally, crises are rarely fixed and static – they typically evolve, unfold and take on 'a life of their own'. Nor can we forget, as one troubleshooting expert has reminded us, that 'while bombs, fires and floods may capture the headlines, almost 90 per cent of crises are quiet catastrophes and it is the quiet catastrophes that have the potential to damage your organization's most valuable asset – its brand and reputation' (Gill, 2008b). What, then, can you plan with any certainty? How can we seek to respond effectively in a crisis? First, we need to ensure the basic elementary steps are in place.

Be clear what constitutes a major incident for your university

Not so straightforward as you might think, since crises that seem minimal can grow. A major incident is typically regarded as being an unplanned, adverse event requiring an institution-wide response to manage it, that:

- has a major impact on students, staff, visitors, the public, the environment and/or the buildings within and around the university;
- affects significant numbers of staff, students, members of the public or the environment;
- affects the operational capability of the university in a material way.

Regularly test the plans you have developed to deal with the major threats you've identified to your university

Your risk assessment will have revealed the major threats which have guided your planning efforts in seeking to offset them. These plans of course are just that – a theoretical modus operandi. They should be tested on an annual basis to learn, develop and improve upon them: initially, as a dry-run desk test exercise, but more importantly also through a 'live' emergency case scenario.

Ensure there is clarity in the roles and responsibilities of the major incident team members – and these are known and understood

All else stems from the initial lead taken by the major incident team. There are several initial critical tasks that the team leader must undertake: determining if there is indeed a major incident; confirming the location of the command centre; establishing a line of communication; appointing a single liaison contact to the emergency services and so on. Confidence from the training and the planning will help with unfamiliarity in this regard.

Also critical is the reaffirmation of team member roles and the requirement that individuals understand and stick to them. Major incident teams – and their 'shadow team' if members of the original team are unavailable at the time of the emergency – typically include individual leaders responsible for logistics, health and safety, communications, buildings, telephony, IT, security, student welfare, staff welfare and legal aspects, as well as an extended network of local leaders in buildings across campus.

Prepare to meet the communications challenge

While you may not be able to plan for every contingency there is always one aspect which is a guaranteed constant in all major incident: it will be a formidable media communications challenge. You can though think and plan ahead in this regard too:

- by remembering to cover the basics (when, what, where, who) and sticking to them on your crisis fact sheet on the incident (see Box 10.9);
- by establishing a communications framework, starting as you mean to go on, with your very first media statement (see Box 10.10);

Box 10.9 Your crisis fact sheet

Spokesperson: 'The facts I can give you at this point are as follows:

Try to cover: 1
When
What
Where
Who   2
Our response

                    3

                    4

                    5

Spokesperson: That's all I can give you at present, but for an update please call

_____

on _____as we would like to keep you

informed.'

Journalist: 'But surely you can tell me . . . . ?'

Spokesperson: 'Sorry, that's all I can give you right now, but we will be issuing updates. I have to go now as there's a lot happening at this end, as I'm sure you can imagine.'

Source: adapted from Cabinet Office, 2001.

- by preparing and practising for interviews with the media through a formal media training programme (see Boxes 10.11 and 10.12);
- by ensuring all your communications are customized to your target audience: namely, they are always NICE: i.e. they meet the Needs, Interests, Concerns and Expectations of the groups and individuals you have identified as having a major interest in the incident;
- by practising with your team in a 'live scenario', on how to 'get your message across' effectively, during a crisis (see Figure 10.6).

Box 10.10 Crisis management: your first contact

DO include the media in your notification process to the relevant authorities.

DON'T fail to inform your local reporters especially.

DO prepare a simple factual statement and issue nothing else.

DON'T rush this process – take time to gather the basic facts.

DO make this statement with source and time widely available – internally as well as externally.

DON'T allow it to go altered or amended, unless you replace it with an update.

DO designate an employee to read out your statement on the phone when reporters ring in.

DON'T frustrate reporters by wasting time with one persistent caller.

DO clarify rules of access to the place and person/s involved.

DON'T allow access to anyone or any location, unless you have prepared carefully.

DO offer to provide an update, and name a time and contact person.

DON'T give in to pressures for more information until you are quite ready.

DO ensure an internal news black-out.

DON'T allow casual communication with the outside world – control it, or it will control you.

Source: adapted from Cabinet Office, 2001.

Box 10.11 Preparing for interviews with the media

DO politely ask the reporter his/her name and which media organization he/she represents.

DON'T start any interview blind – take the initiative from the first moment.

DO ask why the reporter wants to speak to you in particular and the background to the interview.

DON'T agree to give an interview until you are satisfied that you are fully prepared to go through with it.

DO ask for time to find out facts and gather information.

DON'T guess. Always buy time to inform yourself.

DO check how long the interview will last and where it will take place.

DON'T overrun the allotted time and watch for background 'fouls'.

DO try to find out who else is giving interviews on this subject.

DON'T walk into a trap unaware.

DO seek to correct any wrong facts or obvious misunderstandings.

DON'T let misleading information go unchallenged.

DO ask for clarification about the specific area of questioning.

DON'T take part in vague or generalized questioning.

DO remind the reporter about your credentials and area of expertise.

DON'T speak on behalf of others unless authorized to do so.

Source: adapted from Cabinet Office, 2001.

Box 10.12 Handling interviews with the media

DO anticipate the start of the interview with the right body posture and eye-line.

DON'T readjust your position or clear your throat during the interview.

DO listen carefully to the questions and look for the loaded ones.

DON'T allow incorrect statements in the introduction or questions to go

DO use the first question as a springboard for your message, starting with a headline.

DON'T wait to get started with your message – get to the facts fast.

DO complete your sentences and answers, even when interrupted.

DON'T allow the interviewer to break new ground until you are ready.

DO keep the audience in mind at all times and offer examples relevant to them.

DON'T get locked into scoring points off the interviewer.

DO establish the issue before the interviewer does.

DON'T let the interview gain the moral high ground ahead of you.

DO state your decision/proposal/solution/idea before it's too late.

DON'T risk losing the chance to offer your position statement.

DO watch for closing signals and stand by to summarize.

DON'T end on a negative point – prepare your positive finish and stress benefits.

Source: adapted from Cabinet Office, 2001.

Mastering the communications challenge does not mean, of course, that you will have managed the emergency (that will depend on how effectively you implement your crisis management plan also). It will ensure, however, that you've secured the public 'front end' of the incident and with it every possibility of restoring your reputation.

HEADLINE It's all about . . .

○

BACKGROUND The facts are . . . . .

B

○
○
○
○

NEGATIVE SCENARIO If nothing is done . . . .

•
•
•

ISSUE Our shared goal . . . .

I

➤

DECISION The best way to reach it is . . . . . .

Action Plan

D

○
○
○
○

BENEFITS This will make a difference because . . . .

✓
✓
✓
Bonus   ✓

ACTION AGENDA who does what . . . . . .

➤   ➤

Figure 10.6 Crisis management: getting your message across – the BID grid system

Source: adapted from Cabinet Office, 2001.

11 Managing yourself

Let he who would change the world first change himself.

Socrates

I know that the only way to live my life is to try to do what is right, to take the long view, to give of my best in all that the day brings and to put my trust in God.

Queen Elizabeth II, 25 December 2002

To succeed as a leader and manager you must master, as we have seen, a whole variety of different skills and competencies. There is one remaining skill, however, we have yet to consider; one that completes the full complement, and that is, of course, how you manage yourself. This again is a skill, like many others, that is too often taken for granted. As it seems self-evident, many managers tend to overlook it or consciously disregard it in practice: i.e. they either under-use the ability or sacrifice it in the face of (apparently) more pressing concerns. This again is a grave error. For it can harm them both ways, on the one hand by inflicting ill-health on themselves, and on the other by damaging their credibility in the eyes of their staff. The point is: you cannot expect to make a good job of managing other people and situations unless, and until, you can effectively manage yourself.

This ability to self-manage – to keep on learning – is in fact one of the distinctive hallmarks that characterize strong leadership (Eglin, 2003). It is though not nearly so straightforward to master and the evidence suggests that many managers have considerable difficulty in doing so (Quinn *et al.*, 2007). The incessant demands, the competing priorities, the information overload and the degree of expectation in the environment in which we operate, all make it harder than ever; and the inward journey of self-exploration and realization can be an uncomfortable and possibly a painful one too. Even so you owe it to yourself, as well as to others and to your institution, not to shirk or neglect this responsibility. On the contrary, you should indeed be diligent and purposeful in fulfilling it. How, though, can and should you organize yourself – be yourself, look after yourself, and develop yourself? This last chapter seeks to explain just that.

Organizing yourself

> Are the least effective managers the ones who look like they are doing the most?
>
> (Bruch and Ghoshal, 2002)

Many managers in academia as elsewhere are often frenetically busy. Their diaries 'wall-to-wall' with meetings, they dash hither and thither, ubiquitous Blackberry in hand, constantly checking their email, making countless phone calls, dispatching memos and extinguishing fire after fire. It certainly looks impressive. Unfortunately, the sad truth (often acknowledged, if unspoken) is that most of this activity for much of the time achieves very little. Indeed Bruch and Ghoshal (2002) found in their decade-long study of 'busy managers' that fully 90 per cent of them squandered their time in all sorts of ineffective activities: namely, they may have thought 'they were attending to pressing matters' (grappling with strategic issues, focusing on cost savings, devising creative approaches to new markets, etc.) but 'they were really just spinning their wheels' in an unproductive way. Only a 10 per cent minority – the 'purposeful action-takers' – spent their time in a committed, purposeful and reflective manner. The difference between the two groups was that the latter managed to combine two particular traits – *energy* and *focus* – in a far more effective way than the other three categories which made up the 90 per cent majority (see Figure 11.1).

- Forty per cent 'distracted managers': highly motivated and full of energy, they switch from one activity to the next at a rapid rate. They are not driven, however, by any strategic imperative and as such are unable to lead others.
- Thirty per cent 'procrastinators': those managers who can't even get started. Experience has taught them that whatever they do they won't make any difference to anything. They are unable to motivate others.

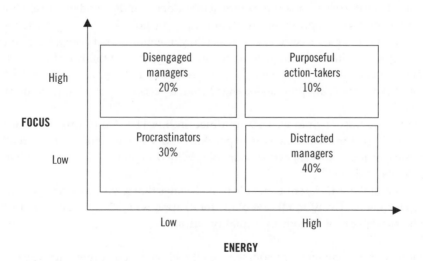

Figure 11.1 The 'busy manager syndrome': managerial behaviours

Source: adapted from Bruch and Ghoshal, 2002.

- Twenty per cent 'disengaged': focused but not driven or excited by what they do, they lack the energy to deal with problems or drive things through.

How can you avoid being a victim of this 'busy manager' syndrome? What can you do to ensure you are a 'purposeful action-taker'?

- Do not confuse being active with being productive. Do not be so absorbed with routine tasks and fire-fighting that you have little time or energy for issues that require reflection, systematic planning or creative thinking.
- Do not blame your institutional environment. Do not spend your time on making the inevitable happen. Focus your energy and your willpower on what you're paid to do – making happen what otherwise won't happen.
- Do not be constrained by extraneous factors – your manager, your peers, your job role. Do not be swayed by those around you even if they look busy and sound busy. Instead decide *first* what it is you must achieve and then manage your way through those around you.

Put positively:

- Stave off the instinctive feeling that you must look busy, no matter how powerful it may seem. Make an appointment with yourself for thinking and develop your own personal strategic plan. Identify 3–4 priorities – *the things that would really make a difference to your department* (e.g. developing an e-learning infrastructure for your courses; establishing a work-based learning programme with local employers; hosting a learning and teaching conference; leading a partnership bid for regional or European funding, etc. Let these be a guide to your actions and your planning over the term, semester and year ahead.
- Set up a seven-day time log and record how you currently use your time. This does not have to be the time-consuming chore it may appear and provided you are honest with yourself can also prove self-revelatory. Simply note down how you spent the hours in a day over a one-week period: teaching, meeting, supervising, telephoning, emailing, socializing, reflecting, etc. Compare how you used this time in proportion to the priorities you set yourself. How does it 'fit'? Is there consistency in your actions? What areas are you neglecting? What aspects can you change to improve matters?
- Consider the 'top 21 time-wasters' outlined in Box 11.1. Go through the list and identify those time wasters you experience. To what extent are they really a necessary or inevitable aspect of your role? Why do you tolerate them? What can you do about them?
- Never forget that the Pareto Principle (which states that significant items of a given group form a relatively small part of the total) applies and 20 per cent of your time produces 80 per cent of your best-quality output.

Enrol on a time management course. We all feel we've been there already. And it is the case that, simply put, time management involves addressing three basic elements: clarifying goals, forward planning and making effective use of time at the time (Maitland,

Box 11.1 The top 21 time-wasters

1. Constant interruptions – telephone or other
2. Indecision
3. Meetings – too long or not really necessary
4. Switching priorities
5. Lack of objectives, priorities or daily plan
6. Personal disorganization
7. Cluttered desk or work area
8. Ineffective delegation
9. Shuffling paperwork
10. Limited access to required equipment or materials
11. Trying to find or track down people
12. Attempting too much – inability to say 'No'
13. 'Butterflying' from job to job, leaving tasks unfinished
14. Inadequate, inaccurate, delayed information or communication
15. Unnecessary socializing
16. Office procedures not clearly established
17. Confused line of responsibility or authority, or the need to get decisions approved
18. Constant checking up on others and their work
19. Plunging into a task without planning
20. Lack of self-discipline
21. Exhaustion!

Source: Industrial Society survey cited in Warren and Toll, 1996.

1995). Nevertheless we should not be so grand that we think we know everything there is to know. There is often something new to pick up, that little extra that could make a difference (Adair and Thomas, 2008).

Pay particular attention to those primary activities that could make all the difference to the way you operate and how effective you may be:

- *Delegation* – Never do a task that someone else can do. Do not let guilt, fear or pride keep you from delegating (see Chapter 6).
- *Meetings* – Challenge the value of all meetings that do not have a clear, useful purpose. A good chair will review the effectiveness of their meetings on a periodic basis (see Chapter 4). Prompt them lest they forget. Alternatively, propose that you use your internal institutional auditors to conduct an independent review to improve the effectiveness of meetings. Always ask the Chair to cancel meetings if there is no substantial business.
- *Brainstorming* – Best done on your own in your own way or in an activity forum specially designed for that express purpose. Ignore the hype and avoid conventional brainstorming group sessions. They never work (Allan *et al.*, 1999). Often dominated by one or two strong personalities (while the others struggle to think in the babble going on around them), such 'free-wheeling, blue-sky' sessions at best typically recycle old ideas and at worst constitute so much 'social loafing': i.e. high-profile activity of the most menial (and wasteful) kind (Furnham, 2002).

- *Handling paperwork* – Process it as soon as you can. If you've let it build up, then set some time aside for a stress-busting blitz. Label four empty filing trays – Deal With; Distribute; Read; File – and arm yourself with sufficient recycling bin bags for the most important category, the Discard pile. *Handle each piece of paper once only*. Don't read it. Skim it and determine what to do with it. Don't use your desk as a filing space – use project folders or 'bring forward' files for work in progress. And don't transfer piles of paper on your desk to piles of paper in other parts of the office.

- *Handling electronic data and emails* – The principles are no different to that of handling paperwork. You need a simple and logical grouping of material arranged in folders, sub-folders and file names. Likewise with correspondence. The message may be instant but your reply need not be. Judge each case on the basis of its merits, not that of 'net-etiquette'. Discipline yourself to checking your email twice a day and no more.

- *Prioritizing tasks* – Distinguish between what is *important* and what is urgent. Prioritizing activities ensures you are not just involved in routine maintenance tasks; that you are proactive, not simply reactive. If you have several items of urgency and importance, do the hardest one first. Do the most important items during that portion of the day when you perform best and the most trivial when your energy levels are lowest.

- *Working with an assistant* – Establish regular one-to-one 'business meetings' every other week. Review your diary with them on a weekly basis. Have them filter your post and phone calls. Don't dump on them. Delegate interesting and responsible work, not simply the mundane. Keep them informed.

Being yourself

> Be not another's, if thou canst be thyself.
>
> Paracelsus (Swiss physician)

The importance of understanding your own values and behaviours – of knowing yourself, valuing yourself and being yourself – is self-evident. If you don't understand yourself and accept yourself it is nearly impossible to understand and accept others. Many managers often find this genuinely difficult, however, while others shy away from it altogether. Either way, their impact on those around them is, as we noted in Chapter 4, often one of the last things they ever learn about themselves.

Much of this apathy, difficulty or resistance is often related to the amount of experience and proficiency that managers have in their role and in particular to the way in which they respond to feedback. One of the main problems about receiving feedback of course – and why we instinctively shy away from it – is that we may not like what we get. Negative information is never particularly pleasant and we often resort to all kinds of strategies to deflect it, including denial ('It's not true'); flight ('I've got another meeting to go to'); rationalization ('I can explain that . . .'); shifting the blame ('That was because somebody else . . .') or attacking the source ('He's an idiot anyway') (Pedler *et al.*, 2006).

To be effective as a manager, however, you must strive to overcome this natural inclination. For the key to overcoming defensiveness in others – to help them learn, to build up trust with them, to better understand them – is, as Socrates reminds us, by *confronting the defensiveness within ourselves first*. Put simply, if you are a role model of sensitivity, openness and learning then you will more than likely cultivate the spread of these same qualities in those around you. It is also the case that if you don't really understand yourself then you will not develop and grow in your role as you should, or realize your latent potential (Quinn *et al.*, 2007).

How then can you be less defensive? How can you understand yourself better, value yourself, be yourself?

Recognize the true scope and flexibility for change in your relationships with those around you

We all have different aspects which we choose to 'open' or 'hide' from view, as well as 'blind spots' which others see and we do not. Likewise we all have aspects that lie 'unknown' both to ourselves and to those around us (as in the Johari Window depicted in Figure 11.2). The size of these quadrants is not fixed. In relationships they will of course change with the passage of time. You can, however, exercise more direct influence through your willingness to, on the one hand, explore your current lack of self-awareness in areas 2 and 4, and on the other reveal more of yourself to those around you; or, put another way, by directing your energy, skills and resources into increasing quadrant 1 at the expense of 2, 3 and 4.

Remember that in any given situation we never see things as they are, only as we are

We always have a choice – to change the situation; to change ourselves; leave the situation; or decide to live with the situation.

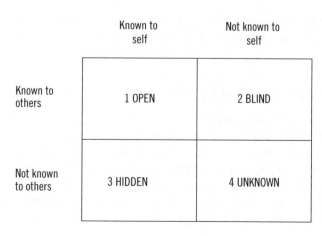

'Your values, motives and behaviours ...'

	Known to self	Not known to self
Known to others	1 OPEN	2 BLIND
Not known to others	3 HIDDEN	4 UNKNOWN

Figure 11.2 The Johari Window

Note: named after the originators, Joe Lufts and Harry Ingham.

Use personal self-reflection: a 'backwards review'

Start a personal journal: a review of critical incidents describing what happened, who was involved and what they did. What did you *want* to say or do? What did you *actually* say and do? On reflection, how do you feel about it now? What have you learned? What are you going to do about it?

Remember that our 'concept of self' is neither fixed nor permanent

It may have been conditioned by powerful external influences (parents, family, school and neighbourhood) in the past but need not be so in the future. Our self-concept is made up of three critical parts: our self-ideal (the person we would most like to be); our self-image (or inner mirror of how we see ourselves and think about ourselves); and our self-esteem (how we feel about ourselves). All three are malleable and can be built up, not so as to create a super-inflated ego (though of course that can and does happen) but rather in nurturing a wholesome self-respect or positive self-image. Put another way, low self-esteem does not have to be a lifetime condition, or the realization of our self-ideal an elusive goal (Turner, 2002).

Recognize how conditioned beliefs can prevent you from managing yourself

These typically manifest themselves in a number of ways, as:

- major debilitating devices: e.g. negative thinking; irrational fear and worry; pro-crastination; complacency; our past mistakes and failures; the conditioned negative attitudes (the 'No syndrome') inherited from childhood ('I'm just no good with maps');
- unrealistic expectations with which to beat yourself up; e.g. 'I must be perfect in everything I do'; 'I must have the love and approval of others at all times'; 'I have a right to rely on others to give me what I want';
- self-fulfilling prophecies: e.g. 'my background, childhood and past must continue to determine my feelings and behaviour' (aka 'Died at 20, buried at 70');
- irrational assumptions, for example: 'Unhappiness is externally controlled'.

Whatever their source, their effect is much the same – to deny us true self-management. Can you identify any of your own conditioned beliefs that may be holding you back from managing yourself?

Seek to overcome your conditioned beliefs, thinking and behaviour

Cultivate your higher self (your inner friend), not your lower self (your inner enemy). This is much easier said than done of course. At its most sophisticated this involves contemplation, visualization and activating your super-conscious often – as in the case of sports players – with the help of a coach. You, too, may wish to consider this option. It is not as fanciful as it may seem. Indeed a half-day at a recognized assessment centre is – as many have discovered – a small investment for the rewards it may bring. Alternatively you can access the wealth of self-development literature on this subject which offers advice on everything from drawing up action plans for 30-day mental diets to practical tips on using the Affirmation method ('Yes, I can do this . . .') (Turner, 2002; Pedler *et al.*, 2006).

Develop your own personal mission statement

Not, that is, a missionary tract but rather an expression of what you want to be, your purpose in life, your values; an anchor, in other words, that you can use as a source of guidance in your professional life. Again this can be a very demanding task. It involves going back to first principles – your basic beliefs about people, work, family, religion, politics, life and death – and teasing out and questioning your 'taken-for-granted' assumptions. The process will force you to articulate and define your personal 'sense of mission'. And the statement will add meaning to what you do, explain what you do and be a source of comfort in good times and bad.

Elicit feedback through formal self-assessment instruments

The Myers-Briggs (Personality) Type Indicator (1977; Quenk, 1999) will provide you with insight on the deeply held ways – Extrovert or Introvert; Senser or Intuitive; Thinker or Feeler; Judger or Perceiver – in which you prefer to work, as well as offering a character profile for your particular category: ENTJ, ISTP, INFP, ESFJ, etc. The Thomas-Kilmann Conflict Mode Instrument (2002) will enable you to assess the particular style – Competing, Accommodating, Avoiding, Collaborating and Compromising – you have learned (and can modify) in handling workplace conflict (see Figure 11.3).

Test your own perceptions against those of others through 360-degree feedback

The Visionary Leader Behavior Questionnaire (Sashkin, 1995) is a well-established formal instrument which will give you 'contextual feedback' on your leadership behaviour, your leadership characteristics and your effect on your institution as a leader.

Undertake a formal psychological assessment

A half-day exploration of your inner psyche (your childhood experiences, family relationships and so on) with a reputable clinical psychologist may seem daunting but it can also yield considerable benefits. It will provide you with insight on your emotional well-being (your capacity for intimacy and independence) and how you react to pressure as well as identifying your strengths (your degree of intuition, creativity and envisioning, your mastery of logic, fact and detail, etc.). You can also compare the findings with the outcomes of the formal self-assessment tools you use above.

Respond to feedback in a constructive way

Don't dodge it in the ways outlined above. If you feel the criticism is justified then listen, ask for details, seek to clarify and understand, ask for examples and try to establish a way forward. If you feel the criticism is unjustified – do not ignore it or dismiss it. You still

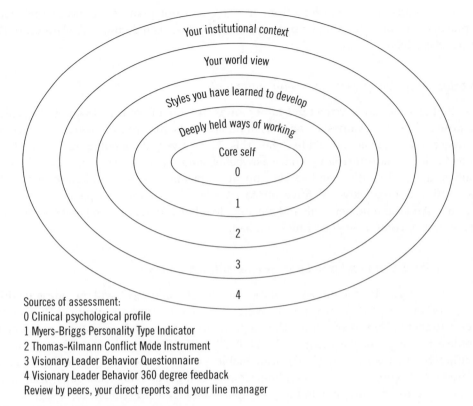

Sources of assessment:
0 Clinical psychological profile
1 Myers-Briggs Personality Type Indicator
2 Thomas-Kilmann Conflict Mode Instrument
3 Visionary Leader Behavior Questionnaire
4 Visionary Leader Behavior 360 degree feedback
Review by peers, your direct reports and your line manager

Figure 11.3 Understanding yourself

need to build and maintain a useful relationship with the person who made it and they must have some reason for making it. Try and establish the source. Is it past history – a case of bad timing – or a legitimate difference of view? If you receive positive feedback, then don't put yourself down by trivializing it ('You're only saying that to be kind'); don't be seduced by your own brilliance either, otherwise you will remain blind to other aspects of yourself; learn to accept it with good grace ('Yes, I was pleased with the way that went').

Looking after yourself

> If you don't control pressure, then pressure will control you.
>> Terry Venables, football coach

> Well, there's work–life balance and then there's work . . .
>> Female Vice Chancellor, UK 'new' university

Rarely a day goes by without one report or another reminding us that stress is the most prevalent health problem of our ever faster-moving world, that we do not do nearly enough to balance work with life and that children are showing increasing signs of the stress-related illnesses that affect their parents. All very true of course – and not surprising. We live in a world in which our personal and private space is more cramped than ever, where the journey to work can be as stressful as work itself, where the noise levels are three times greater than they were in 1970 – a decibel hell that no doubt has Thomas Carlyle spinning in his grave – and where new technology ensures we can not only communicate but are also accessible on a 24/7 basis. Not only that. We often work in environments which encourage – if not celebrate – Stakhanovism as a virtue; those, that is, who work very long hours, regularly go without sleep and rarely take up their full leave entitlement. All of which begs the question: how well do you manage to look after yourself? Or, put another way, what can you do to manage the (apparent) contradiction between sustaining high performance in your role on the one hand, while maintaining a healthy work–life balance on the other?

Appreciate the nature of stress

Stress is particular to each individual and can be good as well as bad. In essence, stress is the response we make to the (perceived) relationship between the demands made upon us and our ability to cope. As such, it varies from individual to individual in circumstances which one – a competitive Type A person, for example – might find stressful and another (more sanguine Type B person) may not. Generalizations are therefore difficult, though it is apparent that we do benefit from 'stress' so long as we perceive it to be healthy. Problems arise when we experience 'over-stress' (see Figure 11.4). We also need to remember that many people do love their jobs and don't regard work as a chore.

If, on the other hand, you do have feelings of resentment, this may be because you are in a role which you don't enjoy, but with commitments that mean you can't quit. Then remember that – as we noted above – you still have options: to change the situation, to change yourself or decide to put up with it. The best way forward very often is to start by reassessing your priorities and changing your attitude and approach to your work (Barez-Brown, 2008; *Change the World*, 2006; Warren and Toll, 1996).

Figure 11.4 The stress curve

Source: adapted from Kelly, 1998; Warren and Toll, 1996.

Learn to recognize the symptoms of stress and how they may apply to you

Stress can affect us in many ways and to varying degrees: from sore eyes (minor) to migraine (major) to ulcers (last chance) and in the worst circumstances 'burn-out' and even death (see Box 11.2). Consider, then, the circumstances when you feel under pressure

---

Box 11.2 What does stress do to us?

Stage 1 – Minor
- Frequent infections/colds
- Sore eyes
- Overreaction to situations
- Speeding up, talking too fast, walking too fast
- Overeating and drinking
- Sweating
- Making more errors than usual
- Absent-mindedness/forgetfulness

Stage 2 – Major
- Emotional outbursts
- Extreme irritability
- Dyspepsia and gastric symptoms
- Heartburn
- Constipation
- Tension headaches
- Aching muscles
- Migraine
- Insomnia
- Loss of energy
- Comfort tricks: smoking/drugs/drinking
- Anxiety/depression
- Clumsiness

Stage 3 – Last chance
- Cottonwool head
- Ulcers
- Palpitations
- Chest pains
- Cardiac symptoms/incidents
- Extreme depression/anxiety
- Exhaustion

Stage 4 – Too late
- Burnout *
- Physical or mental breakdown
- Death

* Burnout can be defined as 'a state of physical, emotional and mental exhaustion marked by chronic fatigue, feelings of helplessness and hopelessness, and the development of a negative self-concept and negative attitudes towards work, life and other people'.

Source: based on Miller *et al.*, 1994; Peiffer, 2005.

or experience a stressful event; notice where in your body you feel the effects. Do these correlate with any of the symptoms listed in Box 11.2? Begin to identify precisely what situations make you feel like this. Talk it over with your doctor if appropriate.

You should also reflect on the fact that while 'burn-out' and recovery from it are not unusual (some even manage to survive a second bout), it is not a condition that you will recover from professionally (and probably as not physically) should you experience it a third time (Kakabadse, 2001).

Assess and monitor your stress fitness level and your work–life balance

Complete the questionnaire in Box 11.3 to assess how vulnerable you are to stress and how it manifests itself in your life. What do you need to do to improve your level of stress fitness?

Box 11.3 How vulnerable are you to stress?

Mark against each of these statements:

F – Frequently
O – occasionally
N – Never

- I manage the time I spend on the different parts of my life satisfactorily ____
- I meet people with whom I can talk ____
- I have at least one close friend in whom I can confide ____
- I am able to express my feelings ____
- I give and receive affection ____
- I keep a check on tensions in my body and have ways of reducing them ____
- I make sure I do something that relaxes me after a stressful time
- I take a quiet time for myself at least once a day ____
- I laugh and have fun ____
- I walk, rather than drive or ride, whenever possible ____
- I use the stairs rather than a lift when practicable ____
- I take reasonably energetic exercise at least twice a week ____
- I choose TV or radio programmes, or books or magazines that interest me ____
- I have an absorbing interest or hobby apart from work ____
- I am clear about my sense of values and what is important in my life ____
- I am the appropriate weight for my age, height and build ____
- I eat at least one balanced meal a day ____
- I limit my drinks of tea, coffee, chocolate and cola to three or less a day ____
- I keep within the recommended limits for alcohol of 21 units (men) or 14 units (women), spread over a week ____
- I give myself treats ____

Now see how many Fs, Os and Ns you have: 17 or more Fs and Os, then you are probably pretty stress fit; 5 Ns or more suggest you have an increasing vulnerability to stress and need to take action to turn them into Os or Fs.

Source: adapted from Warren and Toll, 1996.

Figure 11.5
Balancing your
'nine lives'

Family	Work	Leisure
Partner	Personal development	Financial
Home	Health	Friends

In the case of Figure 11.5 take each one of your 'nine lives' in turn and grade them on a scale of 1–10 on the basis of (a) quality (1–poor; 10–good) and (b) time spent (1–little; 10–a lot). What does your profile tell you? Where are you doing well – less well? What are your areas of neglect? What is the relationship between the time spent and the quality outcome? What can you do to strike a more even balance?

Repeat these two activities on a three-monthly basis to monitor your progress.

Think of stress fitness in a positive, not a negative, way

Think of it as a way of improving your well-being (from within), not of overcoming 'a problem' (from without). Sustained high performance is not simply about managing stress. It is about physical and emotional strength as well as brainpower. It is about aligning mind, body and spirit together in such a way as to achieve peak condition. The 'High-Performance Pyramid' illustrated in Figure 11.6 is a mirror-image of Maslow's hierarchy of needs. Consider the condition of your needs. Identify the ones you must nurture (Barez-Brown, 2008; *Change the World*, 2006; Loehr and Schwartz, 2001).

Figure 11.6
The High-
Performance Pyramid

Source: adapted from
Loehr and Schwartz, 2001

Draw up your own personal stress fitness action plan

Just as the media regularly remind us about the prevalence of stress, so too are we inundated with advice on how to tackle it – from quick fixes on 'how to be happy', 'how to detox', to lifestyle planning and exercise regimes, and to object lessons in full-blown therapy. The difficulty is not that there is a choice, but that there is so much it can seem disabling, even contradictory. That said, these various schemata tend to be built around a number of key organizing principles (the need for exercise, relaxation and so on). These are just some practical 'tips' you may want to consider in drawing up your action plan:

- Always accept 100 per cent responsibility for how you feel. You may not be responsible for all that goes on around you but you can always control your reaction to it.
- Learn to develop positive thinking techniques.
- Do regular physical exercise: cycling, swimming, running or gym work. Two 30-minute cardio-vascular workouts a week will keep you ticking over. Three will increase your fitness levels. Charles Dickens chose to walk 20 miles a day as a means of staving off manic depression.
- Learn to use muscle relaxation techniques.
- Develop a more balanced diet. Avoid processed foods and drink 1.5 litres of water a day.
- Practice the 3Rs: rest, reflection and renewal. Take regular 'time-outs' as well as time off. Stakhanovism is a vice. Those who achieve a good balance between work and leisure have more energy and more commitment to their job.
- Build in treats as a reward for hard work or to sustain you in hard times.
- Find someone you can really talk to, your 'speaking partner'.
- Join a peer support group.
- Learn to listen to the person who knows you best . . . you!
- Do unto others as you would have them do unto you.
- Increase your spirituality through study, meditation, fasting or prayer.
- Go regularly to places that renew you.
- Avoid moaners.
- Put yourself in situations where people are having fun. Management is a serious business but you don't have to be po-faced about it all the time.
- Do all those healthy things you know you ought to do.

Developing yourself

> The life which is unexamined is not worth living.
>
> Socrates

> The end of all our exploring will be to arrive where we started and know the place for the first time.
>
> T.S. Eliot

> If you stop learning, you're dead.
>
> Kirk Douglas, at 92

HE management is held in low esteem not only within the sector, but outside it too. 'Bogus professionalism' is the pejorative term most commonly used by Whitehall departments – in private, if not in public – to describe the way in which universities are led and managed: a criticism that is not without foundation and has more credence in this area – of self-development – than perhaps in any other aspect of the HE manager's role – an outcome, ironically, for which we only have ourselves to blame. Put another way, the strong commitment to – and practice of – continuous professional development (CPD) that is characteristic of so many professional groups has until recently been conspicuous by its relative absence within HE. The point is: CPD should not be, nor should you consider it, a matter of optionality. It is no less than a lifetime obligation and responsibility. You cannot expect staff to do it if you do not practise it yourself. Nor can you expect to create, as we discussed in Chapter 6, an authentic learning climate within your department. More than that, however, CPD is primarily about *you* – about 'doing your best', aspiring to 'be the best', not being complacent, working on improvement, being curious, etc. It is in essence the key to your professional growth and fulfilment. As such, it is an activity you can embrace positively rather than negatively as a forced expectation. Indeed, it is an opportunity for you to relish, not spurn. How then can you make the most of it? What can and should you do to develop yourself?

Conduct a self-assessment of your learning needs

You should by now – if you completed the self-assessment tools earlier in this book – have built up a reasonably clear picture of your own profile as a manager. If not, then consider again Boxes 3.7, 3.8, 4.2, 4.21 and 10.1 in particular, along with any feedback you received. Remember to bear in mind, too, that you should determine your skill needs in terms of three broad areas:

- personal skills, e.g. creativity, problem-solving, decision-making;
- skills involving other people, e.g. communication, negotiation, team-work;
- skills involving things, e.g. new learning technology, IT equipment.

With this in view, reflect on your role and draw up your needs analysis based on a consideration of:

- your levels of personal and professional satisfaction. Write down three major sources of satisfaction, and three of dissatisfaction, in terms of dealing with people and managing activities in each of the following: your job, your career and your life;
- your perception of your degree of 'fit' with your role. Complete the dartboard questionnaire illustrated in Figure 11.7;
- your perception of your needs against a common template. The Competing Values Framework developed by Quinn *et al.* (2007) integrates four contrasting models of management – human relations (collaboration), open systems (creation), internal processes (control) and rational goals (competition) – and identifies the eight specific (and *prima facie* conflicting) roles that every manager must ultimately master if they are to be wholly effective in their post: innovator, broker, producer, director, monitor, coordinator, facilitator and mentor (see Figure 11.8). Each role has three

Figure 11.7
How well do you fit your role?

I understand the university's overall objectives and how I fit in

I have relationships of openness and of trust with my line manager and my team

I am clear about the things which people value and believe are important

I feel motivated to do my job properly and help the university to succeed

I have the skills and experience needed to make sound judgements and do my job

I am certain about my personal limits of authority

I know what rules do matter in the university

I have reliable information about my department's performance

0	On target
1	Nearly there
2	Some way off
3	Long way off

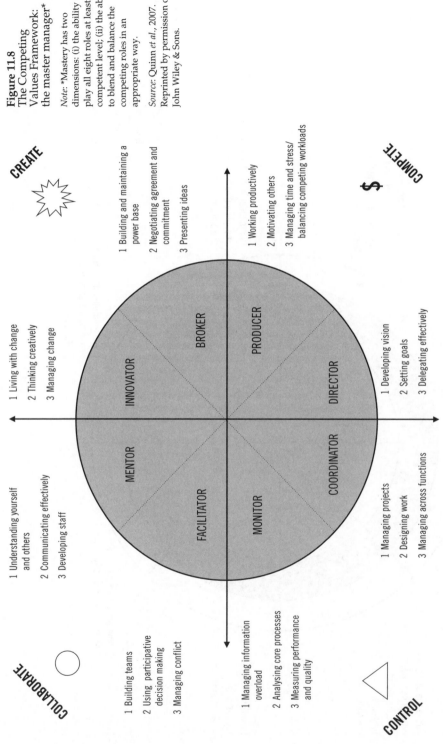

Figure 11.8
The Competing
Values Framework:
the master manager*

Note: *Mastery has two
dimensions: (i) the ability to
play all eight roles at least at a
competent level; (ii) the ability
to blend and balance the
competing roles in an
appropriate way.

Source: Quinn *et al.*, 2007.
Reprinted by permission of
John Wiley & Sons.

CREATE

COMPETE

$

COLLABORATE

CONTROL

1 Living with change
2 Thinking creatively
3 Managing change

1 Understanding yourself
 and others
2 Communicating effectively
3 Developing staff

1 Building teams
2 Using participative
 decision making
3 Managing conflict

1 Managing information
 overload
2 Analysing core processes
3 Measuring performance
 and quality

1 Building and maintaining a
 power base
2 Negotiating agreement and
 commitment
3 Presenting ideas

1 Working productively
2 Motivating others
3 Managing time and stress/
 balancing competing workloads

1 Developing vision
2 Setting goals
3 Delegating effectively

1 Managing projects
2 Designing work
3 Managing across functions

INNOVATOR

BROKER

PRODUCER

DIRECTOR

COORDINATOR

MONITOR

FACILITATOR

MENTOR

competences, thus making 24. Take each of the eight roles in turn and consider: what do I know about myself in this role? How could I play this role more effectively? Which of the 24 competences do I really need to work on?

Identify your developmental stage as a manager

Management is no different to any other activity in that it is a learning process. With appropriate knowledge and experience, as well as skill and ability, there is no reason why we cannot master it. On the other hand, it is not that easy either. Where are you on the road to mastery?

- The novice stage, following rules and procedures;
- the advanced beginner, who has worked out the unwritten rules as well (the norms, conventions and accepted practices in your role);
- the competent, thinking independently for yourself;
- the proficient, who has learned to unconsciously 'read' evolving situations;
- the expert, doing what comes naturally, as if having a 'sixth sense'.

Use the models developed by Pedler *et al.* (2006) and Quinn *et al.* (2007) to determine your stage of development. What do you think of it? How do you feel about it? What can you do to start to move into the next one?

Diagnose your natural learning style and seek to strengthen your ability in others

We all learn in a combination of (four) different ways, as activists, reflectors, theorists and pragmatists. This, in turn, has implications for the kinds of activities and situations that suit – or do not suit – our development as learners. Use the learning style questionnaire developed by Honey and Mumford (2000, 2006) to determine your own personal preference for learning. Consider how you can take advantage of learning opportunities that dovetail with your style. Equally, reflect on how you can build up your learning strength, by developing those learning styles for which you do not currently have a strong preference.

Remember to consider the full range of potential learning opportunities open to you

Opportunities may be planned as well as unplanned, 'within the job' as well as 'away from the job' (see Chapter 6). Some unwittingly restrict the scope of their opportunities – and hence their prospects for development – by making artificial distinctions between these four areas. Make sure you do not fall into the same trap. Try to think of learning as a seamless activity running through all aspects of your life (Forrest, 1995).

Develop your own personal strategic action plan

In Chapter 3 we discussed how you could establish a strategic plan for your department. You can, and should in fact, use and apply the same principles with regard to your professional development: namely, what is your vision – your personal dream? What are your aims, capabilities (resources) and opportunities? Are they aligned with one another? Where are you now? What will help you get to where you are going? What do you have to do today?

Keep a learning log

Underrated, and underused, personal journals of this nature are, as many of the professional bodies now recognize, a powerful means of sustaining professional development. At their simplest, such logs provide a record of your answers to three basic questions: What did you do? What did you learn from it? How might you use this now and in the future? Completing the answers not only helps you to review your experiences and to monitor your progress, but you will also find it disciplines you to search out and take learning opportunities – as well as providing a source of comfort and ideas you can draw on in difficult situations.

And finally – *make a pact with yourself*. Commit to becoming a master manager.

Role map analysis of a principal lecturer in a UK (post-1992) 'new' university

Role definition	Job purpose: why do I exist?
Principal Lecturer	• To take a major responsibility for quality and innovation in teaching and learning within a faculty and for ensuring the continuing academic and professional development of faculty colleagues • To take a leading role in learning and teaching innovation • To act as a role model and mentor for colleagues • To make a major contribution to academic quality in the faculty by providing continuing academic leadership on a subject and ensuring the ongoing development of students, colleagues and the curriculum in that area • To contribute to enriching the learning experience of students within a faculty • To lead on the development of specified, high-quality modules/programmes which understand and meet students' needs • To ensure that these modules/programmes meet the university's commitment to equality through development of the curriculum and by diversifying the range of students • To support colleagues in the delivery of modules/programmes by actively seeking to incorporate student evaluation as part of their continuing improvement

Core responsibility to head of department for	How success is measured (the standard of performance)	Skills, styles and qualities needed (the requisite competencies – the 'how')
Students Key competences (the 'what') • Contribute to enriching the learning experience of students in the faculty • Encourage and enable colleagues and students to develop modules/programmes which identify and meet students' needs • Contribute to the personal tutorial and pastoral care systems of support for students • Encourage and enable students to participate in the work of the faculty	• Students' evaluation of their learning experience is positive and their objectives are achieved • Students' views and opinions are actively sought in the development of new modules / programmes and tutorial/support systems • Faculty committees, task groups, etc., have active student membership or representation	• Ability to encourage and motivate students and to create a culture in which they feel empowered to express views • Ability to resolve issues of concern for students and to achieve conflict resolution
Teaching and learning Key competences (the 'what') • Act as a role model for educational innovation through one's own approach to teaching and learning and utilization of a wide range of techniques and methods, including resource-based learning • Identify internal and external good practice and innovation in teaching and learning strategies; share and promote this within the faculty • Act as a facilitator, mentor and support for colleagues in their professional development as teachers • Utilize and experiment with a variety of self,	• Recognition through the quality management process, including student evaluation • Regular communication, including workshops/seminars, takes place • On-going professional development activities and one-to-one support are offered to colleagues • Recognition through the quality management process • Curriculum content reflects current thinking and developments in the subject area • Curriculum delivery reflects current developments in teaching and learning	• Interest in teaching and learning; willingness and ability to use and experiment with a variety of teaching and learning approaches and methods • Ability to disseminate information and knowledge in an enthusiastic and non-patronizing way to stimulate curiosity • Ability to motivate, coach and support; knowledge of individual learning styles and development needs • Knowledge of assessment and evaluation theory and methods; ability to respond constructively to evaluation

strategies

- Communication, presentation and interpersonal skills
- Ability to be proactive and to manage projects

peer and student assessment and evaluation methods, including resource-based learning
- Communicate effectively one's own subject knowledge and updating to colleagues and students and make a major contribution to curriculum development across the faculty and the university
- Lead on and promote special initiatives in teaching and learning in the faculty and ensure resulting good practice is embedded in the curriculum

Staff
Key competences (the 'what')
- Provide support, advice and guidance to one or more specified subject groups/ programme teams in the delivery of high-quality modules/programmes
- Have a responsibility within the faculty for delivering the university's commitment to equality in all aspects of the recruitment and development of teaching staff

- Members of subject groups/programme teams feel valued and supported and have full access to information and guidance
- The teaching/staffing profile and participation in staff development activities reflect the university's commitment to equality

- Ability to offer advice and guidance in constructive and supportive ways
- Demonstrate a clear commitment to equality and the ability to act as role model in carrying out equal opportunities good practice

Programmes and quality management
Key competences (the 'what')
- Provide proactive, continuing, academic leadership in a subject area and make a major contribution to raising the standards of academic quality in the faculty
- Encourage and enable students and

- Recognition through the quality management process
- Effective and open processes of evaluation are in operation, participated in and acted upon
- The appropriateness of modules/programmes

- Demonstrate a strong commitment to one's own on-going academic development and updating
- Understanding of quality issues, processes and management

Core responsibility to head of department for	How success is measured (the standard of performance)	Skills, styles and qualities needed (the requisite competencies – the 'how')
colleagues to participate in a range of monitoring and evaluation activities to assess the effectiveness and appropriateness of module/programme delivery • Lead on and promote the development of modules/programmes which encourage wider participation and which meet students' needs • Actively promote and meet the university's commitment to equality as integral to the content and curriculum development of modules/programmes	for existing and potential students' needs is regularly evaluated • The extent to which equality issues are explored in the curriculum is regularly evaluated	• Knowledge of needs of existing students and under-represented student groups and a strong commitment to increasing access • Persuading and motivating skills; ability to ensure open debate on equality issues and to take action on negative feedback
Communication Key competences (the 'what') • Make a major contribution to effective communication for students and colleagues in the Faculty • Contribute to and participate in lateral communication across the University	• Information, views and ideas are communicated proactively, openly and consistently • Regular meetings and communication take place with colleagues in other faculties and in university-wide services	• Ability to use effectively a range of communication styles and methods and to encourage people, their ideas and views • Ability to communicate and share ideas in an open, supportive and non-confrontational atmosphere
Strategy and policy formulation Key competence (the 'what') • Contribute to the development of strategies to realize the university's mission and the	• Teaching and learning strategies are developed which inform and are influenced	• Knowledge of the aims and objectives of the faculty and the university and how

faculty's aims and objectives

Additional responsibilities
- A Principal Lecturer would be expected to take on one or more of the following accountabilities during his/her teaching career in the university

Subject quality group coordination
Key competences ('the what')
- Coordinate the activities of a Subject Group within the faculty and be responsible to HoD for its work
- Ensure the effectiveness of the quality management process in module delivery and Subject Group operation and be responsible to the HoD for the assurance of quality management
- Coordinate resources for a subject group

Programme leadership and direction
Key competences ('the what')
- Lead and direct one or more major programme teams within the faculty and be responsible to the programme manager (PM) for their work
- Ensure recruitment and admissions procedures and practices in specified

by the faculty's plans and which help to realize the university's mission

- Achievement of agreed objectives and targets for the subject group
- Recognition through the quality management process of the effectiveness of the subject group operation
- Continuous improvement in the efficient and effective use of resources

- Achievement of agreed objectives and targets for the programme team
- The programme(s) profile broadens and diversifies; equality issues and monitoring are an integral part of all procedures and practices

these relate to teaching and learning strategies; ability to contribute to policy formulation and strategic planning

- Persuading, motivating and negotiating skills
- Strong commitment to quality and excellence; ability to respond to perceptions of quality and to implement and monitor change
- Ability to match resources to needs; ability to predict and identify shortfall and duplication

- Persuading, motivating and negotiating skills
- Ability to develop a common understanding among admissions staff of the meaning and importance of quality and social justice

Core responsibility to head of department for	How success is measured (the standard of performance)	Skills, styles and qualities needed (the requisite competencies – the 'how')
programmes are in accordance with academic board and faculty policy • Ensure the effectiveness of the quality management process in specified programme delivery and programme team(s) operation and be responsible to the PM for the assurance of quality management • Coordinate resources for one or more specified programme teams, including the resources for the provision of personal tutorial and pastoral care systems for students	• Recognition through the quality management process of the effectiveness of programme team(s) operation • Continuous improvement in the efficient and effective use of resources	• Strong commitment to quality and excellence; ability to respond to perceptions of quality and to implement and monitor change • Ability to match resources to needs; ability to predict and identify shortfall and duplication

Research and scholarly activity
Key competences (the 'what')
All teaching staff are required to engage in a programme of self-management scholarly activity for which they will be accountable on an annual basis to their head of department

However, it is recognized that a Principal Lecturer might wish to make a particular contribution to research and scholarly activity in a faculty in the following ways:

Core responsibility to head of department for	How success is measured (the standard of performance)	Skills, styles and qualities needed (the requisite competencies – the 'how')
• Lead and coordinate a research group, including securing research funding	• Achievement of agreed objectives and targets for the Research Group including	• Persuading, motivating and negotiating skills

- Help to create a research environment in the faculty by encouraging and supporting colleagues to engage in research activities
- Make a major contribution to the research profile of the faculty through personal research activities and publications
- Coordinate staff development activities in research methodology and skills
- Develop and promote resource-based learning

increase in research funding
- The number of staff engaged in research activities increases
- Increase in research papers and publications; research profile of faculty rises and is externally recognized
- Increase in workshops, seminars, guidelines, etc.
- Use of resource-based learning materials and techniques increases across the faculty

- Ability to identify, generate and repeat a variety of sources of funding; ability to optimize research opportunities
- Ability to act as coach, mentor and facilitator; ability to motivate and encourage
- Ability to self-motivate and to meet deadlines; commitment to achieving recognition for the faculty as well as for personal academic achievement
- Ability to disseminate information and knowledge in a non-patronizing and empowering way
- Strong commitment to and belief in benefits of resource-based learning

External relations

Key competence (the 'what')

- Contribute to the establishment, development and monitoring of strategic alliances and partnerships with other education and training providers
- Contribute to the development of the external reputation and profile of the faculty
- Contribute to the increase of sources of income for the faculty, including specially funded projects

- Wider and increased participation in programmes at or with the university
- Increase in applications by students and staff wishing to join the faculty
- Increase in faculty representation on external forums and bodies
- Sources of income increase and diversify

- Demonstrate a commitment to widening access and to meeting the needs of the university's partners
- Ability to promote the faculty marketing, liaison and networking skills
- Ability to identify, generate and repeat a variety of sources of income; ability to optimize opportunities

Annual evaluation of department contributions

Annual evaluation of department contributions to institution-building at Arizona State University

Relevance	Status	Grade
PR, of primary relevance	EX, exemplary	A Excellent
SR, of secondary relevance	AVG, typical; average	B Good
NR, not relevant	MIN, absent or minimal	C Fair
		D Unsatisfactory
		E Failing

	Relevance	Status	Grade

I Creating a quality learning environment

A Special classes being offered

  1   Writing intensive
  2   Time flexible (jumbo, stretch)
  3   Honors
  4   New student seminars
  5   Enhancements (lab; reading; recitation; discussion sections; field trips)
  6   Broadened perspective (integrative; capstone; inter-, cross-, and multi-disciplinary; senior seminar)
  7   Enrolment limited
  8   Faculty taught
  9   Undergraduate research experience
  10 Innovative instruction (collaborative learning; critical inquiry; learning cycle; technological enhancement)

	Relevance	*Status*	*Grade*

B   Special facilities/support
1   Mediated learning labs/classrooms
2   Tutors/advisers (hours extended)
3   Modern equipment/adequate stations
4   Colloquia, symposia series
5   Audio/visual support
6   Class scheduled in appropriate facilities

C   Special efforts at enrichment/recognition
1   Honors societies, majors clubs
2   Organized study groups
3   Student awards
4   Development of 'involvement profiles' (job résumé)
5   Junior fellows program
6   Conference paper presentation support

D   Attracting student talent
1   Scholarship support
2   Recruitment activities
3   Campus visits
4   Student preparation for awards competition
5   Co-enrolment of majors in the honors programme

E   Department climate (attentiveness/sensitivity to students)
1   Faculty/student diversity
2   Protected classes mentoring/networks
3   Undergraduate printed guidebook
4   Senior reception
5   Program of study workshops
6   Student interviews (entry, 87 hours, exit)
7   Brown bag lunch discussion groups
8   Social events for all

F   Efforts at continuous improvement
1   TA training/evaluation/mentoring
2   Graduate training attentive to future requirements
    of the professoriate
3   Faculty development
4   Unit development (retreats)

II Building/sustaining nationally prominent programs
A   Encourage and support faculty research/ creative activity
1   External funding
2   Publication
3   Invited presentation
4   Editing/reviewing

	Relevance	*Status*	*Grade*

5 Clusters of strength
6 Collaborate with faculty in other disciplines
7 Career development grants
8 Support of interdisciplinary activities
9 Collaboration with industrial partners/national labs

10 Access to special facilities (e.g. NASA's Space Telescope), collections, archives, etc.

B Provide leadership for the discipline
1 Hold office in the national professional organization
2 Service as program director, section head in federal agencies
3 Serve on panels, boards, accreditation bodies
4 Host/organize conferences and workshops
5 House national/international journals

C Build graduate student quality
1 Graduate student recruitment visits
2 Graduate entry scores of enrolled students
3 PhD, teaching assistants placement
4 Graduate school admission of undergraduate majors
5 Appropriateness of teaching assistant workload
6 Competitive stipends

III Serving the broader institution
A Full and effective use of resources
1 Space and facilities appropriately utilized
2 Faculty time and effort directed and distributed appropriately
3 Staff utilization optimized to work to be accomplished
4 Resourcefulness in handling instructional replacement (due to the unavailability of faculty because of leaves, unfilled positions, understaffing, etc.)

B Responsiveness to institutional needs
1 Offer courses responsive to demand
2 Income generation (protection of the funding base)
3 Provide coursework to support general studies
4 Summer bridge offerings
5 Use of faculty in undergraduate, lower-division courses

		Relevance	*Status*	*Grade*

    6   Support interdisciplinary instruction

    7   Provide quality advising

    8   Support university-wide student recruitment/ career days

C Unit culture

    1   Depth of concern for, loyalty to the university

    2   Service on committees at all levels

    3   Good communication between Chair and faculty

    4   Appropriate levels of consultation/shared governance

    5   Effective internal problem solving mechanisms

D Active outreach

    1   Service on state boards/councils

    2   Sponsorship of external events

    3   Workshops for public school teachers

    4   Campus events for high school students (science fair)

    5   Hosting community college personnel, high school counselors

    6   Participation in faculty ambassador's program

    7   Operation of clinics, labs, museums, galleries

    8   Programs for disadvantaged

    9   Participation in state and local organization

    10   Hosting campus tours

    11   Participation in alumni events

    12   School demonstrations

    13   Radio, television programming

    14   Telefund groups

    15   Friends groups

    16   Newsletters

APPENDIX

3

Staff self-assessment survey

The self-assessment survey is reproduced from R. Harrison (2000) *Employee Development*, pp. 538–41. It is reprinted with the permission of the publisher, the Chartered Institute of Personnel and Development, London (www.cipd.co.uk).

Staff retain Sections 1 and 2 and return Section 3 to you.

Section 1: assessment

Current work performance

(i) Professional knowledge of present job

A   _____   Inadequate

          _____   Tendency to A

          _____   Tendency to B

B   _____   Thorough knowledge of job

(ii) Quantity of work (speed and consistency) in producing required results

A   _____   Fair

          _____   Tendency to A

          _____   Tendency to B

B   _____   Usually high output

(iii) Quality of work (extent to which results meet requirement)

A   _____   Passable

          _____   Tendency to A

          _____   Tendency to B

B   _____   High quality

(iv) Attitude towards job

A   _____   Passable

          _____   Tendency to A

| | Tendency to B |
| B | High quality |

(v) Judgement and analytical ability
Extent to which decisions or actions based on a sound appraisal of the situation and reached by logical reasoning

A	Conclusions sometimes inaccurate
	Tendency to A
	Tendency to B
B	Sound judgement

Personal characteristics in relation to the job

(i) Personality and acceptability

A	Impact and effect on others not always favourable
	Tendency to A
	Tendency to B
B	Makes a very good impression

(ii) Ability to communicate
(a) Verbal (at meetings, discussions, interviews)

A	Verbal communication not always effective
	Tendency to A
	Tendency to B
B	High standard of presentation

(b) Written (reports, memoranda, letters)

A	Limited, basic writing skills
	Tendency to A
	Tendency to B
B	Writes very well

(iii) Mental, alertness and initiative
Initiative, grasp of new ideas, with problem-solving, etc.

A	Tends to follow precedent
	Tendency to A
	Tendency to B
B	Constructive and creative thinker

Section 2: diagnosis

Assessment of learning needs/objectives for continuous development

Learning needs
(tick as appropriate)

Rate your ability in:

	High	Low	
Assessing other people's capabilities			❏
Decision-making			❏
Delegating			❏
Giving instructions			❏
Problem-solving			❏
Judgement			❏
Leadership/initiative			❏
Listening			❏
Planning			❏
Public speaking			❏
Running meetings			❏
Self-discipline			❏
Selling ideas			❏
Thinking/creativity			❏
Understanding other people			❏
Use of time			❏

Section 3: action

Department staff development programme

You can, of course, address your particular learning needs in a number of (informal) ways and in a variety of settings (both at work and outside the workplace).

In order that the department may help you fulfil your learning needs, I would be grateful if, in this particular instance, you would complete the questions below and return this sheet (and this sheet only, not pages 1–2) to your head of department.

1   Please identify (up to) 3 staff development activities that you would like the department to organize and be willing to participate in (e.g. chairing meetings, dealing with people; team-building, minute taking; IT training; self-appraisal; handling discrimination, delivering (better) lectures; writing a PhD, getting published, maximizing research, etc.):

(i) _____

(ii) _____

(iii) _____

2   In what ways would you prefer these activities were provided: via (please rank in order of preference: 1, 2, 3 . . .)

_____ Resource pack	_____ Task group (focus)
_____ Practical demonstrations	_____ Informal, ad hoc

_____	Seminars (Teach-each-other events)	_____	Any of the above
_____	Formal lectures	_____	Other (please specify)
_____	Workshops		

3 When would you prefer these activities were organized? (please tick as appropriate)

_____	Beginning of academic year	_____	Half-day
_____	Inter-semester	_____	Full-day
_____	End of academic year	_____	One-hour-sessions
_____	Year round	_____	Early morning
_____	Other (please specify)	_____	Lunch-time
		_____	Late afternoon
		_____	Evening
		_____	Weekend
		_____	Other (please specify)

Signed (optional) _____ Date _____

Source: CIPD Assessment cited in Harrison, 2000.

References

1994 Group (2007) *Enhancing the Student Experience*, Policy Statement and Report (November).

ACAS (Advisory, Conciliation and Arbitration Service) (2008a) *Employee Appraisal*, London.

ACAS (2008b) *Discipline and Grievances at Work*, London.

ACAS (2008c) *Redundancy Handling*, London.

Adair, J. (1983) *Effective Leadership*, Pan Books, London.

Adair, J. and Thomas, N. (2008) *The Best of Adair on Leadership and Management*, Thorogood Publishing, London.

Alanbrooke, Lord (2001) *War Diaries, 1939–1945: Field Marshal Lord Alanbrooke*, Weidenfeld and Nicolson, London.

Albury, D. (1997) *The Future and Management of Higher Education*, Office of Public Management, London.

Alderman, G. (1999) 'Innocence amid TVU slaughter', *Times Higher Education Supplement (THES)*, July 23.

Alexander, M. (2001) 'Strategy and strategic process: from theory to reality', *Top Management Programme 61*, Cabinet Office, London, unpublished paper.

Alimo-Metcalfe, B. and Alban-Metcalfe, J. (2002) 'The great and the good', *People Management*, 10 January: 18–22.

Allaire, Y. and Firsirotu, M.E. (1984) 'Theories of organizational culture', *Organization Studies* 5 (3): 193–226.

Allan, D., Kingdon, M., Murrin, K. and Rudkin, D. (1999) *How to Start a Creative Revolution at Work*, Capstone, London.

Argyris, C. (1999) *On Organizational Learning*, 2nd edn, Wiley Blackwell Press, London.

Argyris, C. (2008) *Teaching Smart People How to Learn*, Harvard Business School Press, Cambridge, MA.

Argyris, C. and Schon, D. (1978) *Organizational Learning: A theory-in-action perspective*, Addison-Wesley, Reading, MA.

Argyris, C. and Schon, D. (1996) *Organizational Learning II: Theory, Method and Practice*, Addison-Wesley, Reading, MA.

Armstrong, M. (2000) *Strategic Human Resource Management: A guide to action*, 2nd edn, Kogan Page, London.

Armstrong, M. (2001) 'Changing the culture: rewarding and developing staff in higher education', Improving Performance Management in Higher Education Conference, 22 October, Capita, London.

Armstrong, M. (2006a) *Strategic Human Resource Management: A guide to action*, 3rd edn, Kogan Page, London.

Armstrong, M. (2006b) *Human Resource Management Practice*, 10th edn, Kogan Page, London.

Armstrong, M. and Baron, A. (1998) *Performance Management: The new realities*, The Institute of Personnel and Development, London.

Arthur, M. (2008) 'Increasing the talent pool from 2010: 14–19 diplomas and higher education', University of Leeds, 11 November, unpublished paper.

Athena Guide (2003) *Athena Guide to Good Practice, 1999–2002*, The Athena Project 22, Equality Challenge Unit, London.

Athena Swan: Charter for Women in Science (2008) *Annual Report*, ECU, London.

Attwood, R. (2008) 'A measured relationship', *Times Higher Education (THE)*, 10 April.

Babbidge, H.D. and Rosenzweig, R. (1962) *The Federal Interest in Higher Education*, McGraw-Hill, New York.

Baer, M., Hellman, D.A., Porter, R. and Watson, M. (1998) 'Creating a new home for faculty: implementing departmental planning', Northeastern University, Boston, MA.

Barez-Brown, C. (2008) *How to Have Kick-Ass Ideas: Shake up your business, shake up your life*, Skyhorse Publishing, New York.

Bargh, C., Bocock, J., Scott, P. and Smith, D. (2000) *University Leadership: The role of the chief executive*, Society for Research into Higher Education (SRHE) and Open University Press (OUP), Buckingham.

Barnett, R. (1990) *The Idea of Higher Education*, SRHE and OUP, Buckingham.

Barnett, R. (2000) 'The University is dead, long live the University', *THES*, 11 February.

Barrow, S. and Davenport, J. (2002) 'The employer brand', People in Business, London, unpublished paper.

Barzun, J. and Graff, H.F. (2003) *The Modern Researcher*, 6th edn, Harcourt Brace Jovanovich, London.

Bass, B.M. (1985) *Leadership and Performance Beyond Expectations*, Free Press, New York.

Baty, P. (2001) 'Cambridge debacle may lead to inquiry', *THES*, 9 November.

Baty, P. (2006) 'Part-timers merit equality', *THE*, 2 June.

Becher, T. (2001) *Academic Tribes and Territories: Intellectual enquiry and the cultures of disciplines*, 2nd edn, SRHE and OUP, Buckingham.

Beckhard, R. (1992) 'A model for the executive management of transformational change' in G. Salaman (ed.) *Human Resource Strategies*, Sage, London.

Bekhradnia, B. (2007) 'In praise of the quite good', *Academy Exchange*, issue 7 (Winter), Higher Education Academy (HEA), York.

Belbin, R.M. (2003) *Management Teams: Why they succeed or fail*, 2nd edn, Butterworth-Heinemann, London.

Belbin, R.M. (2008) *The Belbin Guide to Succeeding at Work*, Belbin Associates, London.

Bell, D. (1966) *The Reforming of General Education: The Columbia College experience in the national setting*, Columbia University Press, New York.

Bennis, W. and Nanaus, B. (1985) *Leaders: The strategies for taking charge*, Harper and Row, New York.

Benson, L. and Harkavy, I. (2000) *The Role of Community in Higher Education – School partnerships in educational and societal development and democratization*. Paper commissioned by the Joint Educational Trust, Philadelphia.

Bett, M. (1999) *Independent Review of Higher Education Pay and Conditions* ('The Bett Report'), Stationery Office Agencies, London.

Bhattacharyya, G. (2000) 'Feelgood is no good', *THES*, 31 March.

Blackmore, P. and Blackwell, R. (2004) 'How can staff development become strategic?', *In Practice*, Issue 3, LFHE, London.

Blake, R.R. and McCanse, A.A. (1991) *Leadership Dilemmas: Grid solutions*, Butterworth- Heinemann, Oxford.

Blanchard, K. and Johnson, S. (2000) *One Minute Manager*, Harper Collins, London.

Bloom, A. (1988) *The Closing of the American Mind*, Simon and Schuster, New York.

Bolden, R., Petrov, G. and Gosling, J. (2008) *Developing Collective Leadership in Higher Education*, LFHE, London.

Bolton, G. and Lucas, C. (2008) *What Are Universities for?*, League of European Research Universities (LERU), Leuven, Belgium.

Boutall, T. (1997) *The Good Manager's Guide*, Butterworth Heinemann, London.

Boxall, P. and Purcell, J. (2002) *Strategy and Human Resource Management*, Palgrave Macmillan, Basingstoke, Hants.

Boyer, E.L. (1990) *Scholarship Reconsidered: Priorities of the professoriate*, Carnegie Foundation for the Advancement of Teaching, Princeton University Press, Princeton, NJ.

Brew, A. (ed.) (1995) *Directions in Staff Development*, SRHE and OUP, Buckingham.

Bridges, W. (1991) *Managing Transitions: Making the most of change*, Addison-Wesley, Reading, MA.

Bridges, W. and Mitchell, S. (2000) 'Leading transition: a new model for change', *Leader to Leader*, No. 16 (Spring): 26–94.

Brodie, I. (2001) 'Great leaders were grumpy', *The Times*, 1 September.

Brown, H. and Sommerlad, E. (1992) 'Staff development in higher education – towards the learning organization?', *Higher Education Quarterly* 46: 174–190.

Brown, J.S. and Duguid, P. (1996) 'Space for the chattering classes', *THES*, 10 May.

Brown, M. (2004) 'The EFQM European excellence model as a tool in university leadership', *In Practice*, issue 2 (November), The Leadership Foundation for Higher Education (LFHE), London.

Bruch, H. and Ghoshal, S. (2002) 'Beware the busy manager', *Harvard Business Review*, February: 5–11.

Bryman, A. (2007) *Effective Leadership in Higher Education*, LFHE, London.

Buckingham, M. and Coffman, C. (2001) *First, Break All the Rules: What the world's greatest managers do differently*, Simon and Schuster, London.

Bundred, S. (2009) 'Our public debt is hitting Armageddon levels', *The Times*, 27 February.

Burgan, M. (2004) 'Why governance? Why now?' in W.G. Tierney (ed.) *Competing Conceptions of Academic Governance*, The Johns Hopkins University Press, Baltimore, MD.

Burgoyne, J. (2001) 'Tester of faith', *People Management*, 22 February: 32–34.

Burns, J.M. (1978) *Leadership*, Harper and Row, New York.

Butcher, D. and Atkinson, S. (1999) 'Upwardly mobilized', *People Management*, 14 January: 28–33.

Cabinet Office (2001) 'Strategic communication in practice', *Top Management Programme 61*, London, unpublished paper.

Cameron, K.S. and Quinn, R.E. (2006) *Diagnosing and Changing Organizational Culture*, revised edn, Jossey-Bass, San Francisco, CA.

Candy, P.C. (1998) 'Disciplinary discourses, departmental differences and distributed development', University of Ballarat, Victoria, unpublished paper.

Cemmell, J.B. and Bekhradnia, B. (2008) *The Bologna Process and the UK's International Student Market*. HEPI (Higher Education Policy Institute) Report, Oxford.

Chait, R.P., Holland, T.P. and Taylor, B.E. (1991) *The Effective Board of Trustees*, American Council on Education, Oryx Press, Phoenix, AZ.

Chait, R.P., Holland, T.P. and Taylor, B.E. (1996) *Improving the Performance of Governing Boards*, American Council on Education, Oryx Press, Phoenix, AZ.

Change the World 9 to 5 (2006) Short Books, London.

CIPD (Chartered Institute of Personnel and Development) (2002) *The Guide to Work Life Balance*, CIPD, London.

CIPD (2008) *Research Report: Managing diversity and the business case*, CIPD, Wimbledon.

Churchill, W. (1996) *Memoirs of the Second World War*, Houghton Mifflin, Boston, MA.

Clark, B.R. (1983) *The Higher Education System: Academic organization in cross-national perspective*, University of California Press, Berkeley, CA.

Clark, B.R. (1998) *Creating Entrepreneurial Universities: Organizational pathways of transformation*, IAU Press, Pergamon, Oxford.

Clark, B.R. (2004) *Sustaining Change in Universities: Continuities in case studies and concepts*, SRHE and OUP, Maidenhead, Berks.

Coaldrake, P. and Stedman, L. (1998) *On the Brink: Australia's universities confronting their future*, University of Queensland Press, St Lucia, Queensland.

Cohen, D. (1998) 'Universities to the power of 21', *Guardian*, 27 July.

Cohen, M. (2000) 'Poisonous exercises: a dartboard and a map could do better than the RAE', *THES*, 22–29 December.

Cohen, M.D and March, J.G. (1986) *Leadership and Ambiguity: The American College President*, 2nd edn, Harvard Business School, Boston, MA.

Covey, S.R. (1989) *The Seven Habits of Highly Effective People*, Simon and Schuster, London and New York.

Covey, S.R. (2004) *The 8th Habit: From effectiveness to greatness*, Simon and Schuster, London and New York.

CRE (Commission for Racial Equality) (2000) *Strengthening the Race Relations Act*, CRE, London.

CUC (Committee of University Chairs) (2009) *Guide for Members of Higher Education Governing Bodies in the UK*, HEFCE, Bristol.

CUCO (Commission on University Career Opportunity) (1997) *Guidelines on Recruitment, Selection and Promotion for Universities and Colleges in Higher Education*, CVCP, London.

Cunningham, V. (2000) 'Fine mess we're in', *THES*, 13 October.

CVCP (Committee of Vice Chancellors and Principals) (2000) *The Business of Borderless Education: UK perspectives*, London.

Daniel, J.S. (1996) *Mega-Universities and Knowledge Media: Technology strategies for higher education*, Kogan Page, London.

Daniel, J.S. (1998) 'Open as to places: an academic community on which the sun never sets', SRHE Annual Conference, University of Lancaster.

Dann, J. (2001) *Test Your Emotional Intelligence*, Hodder Arnold, London.

Dann, J. (2008) *Emotional Intelligence*, Hodder Education, London.

Davis, A. (2009) 'Funds slashed at research colleges', *London Evening Standard*, 5 March.

Deal, T.E. and Kennedy, A.A. (1982) *Corporate Cultures: The rites and rituals of corporate life*, Addison-Wesley, Reading, MA.

de Alva, J.K. (2002) 'The for-profit university', UUK Conference, The Future of Higher Education: Profits, Partnership and the Public Good, 14 June.

Dearing Report: National Committee of Inquiry into Higher Education (1997) *Higher Education in the Learning Society: Summary report*, HMSO, London.

De Nisi, A.S. (2000) *Human Resource Management*, Houghton Mifflin College, Wilmington, MA.

DfEE (Department for Education and Employment) (2000) *Changing Patterns in a Changing World: Work-life balance*, London.

DRC (Disability Rights Commission) (2002) *The Disability Discrimination Act: A senior manager's guide*, London.

Drucker, P. (1974) *Management: Tasks, responsibilities, practices*, Heinemann, London.

Drucker, P. (1993) *Post-Capitalist Society*, Harper, New York.

Duderstadt, J.J. (2004) 'Governing the twenty-first-century university: a view from the bridge' in W.G. Tierney (ed.) *Competing Conceptions of Academic Governance*, The Johns Hopkins University Press, Baltimore, MD.

Duke, C. (1992) *The Learning University: Towards a new paradigm?*, SRHE and OUP, Buckingham.

Durham, H. (1998) 'Building a learning organization: assessing faculty quality of life', Appalachian State University, Boon, NC.

Durham, H., Claxton, C. and Butts, J. (1998) *Building a Learning Organisation: Assessing faculty quality of life*, Appalachian State University, Boon, NC.

Earwaker, J. (1991) 'Boo to the barbarians', *THES*, 29 March.

Eastwood, D. (2008) 'High drop-out rate? Hardly. We have an excellent record', *Guardian*, 26 February.

ECU (Equality Challenge Unit) (2002) *First Annual Report*, London.

ECU (2004) *Employing People in Higher Education*, London.

ECU (2008) *Briefing: The Equality Bill – Impact on Higher Education* (June), London.

ECU (2009) *Flexible Working: Ensuring success*, London.

Egan, G. (1995) 'A clear path to peak performance', *People Management*, 18 May: 34–37.

Eglin, R. (2003) 'Give the young turks a helping hand to the top', *Sunday Times*, 30 March.

Ehrenberg, R.G. (ed.) (2004) *Governing Academia: Who is in charge at the modern university?*, Cornell University Press, Ithaca, NY.

Elton, L. and Partington, P. (1993) *Teaching Standards and Excellence in Higher Education: Developing a culture for quality*, 2nd edn, CVCP, London.

Erban, P. (2001) 'Competency frameworks in performance management', Improving Performance Management in Higher Education Conference, 22 October, Capita, London.

Farnham, D. and Pimlott, J. (1995) *Understanding Industrial Relations*, 5th edn, Cassell, London.

Farrar, S. (2008) 'Mentors develop the new leaders', *Sunday Times*, 30 March.

Fiedler, F.E. (1978) 'The contingency model and the dynamics of the leadership process', in L. Berkowitz (ed.) *Advances in Experimental Social Psychology*, vol. 11, Academic Press, New York.

Finch, J. (2001) 'Why I believe the drive for equal opportunities needs new impetus', *THES*, 16 February, 2001.

Fitzgerald, M. (1992) 'TVU: academic organization', 17 June, unpublished paper.

Flexner, A. (1930) *Universities: American, English, German*, Oxford University Press, Oxford.

Forrest, A. (1995) *Fifty Ways to Personal Development*, The Industrial Society, London.

Forrest, A. (1997) *5 Way Management: Maximise your all round impact*, The Industrial Society, London.

Forrest, A. (2005) *5 Way Management: Maximise your all round impact*, Excel Books, London.

Forsyth, P. (2000) *How to Motivate People*, Kogan Page, London.

Frand, J.L. (2000) 'The information age mindset: changes in students and implications for higher education', *Educause Review* 35(5): 14–24.

Fraser, A. and Neville, S. (1993) *Team Building*, The Industrial Society, London.

Frean, A. (2001) 'Boardroom is playground for mummy's boys', *The Times*, 8 September.

Frean, A. (2008a) 'Former polytechnics give Oxbridge a run for its money in new research rankings', *The Times*, 18 December.

Frean, A. (2008b) 'Fewer state school students go to elite universities', *The Times*, 5 June.

Freedman, J.O. (2004) 'Presidents and trustees' in R.G. Ehrenberg (ed.) *Governing Academia: Who is in charge at the modern university?*, Cornell University Press, Ithaca, NY.

Frost, P.J., Moore, L.F., Louis, M.R., Lundberg, C.C. and Martin, J. (1991) *Reframing Organizational Culture*, Sage, London.

Fullan, M. with Stiegelbauer, S. (1991) *The New Meaning of Educational Change*, Cassell, London.

Fullan, M. (1993) *Change Forces*, Falmer, London.

Fullan, M. (1999) *Change Forces: The Sequel*, Falmer, London.

Furnham, A. (2002) 'Getting the most from a meeting', *Sunday Times*, 29 September.

Garratt, B. (1995) 'The learning organization: an old idea that has come of age', *People Management*, 21 September: 25–28.

Gaule, S. and Box, M. (2008) 'Making the case for staff networks', *In Practice*, issue 15, LFHE, London.

Gibbs, G., Knapper, C. and Piccinin, S. (2007) 'The role of departmental leadership in fostering excellent teaching', *In Practice*, Issue 13, LFHE, London.

Gill, J. (2008a) 'Accurately target foreign students or lose, sector told', *THE*, 20 March.

Gill, J. (2008b) 'Crisis management must target quiet catastrophes', *THE*, 3 April.

Gill, J. (2008c) 'Look past the usual suspects to foster global exchange', *THE*, 3 July.

Gladwell, M. (2000) *The Tipping Point: How little things can make a big difference*, Little Brown, London and New York.

Goddard, A. and Tysome, T. (2000) 'Admission impossible?', *THES*, 2 June.

Goddard, J. (1999) 'Sign post to the learning corporation', THES, 30 July.

Goleman, D. (1996) *Emotional Intelligence: Why it can matter more than IQ*, Bloomsbury, London.

Gourley, B. (2004) 'Distance learning will offer the winning move', *THES*, 11 June.

Grant, A. (1997) *Presentation Perfect: How to excel at business presentations, meetings and public speaking*, The Industrial Society, London.

Grass Roots Diversity Group (2003) *Respect for People: Charter for diversity*, Tring, Herts.

Gronn, P. (2000) 'Distributed properties: a new architecture for leadership', *Educational Management and Administration* 28 (3): 317–38.

Halsey, A.H. (1992) *Decline of the Donnish Dominion*, Clarendon Press, Oxford.

Handy, C. (1993) *Understanding Organizations*, Penguin, Harmondsworth.

Hanscombe, S. (1998) 'Make the right impression', *The Times*, 21 June.

Harrison, R. (2000) *Employee Development*, Chartered Institute of Personnel and Development, London.

Harrison, R. (2005) *Learning and Development*, 4th edn, Chartered Institute of Personnel and Development, London.

Harvey, L. (1995) Editorial, *Quality in Higher Education* 1: 5–12.

Harvey, L. (2007) 'Understanding quality' in L. Purser, L. Wilson, E. Froment and J. Kohler (eds) *The Bologna Handbook*, European University Association and Raabe Press, Stuttgart, Germany.

Harvey, L. (2008) 'Jumping through hoops on a white elephant: a survey signifying nothing', *THE*, 14 June.

Haselgrove, S. (ed.) (1994) *The Student Experience*, SRHE and OUP, Buckingham.

HEA (Higher Education Academy) (2008) *Ethnicity, Gender and Degree Attainment Project: Final report*, HEA, York.

HEA (2008) *Professional Recognition Scheme*, HEA, York.

HEFCE (Higher Education Funding Council for England) (2000a) *Strategic Planning in Higher Education*, 24, Bristol.

HEFCE (2000b) *Better Accountability for Higher Education*, 36, Bristol.

HEFCE (2001a) *Funding Higher Education in England*, 14, Bristol.

HEFCE (2001b) *Guide for Members of Governing Bodies of Universities and Colleges in England, Wales and Northern Ireland*, 20, Bristol.

HEFCE (2001c) *Rewarding and Developing Staff in Higher Education*, 16, Bristol.

HEFCE (2001d) *Good Practice to Risk Assessment*, 24, Bristol.

HEFCE (2002a) *Rewarding and Developing Staff in Higher Education: Good practice in setting human resource strategies*, 14, Bristol.

HEFCE (2002b) *Financial Strategy in Higher Education Institutions: A business approach*, 34, Bristol.

HEFCE (2003) *Joint Consultation on the Review of Research Assessment*, 22, Bristol.

HEFCE (2008a) *Funding for Higher Education in England*, 33, Bristol.

HEFCE (2008b) *Counting What Is Measured or Measuring What Counts? League tables and their impact on HEIs in England* (April), Bristol.

HEFCE (2009) *Higher Education in England: Achievements, challenges and prospects*, 6, Bristol.

Heller, D.E. (2004) 'State oversight of academia' in R.G. Ehrenberg (ed.) *Governing Academia: Who is in charge at the modern university?* , Cornell University Press, Ithaca, NY.

HEPI (Higher Education Policy Institute) (2009) *The Role of the Market in Higher Education*, Oxford.

Hermalin, B.E. (2004) 'Higher education boards of trustees' in R.G. Ehrenberg (ed.) *Governing Academia: Who is in charge at the modern university?*, Cornell University Press, Ithaca, NY.

Hersey, P. and Blanchard, K.H. (1992) *Management of Organizational Behavior*, 6th edn, Prentice-Hall, Englewood Cliffs, NJ.

Honey, P. and Mumford, A. (1995) *Using Your Learning Styles*, 3rd edn, Ardingley House, Maidenhead.

Honey, P. and Mumford, A. (2000) *The Learning Styles Helper's Guide*, Peter Honey Publications, Maidenhead, Berks.

Honey, P. and Mumford, A. (2006) *Learning Styles Questionnaire*, Peter Honey Publications, Maidenhead, Berks.

House, R.J. (1988) 'Power and personality in complex organisations' in B.M. Shaw (ed.) *Research in Organizational Behaviour* , vol. 10, JAI Press, Greenford, CT.

Hubbard, D. and Sullivan, P. (2006) *Learning from America*, HEFCE, Bristol.

Hunt, J. (1992) *Leadership: A new synthesis*, Sage, London.

Ince, M. (2008) 'Excellence in the round: world university rankings, 2008', *THE*, 9 October.

Jacoby, R. (1997) 'Intellectuals: inside and outside the academy' in A. Smith and F. Webster (eds) *The Postmodern University? Contested visions of higher education in society*, SRHE and OUP, Buckingham.

Jaques, D. (1998) *Supporting Part Time Teachers in Higher Education*, Universities and Colleges Staff Development Agency, Briefing Paper 56, Sheffield.

Jarratt Report (1985) *Report of the Steering Committee for Efficiency Studies in Universities*, Committee of Vice-Chancellors and Principals (CVCP), London.

Jaspers, K. (1946) *The Idea of the University*, Macmillan, London (originally published 1923).

JCPSG (Joint Costing and Pricing Steering Group) (2005) *An Overview of Transparent Approach to Costing* [in universities] *(TRAC)*, HEFCE, Bristol.

Jobbins, D. (2006) 'US colleges hostile to data pooling', *THE*, 17 November.

Jones, E. and Brown, S. (eds) (2007) *Internationalizing Higher Education: Enhancing learning, teaching and the curriculum*, Routledge, London and New York.

Kakabadse, A. (2001) 'Leadership and context', *Top Management Programme 61*, Cabinet Office. London, unpublished paper.

Kakabadse, A. and Kakabadse, N. (1998) *Essence of Leadership*, International Thompson Business Press, London.

Kandola, R. and Fullerton, J. (1998) *Diversity in Action: Managing the mosaic*, 2nd edn, Chartered Institute of Personnel and Development, London.

Katzenbach, J.R. (1997) 'The myth of top management teams', *Harvard Business Review*, November–December: 83–91.

Kay, J. (2000a) 'Dream world', *Guardian*, 28 November.

Kay, J. (2000b) 'So we agree not to agree?', *THES*, 24 November.

Kellaway, L. (2006) 'Why academics make an unfit subject for management', *Financial Times*, 27 February.

Kelly, D. (1998) *The Pressure's On!*, Stress Management Video, BBC, London.

Kelly, G. (2008) 'Upending league tables', *THE*, 15 July.

Kemmis, S. and Maconachie, D. (1998) *Strategic Repositioning: A case study of rapid change at the University of Ballarat*, Department of Employment, Education, Training and Youth Affairs, Canberra.

Kerr, C. (1963) *The Uses of the University*, 3rd edn, Harvard University Press, Cambridge, MA.

Kerr, C. (2001) *The Gold and the Blue: Academic triumphs*, University of California Press, Berkeley, CA.

Kezar, A. (2006) 'Rethinking public higher education governing boards performance', *Journal of Higher Education* 77 (6): 968–1009.

Killick, D. (2006) 'The internationalized curriculum', *Academy Exchange*, 5 (Winter), HEA, York.

Knight, P. and Yorke, M. (2003) *Assessment, Learning and Employability*, SRHE and OUP, Buckingham.

Kotter, J.P. (1990) *A Force for Change: How leadership differs from management*, Free Press, New York.

Kouzes, J.M. and Posner, B.Z. (1995) *The Leadership Challenge*, Jossey-Bass, San Francisco, CA.

Kouzes, J.M. and Posner, B.Z. (2003) *The Leadership Challenge*, Jossey-Bass Wiley, New York.

Krahenbuhl, G., Linder, D. and Collins, J. (1998) 'Faculty work reconsidered: an integrative model', Arizona State University, unpublished paper.

Krinsky, I. and Weber, S. (1997) 'New manager assimilation', *American Association of Higher Education Bulletin* 49 (9): 11–13.

Lambert Review (2003) *Lambert Review of Business–University Collaboration: Final Report*, December, HM Treasury, HMSO, London.

Laurillard, D. (2001) *Rethinking University Teaching: A conversational framework for the effective use of learning technologies*, 2nd edn, RoutledgeFalmer, London.

Leandro, H. (2008) *Viral Change: The alternative to slow, painful and unsuccessful management of change in organizations*, 2nd edn, Meetingminds Press, London.

Leitch Review of Skills (2006) *Prosperity for All in the Global Economy – World Class Skills*, HM Treasury, London.

Lewin, K. (1951) *Field Theory in Social Science*, Harper and Row, New York.

LFHE (The Leadership Foundation for Higher Education) (2003) *Introducing The Leadership Foundation for Higher Education*, LFHE, London.

LFHE (2004) *Leadership Summit: The evolving agenda*, London.

LFHE (2007) *Annual Report, 2006–07*, London.

Likert, R. (1967) *New Patterns of Management*, McGraw-Hill, New York.

Lipsett, A. (2005) 'UKeU was a disgraceful waste of public money', *THES*, 4 March.

Loehr, J. and Schwartz, T. (2001) 'The making of a corporate athlete', *Harvard Business Review*, January: 120–8.

Lucas, A.F. (1995) *Strengthening Departmental Leadership*, Jossey Bass, San Francisco, CA.

Luffman, G., Lea, E., Kenny, B. and Sanderson, S. (1996) *Strategic Management: An analytical introduction*, 3rd edn, Blackwell, Oxford.

Luker, P. (2006) 'Not yet, Prime Minister', *Academy Exchange*, 5 (Winter), HEA, York.

McCall, B. (2006) 'Academics suffer more stress than A&E staff', *THE*, 17 February.

McGregor, D. (1960) *The Human Side of Enterprise*, McGraw-Hill, New York.

Macintyre, B. (2001) 'Bush gets America down to business', *The Times*, 17 February.

McNay, I. (1995) 'From the collegial academy to corporate enterprise: the changing culture of universities' in T. Schuller (ed.) *The Changing University?*, SRHE and OUP, Buckingham.

McNay, I. (1996) 'Work's committees' in R. Cuthbert (ed.) *Working in Higher Education*, SRHE and OUP, Buckingham.

McNay, I. (ed.) (2006) *Beyond Mass Higher Education*, SRHE and OUP, Maidenhead and New York.

McNay, I. and Bone, J. (2006) *Higher Education and Human Good*, Tockington Press, Bristol.

McNay, I. and Dopson, S. (1996) 'Organizational culture' in D. Warner and D. Palfreyman (eds) *Higher Education Management: The key elements*, SRHE and OUP, Buckingham.

MacTaggart, T.J. (2004) 'The ambiguous future of public higher education systems' in W.G. Tierney (ed.) *Competing Conceptions of Academic Governance*, The Johns Hopkins University Press, Baltimore, MD.

Maddix, R.B. (1998) *Team Building*, 2nd edn, Kogan Page, London.

Maitland, I. (1995) *Managing Your Time*, Institute of Personnel and Development, London.

Marcus, J. (2009) 'Tenuous-track positions', *THE*, 5 March.

Marginson, S. (2004) 'Going global: governance implications of cross-border traffic in higher education' in W.G. Tierney (ed.) *Competing Conceptions of Academic Governance*, The Johns Hopkins University Press, Baltimore, MD.

Marshall, S. (ed.) (2007) *Strategic Leadership of Change in Higher Education: What's new?*, Routledge, London and New York.

Martin, E. (1999) *Changing Academic Work: Developing the Learning University*, SRHE and OUP, Buckingham.

Maslen, G. (2006) 'Sell-off jeopardizes e-university venture', *THES*, 15 December.

Maurrasse, D.J. (2001) *Beyond the Campus: How colleges and universities form partnerships with their communities*, Routledge, London and New York.

Melody, W. (1997) 'Universities and public policy' in A. Smith and F. Webster (eds) *The Postmodern University? Contested visions of higher education in society*, SRHE and OUP, Buckingham.

Middlehurst, R. (1993) *Leading Academics*, SRHE and OUP, Buckingham.

Middlehurst, R. (2006) 'Internationalization: a leadership challenge', *Academy Exchange*, 5 (Winter), HEA, York.

Miles, R.E. and Snow, C.S. (2003) *Organizational Strategy, Structure and Process*, Stanford University Press, Stanford, CA.

Miller, L.H., Smith, A.D. and Rothstein, L. (1994) *The Stress Solution*, Pocketbooks, New York.

Mills, M. (2007) 'Universities torn between two masters', *THE*, 14 September.

Mintzberg, H. (1973) *The Nature of Management Work*, Harper and Row, New York.

Mintzberg, H., Ahlstrand, B. and Lampel, J.B. (2008) *Strategy Safari: The complete guide through the wilds of strategic management*, 2nd edn, Prentice Hall, London and New York.

Modood Report (1999) *Ethnicity and Employment in Higher Education*, Policy Studies Institute, London.

Moody, J.A. (2004) *Faculty Diversity: Problems and solutions*, Routledge, London and New York.

Moores, R. (1994) *Managing for High Performance: A practical guide*, The Industrial Society, London.

Morgan, G. (2006) *Images of Organization*, 3rd edn, Sage, London.

Morris, E. (2008) 'Performance tables put successful diversity at risk', *Guardian*, 29 July.

Mortimer, K.P. and O'Brien Sathre, C. (2007) *The Art and Politics of Academic Governance*, Praeger Publishers, Westport, CT.

Mulholland, G., Ozbilgin, M.F. and Worman, D. (2006) *Managing Diversity: Words into action*, CIPD, London.

Murlis, H. and Hartle, F. (1996) 'Does it pay to work in universities?' in R. Cuthbert (ed.) *Working in Higher Education*, SRHE and OUP, Buckingham. .

Myers, M.S. (1991) *Every Employee a Manager*, 3rd edn, Prentice-Hall, Englewood Cliffs, NJ.

Myers, P. and Myers, K.D. (1977) *Myers-Briggs Type Indicator*, Oxford Psychologists Press, Oxford.

NAO (National Audit Office) (2007) *Staying the Course: The retention of students in higher education*, London.

NATFHE (National Association of Teachers in Further and Higher Education) (2001) *Justice for Agency Lecturers*, June, London.

NATFHE (2002) Survey, *The Lecturer*, June.

National Commission on Education (1995) *Learning in the New Millennium*, Briefing 5, Paul Hamlyn Foundation, London.

National Conference of University Professors (1996) *The Case for Universities*, Policy Document No. 6, London.

Newman, J.H., Cardinal (1976) *The Idea of a University*, Oxford University Press, Oxford (originally published 1853).

Newman, M. (2007) 'Students shun foreign peers', *THE*, 5 October.

Newman, M. (2008a) 'Staff give sector managers low marks', *THE*, 27 March.

Newman, M. (2008b) 'Infantilised students and staff rapped', *THE*, 12 June.

Oswald, A. (2003a) 'The quest for job satisfaction', *Sunday Times*, 13 April.

Oswald, A. (2003b) 'Life can be a beach, if you let it', *Sunday Times*, 2 February.

Owen, G. (2001) 'Cambridge amateur culture led to chaos', *The Times*, 3 November.

Oxford, E. (2008) 'Still second among equals', *THE*, 27 March.

PA Consulting Group (2008) *Keeping our Universities Special: Surviving and thriving in a turbulent world*, London.

PA Consulting Group (2009) *Positive Accountability: Review of the costs, benefits and burdens of accountability in English higher education*, HEFCE, Bristol.

Pearson, M. (2009) *Getting to Grips with Finance: Resources for governors of UK universities and higher education colleges*, LFHE, London.

Pedler, M., Burgoyne, J. and Boydell, T. (1991) *The Learning Company: A strategy for sustainable development*, McGraw-Hill, London.

Pedler, M., Burgoyne, J. and Boydell, T. (2001) *A Manager's Guide to Self-Development*, 4th edn, McGraw-Hill, London.

Pedler, M., Burgoyne, J. and Boydell, T. (2006) *A Manager's Guide to Self Development*, 5th edn, McGraw-Hill, London.

Peiffer, V. (2005) *Total Stress Relief: Practical solutions that really work*, Piatkus Books, London.

Pelikan, J. (1992) *The Idea of the University: A re-examination*, Yale University Press, London.

Pennington, G. (2006) *Guidelines for Managing and Facilitating Change: A guide for heads of department, programme leaders and other change agents in higher education*, 2nd edn, HEA, York.

Peters, T. (1987) *Thriving on Chaos: Handbook for a management revolution*, Pan Books, London.

Pettigrew, A., Ferlie, E. and McKee, L. (1992) *Shaping Strategic Change: Making change in large organizations: The case of the National Health Service*, Sage, London.

Philips, S. (2007) 'Phoenix soars but still dogged by turbulence', *THES*, 20 April.

Pickard, J. (2001) 'Ruling classes: what does it take to be a leader', *People Management*, 9 August: 21–5.

Port, J. (2008) *Measuring Institutional Key Performance Indicators for Governors: CUC Implementation Project*, LFHE, London.

Porter, M.E. (1998) *The Competitive Advantage: Creating and sustaining superior performance*, Simon and Schuster, London.

Pratt, J. (2000) 'How will our soul be saved', *THES*, 29 September.

QAA (Quality Assurance Agency for Higher Education) (1998) *Special Review of Thames Valley University*, 9 November, Gloucester.

QAA (2004) *Code of Practice for the Assurance of Academic Quality and Standards in Higher Education*, September, Gloucester.

Quenk, N.L. (1999) *Essentials of Myers-Briggs Type Indicator Assessment*, John Wiley and Sons, London and New York.

Quinn, R.E., Faerman, S.R., Thompson, M.P., McGrath, M. and St. Clair, L.S. (2007) *Becoming a Master Manager: A competing values approach*, 4th edn, John Wiley and Sons, London.

Ramsden, P. (1998) *Learning to Lead in Higher Education*, Routledge, London.

Ramsden, P. (2006) 'The student learning experience: editorial', *Academy Exchange*, 4 (Summer), HEA, York.

Ramsden, P. (2007) 'Inspiring tomorrow's students', *Academy Exchange*, 7 (Winter), HEA, York.

Reed, M. and Hughes, M. (eds) (1992) *Rethinking Organizations: New directions in organization theory and analysis*, Sage, London.

Reid, E (1997) 'Run-around nightmare', *Guardian*, 14 October.

Reilly, J. (2006) 'UK students and European mobility', *Academy Exchange*, 5 (Winter), HEA, York.

Revans, R.W. (1984) *The Origins and Growth of Action Learning*, Chartwell Bratt, Bromley.

Ritchie, E. (2006) 'Internationalization: where are we going and how do we know when we have got there?', *Academy Exchange*, 5 (Winter), HEA, York.

Roberts, G. (2003) *Joint Consultation on the Review of Research Assessment*, HEFCE, 22, Bristol.

Robins, K. and Webster, F. (eds) (2002) *The Virtual University? Knowledge, markets and management*, Oxford University Press, Oxford.

Roderick, C. (1993) 'Becoming a learning organization', *Training and Development*, March: 14–22.

Rose, M. (2000) 'Target practice', *People Management*, 23 November: 44–5.

Rothwell, J. (2000) 'How to break the news of redundancies', *People Management*, 23 November: 46–8.

Russell, C. and Parsons, E. (1996) 'Putting theory to the test' at the OU', *People Management*, 11 January: 30–4.

Sanders, C. and Goddard, A. (2001) 'Cambridge is worth 170 Guildhalls', *THES*, 13 July.

Sashkin, M. (1995) *The Visionary Leader*, HRD Press, Amherst, MA.

Sashkin, M. and Rosenbach, W.E. (1993) 'A new leadership paradigm' in W.E. Rosenbach and R.L. Taylor (eds) *Contemporary Issues in Leadership*, Westview Press, Boulder, CO.

Schein, E. (2004) *Organizational Culture and Leadership*, 3rd edn, Jossey Bass Wiley, London.

Schmidt, P. (2008) 'Most colleges chase prestige on a treadmill', *The Chronicle of Higher Education*, 10 November.

Schneider, R. (2001) 'Managing diversity', *People Management*, 3 May: 27–31.

Schofield, A. (2009) *What Is an Effective and High Performing Governing Body in UK Higher Education?* LFHE, London.

Schuller, T. (ed.) (1995) *The Changing University?*, SRHE and OUP, Buckingham.

Scott, P. (1995) *The Meanings of Mass Higher Education*, SRHE and OUP, Buckingham.

Scott, P. (ed.) (1998) *The Globalization of Higher Education*, SRHE and OUP, Buckingham.

Scott, P. (2008) 'Leadership and management in higher education', LFHE Conference 12 February, unpublished paper.

Scott, P. and Watson, D. (1994) 'Managing the curriculum: roles and responsibilities' in J. Bocock and D. Watson (eds) *Managing the University Curriculum: Making common cause*, SRHE and OUP, Buckingham.

Seel, R. (2000) 'Complexity and culture: new perspectives on organizational change', *Organizations & People* 7 (2): 2–9.

Seel, R. (2004) *The Nature of Organizational Change*, Change Academy Paper 3, HEA, York.

Scott-Morgan, P. (1999) 'Hidden depths', *People Management*, 8 April: 38–46.

Senge, P. (1990) 'The leader's new work: building learning organizations', *Sloan Management Review* 32 (1): 7–23.

Senge, P. (1994) *The Fifth Discipline Fieldbook: Strategies and tools for building a learning organization*, Nicholas Brealey, London.

Senge, P. (1995) *Leading Learning Organizations: The bold, the powerful and the invisible*, MIT Press, Cambridge, MA.

Senge, P. (1998) 'Faculty work in learning organizations', Sixth American Association of Higher Education Conference on Faculty Roles and Rewards, Orlando, FL.

Senge, P. (2006) *The Fifth Discipline: The art and practice of the learning organization* (special revised edn), Random House, London.

Senge, P., Kleiner, A., Roberts, C., Ross, R., Roth, G. and Smith, B. (1999) *The Dance of Change: The challenge of sustaining momentum in learning organizations*, Nicholas Brealey, London.

Shattock, M. (2006) *Managing Good Governance in Higher Education*, OUP, Maidenhead.

Shiel, C. (2006) 'Developing the global citizen', *Academy Exchange*, 5 (Winter), HEA, York.

Shulman, G. (1998) 'Leading a quality department: a learning organization perspective', Miami University, Oxford, OH, unpublished paper.

Siddons, S. (1998) *Presentation Skills*, Institute of Personnel Development, London.

Sizer, L. (1982) 'Assessing institutional performance and progress' in L. Wagner (ed.) *Agenda for Institutional Change in Higher Education*, SRHE, Guildford.

Smith, A. and Webster, F. (eds) (1997) *The Postmodern University? Contested visions of higher education in society*, SRHE and OUP, Buckingham.

Smith, P.B. and Peterson, M.F. (1988) *Leadership, Organizations and Culture*, Sage, London.

Snoddy, R. (2002) 'The BBC's popular vulgarian', *The Times*, 15 February.

Soames, M. (ed.) (1998) *Speaking for Themselves: The personal letters of Winston and Clementine Churchill*, Doubleday, London.

Spellings Commission Report (2006) *A Test of Leadership: Charting the future of U.S. higher education*, U.S. Department of Education, Washington, DC.

Spillane, J.P. (2006) *Distributed Leadership*, Jossey-Bass, San Francisco, CA.

Stamp, R. (2002) *Positioning Statement Development*, Riley Consulting, London.

Stothart, C. (2008) 'Fires, floods, pandemics: planning for the worst', *THE*, 17 April.

Syrett, M. and Hogg, C. (eds) (1992) *Frontiers of Leadership*, Blackwell, Oxford.

Tahir, T. (2007) 'For some, campus is still another country', *THE*, 31 August.

Tahir, T. (2008) 'The in-betweeners', *THE*, 10 July.

Talloires Declaration (2005) *Strengthening the Civic Roles and Social Responsibilities of Higher Education: Building a global network*, Tufts University, Medford, MA.

Taylor Report (2001) *New Directions in Higher Education Funding*, Universities UK, London.

Teaford, J.C. (1984) *The Unheralded Triumph: City government in America, 1870–1900*, Johns Hopkins University Press, Baltimore, MD.

Tear, Y. (1998) 'Mike Fitzgerald: The man with the plan', *Ealing Gazette*, 20 November.

Thackwray, B., Chambers J. and Huxley, L. (2007) *Enhancing Organizational Development in English Universities*, HEFCE, Bristol.

THES (2000) 14 April, 25 February, 31 March.

THES (2003) 7 February.

Thomas, K.W. and Kilmann, R.H. (2002) *Thomas-Kilmann Conflict Mode Instrument*, Consulting Psychologists Press, Palo Alto, CA.

Tichy, N.M. (1983) *Managing Strategic Change*, John Wiley and Sons, New York.

Tierney, W.G. (ed.) (2004) *Competing Conceptions of Academic Governance: Negotiating the perfect storm*, The Johns Hopkins University Press, Baltimore, MD.

Toffler, A. (1991) *Power Shift: Knowledge, wealth and violence at the edge of the 21st century*, Bantam Press, London.

Tollyfield, H. (2007) 'UK strategy for world class skills', Learning after Leitch Conference, DfES, 24 May.

Torrington, D., Taylor, S. and Hall, L. (2007) *Human Resource Management*, 7th edn, Prentice-Hall, Englewood Cliffs, NJ.

Trow, M. (1973) *Problems in the Transition from Elite to Mass Higher Education*, Carnegie Commission on HE, Berkeley, CA.

Trowler, P.R. (1998) *Academics Responding to Change: New higher education frameworks and academic cultures*, SRHE and OUP, Buckingham.

Trowler, P., Saunders, M. and Knight, P. (2003) *Change Thinking, Change Practices: A guide to change for heads of departments, programme leaders and other change agents in higher education*, Learning and Teaching Support Network, Generic Centre, York.

Turner, C. (2002) *Born to Succeed: Releasing your business potential*, Texere, London.

Turner, D. (1998) *Liberating Leadership: A manager's guide to the new leadership*, The Industrial Society, London.

Tutt, N. (1985) 'The unintended consequences of integration', *Educational and Child Psychology* 2: 20–38.

UCEA (Universities and Colleges Employers Association) (2000) *Guide to Good Practice on Fixed Term and Casual Employment in Higher Education*, UCEA, London.

University of Western Australia (1998) 'Challenging conceptions of teaching: some prompts for good practice', available online at http://www.osds.uwa.edu.au/other_services/publications/herdsa/conceptions (accessed 27 September 2009).

Urry, J. (1999) 'Locating HE in the global landscape', *SRHE News*, Society for Research into Higher Education 39, London.

UUK (Universities UK) (2002) *Student Services: Effective approaches to retaining students in higher education*, UUK, London.

van Ginkel, H. (1995) 'University 2050: the organization of creativity and innovation', *Higher Education Policy* 8 (4): 14–18.

Vroom, V. and Yetton, P.W. (1973) *Leadership and Decision-Making*, University of Pittsburgh Press, Pittsburgh, PA.

Warner, D. and Palfreyman, D. (eds) (2001) *The State of UK Higher Education: Managing change and diversity*, SRHE and OUP, Buckingham.

Warren, E. and Toll, C. (1996) *The Stress Work Book: How individuals, teams and organizations can balance pressure and performance*, Nicholas Brealey, London.

Waterhouse, R. (2002) 'Serve the customer', *THES*, 20 December.

Watson, D. (2007a) 'Listen carefully: I shall say this only twice', *Academy Exchange* 7 (Winter), HEA, York.

Watson, D. (2007b) *Managing Civic and Community Engagement*, OUP, Maidenhead.

Watson, D. and Amoah, M. (eds) (2007) *The Dearing Report: Ten years on*, Institute of Education, London.

Webb, G. (1996) *Understanding Staff Development*, SRHE and OUP, Buckingham.

Wedgewood, M. (2006) 'Mainstreaming the third stream' in I. McNay (ed.) *Beyond Mass Higher Education: Building on Expansion*, SRHE/Open University Press, Maidenhead.

Weick, K. (1976) 'Educational organizations as loosely-coupled systems', *Administrative Science Quarterly* 21 (1): 1–19.

White Paper (2003) *The future of higher education*, DfES, London.

Whyte, W.H. (1956) *The Organization Man*, Simon and Schuster, New York.

Williams, P. (2007) 'Quality assurance in the UK' in L. Purser, L. Wilson, E. Froment and J. Kohler (eds) *The Bologna Handbook*, European University Association and Raabe Press, Stuttgart, Germany.

Wood, J. (1997) 'Engaging the future: report of the president's faculty task force on the future of the university', George Mason University, Fairfax, VA.

Wood, J., Brinig, M. and Clark, R. (1997) *Engaging the Future: Report of the President's Faculty Task Force on the future of the university*, George Mason University, VA.

Woodcock, M. (1989) *Activities for Team-Building*, Gower, London.

Woods, P.A. (2004) 'Democratic leadership: drawing distinctions with distributed leadership', *International Journal of Leadership in Education* 7 (1): 3–26.

Woolcock, N. (2008) 'Universities pricing out foreign students', *The Times*, 22 May.

Work Foundation (2006) 'Effective middle management: essential skills', London.

Worman, D. (2008) 'Stepping up the pace of progress for managing diversity', *Impact* (May), CIPD, London.

Wynne-Jones, R. (1997) 'The University that's hip, cool and loses its degree results', *Independent on Sunday*, 30 November.

Yorke, M. and Longden, B. (2004) *Retention and Success in Higher Education*, SRHE and OUP, Maidenhead.

Yorke, M. and Longden, B. (2008) *The First Year Experience of Higher Education in the UK: Final report*, HEA, York.

Index